THE RAINBOW DIVISION
IN THE GREAT WAR

Typical Rainbow Trench Arts Helmets, Germany, 1919. Courtesy of Great War Militaria.

THE RAINBOW DIVISION IN THE GREAT WAR

1917–1919

James J. Cooke

 PRAEGER

Westport, Connecticut
London

Library of Congress Cataloging-in-Publication Data

Cooke, James J.
    The Rainbow Division in the Great War, 1917–1919 / James J. Cooke.
       p.   cm.
    Includes bibliographical references and index.
    ISBN 0–275–94768–8 (alk. paper)
    1. United States. Army. Infantry Division, 42nd—History.
  2. World War, 1914–1918—Regimental histories—United States.
  3. World War, 1914–1918—Campaigns—France. I. Title.
D570.3 42d.C66 1994
940.4'1273—dc20   93–37024

British Library Cataloguing in Publication Data is available.

Library of Congress Catalog Card Number: 93–37024
ISBN: 0–275–94768–8

First published in 1994

Praeger Publishers, 88 Post Road West, Westport, CT 06881
An imprint of Greenwood Publishing Group, Inc.

Printed in the United States of America

The paper used in this book complies with the
Permanent Paper Standard issued by the National
Information Standards Organization (Z39.48–1984).

10 9 8 7 6 5 4 3 2 1

Dedicated to the memory of my Great Uncle,
Private Charles Wise, Doughboy, AEF, 1917-1918

Contents

Maps   ix

Acknowledgments   xi

Introduction: Birth of the Rainbow   1

Chapter 1: From Camp Mills to France   7

Chapter 2: Training for the Fight: Rolampont   29

Chapter 3: In the Trenches at Lunéville   53

Chapter 4: From Baccarat to Champagne   75

Chapter 5: From Champagne to the Marne   97

Chapter 6: Crossing the Ourcq River   117

Chapter 7: The St. Mihiel Offensive   139

Chapter 8: The Meuse-Argonne Campaign   163

Chapter 9: From Sedan to Belgium and Luxembourg   187

Chapter 10: Rainbow on the Rhine   209

Chapter 11: The End of the Rainbow   233

Appendix A: Organization of the 42nd Division, 1917   247

Appendix B: Equipment Taken into the Trenches, February 1918   251

Bibliography   253

Index   261

Photographs follow page 116 (end of Chapter 5)

MAPS

2.1	42nd Division Training Areas	31
4.1	The Baccarat Sector	77
5.1	The Champagne Defense	99
6.1	The Ourcq River Battlefield	119
7.1	The St. Mihiel Battlefield, 1	141
7.2	The St. Mihiel Battlefield, 2	142
8.1	Meuse-Argonne Battlefield	165
9.1	Positions of AEF Divisions, 7 November 1918	194
9.2	The Sedan Operation	194

ACKNOWLEDGMENTS

My first association with the Rainbow Division in the Great War came when a good friend, Celia Flyshacker of Tupelo, Mississippi, handed me a bag containing over 125 letters written by Pfc. Everett Scott of the Iowa 168th Infantry Regiment. Mrs. Flyshacker, who knew my interest in military letters from the period of the two world wars, owns a nostalgia shop and is a constant visitor at estate sales. The more I read of Scott's adventure with the Rainbow Division, the more interested I became. As I checked bibliographies, I found that the last major work on the division was Colonel Henry J. Reilly's *Americans All*, published in 1936. I then decided that an analysis of the 42nd Division was overdue.

Dr. H. Dale Abadie, dean of the College of Liberal Arts at the University of Mississippi, assisted me with a small research grant, which took me to the archival holdings of the U.S. Army's Historical Institute at Carlisle Barracks. There Dr. Richard J. Sommers, chief of the archival branch, and his excellent staff assisted me in perusing the Rainbow collection and the responses to their World War I questionnaire program. Dr. Sommers, a rock-solid professional, not only knew the sources but also took a great deal of time to answer questions through the mail. During the summer of 1990 I went to the Alabama State Archives, which houses an important collection relating to the Alabama "Wildmen" of the 167th Infantry Regiment. The archival staff in Montgomery were extremely helpful. The staff at the Mitchell Library, Mississippi State University, and at the Emporia (Kansas) Public Library were also giving of their time and efforts. The Auburn University Library's Special Collections staff located two important collections relating to the 167th Infantry.

Also, during the summer of 1990 I traveled to the National Archives in Washington, D.C., where Joe Knapp guided me through several records groups. Records Group 120 pertaining to the Rainbow Division was extensive, but by August I had completed my research work there. When I returned to Oxford, Mississippi, in August, I began to write and had finished six pages when I volunteered to go to the Persian Gulf. There I served with the 18th Airborne Corps, which took a chance on a National Guard lieutenant-colonel and sent me first with the Saudi Army until January 1991, and then with the 6th French Light Armored Division during ground combat. Upon returning home from Southwest Asia in late March 1991, I put aside the Rainbow while I wrote of my experiences with the French army in Desert Storm.   I was offered an opportunity to be a visiting professor of military history at the U.S. Air Force's Air War College, Air University, during the 1992-93 academic year. While at Maxwell Air Force Base, Alabama, I began to work in the Air Force Historical Agency archives and found a facet of the Rainbow Division's existence that I had not researched before. The agency's staff of archivists could not have been more helpful. In the Air University Library, one of the best military libraries in the United States, I was helped considerably by Sue Goodman, bibliographer. The Interlibrary Loan department with Ruth Griffin, Joan Phillips, and Wendi Cowart went above and beyond the call of duty to assist me in finding rare volumes pertaining to World War I.

I cannot say enough about my colleagues—civilian and military—in the Department of Military Studies. Colonels Fred Beatty and Bryant Culberson, as well as Dr. Bill Snyder, guarded my research and writing time.   Dr. Steve MacFarland of Auburn University, also a visiting professor and a first-rate airpower historian, gave generously of his time to hear ideas, give suggestions, and be simply an all-round friend. Secretaries Audrey Danziger and SSG Ronda Boutté put up with me, while Joann Law and Barbara Winton puzzled over my poorly typed manuscripts.

Rick Keller and Dean Gelwicks of Great War Militaria in Chambersburg, Pennsylvania, must be thanked for answering many, many questions about the uniforms and equipment of the doughboy. I also wish to thank Professor T.J. Ray, Department of English of the University of Mississippi, who prepared the maps for this work. Johnette Carwyle, of the University of Mississippi, worked with my many revisions. Certainly, my wife of thirty-plus years must be singled out for reading, proofing, and being one of my severest critics and my loudest cheerleader.

Introduction

Birth of the Rainbow

April 6, 1917, promised to be a warm day in Primgihar, Iowa, and for Everett Scott it was a day to turn his attention to his two main interests—farming and Louise, the girl he hoped to marry someday if he could only convince her father, a stern man. He watched his high-spirited brother Leslie leave for school, then turned his attention to chores.

In Bessemer, Alabama, Joe Romano was enjoying being back home from a year's duty with the Alabama National Guard on the Mexican border. The old Fourth Alabama—the "Bloody 4th" of Civil War Confederate fame—had answered the president's call-up of the guard to protect American territory and citizens from the Mexican banditos. Now the great adventure of his life was finished, and Romano contemplated whether or not to sign up for another hitch with the Alabama Guard.

Dodge City, Kansas, was similar to Primgihar, Iowa, and Bessemer, Alabama, in that the day started out quiet enough, as befits small-town America. For Calvin Lambert, a recent graduate of Kansas State University, the prospects for a solid future were definitely there, because he had a job with the local newspaper and had attracted the attention of the renowned editor, William Allen White. Lambert realized the import of President Woodrow Wilson's April 2nd message to Congress asking for a declaration of war against Germany. Certainly, Lambert thought, America's contribution would be heavy—her farm produce and her industry might be enough to sustain the allied troops in the field.

In Washington, D.C., Major Douglas MacArthur, serving on the American General Staff, recognized that Europe wanted more than just produce and machinery. Europe would need men to fill its dangerously depleted ranks, and if America was forthcoming, U.S. soldiers would then go to France. MacArthur wanted to be among those soldiers sent to do battle in this great world war. Major MacArthur lived in the shadow of his father, General Arthur MacArthur. On 25 November 1863, Captain Arthur MacArthur seized the flag of the 24th Wisconsin Infantry and led the regiment up Missionary Ridge, winning promotion, fame, and the Congressional Medal of Honor. By the end of the Civil War, he had again been cited for gallantry at Atlanta and at the terrible slaughter at Franklin, Tennessee. He never forgot his old 24th Wisconsin, and the aging, retired Major General MacArthur was attending a reunion of the Yankee veterans in 1912 when he was stricken with a fatal heart attack. Douglas had been close to his father, and had learned a lesson that was not popular among Regular Army officers: When well-led, the militia (now called the National Guard) could fight as well as any troops.

William J. Donovan was the archetypal New York National Guard officer. He was a lawyer, well-educated, articulate, well-connected with the New York Republican Party, a faithful Catholic, and a handsome man with an Irishman's flair for the phrase and the dramatic. Like many of the National Guard officers in New York City on that April day, he wondered what role he would play. Bill Donovan had political ambitions and knew that war could bring fame, but for his acquaintance, Father Francis P. Duffy, war meant death and suffering. Father Duffy knew, however, that wherever Irish National Guardsmen of the 69th Regiment went, he would go also. Fiercely proud of his Irish background, Duffy had doubts about serving in any cause with the British, but the French were another matter. The old Irish Brigade and the Fighting 69th Regiment had a long Catholic tradition; there was a monument to Father Corby, who gave absolution to the Irishmen before they stormed into the maelstrom of the Wheatfield at Gettysburg. Duffy was certain that the blood of old Eire surged through the veins of the 69th. The Irish were poets, and now in its ranks was the intellectual Sergeant Joyce Kilmer, whose poetry had been well-received. Kilmer was a favorite of Duffy and of Donovan, and there was little doubt that Kilmer, like the Irish warrior-poets of old, would acquit himself well once the old 69th advanced—with Father Duffy's prayers, of course.

Prayers of absolution, brave charges against the enemy, medals and glory were far from the thoughts of Dr. William W. van Dolsen of Washington, D.C. While Douglas MacArthur agonized in the same city over his military future, van Dolson was content. He had finished medical school, and the world was, as he saw it, his oyster. He looked forward to a good practice in the capital city and all the worldly comforts that could bring. Like many young men he dreamed of adventure, but the declaration of war seemed to him to be of very little interest. He had been approached to join the National Guard ambulance unit, and membership in the Washington, D.C. National Guard held certain social advantages.

Martin J. Hogan of Brooklyn, New York, was not pondering any social advantage of the National Guard that spring day. His interests in the military stemmed from hero worship. Seventeen-year-old Martin had just visited his older brother, Sergeant Tom Hogan of Brooklyn's 23rd Infantry regiment. Tom Hogan had returned from a year on the Mexican border and had tales to tell, and Martin was certain that if the National Guard was good enough for his older brother, it was just right for him. But there were problems in that Martin Hogan was a year under the enlistment age, and as an orphan he lived with an aunt and an unmarried sister.

Charles MacArthur's thoughts were far from the military. He was a student at the University of Illinois, and the school year had gone well for him. To a fraternity man in good standing, Illinois offered great opportunities to learn, meet pretty co-eds, and watch football. With the summer vacation approaching, MacArthur was interested in a summer job and what the hot sun of July and August could bring for a young man.

Another University of Illinois man, Leslie Langille, was also looking forward to returning to Chicago and his home. He enjoyed singing in his church choir and anticipated a good vacation, even though summers could be boring if a summer job could not be found. The rumors of war did not bother Leslie Langille, and certainly on 6 April 1917 military service was not in his future.

The news that the United States was at war was heard by 28,000 such young men, in twenty-six states, who would become soldiers of the Rainbow Division. That news really did not seem possible, because in 1916 President Wilson had campaigned on a promise to keep America out of the threatened European war, and the same year Tin Pan Alley's most purchased song was "I Didn't Raise my Boy to be a Soldier." However, America had been provoked, and finally Wilson, obviously regretting the move, asked Congress to issue the declaration. Many believed the response to Europe's needs resided in the great farms of America and in her industrial potential, not manpower. Yet on 5 June, after a slow and acrimonious debate, Congress passed a draft law that went into effect a few weeks later, for there was a desperate need for manpower to dispatch to Europe.

In Washington, the initial plan put forth by the regular military establishment was to raise a Regular Army of nearly a half-million men and send them to France, making this war strictly a Regular Army show. But there were those who disagreed. The newly appointed commander of the American Expeditionary Force (AEF), John J. Pershing, worried that the slow, cumbersome, and inexperienced general staff could not react quickly enough to get a half-million regulars to France with any alacrity. Within the staff, Douglas MacArthur argued for the full utilization of the National Guard, and his view found favor with Secretary of War Newton Baker and, more important, with President Woodrow Wilson. There were perfectly good reasons to call the Guard into active service. They were already organized, and many Guard units had seen active service on the Mexican border, putting into practice what they had learned at musters. Three National Guard infantry divisions already were organized in Pennsylvania, New England, and New York, and their deployment to France would certainly take a lot less time than waiting for the draft Army divisions to be organized. Last, but not least, the National Guard, more than the Regular Army, represented the people in a democratic state. To call the Guard was to insure patriotic support by the "folks back home," who would take a deeper interest in the war effort since their sons and husbands, as represented by the National Guard, would be involved.

The argument that the Regulars were the professionals, the real war-fighters, did not corresponded to reality. Very few Regular units had ever seen the type of combat that awaited the AEF in France; they were just as much a group of novices as were the National Guardsmen. The Regulars would have to promote officers rapidly to make them available for assignments to divisional command and staffs, and many new colonels and brigadiers would be just as ignorant of their jobs as the National Guard officers of similar rank. What remained at the bottom of the tally sheet was the idea that Regular Army officers simply did not like the idea of calling on the National Guard.

To many in the regular ranks, the Guard appeared to be a social organization that only played at soldiering. There were state politics that often governed promotions within the Guard's Officer Corps, and, as the general staff and General Pershing would soon find out, in time of war the politicians in state capitals and in the halls of the U.S. Congress would watch over those men who would return home to vote.

There was always a disturbing tendency in Guard ranks to be democratic. A man who commanded a company might find that his sergeant was his employer during the week, and this could lead, in the eyes of the regulars, to a lamentable lack of military discipline. By and large, the Guardsmen were older, well-educated, and prided themselves on initiative and independent thought. Did one really need a thinking corporal or, worse, a lieutenant capable of independent thinking? The staff in Washington viewed the National Guard as having many regrettable traits.

What the National Guard did have was men who had at least been introduced to the rudiments of training, and many had service on the Mexican border. These units would be called and used. That did not solve the problem of getting Guard units to France as quickly as possible, however.

A plan was proposed in the War Department to form a new 28,000-man division from the best of the National Guard units from twenty-six states. While certainly an unorthodox approach to the utilization of the militia in time of war, this new formation served several purposes. First, it would be made up of units from every section of the country. Also, the War Department would have control over the naming of the commanders and the higher staff of the newly created formation. It was hoped that the training of this division and its commitment to combat would present fewer political problems than would state units with their own home-grown commanders.

The plan was presented to Secretary of War Newton Baker by Major Douglas MacArthur, who immediately saw its military and political advantages, and it was approved. MacArthur, after lobbying heavily, was named the new chief of staff of the division, with the commensurate rank of full colonel. Brigadier General William A. Mann was selected to command the new unit and to give a regular's discipline. At a news conference later, Colonel MacArthur described the unit, designated the 42nd, as having the structure of a rainbow, covering the country from one end of the sky to another. Evidently a newspaper reporter used the term "Rainbow Division" in a dispatch, and the name stuck.

The Rainbow Division was to have four divisional commanders from 1917 to 1919, and William A. Mann was a good choice to be its first commander. A West Pointer, Mann had served during the Sioux Insurrection of 1890-91, the Spanish-American War, the Philippine Pacification Campaign in 1899, the Cuban Occupation of 1906-07, and the Mexican Border Operation in 1916. When Baker selected him to command the 42nd, Mann was chief of the Militia Bureau. Perhaps too old for the rigors of combat, the new major general was known as a man with an eye for talent and for the judicious selection of staff officers. Besides MacArthur, Newton Baker's choice to be chief of staff, Mann selected several other majors to flesh out his staff. The division was to begin gathering at Camp Alvord L. Mills on Long Island, near New York, in early September and start training for deployment to France. Mann and his staff arrived in New York, and on 6 September he formally assumed command of his division.

Where were the troops these regulars were to train? They were en route from twenty-six states, from as far away as California and as close as New York City. These were the men, the raw material that would win or lose a war. It was an experiment with military and political overtones, but one thing was certain. They would go to France and would be in combat. Major William Donovan's trip to Camp Mills would be short. Joe Romano had never been farther from Alabama than the Mexican border. Everett Scott had never been away from his Iowa farm. The time had come to make a fighting division out of twenty-six separate state units. The odyssey of the Rainbow Division was beginning at Camp Mills, New York.

1

From Camp Mills to France

It was one thing to declare war on Germany in the spring of 1917, and it was another matter entirely to equip an army to fight. The United States did not have the troops or the equipment to send to France until the late fall of 1917, and to make the situation even more critical, a large number of officers and non-commissioned officers had to be created from a body of raw recruits or taken from the ranks of the Regular Army and the National Guard. Since 1916, the nation had had the power to conscript and raise a national army that would be separate and distinct from the volunteer Guard. Wilson was not totally sure of his powers and authority, and he complicated the military picture by drafting the National Guard into active service, a move that caused anger and bitterness and would have repercussions in Guard-Regular Army relationships for generations. The draft of the volunteer National Guard also presented administrative and control problems. The orders from the War Department, dated 28 July 1917, made the new relationship between National Guard and Regular Army very clear in that:

The draft of the President completely separates from the National Guard all persons included in the draft....and all other provisions of existing orders and regulations calling for the rendition of reports and returns by National Guard commanders to the adjutant generals of their respective states become inoperative from, and on the date of this draft. This was to take place on 5 August 1917, and all enlisted men would receive a discharge from the Guard on that date.[1]

This served to separate the troops from their state affiliation—the adjutants general, governors, and legislatures. More important, it opened the door for placing Regular Army officers as commanders of the newly formed National Guard and National Army brigades and divisions. For a Regular, this meant automatic, although temporary, promotion through the newly formed National Army. It also allowed for the removal of National Guard officers from their respective commands, and this was done sometimes on the flimsiest excuse. But in many cases the National Guard officers were veterans of regular or wartime service (including the Mexican Border Operation of 1916-17) and had as much combat command time as did the incoming Regular Army replacements.

The task of building camps and training the troops needed to staff the newly formed American Expeditionary Force was staggering. However, the 42nd Infantry Division could be trained in the basic school of the soldier at the massive tent city that was Camp Mills, New York. Since the Rainbow would come from twenty-six states, the problems of getting all of the forces to Mineola, New York, by rail were complex. Officers and sergeants were totally ignorant of sanitation and subsistence requirements for the lengthy trips from as far away as California, Wisconsin, and Minnesota in the West, Alabama and Georgia in the South, and Illinois in the heartland. When the division began to form in June and July, many of the soldiers were lacking even uniforms and decent Army marching shoes. Some troops were training in overalls and leftovers from the Mexican Border Operation.

The Rainbow Division had a structure, a table of organization and equipment (TO&E), like all other World War I divisions. Those divisions were huge: 991 officers and 27,114 enlisted men. This was the size of a very large Civil War corps, and was double the size of any division in the next war the United States would fight. The heart and soul of the World War I division was the 4,000-man infantry regiment. Four regiments were organized into two equal-sized brigades, each commanded by a brigadier general and a small staff. A number of Regular Army colonels suddenly found themselves wearing the star, and a large number lost them just as quickly. An artillery brigade consisted of three regiments and had a total of twenty-four 155mm howitzers, forty-eight 75mm guns, and a trench mortar battery. Each infantry brigade was supported by a machine gun battalion, with another machine gun battalion located with divisional or non-brigade troops. This gave the division an impressive 260 machine guns to commit to battle. But it was the 16,000-plus rifles that would carry the day for the AEF.

Pershing and many of his key subordinates firmly believed that the war would be won by the rifleman, supported by artillery and assisted by the support units that kept him fighting. During his tenure as AEF commander, Pershing came into contact with the tank, and he had a brilliant Air Service officer on his staff named Billy Mitchell. But neither air nor the tank would be of great interest to Pershing. Those technological innovations in modern war were, in his view, exotic and peripheral. The foot soldier would carry the day, and in Pershing's mind, he had to be led by competent and fearless officers.

Black Jack Pershing's training and his reading all pointed to the historical necessity of ultimate reliance on the infantry regiments. Regrettably, the Spanish-American War yielded few, if any, positive examples or lessons for the modern soldier. The Indian Wars and the Mexican Border Operation of 1916 were so different from France in 1917 that little could be gleaned from those experiences. Pershing continued to believe in an exaggerated view of the effectiveness of the horse cavalry, but mainly he looked at the force of the rifle to prevail. Where, then, did he find examples that would guide his thinking and affect all American troops, including the 42nd Division? Pershing's ideas were largely formed by that great conflict called the Civil War, which was, after all, only fifty years in the past.

The combat arms—infantry, machine gun, and artillery—made up three-fourths of a division, a force to maneuver on the battlefield and to wage decisive battle with the enemy. The infantryman was the ultimate weapon that commanders had at their disposal.

Pershing, who was surprised to have received command of the AEF, went to France with several objectives in mind. First, he would create and keep intact a totally American force, and second, he would commit that force to combat based on maneuver. But he knew that the worst thing that could happen would be to send a green, untrained Army into the fight, and this belief affected every division, including the Rainbow. Again, lessons of history determined the future of the AEF. Combat divisions would spend a great deal of time preparing for combat and would receive actual experience by serving in the line with British and French combat units. Allowing Americans to serve in the trenches did not violate Pershing's commitment to a total American force. For the Rainbows, as for everyone else in the AEF, time would be taken to prepare the troops to fight as large units. The school of the soldier and preliminary physical toughening would take place in the United States, but the real business of defeating hardened German troops in battle would be learned in combat in France.

Very quickly, units throughout the 42nd lost promising privates and non-commissioned officers (NCOs) to the Officer Training Program, where they were turned into "ninety-day wonders." However, the old West Point school ring remained a ticket for most for advancement to higher grades. Certainly of value was the Mexican Border experience, and the 4th Alabama and the 69th New York regiments had a large number of border veterans. But when arriving at Mineola, New York, most officers and NCOs had not the faintest idea of how to train and care for large numbers of soldiers on extended duty.

In Dodge City, Kansas, Calvin Lambert had decided to enlist in something, but the infantry did not appeal to him. While drilling with a volunteer home guard unit he decided to enroll in a new company—a mule-drawn ammunition train that, to his delight, was changed to a motor truck company to haul ammunition. There was a problem: The company had no troops and no vehicles. Consequently, Lambert and the few stalwart ammunition-train men went on the road like a traveling medicine show to recruit members. Four men in a Ford Model T would arrive in a town, one of the four would blow an antique bugle, assemble the town's young and curious, and then make his pitch. And they lied shamelessly. "We promised them," Lambert recalled, "there would be no drilling, no loading or unloading, we probably would have big white trucks and we even pictured a trip across the United States from the truck factory to the seaboard."[2] On 25 June, the 100-man truck company of the Kansas Ammunition Train was sworn into the National Guard.

On 1 July, Joe Romano decided to re-enlist in his old Mexican Border unit, Company D, 4th Alabama. The 4th was now the 167th Infantry Regiment and was scheduled to move soon to the state capital at Montgomery. Volunteers came quickly to the Alabama regiment, and soon it had attained its assigned strength of 4,000 men.[3] The 4th Alabama had arrived in Montgomery from the Mexican border on 22 March 1917, and now, less than six months later, it was again preparing for active duty. The regimental commander, Regular Army Colonel William Screws of Montgomery, had been a lieutenant colonel with the regiment in Mexico. After the regiment's return, he was elected by the troops to be colonel of the unit. Screws tried to train his Alabamians as best he could, given the constant influx of new recruits and the shortage of equipment.[4] On 28 August, in secrecy, eight trains took the 167th Infantry on the first leg of its World War I odyssey.

For Father Francis Duffy, Major William "Wild Bill" Donovan, Sergeant Joyce Kilmer, and Private Martin Hogan, the move to Camp Mills would be simple, only a few miles. Once it was announced that the old Irish 69th Regiment would be sent to the 42nd Division there was a rush to fill the ranks up to 4,000 soldiers. Father Duffy, a leading Catholic intellectual and former editor of the Catholic *New York Review*, had built up his Church of the Savior in a tough Irish area of the Bronx, and when the 69th was mobilized for duty on the Mexican Border in 1916, Duffy left his pulpit for duty as senior chaplain.[5]

Wild Bill Donovan had just been transferred into the 69th from the staff of New York's 27th Division. Duffy respected Donovan as an Irish leader, but there were many rumors that the wealthy Donovan was a glory hunter, a man with a career filled with success and adventure. Born in 1883 to an Irish Catholic, but Republican, family in Buffalo, New York, Donovan was a well-known football player at Columbia University, where he graduated in 1905. In 1914 the rising young lawyer met and married Ruth Rumsey, a beautiful socialite and member of a prominent Buffalo family, possibly the city's wealthiest and best connected politically. Despite their obvious deep affection for each other, Ruth Donovan had a formidable task ahead of her if she wished to domesticate Wild Bill Donovan, especially since he had become involved deeply in the New York National Guard, taking every opportunity to be with the cavalry troop he commanded as a captain.

In 1916, Donovan traveled to Europe as part of a war relief commission. In London he met and befriended Herbert Hoover, but his time in Europe was cut short when President Wilson called up units of the National Guard to serve on the Mexican border. Donovan then spent eight and a half months there and acquired a reputation as a hard trainer and a demanding officer, attracting the attention of Brigadier General Pershing. When Donovan returned to New York, he was offered a colonelcy in the 27th New York National Guard Division, but he turned it down, pulled strings, and transferred to the 69th New York Infantry as its First Battalion commander. What worried Duffy were the stories of Donovan's being brave to the point of recklessness, and possibly putting military advancement ahead of the lives and safety of his troops.

Duffy had no such worries about the poet Joyce Kilmer. Kilmer, a recent convert to Catholicism, was serving with the prestigious 7th New York Regiment when he decided to transfer to the 69th. Twice he went to the 69th's armory and found no recruiting officers there. He discussed his inability to join the 69th with his parish priest, Father John Kelly, who quickly took him to Duffy. Duffy immediately liked the intellectual and devout Kilmer, and he assured him that when the 69th completed muster, Kilmer's name would be on the rolls.[6] Martin Hogan, who had permission now to join, was added to the rolls just as word reached the National Guardsmen that by the end of August they would depart for Camp Mills to begin preparation for going "Over There." On 16 and 19 August, advanced details went to Camp Mills to prepare for the arrival of the main body.[7] The *New York Times* announced the scheduled departure of the main portion of the regiment for Camp Mills on 20 August. Amid cheers from families and patriotic well-wishers, the Irish regiment paraded through New York to the ferry that would take them on the first leg of their wartime journey.[8]

Everett Scott enjoyed his initial sojourn as a soldier, since his regiment mustered into service in Des Moines. Besides drilling and marching, they enjoyed a feast of entertainment and food provided by the patriotic citizens of the state, who took pride in their old 3rd Iowa regiment, now the 168th U.S. Infantry. The troops were treated to car races and picnics, but by 5 September, although the trains had not arrived to take them to New York, the rookie doughboys were ready to go.[9] Quietly, on the night of 6 September, the regiment departed for the East Coast, arriving at Camp Mills on 13 September. What first impressed Scott about Camp Mills was its size and the aircraft, which he had never seen before. He wrote to his mother, "I have to stop writing once in a while to hear the airoplanes. There is some of them in the air all the time here now. They are all government airoplanes. There are seven of them in the air at one time. Its quite a sight...."[10]

Calvin Lambert's promised motorcade of gleaming new white trucks did not materialize, much to his dismay, but Lambert and the Kansas Ammunition Train were on the way to Camp Mills. "The Rock Island," Lambert complained, "must be a pacifist road or at any rate it has no love for soldiers. For our special consisted of the oldest and dirtiest sleepers I ever saw."[11]

What the men Lambert recruited with visions of the big parade of new trucks thought about the change in plans, Lambert did not say, but he heaped scorn on the 117th Ammunition Train's commissary officer, who saw a good buy in potted ham for the trip from Kansas to Camp Mills and served it without variation. To make matters worse, the Ammunition Train's commander refused to allow his soldiers to leave their cars in St. Louis, Missouri, to buy food and drink.

Leslie Langille had decided to enlist in the National Guard of Illinois, and by July he was a member of B Battery, 149th Field Artillery (without guns), descended from the Chicago Board of Trade Battery which was organized in 1862 and saw service in every battle in Tennessee and Georgia. While waiting for the trains to take them to Camp Mills, members of the 149th found out that they were to be part of a brigade that had two other midwest regiments—the 150th Field Artillery, formerly the First Indiana, and the 151st Field Artillery, which had been the First Minnesota Field Artillery Regiment. From a mobilization site at Fort Sheridan, Illinois, the troops departed in secrecy for Camp Mills, arriving on 5 September.[12]

Charles MacArthur of the 149th Field Artillery Regiment arrived at Camp Mills having never fired an artillery piece. He and most of his battery had been recruited into the National Guard during the summer, immediately after war was declared. Like the rest of the regiment, MacArthur and his college pals went to Fort Sheridan and then to Long Island. So far, it had been a lark, and the greatest concerns facing the Illini involved finding decent-fitting military clothes, a way to get into the fleshpots of New York, and a method of teaching the University of Illinois Alma Mater and fight song to the non-college men of the battery.[13] What the college boys did not reckon on was the presence of a tough, former Regular Army field artillery colonel by the name of Henry J. Reilly, who was determined, once all of his artillerymen were in camp, to turn the boys of the Chicago Battery and the rest of the Illinois gunners into a first-rate artillery regiment.

The Minnesota artillery regiment had assembled near Fort Snelling and came under the command of Colonel George Leach, a longtime member of the Minnesota National Guard. Leach's family had a long, distinguished militia history. His father had been a captain and the adjutant of the gallant 1st Minnesota infantry in the Civil War. The old 1st Minnesota Artillery had seen service on the Mexican border and should have been prepared to begin active service. The colonel was worried, however, because almost a majority in the ranks preparing to go to Camp Mills were infantrymen the state had transferred into the artillery as a money-saving device. Both infantry and artillery were on active service, but the artillery was on state service making two dollars a day, while the infantry on federal duty was making fifty cents a day. The Minnesota Public Safety Commission decreed that as many artillerymen as possible be released to save the state money, and Leach was concerned about the quality of his regiment, for good reasons.[14] Over the next few weeks, more Minnesota artillerymen would return to the ranks, but the war was not starting out well for the Gopher Gunners.

Private Franklin Ashton Croft of the Alabama Regiment had initially enlisted in the machine gun company of the 2nd Alabama Infantry Regiment at Andalusia, but on 14 August, ten days after his enlistment, he was informed that he would be part of a contingent of 800 2nd Alabama men to be transferred to the 167th Infantry at Montgomery. Clark did not mind, as the rumor was that the 167th would be the first state unit to go to France. Only two weeks later he was in Camp Mills, and he confided in his diary that the aircraft, in the air all day, fascinated him.[15] He had never seen an airplane before.

Calvin Lambert and his fellow Kansans were greatly upset. They had to move their tents almost every day for a week due to errors made by inexperienced division and camp engineers. The continual distribution of clothing, the medical exams, and the mounds of paperwork kept Lambert from visiting either Hempstead, New York, or New York City.[16]

Martin Hogan, now a private in Company K, part of the Third, or Shamrock Battalion, 165th Infantry, had no great desire to visit the dens and dives of New York City. He was bored. His day consisted mainly of physical training, bayonet drill with no dummies, and marching. His stomach muscles hurt badly from constant sit-up exercises. Before his arrival at Camp Mills, he and other recruits were taught the school of the soldier in a vacant lot near the 69th Infantry Armory, but his best memory was the march through New York clad in new uniforms, and worse luck, new shoes. The regiment, when it turned on to Fifth Avenue, was greeted by a wildly cheering throng, which included parents who dashed into the ranks to kiss their sons good-bye. Most of the tough Irishmen of the old Fighting 69th were in tears as they left their city for the war.[17]

Early in August, Major General Mann had complained that it was one thing to create a division of 28,000 men on paper, but it was another matter to form that unit and prepare them for embarkation, let alone combat operations. Within one month, from 7 August to 8 September, the division was formed, units were ordered to move from home station to Camp Mills, and training was started. Moving the Rainbows to France in September was out of the question.[18] Mann, MacArthur, and the staff knew that the War Department was determined that John J. Pershing have troops in France as soon as possible to lend credibility to the American commitment to the war effort. Pershing's position was that once the soldiers were in France, a more important detailed training program would prepare them for the trenches and open warfare. The best that could be hoped for was a unit composed of subordinate commands that at least had physical training, uniforms, and a basic knowledge of the school of the soldier.

Although many of his young officers had not yet arrived from their training programs, Mann had to begin the process of training what was there. On 8 September, his training officer and MacArthur issued a schedule that had three simple and basic directives. Building discipline and unit cohesion had priority. Second, physical fitness was to be emphasized. Last, Mann expected that his troops would learn the school of the soldier, including drill, personal hygiene, and maintenance of personal combat gear (such as they had at that point). Company officers were expected to know the drill and be ready to conduct drill and physical training. They instructed the non-commissioned officers prior to each training day while the troops ate and made preparation for drill.[19]

The day began at 5:30 A.M. and ended at 4:30 P.M., six days a week. By 9:45 P.M. lights were to be out in the enlisted men's tents, while the officers continued to review and practice training for the next day. There were attempts to allow the troops a little time off on Saturday night and part of the day on Sunday, but it was obvious that there was a sense of urgency to train the troops in the basics.[20]

Mann and his staff knew that the training of the troops was basically an exercise in repetition and tedium, and with so many young, healthy men present in a small place, there were many opportunities for them to find trouble. Most of the non-New Yorkers were determined to see America's largest city, so famed for diversions a soldier would not dare write home about. For the men of the old 69th, home was a few miles away, and the temptation to see a girlfriend, have a home-cooked meal, or lift a glass with those who remained behind was great.

Ettinger found himself being court-martialed by Major Wild Bill Donovan for going back to New York without a pass. He pled guilty to being AWOL, whereupon Donovan fined him a month's extra duty and two-thirds of a month's pay. What made things worse for Ettinger was the twist of fate that caught him the very next morning. Now restricted to Camp Mills, Ettinger decided to enter into a quiet Sunday morning craps game, where he was caught by Father Duffy. Duffy took exception to crap shooting before Mass, and he gave Ettinger and his Irish comrades a severe tongue-lashing. The young Ettinger, having run afoul of both Donovan and Duffy, frankly wished he were in France.[21]

The longer they stayed, the greater was the possibility for trouble. Everett Scott told his brother that there were fist-fights between Iowa troops and men from other states.[22] When time allowed, Scott and his buddies went to the YMCA in Hempstead.[23]

Private Ashton Croft of Alabama was worried that the Alabamians seemed a sickly lot. They were continually being quarantined for one ailment or another. On 13 September, Croft was disgusted to find out that the regiment had been restricted due to several cases of spinal meningitis within the unit. The quarantine lasted a full seven days.[24] General Mann and his staff really did not want the Alabama troops to have too much freedom while at Mineola, New York, because there had already been health and discipline problems with the regiment in camp and in the nearby town of Hempstead.

Major James W. Frew, a doctor from the Wisconsin National Guard and one of the original members of the Rainbow staff, recorded:

From a medical standpoint the Alabama regiment caused us a great deal of worry and trouble. They were nearly all boys from the mountains and rural districts and as soon as they hit camp they began to have their baby diseases. Measles, diphtheria, and scarlet fever were soon raging and the whole regiment was put under strict quarantine. After we arrived in France over 600 of them came down with mumps inside of two weeks.[25]

The Alabamians were also hard to discipline, and the division leadership did not like them to go to Hempstead for recreation. While on the Mexican border, there had been an incident between the 4th Alabama and some black U.S. cavalry troops, and at Camp Mills there were several racial incidents.[26]

Alcohol became very quickly a source of trouble for the division. Young soldiers enduring the tedium of repetitive training had a tendency to drink, and many had never drunk alcohol before. By mid-September the sale or possession of intoxicants was forbidden, and bars in Hempstead and in Jamaica, now thriving towns based on the soldier trade, were put off-limits.[27] This still did not curb the antagonisms between the troops, especially the Alabama and the New York soldiers, who took an instant dislike to each other. No two regiments could have been more unlike than the 167th Alabama and the 165th New York, with vast differences in education, religion, and background, as well as the obvious sectional antagonisms.

At one point, a series of fights erupted between the two regiments. During one particularly bad incident, the Virginia Military Police were called in to separate the fighters, and one soldier from Alabama was killed.[28] Even though the division staff, the officers from the two regiments, and the ever-present Father Duffy immediately began the work of repairing the damage, bad blood would continue between the two units, even in France.

The antagonism seemed to be limited to New York and Alabama, however. The Iowa 168th Infantry found itself in the same brigade with the Alabamians, and upon its arrival the rumor made the rounds that there would be a clash. The first night a large number of Southerners wandered into the Iowa camp, but it became clear that the descendants of old Rebels were there to greet their brigade mates peacefully.[29] It was wise to brigade the Iowa and the Alabama regiments together because both were predominantly rural and small-town. Big-city New York and rural Alabama made too volatile a mixture.

Everett Scott was surprised how cold it could be on the East Coast. On 4 October, he wrote to his mother about the hard drilling and marching, and added, "Well they gave us another blanket last night and it sure feels good. It gets awful coald here nights and it is real damp."[30] While Scott was luxuriating in his new Army blanket, Major Hugh W. Ogden, staff judge advocate of the 42nd Division, was scratching his head over a letter he had just received through channels from a mother asking that her son be released from service. She stated that he needed a discharge, "because he is my only sport." How he would answer that, he did not know.[31]

Calvin Lambert, now a sergeant, spent more time in camp while waiting for an opportunity to visit New York City. His appraisal of the area surrounding Camp Mills was sour indeed. He later stated that he disliked Hempstead, and added, "Another village made famous by its crullers and bootleggers, was Westbury, about 2 miles northeast of camp." Here the soldiers found prices a little more reasonable, the booze a little freer, and the crowds smaller. "I visited Waterbury but once....Jamaica was a larger city.... Its chief attraction was booze and a few women of doubtful morals."[32]

Corporal Herman Hillig of C Company, 1st Battalion, 165th Infantry, had no desire to leave Camp Mills. He was a quiet man, an intense soldier seemingly consumed by some inner hate. Often he declared that the Kaiser was totally responsible for this war and the whole German system had to be crushed unmercifully. Hillig, a German immigrant who spoke with an accent, had learned that his father and three brothers who remained behind in Germany had all died in battle for the Kaiser. He had a score to settle in France.[33]

Ashton Croft and Joe Romano found that being quarantined so often in a camp where there were heavy rains and cold nights was not very glamorous at all. On 22 September, the quarantine was lifted and the Alabama boys, eager to sample the fleshpots of Hempstead, Waterbury, and Jamaica, vacated the camp quickly. Croft looked around and suddenly felt very lonely; the camp seemed like a ghost town.[34]

While doughboys were rushing off to savor the dubious pleasures of the surrounding area, others were turning their attention to the more honorable state of matrimony. Camp Mills had its share of these events. Father Duffy was delighted to see young couples married, especially in the church. It was eminently preferable to what went on in the towns near Camp Mills. He explained, "I have become a marrying parson."[35] Most of the time Duffy preferred to perform a quiet Mass, the couples entering his chapel from the rear, but every once in a while things got out of hand and detracted from what Duffy wanted.

Private Michael Mulhern of the 165th's band announced to Duffy that he had decided finally to wed his Irish sweetheart, Peggy O'Brien. For Duffy, this was a marriage made in old Ireland, to be celebrated in the house of Holy Mother Church with decorum. On the way to the chapel to officiate at the nuptials, he encountered the regimental band marching to the chapel with Private Mulhern in the lead. Duffy found out that Mulhern had let it slip that he and pretty Miss O'Brien were to be wed. Naturally, the band wanted to be there, as well as the rest of the regiment and other curiosity seekers. After the wedding it was found that many of the soldiers had stolen a vast quantity of rice from the kitchen, and some even had contraband bottles of whiskey—Irish, of course.[36]

When Protestant Private Samuel S. Darmstedt needed a minister in order to marry nineteen-year-old Elizabeth Ryman of New York, the good ladies of the Hempstead Garden Club arranged for the happy event at the local YMCA.[37] One of the longest engagements finally came to an unorthodox end for Lieutenant James O. Taylor, a Regular Army officer now assigned to Company M, 3rd Battalion, Alabama's 167th Infantry. Taylor and Ruby R. Knight of Bainbridge, Georgia, were engaged in 1914, but the Army sent Taylor to the Presidio of California, and then, much to Miss Knight's distress, to China. Since it was only for a year, she could wait. On his way back from China, Taylor was diverted to the Mexican border, where he spent almost another a year. When it became painfully clear that within a few weeks the Rainbows would be on their way to France, Taylor requested leave to get married and was refused because of the training schedule. At that point, the patient, long-suffering Miss Knight lost her composure. What had worked into a three-year engagement could stretch on indefinitely. Taking advantage of the new technology, Taylor wed his fiancee of many years by telephone. Sadly, there could be no honeymoon.[38]

By the end of September, the Rainbows had been toughened by several ten-mile marches with full gear every week. The school of the soldier had been learned, but many of the men were yet to be trained in their new weapons systems. The 117th Trench Mortar Battery had been a Maryland Coastal Artillery unit, but its members had not even seen a trench mortar. They were promised that once in France they would receive special instruction.[39]

The gleaming white trucks that Sergeant Calvin Lambert had promised back in Kansas had yet to materialize. In an age when vehicles were a rarity in the hinterlands, time would have to be taken for driver training, and, even more important, the critical area of vehicle maintenance. For the infantry, however, drill and training went on as usual; each battalion of each regiment ran a two-mile course over rough terrain and obstacles. Still, there was an avoidance of any discussion of trench warfare.[40]

If there was any question about the primacy of the infantry, it was answered when all officers received General Pershing's guidance in regard to pre-embarkation training. Pershing's thoughts, in the form of a small booklet, stressed the need to perfect rifle marksmanship while at camp in the United States. He ended his admonitions by pointing out that, once in France, military discipline and courtesy would be stressed. It was clear that the 42nd was nearing the end of its time at Camp Mills.[41] On 8 October, the commanders of all of the units of the Rainbow Division held a formation and told their men that if any soldier had qualms about going into battle, they were to step out of the ranks. None did. General Mann was not aware of the dramatic scene, but he was informed of the formation late in the evening.[42]

On 24 October, the Daughters of the American Revolution (DAR) presented a flag to the Rainbow Division. It was a blue silk banner with a rainbow embroidered on it, and below the insignia were the words, in gold thread, "Rainbow Division." Ladies from twenty-six states and the District of Columbia were present for the ceremony, which concluded when Brigadier General Michael Lenihan, commander of the 84th Brigade (New York and Ohio Infantry regiments), accepted the flag. Father Duffy made appropriate remarks, as did a DAR member from South Carolina.[43] It had already been ordered that all regimental and divisional colors and unit guidons would go to France, but, "they will be left well in the rear."[44]

Everett Scott noted with relief that the hours spent on drill were being reduced from more than eight to about five and a half a day.[45] Father Duffy knew that the time to depart was growing near, and he began to contact several hundred priests to come to Camp Mills to hear confession and celebrate Mass before the troops moved to their ships for the hazardous trip across the Atlantic.[46] Ashton Croft was tired of drilling, and the fall rains were damp and heavy. While packing up his gear for the trip to France, he felt ill and went to sick call, where it was determined that he had mumps. In the hospital, in a leaky tent, the young soldier from Alabama wondered if his swollen cheeks would keep him from going to France with his regiment.[47]

While the men at Camp Mills were anxious to be off for France, there were problems that would come back to haunt them later. The troops did not have all of the uniforms and combat gear that they would need. There was a critical shortage of warm sweaters, underwear, and shoes. Local charitable and service groups set about obtaining over 15,000 sets of sweaters, mufflers, and socks. Acting in his capacity as aide to General Mann, Captain Oscar W. Underwood, Jr., the son of the Alabama senator, informed the organizations that contributions would go through the Red Cross.[48] Father Duffy was also concerned about the clothing shortages, but at least he could take comfort in the large number of priests who were arriving in camp.

Leslie Langille heard the news that the Illinois Artillery Regiment would soon depart for France, and he felt ready. Only a few days earlier, the Illinois men watched as a member of their battery who had enlisted with such great patriotic fervor only a few months before was literally kicked out of camp by the battery commander. As departure time grew near, this young man had second thoughts about going into combat, and he prevailed upon political friends in Illinois to secure his release from the service. When the battery commander received the discharge orders, he escorted the man to the end of the Illinois tents and sent him on the way with a well-aimed boot to the rear. Langille and his comrades watched this spectacle with a mixture of disgust and amusement.[49] Calvin Lambert and his 117th Ammunition Train comrades were busy packing their bags, but they were not worried about sweaters; they were packing as many packages of cigarettes and Bull Durham smoking tobacco as they could. Lambert and his buddies had heard that smoking tobacco could be very scarce at the front.[50]

The 166th Ohio Infantry Regiment was tired of Camp Mills, particularly the "lynx-eyed Regular Army officers, some assigned to the division, some as instructors, who watched every move, ordered, hounded, harried unmercifully the men of the 42nd Division." The Ohio boys near the middle of October received new equipment, including the heavy, knee-length overcoat that, in their minds, was associated with service in the trenches. France could not be far off.[51] Martin Hogan of the 165th Infantry was concerned over his training. He understood that trench warfare training would take place in France, but as yet he had never fired his rifle.[52]

During the night of 18 October 1917, the 42nd Infantry Division left Camp Mills for ships at Hoboken, New Jersey; New York; and Montreal. The Hoboken contingent began departing for France that night, and its trans-Atlantic embarkations continued up to 31 October. Those departing from New York City began their voyages on 3 November; the last ship left on 23 November. This group stopped in Liverpool, England, and remained there until 1 December, when they departed for Le Havre, France. The troops that assembled in Montreal left as a convoy on 27 October and landed at Liverpool on 11

November. After a short rest in England, they also departed for Le Havre. The Rainbows were not to be reunited for several months, as different sections went to special training areas.[53]

The vast majority of Rainbow men had never seen such large ships, let alone sailed on one. Ettinger was particularly aggravated at being selected as a lookout for submarines, but he managed to get out of the duty by hiding behind a lifeboat every time his lieutenant walked by. Ettinger was on the USS *America*, which had been a German liner impounded at the start of the war, and there were ten other ships, all escorted by U.S. Navy vessels, taking this section of the Rainbow Division to France.[54]

Private John B. Hayes of Company I, 167th Alabama, observed that most of the Alabama troops afflicted with the mumps were pronounced well enough to undertake the rigors of the sea voyage. But, as Hayes recalled, the portholes leaked, and the floors were covered with the vomit of troops who had yet to find their sea legs.[55] Among the sick was Ashton Croft.

Major Ogden, the lawyer who had pondered so many strange letters while at Camp Mills, had a pleasant voyage, sharing his cramped quarters with southern Rainbow officers. Most officers shared staterooms. Being a Massachusetts man, he described his compatriots as being "all churchmen. At any rate they all go to church."[56]

Everett Scott was not thrilled at all at being on the Atlantic Ocean. For a farm boy from Iowa, this was a new experience that turned out not to be a happy one. Scott was in the first contingent to leave on the night of 18 October, and had been on the seas for five days when one of the main engines broke. Those aboard had to return to Hoboken to wait for another ship. "We seen a lot of interesting things on our trip," he wrote, "and a lot I never want to see again."[57]

Charles MacArthur found himself living in what had once been a ship's coal bin, a far cry from his clean, airy room at the University of Illinois. The best story was that the Alabama regiment had put to sea on the USS *President Grant*, an awful fate for the heirs of the Bloody 4th Alabama. The Illinois men were on the USS *President Lincoln*. It was a good omen for Yankee heroes, and they remained on board for thirteen days. To MacArthur's irritation, Captain Bruce Benedict, his battery commander, continually predicted a submarine attack and pointed out to his soldiers that since they were in the direct center of the ship, well below the water line, they had to train to abandon ship rapidly and they had to wear their newly issued woolen mittens because the waters of the Atlantic would be terribly cold.[58]

Martin Hogan set sail on the USS *America*, and he was upset that there had not been time to get into the city to say good-bye to his mother and his friends. Rumors flew around the *America* that a naval officer had been caught in a life boat with a flashlight, signaling to the feared German submarines. According to Hogan, the spy was caught, but everyone felt uneasy for the rest of the trip to Brest, France.[59] Leslie Langille was tired of wearing his life vest all the time. At night when the officers had retired to their cabins, Langille took off the filthy vest and used it as a pillow, but the fear of the submarine was always there. A religious young man, Langille took comfort in singing hymns while on watch.[60]

Father Duffy was on the *America* also, but once anchored in the French harbor of Brest, Duffy's patience was about gone. The Rainbows were idle on their ships, since no one had prepared for their arrival at the port. There was also no transportation to take the men to the various training areas. Duffy, in need of Communion wafers and wine, was allowed to leave the ship. As Providence would have it, he arrived at a convent at mealtime and dined well, sitting on a chair, with china rather than a mess kit in front of him.[61]

While the Americans sat on ships in the harbor for three to four days waiting for transportation to the training areas, the officers in charge of procuring offloading facilities and railcars to carry troops and equipment faced a task for which they had no training and no precedent. Within the first six months of the war, half a million soldiers made the trip to France. During the summer and fall of 1918, another one and one-half million made the journey. In July 1918, 306,000 doughboys made the one-month trip from East Coast ports to ports in either England or France.[62] No course taught in the Army prepared anyone for this task, and those involved, while roundly cursed (as they were by the Rainbows in November 1917), worked miracles. That did not ease the aggravation on the ships, however. Many of the men bobbing up and down in Brest harbor could clearly see French and American soldiers on the shore going into and out of bars, and there were local women there as well. It was not lost on the Rainbow officers that it would be best to get the men from the ships to the railcars as quickly as possible to avoid any bad incidents.[63]

While in transit across England, the Alabama Regiment experienced a severe outbreak of mumps. Before the Alabamians could leave England, they had over 600 cases of mumps and the entire unit was quarantined.[64] Over 200 167th men had to be hospitalized in the Belmont Military Hospital in Liverpool. A number of them, some recovering and some free of infection, obtained passes to visit the city, and there were fights with other Americans, with British soldiers, and with the Military Police.[65] December 1917 in France promised to be cold and wet, and a large portion of the Rainbow Division was simply not prepared for it. Albert Ettinger recalled that in his boxcar, one of the famed 40 and 8's (a French boxcar capable of transporting forty men or eight horses), there was one soldier who had been issued a uniform and a few basic items of equipment, but no pack, no blankets, no overcoat. Ettinger shared his few blankets with the man, but by the time the 165th Infantry reached their training area the soldier was sick from exposure and had to be taken to the hospital.[66]

On 15 December 1917, a surprised General Mann received orders to turn his command over to Major General Charles T. Menoher, recently a colonel in the Regular Army. Mann was much older than his successor, and Pershing felt that Mann would not be up to the rigors of combat. An 1886 graduate of West Point, a career field artillery officer, and a graduate of the Army War College, Menoher had served for four years on the general staff in Washington, where he attracted the attention of his seniors. He saw service in the Spanish-American War and in Manila in 1899, returning to the United States in 1901. While in the Philippines, Menoher served with Pershing, his old West Point classmate.

During the Mexican Border Operation, as a colonel of artillery, Menoher commanded a brigade at El Paso, Texas. He had an affinity for the French language, and he was given the task of going to France early in September 1917 to establish an artillery school at Samur. Menoher was trusted by Pershing as a solid professional soldier, a man with a forceful personality, and, most important, an officer selected by John J. Pershing. Menoher's personality never invited liberties or joking, but he could be very loyal to subordinates who, in turn, were loyal to him.[67]

Brigadier General Charles P. Summerall, a Regular Army artillery officer, had been in command of the 67th Field Artillery Brigade since its formation at Camp Mills. Noted for his sharp tongue and never liked by his National Guard gunners, Summerall left the brigade to command the 1st Infantry Division's artillery. To no one's surprise, AEF General Headquarters (GHQ) sent another Regular to take his place. Charles H. McKinstry, a few months before a colonel of engineers, took command of the brigade. McKinstry had graduated from West Point in 1888 and had attended all of the Army's schools for engineer officers.[68]

The appointment of McKinstry, an engineer, to command an artillery unit was strange, to say the least, but it did appear that Pershing was determined Regular Army officers would command whenever possible. This left a distinctly bad taste in the mouths of officers and soldiers alike, as they continued to perceive a definite bias on the part of Pershing and the West Point graduates for their own.

Pershing had a policy that was strictly enforced. The commander of the AEF put it simply:

Probably the most important factor in building up an aggressive army is the selection of leaders. Without efficient leadership, the finest of troops may suffer defeat by inferior forces skillfully led.... Inasmuch as our success would depend upon the offensive spirit among combat troops, it was essential that vigorous and intelligent leadership should, if possible, be assured at the outset.[69]

Pershing had an agenda. First, he viewed the AEF as an offensive army, not tied to trenches, not committed to the type of stalemate war that had gripped the Western Front since the end of 1914.

Second, Pershing was determined to mold the AEF and the future Army in his own pattern. In his mind, the Army would be young, robust, intelligent, and professional, and he was antagonistic to the Army system of seniority. Pershing believed:

In our Regular Army, in time of peace, the system of promotion by seniority, instead of by selection, deprives many capable and energetic officers of the opportunity to command the larger units, which would help to prepare them for higher places in time of war. The same comment applies with equal or greater force to our National Guard, in which politics adds another factor often adverse to efficiency in the higher grades.[70]

Regular officers and National Guard officers who did not fit the mold set by Pershing would quickly, ruthlessly be removed from command.

General Mann proceeded immediately to the United States for reassignment and for physical evaluation. On 10 April 1919, Mann was discharged from the National Army, the source of his major general's commission, and reverted to his previously held rank of brigadier general.[71] Certainly, newly minted Major General Charles Menoher gave the appearance of youth and was a Regular Army officer, but one might ask why Mann was not replaced before leaving the United States. Simply put, once Mann reached France he came under the jurisdiction of Pershing.

Mann had also challenged the AEF's concept of replacements, and this did not endear him to Pershing. On 10 November 1917, Colonel Fox Conner at AEF Headquarters issued a memorandum for the chief of staff recommending that "the 42nd Division be designated as the 1st Replacement Division of the I Corps, and that its equipment, organization, and training be made accordingly."[72]

Mann immediately went to Pershing's headquarters at Chaumont to protest this memorandum, arguing that this National Guard division, "had been a uniting force as the nation mobilized for war," and at any rate, replacements could come from those troops arriving from the United States. Douglas MacArthur claimed that he personally went to see Brigadier General James G. Harbord, whom he had known in the Philippines, and convinced him to reconsider.[73]

What happened was that Mann, MacArthur, and the National Guard officers immediately wrote to political friends in the United States for help. Mann, a former chief of the National Guard Bureau, had many such friends, and a flood of letters and telegrams poured into the War Department and into Chaumont. Pershing, Connor, and the staff of Regulars found that they had a serious fight on their hands. Connor, obviously reflecting Pershing's views on the matter, saw this as a test case for control of American troops by the AEF in France. On 22 November 1917, Connor wrote, "The decision in this case is fundamentally important. It will probably establish the policy relating to the employment of National Guard divisions for replacements."[74]

In Washington, the chief of staff's office was less enthusiastic about the breaking up of the Rainbow Division. For good military and political reasons, the chief's office understood the necessity of holding the 42nd intact. The nineteenth-century German military commentator Karl von Clausewitz had warned that there existed, in war, a trinity of the army, the government, and the people, which must be in accord. In a document with echoes of Clausewitzian philosophy, the War College Division advised the chief of staff:

No one should have been surprised that this particular issue should have surfaced and that it would be one that would be hard fought with the advantage being with the National Guard in this case. On 30 August 1917, Major General Tasker Bliss, the Army Chief of

Staff, addressed the idea of using either the 26th Yankee Division or the 42nd Rainbow Division as a replacement unit, and the Chief argued against breaking up either, but especially the 42nd. The Chief of Staff pointed out that, ". . . there is another phase of the question with regard to the 42nd Division which is psychological. It is composed of National Guard units from 24 [sic] states and publicity was given to the fact that it was organized for combat. To convert it into a replacement troop now may invite criticism of bad faith on the part of the War Department. Its engagement in battle will bring home to our people in every section of the country that we are at war."[75]

MacArthur was well aware of this position paper by the chief's office because a copy appears in the 42nd Division's records addressed to him. How quickly support was mobilized back in the United States might seem extraordinary, but the danger of seeing the Rainbow Division broken up had existed for months, and old hands like Mann and MacArthur were prepared for it. Of importance also is the fact that Newton Baker regarded the Rainbow as partially his creation. With the war effort not going smoothly in America, neither President Wilson nor Newton Baker wanted complications over the much publicized 42nd Division. Despite his efforts to appear philosophically above the political fray at times, Woodrow Wilson needed a happy Tammany Hall, a contented state house in Montgomery, Alabama, and support from Midwest Democrats. Those people saw the National Guard as representing the state and the citizen soldier at its best.

AEF Chief of Staff Brigadier General James G. Harbord, who had approved Fox Connor's initial memorandum, now did an about-face fifteen days later and argued forcefully against disbanding the 42nd Division. One of the reasons Harbord gave was, "The division commander is an inactive man, but an active politician," and the Rainbow "has figured more in the press and has more friends to resent the matter."[76] Harbord recognized the political reality of the situation when he concluded, "I much fear that if you used it as replacement without notice to the War Department that you would be reversed; on the other hand if you ask the War Department that you will not be permitted to do it."[77]

There was the crux of the matter. It was politically a hot potato, and Pershing had to agree to retain the Rainbows as a division. Pershing, however, never forgot or forgave this challenge to his authority. He consequently kept a distance from MacArthur, who had dared to circumvent his wishes—and for a National Guard unit at that. The newly arriving 41st Infantry from the National Guards of Idaho, Washington, Oregon, Montana, and Wyoming were designated on 8 December 1917 as the I Corps replacement division, many of the troops going to the Rainbow.

The removal of Mann was just the first in a long series of incidents in which Rainbow officers were removed from command. The situation constantly affected the 42nd Division, as it would all other AEF combat units until after the Armistice in November 1918. Usually, the removed officer was sent to the rear, to the city of Blois "to receive instructions." Often, an officer would find a place of duty, an assignment, in the SOS, the Service of Supply. It was not then uncommon to find relieved infantry or artillery officers in command of quartermaster units, depots, rail yards, and the like. If there were problems in the SOS, some of the blame must rest with Pershing and his staff, who used it at times as a dumping ground. Also, Pershing carried on a continual and dangerous feud with General Payton Marsh, the Army chief of staff in Washington, over the assignment of officers to the AEF. Pershing argued that the assignment to AEF forces should be controlled by himself, being present in France with the knowledge of what was needed and what was not. March rejected this, and the conflict continued throughout the war, often becoming petty and giving a Byzantine nature to World War I Army politics.

By mid-December the division was informed that the majority of the Rainbows would move to the 5th Training Area at Vaucouleurs. Vaucouleurs was a town southwest of Toul and about seventy-five kilometers northeast of Chaumont, Pershing's headquarters. The infantry regiments would go to small towns for billeting and training. The artillery regiments, still devoid of serviceable artillery, went to Camp Coetquidan in Brittany for training.

The Rainbows were separated as each component part went to its own areas to receive training. At some point, they were informed, the infantry and artillery would receive partial hands-on training in the trenches alongside French units. While Pershing did not like this, there was little he could do at that point. The AEF, by December 1917, consisted of the 1st and 2nd Regular Divisions, the 26th Yankee Division and the Rainbow Division. All four units were green, and the American supply system had yet to function to support combat divisions. The headquarters of the SOS (Service of Supply) was in Tours, a city on the Loire River with a key rail line, but during the Christmas season of 1917 the SOS was small and inefficient in operation. Later, Tours and other towns would resemble huge mountains of supplies, but that was weeks away. Pershing recognized the problems in getting the flow of supplies from America to the AEF, but his main problem was that with only four divisions in France, and those incapable of combat, he had few bargaining cards when dealing with the French or British armies.

At least the cold, wet, and thoroughly miserable doughboys of the Rainbow Division were on their way to their training areas. They were indeed "Over There."

NOTES

1. Memorandum from Adjutant General's Office to the commanding general, Southeastern Department, Washington, 28 July 1917, as found in the National Archives, Washington, D.C., *Records Group 120 Records of the AEF, 42nd Division*, carton 126 (hereinafter, RG 120).

2. Sergeant Calvin Lambert Diary, manuscript, Emporia Public Library, Emporia, Kansas, 3.

3. Notes provided by Joseph O. Romano, Jr., Birmingham, Alabama, based on his extensive conversations with his father, Corporal Joseph O. Romano, 167th Infantry

(hereinafter, Romano Notes).

4. William H. Amerine, *Alabama's Own in France* (New York: Eaton and Gettinger, 1919), 51-54.

5. John B. Hayes (company clerk, Company I, 167th Infantry), *Heroes Among the Brave* (Loachapoka, Ala.: Lee Country Historical Society, 1973), 6-7.

6. Francis P. Duffy, *Father Duffy's Story* (New York: George H. Doran Company, 1919), 16-17.

7. *New York Times*, 16 and 19 August 1917.

8. Ibid., 20 August 1917.

9. Scott to his mother, Des Moines, 2 September 1917, in Scott's letters, manuscripts in the author's collection (hereinafter, Scott Letters).

10. Scott to his mother, Camp Mills, 13 September 1917, ibid.

11. Calvin Lambert Diary, 26-27.

12. Leslie Langille, *Men of the Rainbow* (Chicago: O'Sullivan Publishing House, 1933), 16-21.

13. Charles MacArthur, *War Bugs* (Garden City, N.Y.: Doubleday, Doran & Co., 1919), 29.

14. Louis L. Collins, *History of the 151st Field Artillery Regiment, Rainbow Division* (Saint Paul, Minn.: Minnesota War Records Commission, 1924), 12-15.

15. Entry dated 31 August 1917, Franklin Aston Croft diary, 1917, Auburn University Archives, Auburn, Alabama.

16. Calvin Lambert Diary, 30.

17. Martin J. Hogan, *The Shamrock Battalion of the Rainbow: A Story of the Fighting 69th* (New York: D. Appleton and Company, 1919), 10-13.

18. Memorandum from Mann to chief of staff, Washington, 7 August 1917, RG 120, carton 3.

19. General Orders No. 5, Camp Mills, 8 September 1917, ibid., carton 25.

20. Ibid.

21. A. Churchill Ettinger (ed.), *A Doughboy with the Fighting 69th* (Shippensburg, Penn.: White Main Publishing, 1992), 15-16.

22. Scott to his brother, Hempstead, N.Y., 21 September 1917, Scott Letters.

23. Scott to his mother, Hempstead, N.Y., 7 October 1917, ibid.

24. Entry dated 13 September 1917, in Croft diary.

25. From the James W. Frew Papers, a memoir written c. 1921, in *U.S. Army Military History Institute Archives, Carlisle Barracks, Pennsylvania, 42nd Division AEF Collection* (hereinafter, MHIA).

26. *New York Times*, 2 September 1917. The 167th's official history mentions the incident, which took place at Nogales between the 4th Alabama and two troops of the black 10th U.S. Cavalry. According to William Amerine's account, two black cavalrymen were arrested by an Alabama corporal because they violated standing orders and brought loaded weapons into Nogales. The official history lays the blame for the ensuing fistfights between groups of the black cavalrymen and the Alabama infantrymen to anger over their being arrested, as Regulars, by National Guardsmen. More than likely, racial antagonism played a major role in the situation, but Brigadier General Edward H. Plummer, who commanded the Nogales area, sent the 10th Cavalry away from the town on scouting missions. See Amerine, *Alabama's Own*, 44-45.

27. *New York Times*, 19 September 1917.

28. Ettinger, *Doughboy*, 7-8. The local newspapers, including the *New York Times*, do not mention this fatal riot, but stories about it appear in Rainbow legend. In the 1940 movie with James Cagney and Pat O'Brien, the fight is depicted as a harmless altercation between the troops. It was anything but that. The official history of the Alabama 167th Regiment tells a different story and plays down the incident (Amerine, *Alabama's Own*, 55-56). Father Francis Duffy, whose personal account is very pro-165th, saw no need to mention the fracas between the two.

29. John H. Taber, *The Story of the 168th Infantry*, Vol. 1 (Iowa City: State Historical Society of Iowa, 1925), 8-10.

30. Scott to his mother, Camp Mills, 4 October 1917, in Scott Letters.

31. Ogden to his wife, nd, written while in transit to France, in the Major Hugh W. Ogden Letters, MHIA.

32. *Calvin Lambert Diary*, 30-31.

33. *New York Herald*, 25 September 1917.

34. Entry dated 22 September 1917, in Croft Diary.

35. Duffy, *Story*, 21.

36. Ibid.

37. *New York Herald*, 16 September 1917.

38. *New York Times*, 8 October 1917.

39. Peter H. Ottosen, *Trench Artillery, AEF* (Boston: Lothrop, Lee & Shepard, 1931), 99.

40. *New York Times*, 6 October 1917.

41. *New York Herald*, 9 October 1917.

42. Ibid.

43. Ibid., 24 October 1917.

44. Memorandum, HQ, 42nd Division, Camp Mills, 7 October 1917, in RG 120, carton 150.

45. Scott to his mother, Camp Mills, 7 October 1917, Scott Letters.

46. Duffy, *Story*, 33-35.

47. Entries 22, 30, 31 October, and 1 and 2 November 1917, in Croft diary.

48. *New York Herald*, 3 October 1917.

49. Langille, *Men of the Rainbow*, 33-35.

50. Calvin Lambert Diary, 39.

51. R. M. Cheseldine, *Ohio in the Rainbow: Official Story of the 166th Infantry, 42nd Division in the World War* (Columbus, Ohio: F. J. Heer Printing Co., 1924), 59-60.

52. Hogan, *Shamrock Battalion*, 12-13.

53. American Battle Monuments Commission, *42nd Division, Summary of Operations in the World War* (Washington: Government Printing Office, 1944), 3-4.

54. Ettinger, *Doughboy*, 20-21.

55. Hayes, *Heroes Among the Brave*, 8-9.

56. Ogden to his wife, nd., Ogden Letters, MHIA.

57. Scott to his mother, Hempstead, N.Y., 27 October 1917, Scott Letters.

58. MacArthur, *War Bugs*, 3-4.

59. Hogan, *Shamrock Battalion*, 22-23.

60. Langille, *Men of the Rainbow*, 39-40.

61. Duffy, *Story*, 36-38.

62. War Department, *The Official Record of the Great War* (New York: Parke, Austin, and Lipscomb, 1923), 48.

63. Ettinger, *Doughboy*, 21-22.

64. Memoir, c. 1921, in Frew Papers, MHIA.

65. Hayes, *Heroes Among the Brave*, 9-10.

66. Ettinger, *Doughboy*, 23-24.

67. Henry J. Reilly, *Americans All: The Rainbow at War* (Columbus, Ohio: F. J. Heer Printing Company, 1936), 111.

68. Ibid.

69. General John J. Pershing, *My Experiences in the World*, Vol. 1 (New York: Frederick A. Stokes Company, 1931), 124.

70. Ibid., 124.

71. Pershing's Files, "In the Matter of the Relief and Discharge of Major General William A. Mann," 23 May 1919, found in National Archives, Records Group 200, Pershing Papers, AEF, carton 8 (hereinafter, RG 200.)

72. Colonel Fox Connor, AEF General Headquarters, "Memorandum: 42nd Division Recommended for Replacement Division," 10 November 1917, in Center of Military History (CMH), *United States Army in the World War, 1917-1919. Vol. 3: Training and Use of American Units with the British and the French* (Washington: Government Printing Office, Reprint, 1989), 666-67.

73. Douglas MacArthur, *Reminiscences* (New York: McGraw-Hill, 1964), 53. See also Donald Smythe, *Pershing: General of the Armies* (Bloomington, Ind.: Indiana University Press, 1986), 61-62.

74. Colonel Fox Connor, AEF General Headquarters, "Memorandum: Recommendation to Designate 42nd Division as Replacement Division," 22 November 1917, in CMH, *US Army in World War*, Vol. 3, 667-68.

75. Chief of staff, Army Memorandum for the chief, War College Division, Washington, 30 August 1917, in RG 120, carton 58.

76. James G. Harbord, "Memorandum," 25 November 1917, in CMH, *US Army in the World War*, Vol. 3, 669-70.

77. Ibid., 670.

2

TRAINING FOR THE FIGHT: ROLAMPONT

Lieutenant William van Dolsen of the District of Columbia National Guard, now with the 117th Sanitary Train, was not enjoying his first weeks in France. His feet stayed wet and a newly purchased pair of rubber boots did no good. He wore two pairs of wool socks, but still his feet remained damp and cold. On arriving in France, he, like all other officers, was required to buy the Sam Browne belt (the symbol of the AEF officer) and a French-made overseas cap. Try as he would in front of a mirror, he couldn't make the cap look quite right. "It...is just like the bonnet of a Scotsman...without the ribbon. Some hat," he complained to his mother.[1]

Major Ogden, the staff lawyer, was amused to find out that he was about to be issued a steel helmet. Frankly, Ogden did not think he would need such an item, and he told his wife, "I shall preserve it with jealous care to show to admiring friends. They say the thing to do is to wait til you get ready to sail for home and then hit it an awful dent in the side with an axe, so you can point out to the proud ones what an awful peril you endured at the battle of vin ordinaire."[2]

Martin Hogan was on his way to Vaucouleurs in a drafty 40-and-8 boxcar and was out of tobacco and money. To make matters worse, the New York doughboys had just been introduced to the standard fare of the American Western Front soldier—Corned Willie and hardtack. Corned Willie was corned beef—dry, tinned, evil-smelling and equally bad-looking. Hardtack had been a soldier's bread for generations, made of flour, water, a little salt, and a very small amount of leavening. This formed a very hard cracker, impossible to bite and difficult to moisten. Most often in training or at the front, the Corned Willie was turned into a stew called Slum (for the Irish Slumgullion stew), to which might be added some dried vegetables or whatever was handy.[3]

Ettinger's company had already arrived at a small town named Naives-en-Blois, and their first drills were held in a rain that turned to snow. He and his buddies slept in a cold hayloft; the battalion commander had ordered that there be no fires built. Ettinger's shoes were completely soaked from the weather outside.[4] Father Duffy's main concern, as chief chaplain for the regiment, was an uplifting celebration of Christmas for these men so far from home. Wanting a midnight Mass, Duffy had approached his regimental commander, Colonel Charles Hine, who pointed out that they were under blackout conditions. But an amused Brigadier General Michael J. Lenihan agreed to holding the Mass, since they were so far from the front it certainly could not be seen by the Germans. Duffy had been put in charge of a special fund raised by the citizens of New York City, and could afford a fine meal for the Irish regiment.[5]

While Everett Scott was as cold and wet as everyone else in the 168th infantry, he was still captivated by what he had seen so far. "All of the houses here," he wrote to his mother, "both in Ingland and here are made of stone or bricks. There are very few wooden buildings. And all of the people wear wooden shoes. It sure was fun to watch them at first, but we are getting used to it now."[6] What was not remembered with fondness was a severe outbreak of scarlet fever, which necessitated the Iowans' being quarantined. A sparse diet, coupled with the cold, rain, and snow, produced a large number of pneumonia cases, and ten Iowa soldiers died.[7]

A problem for all the infantry regiments undergoing training was the weather and the lack of heat in the billets, usually a barn's hayloft where fire was prohibited. Outside, in the elements, the Iowans had a formation at 5:45 A.M., ate a dull breakfast, usually of bread, bacon, and coffee, and then trained in vacant fields. The training now consisted of learning to assemble, disassemble, maintain and fire the French automatic rifle, throw grenades, care for and put on the newly issued gas mask, and hold maneuver formations. There still was no trench training, because the directives to train the soldiers in open warfare came directly from Pershing's G3 (operations officer) at Chaumont.[8]

As could be expected, the infantry regiments and their assigned machine gun battalions would have the most difficult, demanding, and taxing training. In January 1918, Pershing and General Philippe Pétain hammered out details concerning the French responsibilities in relation to the four American divisions in France, including the 42nd. Their agreements came after some hard, contentious bargaining between the two men. The Rainbows would have one brigade soon ready to move into the line with a French division, while the other brigade continued to train. The divisional staff would also receive training and exercises in staff functions and would have only minimal control over the Rainbow brigade, which was in the line.

Pétain felt that the training of the infantry was a simple matter, but the education of the staff was another thing entirely. During the discussion, Pershing stated that he believed April or May would be a good time for the Americans to have their own sector of the line. Pétain was not sure such a rapid schedule could be met, but it was agreed that the 42nd Division would proceed to train and that efforts would be made to have the whole division ready soon for combat.[9]

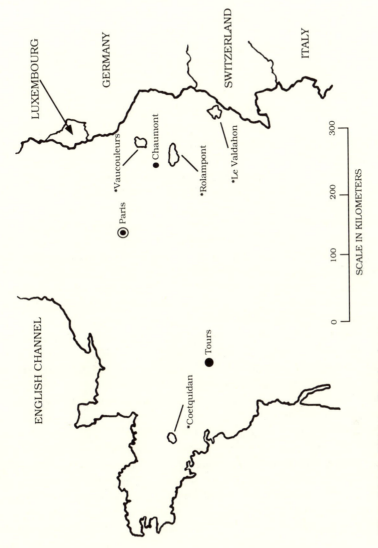

Figure 2.1 *42nd Division Training Areas

As the troops moved into Vaucouleurs, they found a large number of second lieutenants waiting for them. The Rainbow Division had received nearly two dozen young officers to make up for the shortage in the lowest officer ranks. Among them was Second Lieutenant Hugh S. Thompson, the son of the mayor of Chattanooga, Tennessee, and a graduate of the University of Virginia. He had joined the service immediately after the declaration of war and was sent to Officers Training School, where, after ninety days, he received his gold bars. He had arrived in France several months before the 42nd and was sent to a trench-warfare training school run by the French army at Valbonne, near the Alps of the Savoy.

When Thompson left Valbonne in late December, he had no idea where his assignment would be. A few days later he found himself with other young officers assigned to the 168th Iowa at Vaucouleurs. "Of the twenty-seven officers who reported to my regiment, under this order," Thompson recalled, "and remained for active service, seven were killed in action and fourteen were wounded. Several of the latter were twice wounded and two of them were wounded three times." Thompson himself sustained two serious wounds.[10] He had also been in France long enough to have met, in Valbonne, a pretty French girl named Charlotte. He had a girl back in Tennessee, but the war, the champagne, and the distance made Charlotte the object of his attentions. But Valbonne and Charlotte were now far away, and he had to concentrate on his Iowa troops, which he met in a heavy snowstorm only a few days after his arrival and assignment.[11]

While the infantry was the focus of the training in late December, the other components of the division were also taking instruction. The 117th Trench Mortar Battery arrived at the trench mortar school at Fort de la Bonnelle, near the town of Langres. The battery, like so many National Guard units, was made up of patriotic, adventurous youths, the majority of them college men from the Baltimore area who enlisted at the outbreak of the war. They had been associated with military life for only six months and had few skills. The trench mortar men had billets in the old fort, and they had heat; moreover, they could visit the town of Langres for some recreation.[12]

The artillery arrived at Camp Coetquidan in Brittany for training. Leslie Langille noticed that near the entrance to the camp there was a hastily constructed hut and tent boomtown. On some of the crude structures hung signs like "The Stars and Stripes Bar," and the "Franco-American Bar." There were also other diversions, and the artillerymen from Illinois were ready to begin training and exploring.[13]

When the Illinois Field Artillery Regiment arrived at Camp Coetquidan, they found their billets to be vermin-ridden, tar-paper shacks that sat in a sea of French mud. Like most of the 67th Field Artillery Brigade, Charles MacArthur quickly realized that those enterprising Frenchmen who ran the saloons and dives outside the main gate would display, "French and American flags and proceed to gyp the pants off us." At any rate, the proprietor of the Stars and Stripes

Saloon was giving away a hardboiled egg with each drink purchased in the bar.[14]

Colonel George Leach, of the Gopher Gunners, was delighted to be at Camp Coetquidan because his regiment had just received gleaming new French 75mm howitzers, and he was told by the French artillery instructors that on the morrow, 19 November, the regiment would begin formal training.[15] Leach and his officers were worried about the health of the entire regiment, because after Christmas two cases of infantile paralysis appeared. Men had died of pneumonia, but the fear of this dread crippler was intense. Much to the Minnesotans' relief, no new cases appeared while in Europe.[16] Throughout January and into February, the brigade trained on those tasks particular to artillery: crew drills, movement of the batteries, reconnaissance and selection of new firing positions, and artillery marksmanship. The artillerymen became so professional with their French 75mm guns that they could fire an average of thirty-two shells per three-gun battery per minute. They achieved such proficiency because of commanders like Colonel Henry J. Reilly, who was a strange hybrid of the Regular Army and the National Guard. Reilly was born into a Regular Army family in 1881 and went to West Point, graduating in 1904 with Douglas MacArthur. From the beginning of his career, there was something different about Reilly, whose father had been killed in action at Peking during the Boxer Rebellion in China. After graduation, Reilly served in the Philippines as head of the secret service division of the Far East Military Information (Intelligence) Division, and upon his return to the United States he was assigned as an instructor of history at West Point. While at West Point he wrote a weekly military column for the Chicago *Tribune*.

When the war broke out in 1914, the paper wanted him as a military correspondent, but because of his military affiliation, the British and French refused to issue him a permit. Frustrated, Reilly resigned his commission and served in a volunteer ambulance unit on the Western Front until 1915, which gave him a deep appreciation for the lethal nature of World War I artillery. After his return to Illinois, he joined the 1st Illinois Field Artillery as a captain and went with that unit to the Mexican border in 1916. In 1917, when the 1st Illinois was called to the colors, Reilly was a colonel in command of the regiment, and as one of the few Rainbow officers who knew the horrors of trench war, he went at training his regiment with intensity.[17] Reilly also understood his National Guardsmen, and he looked the other way when on Christmas 1917, "Dissipation started after morning stables and lasted until sometime the following morning."[18] On New Year's, also, the college boys of the Illinois regiment celebrated well into the night.

Leslie Langille and his battery mates devised a new game—sitting on the 75mm artillery pieces when fired! The French instructors constantly complained that their students were insane. The gun sitting continued until the battery went into action, and then there was no time for the highjinx of youth.[19] French instructors were everywhere teaching the 67th Field Artillery Brigade the fine points of the gun. Besides the 75mm gun, the Rainbow also received the 155mm howitzer, and training for one regiment equipped with this heavier, yet movable artillery piece had to go on as well.

Of all the units within the Rainbow Division, the 117th Sanitary Train had the most perplexing professional problems as far as preparation for combat was concerned. The train came from eight different states, and not one of its members had any idea of the magnitude of the medical problems they would face in combat. The 117th Sanitary Train was both motorized and animal-drawn, which meant that horses or mules had to be tended to. The motorized sections could move very quickly on dry road, but rainy weather presented problems now very apparent to medical personnel. Animal-drawn sections could use muddy roads, while motor vehicles, trucks, and ambulances had grave difficulties.

After arriving in France, AEF Headquarters published an ambitious three-month training program for the 117th Sanitary Train. The division surgeon was charged with overseeing the established training, and the train received invaluable instruction in preparation for moving to the front. Often, this learning period was interrupted by an influx of soldiers suffering from all manner of diseases, including trenchfoot and frostbite. Non-commissioned officers were required to attend special schools, and drivers were required to perform maintenance on vehicles every day for one hour.[20]

Besides having to keep up with the 117th Sanitary Train's demanding training schedule, while at the same time caring for patients, Lieutenant van Dolsen was made a mess officer, something for which his training as a doctor did not prepare him. However, being resourceful, van Dolsen found a French woman to cook who also had a vacant room that could be used for officers' dining. He wrote to his mother,

You should see me hustling around trying to find green vegetables and fresh eggs and when I am not doing that I am trying to show our French woman how to make a pie which is something she never heard of before. There is just one thing that I don't have to bother with—ice. You could hang a quarter of beef up in my room in this snow covered town.[21]

Wisconsin National Guard doctor James Frew was becoming increasingly alarmed over the lack of warm clothing for the troops in such cold and wet weather.[22]

Calvin Lambert could breathe easier because the 117th Ammunition Train finally had vehicles, and they, too, were at Camp Coetquidan. In a short time the troops were busy finding ways to visit the large number of saloons outside of the camp. But all was not cleaning and carousing. In mid-December, Lambert took a detail of Nash trucks to St. Nazaire to pick up a load of sugar and syrup, but the weather worsened and rain turned to snow, making the roads a slippery mess. During the return trip one truck turned over and spilled sugar and syrup in a farmer's inundated field. Those men who were so eager to drive while the infantry marched were finding out that life in an ammunition train was difficult and dangerous.[23] After January, the 117th Ammunition Train troops began to train with the 67th Field Artillery Brigade, where they found Colonel Reilly to be as demanding of ammunition haulers as of his artillerymen.

While the troops were preparing for a bleak Christmas at Coetquidan and at Vaucouleurs, a number of battalion officers were in school. On Christmas Day they, including Wild Bill Donovan, got an opportunity to go into the forward French trenches. Donovan, who felt at home with the French, engaged an officer in conversation. On the question of leadership, the French officer believed that the British soldier was very good, but he was poorly led, while the German soldier was equally as good, but his leadership was usually first rate. Donovan agreed, basing his views on what he had seen of the British in the trenches.[24] On 26 December, Donovan came under shell and small-arms fire for the first time, and he became the first Rainbow soldier to fire a shot in anger at the enemy. Donovan was exhilarated by the experience, writing in his diary he "was...under shells and rifle fire for the 1st time. Curious but easily accustomed to it. Got my first shot at a Boche. Missed at 1200 yards....Germans attempted a raid, moon, cloudless, snow, flashing signals, thundering noise all seen from a little knoll about 1 km away."[25] Perhaps Father Duffy had not been far wrong about Donovan's being a glory hunter.

Duffy celebrated Mass on Christmas Eve, and on Christmas Day the Irish regiment had turkey, but in the back of everyone's mind was the order that would move the division from Vaucouleurs to training area No. 7 at Rolampont, south of Chaumont.[26] Martin Hogan recalled, "A heavy snow set in the day before Christmas. It was as though a kindly disposed Fate was to make this last Christmas, as many among us would know, a good old fashion one."[27]

Duffy confided to his diary, "I cannot tell just what hard fates this New Year may have in store for us, but I am quite sure that no matter how trying they may be they will not let us forget the closing days of 1917...It was everybody's hike and everybody's purgatory."[28]

The movement of the four infantry regiments, three machine gun battalions, and other divisional troops would take four days to cover about eighty miles. A day's march, or for that matter, a four-day hike, should have presented little problem after the intense physical conditioning at Camp Mills or Vaucouleurs. Some men still did not have a heavy wool overcoat, however, and other problems included severely cold weather, constant heavy snows, and poor shoes. There was also a shortage of motor transport and motorized ambulances for the movement. The animal-drawn train carrying extra supplies was positioned in the center of the divisional column, and it had a hard time in the ice and snow maintaining any pace of march, constantly making the troops behind it stop.[29] To complicate the infantryman's life, the ten-minute halts normally made each hour in training were not made on the first day of the march, and many had a difficult time leaving the line of march to relieve themselves.

Conditions within the Irish regiment began to worsen as the march continued. Major Frew observed the condition of the unit with increasing alarm. He recalled,

The real trouble started on the second day [of the march] and become worse each day thereafter. When the men went into their billets at the end of the first day's march, most of them took off their water soaked shoes to warm their feet. In the morning their shoes were frozen hard and could not be worn, but the column had to move. Men hung their shoes around their necks, wrapped their feet in burlap... and started to hike with the roads two feet deep in snow.[30]

Father Duffy was worried, too, because the men carried no extra rations, and the mule train with food and cookers simply could not keep up with the marching column.[31] Ettinger, definitely a city boy, was surprised to see soldiers having to push and pull exhausted mules over the ice and snow-covered hills.[32]

Joe Romano, Ashton Croft, and other Alabamians endured the march even though a number of the southerners still had not received overcoats. One of the 167th Infantry men recalled, "It was too cold to sit down in the snow during rest periods and the weight of the pack, rifle and equipment became intolerable. Meals at breakfast and supper were meager. Skimpy mid-day rations were issued each man at breakfast."[33]

The Iowa regiment also suffered from a lack of decent shoes and heavy clothes, but despite their condition, the troops were horrified at what they saw when the rest of the division passed them on the road. Captain John H. Taber of the 168th stood in amazement at the spectacle before him.

Because of the condition of their shoes, the feet of some of the soldiers had grown so sore that they could not wear any at all. Instead they wrapped them in burlap and rags and marched on the sharp icy roads with their heavy packs. Their condition was unbelievable... There was not a sufficient number of ambulance to pick up the stragglers, and for days they wandered along the roads, trying to catch up with their outfits.[34]

When the division finally reached Rolampont, one Ohio regiment soldier "limping with his feet in rags crossed the bridge at Rolampont. Sliding and slipping under the weight of his pack and covered with snow from the gale that he was combatting [said], 'Valley Forge—hell!...There ain't no such animal'."[35]

To aggravate the situation of the Rainbow, AEF Headquarters at Chaumont sent the highly professional Major General Hunter Liggett to the march, and his reports back to Pershing's headquarters were devastating. Lieutenant Colonel William N. Hughes, a Regular Army officer and the assistant chief of staff of the Rainbow Division, found nothing right either, despite the cold and wet weather. In a report for Menoher he reserved his greatest criticisms for the New York 165th Infantry. Hughes found the men "surly, insubordinate, and out of hand." The supplies of the regiment were in shambles, and upon questioning Rainbow soldiers, he found that no one really knew what the regiment wanted done with critical supplies. Food and equipment had been dumped as vehicles had to be lightened to negotiate the difficult roads. As the march went on, the state of morale and discipline worsened, and, Hughes suspected, men began to malinger, blaming their conditions on poor shoes.[36]

The report by Hughes would attract the attention of Colonel Douglas MacArthur, since they were childhood friends when their fathers commanded companies at Fort Selden, New Mexico territory, in 1885. In 1914 MacArthur and Hughes had a joyous reunion in Vera Cruz, Mexico, when they served together during the American operation there.[37] MacArthur, as chief of staff, organized the Rainbow's general staff, bringing Hughes into the division in the vitally important post of G3, Operations. With a very demanding training schedule at Rolampont, where the division would prepare for trench warfare and for a period in the trenches with the French, there could be no time wasted.

Consequently, Menoher ordered that a board of officers convene as quickly as possible to look into conditions within the 165th Infantry to decide if Colonel Charles Hine was indeed incompetent. Brigadier General Robert Brown was the president of the board, with Colonel William Kelly commanding the 117th Engineer Regiment and Colonel William P. Screws commanding the 167th Infantry Regiment, all Regular Army officers, as board members. They gathered on 1 January 1918, wasting no time. The first witness was Hine, who had waived the right to counsel. There had been problems with sick reports not being properly sent to brigade and divisional headquarters, and there appeared to be chronic indiscipline within the ranks of the Irish regiment. Lest anyone think that the complaints against Hine simply showed the army's traditional love of paperwork, it is wise to remember that a commander, be he over a brigade or a division, must know the physical condition of his soldiers. The G3 must also be aware of the physical state of the soldiers when he schedules training or plans for combat. One would certainly not want to send soldiers to important training when a large percentage would miss that instruction due to illness.

Charles Hine was not new to military service, however. A West Point graduate, he had spent five years in the army, resigning his commission to attend Cincinnati Law School. He had experience during the Spanish-American War, performing well as commander of a battalion in combat. After the war, Hine went to work for the Harriman railroad system, where he rose up through the ranks. At an annual salary of $20,000 per year, very handsome by 1917 standards, Hine had no reason to join the National Guard other than a patriotic desire to serve. Hine pointed out that all three of his battalion commanders and six company commanders were still in school, and four other companies were under the command of newly commissioned, recently arrived reserve officers of very limited practical experience.

To make matters even worse for the 165th Infantry, the regimental supply officer was ill, and the mules received for pulling the supply train were new, with no experience in harness, let alone working together. Hine had no help, either, as his deputy, a lieutenant colonel, and his senior majors were in staff school at Chaumont. According to Hine, then, the leadership of the 165th Infantry Regiment was simply nonexistent as the regiment began to prepare for the march. The board remained skeptical of this account when other regiments had equal numbers of commissioned officers at various AEF schools. Hine's argument about shoes being a critical problem was certainly correct, but the march to Rolampont had been scheduled for several days, ample time to prepare and ask for assistance if the regiment was in such dire straits as far as leadership was concerned.

The most damaging piece of evidence against Hine was General Order No. 22, issued by Douglas MacArthur on 22 December 1917, detailing the requirements for the march to Rolampont. This order was issued four days prior to departure of the units, which should have allowed enough time for Hine to make known his critical shortages. Hine was relieved of his command, and in a few days he departed for service with the SOS, where he rendered good service due to his extensive civilian experience with the railroads.[38]

A few days later, Colonel John W. Barker, a West Point-educated Regular who had been on Pershing's staff since the AEF commander arrived in France, came from Chaumont and took command of the 165th Infantry. Father Duffy, always ready to defend his Irishmen, took to Barker right away.[39] Major Donovan, who was not present for the march, did record in his diary that just hours before the regiment began its movement, sixty new replacements were received from the 41st National Guard Division, and they had little experience and incomplete uniform issues.[40] Wild Bill Donovan went on to write:

On the day before the march from Vaucouleurs started, regiment received 65 mules. These had traveled from the point of debarkation for 3 days without water. All had sand colic, 1 died within one hour after arrival, 3 others went down and not yet recovered. Mules undersized and underfed and untrained. 20 had to be thrown to be harnessed. Not a shoe on their feet. No government harness. French harness delivered day before the hike—men unfamiliar with it. Harness too large—breast collars hung nearly to their knees."[41]

What now occupied the attention of the Rainbow Division was the rigorous training program to be conducted at Rolampont. Up to that point the division had little, if any, instruction in trench warfare, but there were French instructors, all with extensive combat experience, who would conduct the needed course. However, Pershing and his staff were determined that the training of AEF combat divisions proceed along defined, standardized lines. To ensure that this occurred, in November 1917 Pershing approved his G3's plan and principles for training the 42nd Division.

Those principles reflected Pershing's personal tactical and operational concepts, and they would apply to all AEF combat units. They were outlined in the G3's document and were not subject to any interpretation or modification. First, AEF training principles "must remain or become distinctly our own." The French and the British could train, but the AEF would maintain control of the direction of that instruction. The direction was the second principle: "All instruction must contemplate the assumption of a vigorous [i.e., maneuver] offensive. This purpose will be emphasized in every phase of training until it becomes a settled habit of thought." The third principle stated that standards of proficiency would be found in *Drill Regulations*, *Small Arms Firing Manual*, *Field Service Regulations* and other service manuals. By following them to the letter, standardization of excellence could be achieved throughout the AEF from combat formation to combat formation.

The fourth principle reflected Pershing's belief in the combat infantryman. The document stated: "The rifle and the bayonet are the principal weapons of the infantry soldier. He will be trained to a high degree of skill as a marksman....An aggressive spirit must be developed until the soldier feels himself, as a bayonet fighter, invincible in battle."

Discipline, the next principle, was the cornerstone of victory on the battlefield. "The standards of the American Army will be those of West Point," the document stated, "The rigid attention, upright bearing, attention to detail, uncomplaining obedience to instructions required of the cadet will be required of every officer and soldier of our Armies in France." Another principle was a sound awareness that training had to be progressive, conducted by knowledgeable and energetic leaders, from squad to company, to battalion to regiment, and then higher. Unit integrity in training, therefore, was a must, and units were to be quartered, marched, and put in combat together. Last, but equally important, was the principle that every exercise, regardless of level, would be followed by an in-depth critique. The best time for the critique was immediately after the tactical exercise, and the best location for that review would be on the same ground on which the maneuver was conducted. Within the exercise, "the adoption of 'normal methods' of attack and defense which limit the use of troops to fixed formation is prohibited." In other words, there would be no "schoolhouse solution." If tactics were sound and the troops trained aggressively, then the exercise was judged a success. Flexibility, not rigidity, was the key to a good day's training.[42]

For the staff and the troops of the Rainbow Division there was little time to ponder the fine points of emerging army doctrine. They had a program to put into operation, and they did not really know how much time they had to do it. As far as the division was concerned, it was not a complete unit. As training for the infantry began in earnest at Rolampont, the artillery brigade was still firing at Coetquidan and was scheduled to continue training until early February. There would be little opportunity for Menoher and his staff to coordinate artillery with ground action as they would have to do in actual combat.

The 117th Trench Mortar Battery was to arrive at Rolampont in mid-January, however, and the trench mortars would have some time to work with the infantry.[43] The 117th Ammunition Train prepared to leave Camp Coetquidan for the division in mid-January, and its troops were happy to go. Calvin Lambert would not be going with his unit to rejoin the Rainbows, however, because he was sixty kilometers away, in Hospital No. 8 at Savenay, for a knee operation. A bad fall on the ice at Coetquidan had damaged his knee, and it would be several months before Lambert could rejoin his Kansas comrades.[44]

Lieutenant van Dolsen was just as frustrated at Rolampont as he was at

Vaucouleurs, because he was still the mess officer: "I often have chicken because I can get an adult chicken for 6 francs —$1.20, which is enough for six or seven of us, but everyday I am picking up some new stunt for the menu."[45] Van Dolsen had not had a real bath for six weeks and had to content himself with washing out of a basin. There was not enough hot water for a full bath; besides, who would want to bathe in a freezing room? Martin Hogan had discovered a new enemy during his training at Rolampont—the cootie. Every man training in the field had become infested with lice, but after a day's digging trenches and then practicing assaulting or defending them, Hogan ignored the cooties and usually fell fast asleep.[46]

Joe Romano, Ashton Croft, and the other Alabamians had a good laugh at their own expense. They had their heads shaved after a few days training because of the ever-present cooties. Looking at each other, they were convinced that such a set of thugs and convicts could only have come from Alabama.[47] Iowan Everett Scott was now a dispatch runner, and despite the cold weather he was very pleased with his work. He was still concerned about Louise, however, who had not written in months.[48]

It was no secret that the French were now eager to place elements of the Rainbow into the line as quickly as possible, and tactical training intensified. Here the French differed from Pershing, for they believed the best and most practical training would occur in the face of the enemy, actually in a trench. Pershing, obviously hostile to trench warfare, preferred that American units spend as much time as was practical in maneuver training as well as receiving some instruction in trench warfare outside of the real trenches. The French 32nd Infantry Regiment had been detailed to train the Americans with experienced soldiers from one French battalion in support of an American infantry regiment.

Training exercises would be agreed upon by the French battalion commander and the American regimental commander, with the G3 section of the division overseeing the entire operation to ensure that Pershing's directives were implemented and that Americans continued to maintain control over the direction of the training. The ground rules for French participation had been set by Pershing and were contained in instructions sent to the 42nd Division in December. A key paragraph stated:

It is highly important that the most cordial relations be preserved with our allies, especially with those with whom we must be intimately associated in battle. Nevertheless, the instructions contained in the program of training for your division will be rigorously enforced. The training of American troops must remain in the hands of American officers. Neither the French officers furnished to your division nor the French battalion commanders will be permitted by you to dictate methods of training, substitute programs for those contemplated by these headquarters, or relieve American officers in any way from the responsibility for the training of their units as prescribed in the programs of training by these headquarters.[49]

Pershing had agreed to the training of American divisions in quiet sectors by the French, but he continued to be concerned about the trench mentality of the French,

as their units coming out of the battle line, worn and weary, failed to set an example of the aggressiveness which we were striving to inoculate in our men. Of course our own officers were immediately responsible, but they were frequently handicapped by the lack of energy of tired French officers. After considerable experience, it was the inevitable conclusion that, except for the details of trench warfare, training under the French or British was of little value.[50]

By and large, conflicts between the French and the Americans at the regimental training level were kept at a minimum. The French seemed impressed with the quality of the Rainbow Division's men, and many of the older French officers made the obvious comparison of the morale and esprit de corps of the 42nd Division to French divisions in existance at the time of the great battles that produced the "Miracle of the Marne" in September 1914. The aggressive spirit that confronted the mass of the German army near Paris had been sapped during three years of trench warfare. Both Menoher and MacArthur realized that their French comrades-in-arms thought more of the combat capabilities of the Rainbow than did Pershing's staff at Chaumont.[51] In fact, the French were urging the 42nd Division's infantry regiments and artillery brigades to move into the line with French units as soon as possible.[52]

Before the Rainbow Division could be committed to any sort of combat, however, the question of uniforms and shoes had to be addressed. The Irish regiment was in a state of near rebellion over the issue of British-made uniforms, for it was discovered that on the tunics, which otherwise resembled the standard doughboy's wool jacket, there were British army buttons. A number of the Irish soldiers began to build a bonfire to burn the whole lot of the offensive, though much-needed, tunics, and their officers were hard-pressed to maintain order.[53] Father Duffy was immediately sent to the fire, warning the irate soldiers about the dire consequences of destroying government property, and this calmed the matter for a while. Many buttons were salvaged from torn and tattered American-made uniforms, but the issue smoldered. Duffy went to Colonel Barker, and there, in private, he sided with the outraged troops. Barker at first dismissed Duffy's warnings about the troops' deeply held dislike for the British, but then realized that he was serving as the colonel of a predominantly Irish National Guard regiment. He promised Duffy he would overlook the bonfire incident and, while still not certain of the reasons, promised the chaplain that he would see that no other British tunics ever came to the 165th Infantry.[54]

While this incident seems amusing and harmless enough, it was not. In fact, it came very quickly to Pershing's attention and to the attention of the staff at Chaumont, who had authorized the issue of the British uniforms to help alleviate the suffering of the front-line troops. On 1 February 1918, Brigadier General William Connor of AEF Headquarters had informed the 42nd Division that

British uniforms were authorized for wear to make up for shortages. The plan called for the British issue to take place only in the rear, or the Line of Communication (LOC); the troops at the front, the Zone of Advance (ZA), would have priority for American-made goods. But the situation was critical enough that the British goods were sped to the front-line units.[55] Pershing thought this to be a good idea because

Much of the [American-made] clothing that we received for our troops was reported to be shoddy. I saw numbers of men wearing uniforms which were light and thin and which, of course, offered insufficient protection. The lack of clothing had been met in part by purchase from the British. Our troops did not take kindly to the idea of wearing the uniform of another nation."[56]

Pershing cited the 165th as being particularly incensed at the British uniforms with the English coat of arms emblazoned on the buttons. To avoid further attempts to destroy uniforms, AEF Headquarters sent an officer in an automobile with a large box of replacement American eagle buttons, and the offending buttons were changed. Pershing recalled, "The changes were made, and the regiment turned out looking both smart and serene."[57] Pershing and his staff were not amused, especially when decent uniforms were in such critically short supply.

Brigadier Generals Michael J. Lenihan and Robert Brown began a series of in-depth inspections into the condition of their troops. The troops had to be in condition to move into the line, probably sooner than anticipated. It was critically important that shoes be serviceable in the wet trenches. A litany of complaints came from the regiments about the shoes provided so far. When the shoes were issued at Camp Mills, New York, the units had been training and not involved in continuous operations in the trenches. As it was, the shoes issued deteriorated quickly and fit poorly.

The problem for the Rainbow Division was the same one that faced the other four divisions in France in January 1918. These units left the United States prior to the development of a good army marching shoe or a method of properly fitting the shoe. The traditional army shoe did not have the thick soles necessary to endure hard marching and campaigning over a long period of time. It had two heavy leather soles, the bottom sole being hobnailed, but they simply deteriorated in the wet conditions of France.

The Quartermaster Corps Clothing and Equipage Division had decided on a new shoe, called the Pershing shoe, with three very heavy soles that were screwed and nailed together, with the bottom sole having hobnails. The new shoes were on the way to France as quickly as the factories could turn them out, but in the meantime the Rainbows had to wait and hope that they arrived.[58] Another major problem for the division was that the regulations of 1912 required that a commissioned officer, preferably the company commander, should fit the shoe to the soldier. This was fine for the smaller, prewar Regular Army with a good deal of time to do such chores, but not too practical for wartime France.

The infantry and artillery were especially concerned about replacing damaged or wornout puttees, a vital part of the uniform. The leg wrap seems quaint and perhaps a little foolish to us, but it did not to the doughboy, who used it to keep dirt and dust from going up the trouser leg. On dry and dusty roads, with tens of thousands of infantrymen, wagons, and motorized vehicles on the move, it was vital that grit be kept out of the soldier's trousers. Without some protection, that dirt and grit could cause chafing which, if not tended to, could very well render him incapable of walking.

The reports coming into General Menoher's headquarters all told the same story. Training went well and morale was good, but uniforms were worn out and shoes were a critical problem that might very well keep the Rainbows from performing their combat mission.[59] So critical was the problem that the Inspector General's office at AEF Headquarters sent an inspecting team to Rolampont to see about the condition of clothing, equipment, billets, food, and morale. The Inspector General's report was not encouraging.

Menoher then ordered a follow-up inspection from the divisional Inspector General (IG) section to confirm what GHQ had found out. Major Battle, the inspector, found that almost every soldier in Company F, 165th Infantry, complained about his shoes. One Company F infantryman had one worn-out shoe and one French wooden shoe. Most soldiers had but one set of underwear and one uniform, since their barracks bags had not yet reached the unit from Vaucoleurs. Most had not had a real bath in weeks, because an outdoor shower into which hot water had to be fed by hand required well over five hours to bathe one full company. Even then, the company only allowed showers at night, the coldest time of the day.[60]

The surgeon was appalled with the reports and went to inspect. When Lieutenant Colonel D. S. Fairchild of the Medical Corps, a National Guard officer, went to the training areas, he found that Battle's report was accurate. Over 80 percent of the men he saw had lice, and a full quarter of all troops drilling had worn-out shoes, with rips and holes that exposed the feet to the wet and the mud. Fairchild noted:

A most deplorable condition exists here and it is most imperative that these men be equipped promptly with clothing, shoes, and socks. They are not only unclean, uncomfortable and unsoldierly, but the tremendous menace [exists] to health conditions such as liability to epidemic diseases, and also to the individual possibility of developing "Trench feet," through open skin lesions from improper care of the feet."[61]

Fairchild's report went to Divisional Chief Surgeon Lieutenant Colonel Jay W. Grissinger, who brought it to Menoher's attention. Immediately, corrections were made, with special emphasis on getting the troops' barrack bags to them so that underwear and uniforms could be changed and the old clothing boiled to rid them of cooties. The number of showers were increased, with part of each Sunday being given over to personal hygiene, and last, but most welcomed, disinfectants were sent to the units. The surgeons, under Grissinger's direction, took on the responsibility of fitting the new shoes as they arrived, relieving inexperienced and overworked officers of that unfamiliar but very critical duty.[62] Ten days after the inspection, on 29 January 1918, the AEF Headquarters Inspectors General were back, and they found conditions improved. Colonel P. A. Murphy, serving as the Rainbow Division's IG, also inspected the same units and was able to confirm their assessment: There was considerable improvement. The long-awaited barrack bags had arrived, though some of them had been rifled and items were stolen. The vast majority of men were clean, as showers were in operation, and cooties, while not eradicated, were at least fewer in number.

Murphy also suggested that, while training was vitally important, a part of each day had to be set aside for hygiene and foot care. Company officers had to be aggressive in inspecting shoes, socks, and feet, and work out a plan that would allow a soldier a proper bath at least every four days.[63]

While shoes, uniforms, equipment, and food slowly improved for the Rainbow soldiers, training continued to increase in intensity. The division was working under two factors. First, the French wanted to move the 42nd Division into the line by regiments as quickly as possible. Second, AEF Headquarters simply did not believe that the division was ready for such a move. It was the opinion at Chaumont that the division's training status did not justify putting men into the trenches, a view not shared by Menoher or MacArthur. From 11 to 13 February, a large inspection team from Chaumont visited all the units training at Rolampont, and its members were highly critical of what they saw. The team of six field grade officers was headed by Major General A. W. Brewster, who signed the final report. Brewster was one of the original AEF staff who made the trip to France with General Pershing in 1917, and was handpicked for the position of AEF IG. He was a constant companion of Pershing's, and the commanding general relied on Brewster for detailed reports about the progress of the troops.

Brewster observed training and found the 83rd Brigade's two regiments to be gravely wanting. According to the inspector, the 166th Infantry under Colonel Benson Hough did poorly. Brewster commented, "Neither the regimental nor the battalion commander seemed to understand the purpose of a formation in depth." In the opinion of the IG, the 149th Machine Gun Battalion, the 117th Engineers, 117 Signal Battalion and the 117 Sanitary Train were unfit for active service in the line. Only the 84th Brigade, under Brigadier General Robert Brown, appeared to be on the road to any sort of combat readiness. In closing, Brewster added a recommendation that "Colonel E. R. Bennett, 168th Infantry, NG, and Colonel B. W. Hough, 166th Infantry, NG, are believed to be officers of doubtful ability, and if improvement is not manifested during the next period in the training that they be replaced by competent regular army officers."[64]

The last recommendation infuriated both Bennett and Hough. The report on Hough touched on the very sore relations between the National Guard, still angered over the 5 August draft decree, and the Regular Army, which distrusted

Guard officers. Hough was a lawyer who had won academic and athletic honors at Ohio State University. Upon graduation, he enlisted as a private in the Ohio National Guard, and rising through the ranks, in January 1915 he became adjutant general of Ohio with the state rank of brigadier general. When it became clear that the 4th Ohio was to be sent to the Mexican border, Hough resigned his state commission and joined the regiment as a private soldier. A few days later he received a commission as lieutenant colonel and went with the regiment to the border.

Upon the 4th Ohio's return from the Southwest, Hough received a colonel's commission and command of the regiment, and on 15 July 1917, he was taken into federal service with that rank as the old 4th Ohio became the 166th Infantry Regiment.[65] The experienced Hough was extremely popular with his soldiers and had the respect of Menoher and the staff. While the 166th Regiment had none of the dash of the Irish 165th or any of the color of the Alabama 167th, it maintained a steady degree of combat competence. Both Benson Hough and Edward Bennett interpreted this report as a personal affront and as an attack on National Guard leadership. Menoher had now seen two devastating reports, steps were underway to correct clothing and sanitary conditions, and the movement of the division into combat in the line was only a few days away.

The arrival of new clothing and equipment signaled that the Rainbow infantry and machine gunners would soon be in the line with French units to receive some very practical experience. Donovan heard the rumors that the Rainbow Division was about to move into the line, and he was disgusted that the division would not occupy their own section of the line. Donovan also believed that the battalions were to be divided between the British and the French. "Incredible," Donovan thought, but he had other worries. Forty new replacements reached his battalion on 9 February, and out of that number five men were straight from their basic instruction at Camp Meade, near Baltimore, Maryland. They were draftees, not National Guardsmen. "They had two months training," Donovan observed, "and all of it in close order drill. They did not know how to clean a rifle nor did they know how to fire one. And this one week before going up."[66]

Father Duffy was more concerned about the conduct of his Irishmen. It seems that during bayonet training the men had taken to screaming obscenities and cursing as they attacked the straw dummies that were constructed to represent "the Boche." Duffy had heard enough of the swearing and called the lieutenants to account for the irreligious conduct of his doughboy parishioners. "I see neither grace nor sense in it," Duffy warned, "If a man swears in the heat of battle I don't even say that God will forgive it; I don't believe He would notice it. But this organized blasphemy is an offense. And it is a farce—a bit of Cockney Drill Sergeant blugginess to conceal their lack of better qualities."[67] Obviously, the British were behind it all.

An exasperated Father Duffy had every reason to be pleased with Joyce Kilmer, who had been transferred to the regimental intelligence section. Kilmer had grown more devout every day, and Duffy enjoyed his conversations with the aspiring poet. Over the weeks he had drawn closer to Wild Bill Donovan, too, but the chaplain still harbored doubts about the handsome New Yorker. Duffy had called on Donovan, finding him sitting in an old chair in a rather big room. He confided to Duffy, "I have just been thinking that what novelists call romance [of war] is only what men's memories hold out of the past, with all actual realization of the discomforts left out, and only the dangers past and difficulties conquered remaining in the imagination."[68] Perhaps Donovan was not a glory hunter, but then the fighting had not started yet. Duffy might have been less hopeful about Donovan had he seen the text of a letter he sent to his beautiful socialite wife. Donovan, who spoke French quite well, had been observing as the French assisted with training. He found, "They have here a French disciplining section of the French soldiers who have been bad. They put them in a group properly guarded and make them dig trenches and do all the dirty work. They are mostly Apaches and pretty bad men. To me they have a certain air that is quite attractive."[69]

Donovan had a scare when rumors reached him that he was to be transferred to an AEF school at Chaumont to instruct officers. As soon as he heard that, he went to see MacArthur to verify the rumor and then protest it. MacArthur had no intention of allowing Donovan to leave his battalion command when it appeared that the 42nd Division might be going into the line, and twice, with Menoher's agreement, he had simply shelved the request. While Donovan and MacArthur were talking, Pershing's chief of staff, Brigadier General James Harbord, telephoned Rainbow HQ about the matter. Menoher informed Harbord that he had considered bringing Donovan up to divisional staff, but, given the condition of the 165th Regiment, he decided against it. Harbord became aggravated with Menoher and told him flatly that if the Rainbow Division did not send an officer immediately, they would simply order Donovan to Chaumont.[70] Quickly MacArthur dispatched another officer to Chaumont. Donovan, much relieved, returned to his battalion, and there the matter ended.

Joyce Kilmer had been asked by Colonel Barker to consider becoming an officer, but Kilmer refused. He told a friend in a letter that he would rather remain a sergeant in the old Irish Fighting 69th than be an officer. Besides, he would have to be away from the 165th Infantry for over three months, and he did not want to miss being in the thick of it with his old friends.

Colonel William Kelly, commanding the 117th Engineers, had been informed that the division would soon leave Chaumont for the line. The engineers had to assemble the equipment and material to support units in the line, but Kelly was also furious over Brewster's critical comments after the inspection. The commander felt that his 117th Engineers from North and South Carolina and California had been quite busy, involved in extensive engineering work. In a report Kelly pointed out that the regiment in Training Area 7 built eighty barracks, seventy horse stables, installed eighteen bath units, built pigeon lofts and latrines, and reworked electrical and water systems. Once the work day was over, the Rainbow Engineers conducted night classes for officers and NCOs as well as small-arms ranges, marches, and close-order drill. He also pointed out that as the time to leave Rolampont drew near, the engineers were busy collecting what would be needed by the infantry in the trenches.[71]   On 12 February 1918, AEF Headquarters alerted the division that the troops would move in a few weeks to the French trenches at Lunéville to gain practical experience. The Artillery Brigade would begin its movements from Coetquidan to Lunéville and would rejoin the division there. The last unit to join the 42nd Division was the 117th Mobile Ordnance Repair Company, which arrived just prior to departure.

It is one thing to order a division, especially one spread out in several training locations, into combat, and it is another thing again to issue the orders, make the plans, and support such a movement. Although less than 100 miles, the movement from Rolampont to Lunéville simply could not be made overnight. Menoher's staff was fully aware of the difficulties of such activity, since they had moved from the embarkation points to Vaucouleurs, and then to Rolampont. The plan was to place one regiment with each division of the French VII Corps, then holding a sixteen-mile front.[72] Menoher, MacArthur, and the remainder of the staff would depart for the Lunéville sector on 16 February, leaving behind a small number of staff officers to ensure that the movement went as ordered. By noon on 17 February, the headquarters would be in full operation.[73]

Between 17 and 21 February, all of the Rainbow units, including the artillery, would close on Lunéville and come under the operational and tactical control of the French. Once that was completed, the troops would move into the reserve trenches for an acclimation period of two days. After that, the regiments would go forward to the support trenches for a three-day period, then to the main trench for a seven-day tour in the line.   Once with the French, the divisional commander and the brigade commanders would lose tactical control of their men, having only the duties of inspection, coordination, and normal American administration.

By order of AEF Headquarters at Chaumont, the three headquarters—divisional, 83rd Brigade, and 84th Brigade—would be in separate towns, the division remaining at Lunéville because of roads and communications facilities.[74] The ground rules had changed. Menoher, MacArthur, Brown, and Lenihan did not record what they felt about not having operational or tactical control of their troops, but these men were from the old Regular Army and used to obeying orders. They all felt that with Pershing's insistence on a completely American Army, they would regain control of their troops in combat soon after the Lunéville period.

AEF Headquarters was not about to allow the 42nd Division to go into the line with the French without establishing the ground rules for everyone. The Rainbows, under Major General Hunter Liggett's I Corps, were issued a very specific set of instructions. Liggett, who had the dubious distinction of being the fattest general in the AEF, forbade the division or brigade commanders to issue any tactical orders to their units while they were in the trenches with the French.

The instructions issued on 15 February left nothing to interpretation, stating,

The French commanders have been requested to require of you and your subordinates the actual preparation of order, but IN NO CASE [Liggett's emphasis] will you or your brigade commanders give tactical orders or instructions DIRECT while serving with the French with whom rests in its entirety the responsibility for the tactical command.

Infantry regimental commanders were also informed that they would not assume any tactical authority until eight days had passed, corresponding to a full cycle of a battalion in the reserve, support, and forward trenches.[75]

Why was this done when Pershing had made so much of the Americans' being a separate and distinct entity on the Western Front? The first response is the obvious one: The French had over three years' experience in lethal trench warfare. Probably an equally valid reason, if not more important, was that Pershing knew that men like Menoher, MacArthur, and others wanted a chance to prove themselves as competent combat leaders. For a Regular, success in this Great War—"the war to end all wars," as President Wilson had put it—would mean decoration, promotion, and higher command. The same would be true of a National Guard officer. Both Regular Army and National Guard officers had sought commissions and command, knowing full well that it could lead to mortal combat at some time. These men were not shrinking violets by any stretch of the imagination, and Pershing and Liggett, who were themselves possessed of strong, even overbearing personalities, knew what motivated officers.

For the troops, however, the movement to Lunéville was just another shift from one uncomfortable situation to another. Privates, corporals, sergeants, and even lieutenants were less concerned with going to Blois than were the colonels or generals. Their concerns were very basic. What would life be like in the trenches? And, more important, could they survive in that very dangerous world? They had not faced the Germans before, but there seemed to be no mistaken idea that the job would be easy. With questions unanswered, the Rainbow prepared to leave Rolampont for a new phase in its odyssey on the Western Front.

NOTES

1. Van Dolsen to his family, no place, 28 November 1917, in the W. W. van Dolsen Papers, U. S. Army Military History Institute Archives, Carlisle Barracks, Pennsylvania, 42nd Division AEF Collection (hereinafter, MHIA). Note: All correspondence from France was censored by an officer. The location of troops was not to be mentioned. Most soldiers simply wrote "somewhere in France." Consequently, unless specifically noted, all letters will be noted as np.

2. Ogden to his wife, np, 5 December 1917, in Ogden letters, ibid.

3. Martin J. Hogan, *The Shamrock Battalion of the Rainbow: A Story of the Fighting 69th* (New York: D. Appleton and Co., 1919), 28-29.

4. A. Churchill Ettinger (ed.), *Albert Ettinger, A Doughboy with the Fighting*

69th (Shippensburg, Penn.: White Main Publishing, 1992), 24.

5. Francis P. Duffy, *Father Duffy's Story* (New York: George H. Doran Co., 1919), 46-47.

6. Scott to his mother, np, 29 December 1917, in Scott Letters, manuscripts in the author's collection.

7. John H. Taber, The Story of the 168th Infantry (Iowa City: State Historical Society of Iowa, 1925), 45-48.

8. Ibid., 48-49.

9. Center of Military History, *United States Army in the World War, 1917-1919. Volume 3: Training and Use of American Units with the British and the French* (Washington: Government Printing Office, 1989), 266-67.

10. Hugh S. Thompson, "Following the Rainbow," *The Chattanooga Times*, 21 January 1934.

11. Ibid., 14 January 1934.

12. Peter H. Ottosen, *Trench Artillery, AEF* (Boston: Lothrop, Lee & Shepard, 1931), 47-48.

13. Leslie Langille, *Men of the Rainbow* (Chicago: O'Sullivan Publishing House, 1933), 46-47.

14. Charles MacArthur, *War Bugs* (Garden City, N.Y.: Doubleday, Doran & Co., 1919), 12-14.

15. Diary entry, 18 November 1917, in George E. Seaman (ed.), *War Diary of George E. Leach, Colonel, 151st Field Artillery* (Roanoke, Va.: National Association of Rainbow Veterans, Reprint of the 1923 edition, 1962), 12.

16. Louis L. Collins, *History of the 151st Field Artillery Regiment, Rainbow Division* (Saint Paul, Minn.: Minnesota War Records Commission, 1924), 27-28.

17. *The Rainbow Reveille*, (Monthly magazine of the Rainbow Divisions' veterans organization) November 1957 and February 1964.

18. MacArthur, *War Bugs*, 17.

19. Langille, *Men of the Rainbow*, 48.

20. AEF Headquarters, *Program of Training for the Sanitary Units of the 42nd Division, AEF* (November 1917) in *General Documents WWI*, 42nd Division, Infantry, U.S., MHIA.

21. Van Dolsen to his family, np, 4 January 1918, ibid.

22. From the Frew Papers, c. 1921, ibid.

23. Calvin Lambert Diary, manuscript, Emporia Public Library, Emporia, Kansas, 56-57, 59.

24. Entry 25 December 1917, in William J. Donovan Diary, 1917-1918, in MHIA carton 13A (hereinafter, Donovan Diary).

25. Entry 26 December 1917, ibid.

26. Walter B. Wolf, *Brief Story of the Rainbow Division* (New York: Rand McNally Co., 1919), 8-9.

27. Hogan, *Shamrock Battalion*, 34.

28. Duffy, *Story*, 48.

29. Report by Major Marion R. McMillan, director, Field Hospitals Section, 117th Sanitary Train, 42nd Division, 31 December 1917, in the National Archives, Washington, *Records Group 120 Records of the AEF, 42nd Division*, carton 57 (hereinafter, RG 120).

30. From the Frew Papers, c. 1921, MHIA.

31. Duffy, *Story*, 48-49.

32. Ettinger, *Doughboy*, 33-35.

33. John B. Hayes, *Heros Among the Brave* (Loachapoka, Ala.: Lee County Historical Society, 1973), 11, Romano Notes.

34. Taber, *168th Infantry*, 49.

35. Henry J. Reilly, *American All: The Rainbow at War* (Columbus, Ohio: F.J. Heer Printing Co., 1936), 102.

36. Memorandum by William H. Hughes, 29 December 1917, in RG 120, carton 59.

37. D. Clayton James, *The Years of MacArthur. Vol. 1: 1880-1941* (Boston: Houghton-Mifflin, 1970), 54, 123, 155.

38. Pershing's Files, "In the Matter of the Relief of Colonel Charles Hine, Infantry," 15 May 1919, RG 200, carton 10.

39. Duffy, *Story*, 58-59; Reilly, *Americans All*, 111-12.

40. Entries 26 and 27 January 1918, Donovan Diary. Here Donovan is recounting stories told to him by Duffy and others. His knowledge is second-hand.

41. Entry 28 January 1918, ibid.

42. Training Section, AEF General Staff, "Program of Training for the 42nd Division," 26 November 1917, in RG 120, carton 18. This document is vitally important in that it lays out in clear and coherent terms what doctrine is to be, and it does not prescribe operational and tactical guidelines.

43. Ottesen, *Trench Artillery*, 99.

44. Calvin Lambert Diary, 61-63.

45. Van Dolsen to his mother, np, 13 January 1918, MHIA.

46. Hogan, *Shamrock Battalion*, 47-48.

47. Hayes, *Heroes Among the Brave*, 12-13, Romano Notes.

48. Scott to his mother, np, 9 February 1918, in Scott Letters.

49. AEF Headquarters, Memorandum, 20 December 1917, in CMH, *United States Army in the World War*, Vol. 3, 673.

50. John J. Pershing, *My Experiences in the World War*, Vol. 2 (New York: Frederick A. Stokes Co., 1931), 114.

51. James, *Years of MacArthur*, 152.

52. GHQ, G3, French Armies of the North and Northeast, 9 February, 1918, in CMH, *United States Army in the World War*, Vol. 3, 675.

53. Ettinger, *Doughboy*, 49-50.

54. Duffy, *Story*, 54-56.

55. HQ, 42nd Division, Memorandum No. 25, 6 February 1918, in RG 120, carton 1.

56. Pershing, *My Experiences*, Vol. 1, 315.

57. Ibid., 316.

58. U.S. War Department, *American's Munitions 1917-1918: The Report of Benedict Crowell* (Washington: Government Printing Office, 1919), 473-74.

59. These reports were required of each company within the two brigades and were consolidated at the brigade staff level. They were then sent to the Divisional Surgeon, who briefed Menoher and MacArthur. These reports are found in RG 120, carton 24.

60. Major M. S. Battle, IG Investigation and Report, 18 January 1918, in RG 120, carton 24.

61. First Endorsement to Battle's Report by Lieutenant Colonel D. S. Fairchild, ibid.

62. U. S. Office of the Surgeon General, *The Medical Department of the United States Army in the World War.* Vol. 6: Sanitation (Washington: Government Printing Office, 1926), 631.

63. Colonel P. A. Murphy, Inspection Report (Company F, 165th Infantry), 29 January 1918, in RG 120, carton 24.

64. Major General A. W. Brewster, IG Inspection and Report, 20 February 1917, ibid., carton 21. While this report is dated 20 February, there is evidence that it was in Menoher's hands at least a week earlier.

65. Alison Reppy, *Rainbow Memories: Character Sketches and History of the First Battalion, 166th Infantry* (np: Privately printed by the 1st Battalion, 166th Infantry, 1919), 7-8.

66. Entry 10 February 1918, Donovan Diary.

67. Duffy, *Story*, 58.

68. Ibid., 56-57.

69. Donovan to his wife, np, 30 January 1918, in the William J. Donovan Papers, MHIA.

70. Entry 3 February 1918, Donovan Diary.

71. "Monthly Activity Report" by Colonel William Kelly, 3 February and 3 March 1917, in RG 120, carton 40.

72. 3rd Section, GHQ, French Armies of the North and Northeast, "Memorandum for the Commanding General, The Group of Armies of the East at Mirecourt," 9 February 1918, in CMH, *United States Army in the World War*, Vol. 3, 675.

73. AEF Headquarters, GE, "General Plan for Occupation of Trenches by 42nd Division and Subsequent Training," ibid., 676-77.

74. Ibid., 677-78.

75. Headquarters, 42nd Division Memorandum No. 42, 15 February 1918, in RG 120, carton 1. This Rainbow-produced memorandum repeated I Corps instructions. It was issued to all brigade, regimental, and battalion commanders.

3

IN THE TRENCHES AT LUNÉVILLE

Al Ettinger and his comrades moved to Lunéville on a 40-and-8 train that did not stop for anything. Consequently, a number of men from the Irish regiment were seen hanging from a boxcar by one hand to relieve themselves as the train moved rapidly along. The wind whistled through the old boxcars while the soldiers made do with unheated Corned Willie and hardtack for meals. Once in Lunéville, the whole regiment was marched to the château that would be their headquarters for a few days prior to moving into the line. The men actually had time in the evening to see Lunéville, where "we encountered our first ladies of the night since landing in France, and some of us had an introduction to sex with a capital S."[1]

Martin Hogan would have little to divulge in Father Duffy's confessional, however: "For the first time we took a regular, old-fashioned interest in life again. Discipline was easy. We went to picture shows and restaurants. Some of us promenaded dumbly up and down with French girls. Some of us became engaged. Some of us, even, set about learning French."[2]

The Alabama troops had just as uncomfortable a ride on the French boxcars, and their greatest problem was taking care of the calls of nature. For once, the New York Irish and the Alabama Southerners had something in common: "As these troop trains sped through the French towns and countryside the undraped posteriors of soldiers usually shone protruding from open doors with shirttails flapping in the breeze."[3]

Private Lawrence O. Stewart, a medic of the Iowa 168th Infantry's Sanitary Detachment, was sorry to leave the Rolampont training area. His billets were in the home of a congenial family with a black-haired, flirtatious daughter named Annette. But when the regiment moved, Stewart left his pleasant surroundings, boarded the 40-and-8, and traveled to Lunéville with only memories of Annette. There were only forty-eight medics to serve a regiment of nearly 4,000 doughboys. Ten medics went to each of three combat infantry battalions, with eighteen assigned to keep supplies moving and to maintain what would become a mountain of casualty reports. Now that they were ready to move into the trenches, Stewart and his buddies were issued white armbands with red crosses. Each had a serial number filed with the Red Cross in Geneva, and in case a medic was captured or fell in battle, the number would serve as a quick identifier.[4]

Douglas MacArthur arrived in Lunéville ahead of most of the troops, and he selected a working headquarters and billets for General Menoher and the staff. Menoher preferred to conduct the battle from a fixed divisional command post, which the doughboys called a PC (from the French *Poste de Command*). MacArthur approached General Georges de Bazelaire, the French VII Corps commander under whom the Rainbows would learn the real lessons of trench warfare, and asked to join a French raiding party to see how a crossing of No Man's Land was conducted. De Bazelaire was very reluctant to agree to such a request.[5] What would happen, he asked, if MacArthur were killed, severely wounded, or, even worse, if he were captured? The French liked panche, to be sure, but perhaps this was not the time for such a gesture.

The artillery of the Rainbow began to arrive in Lunéville. It had been nearly two months since Menoher had his now well-trained gunners. Leslie Langille had had enough training under the demanding Colonel Reilly, and when word reached Camp Coetquidan to prepare for departure to Lunéville to rejoin the Rainbows, there was relief. But with guns loaded on flatcars and men jammed into the 40-and-8s, there was a delay.

It seems that the 149th Field Artillery had adopted a small dog, and just before the cars departed a distraught French woman descended on the officers demanding that the Illinois gunners return her "Fluffy." When one doughboy of Battery B (which had hidden the dog, now named Shorty) was questioned by an officer, he simply replied with an innocent expression, "Why, Lieutenant, I never even knew that woman had a fluffy." The red-faced young officer, not wishing to translate the response into French, simply took the outraged woman to another 40-and-8 to search for the missing canine. Shorty was going to Lunéville, too.[6]

Charles MacArthur arrived at Lunéville (which the doughboys had quickly renamed Looneyville) fairly drunk. During the train ride from Camp Coetquidan, the troops were provided with a few sandwiches and hot coffee from the local YMCA, but this was soon consumed. From a French-operated troop comfort station (a *revitaillement*), the doughboys obtained a quantity of rum. An enterprising French soldier sold the artillerymen cognac by the gallon for ten francs (about $3.00) per jug, so the American gunners soon had a large supply. Crap games were the order of the day, and the harsh and very strong cognac comforted the soldiers, who were now reduced to opening cans of the ever-hated Corned Willie. The three-day train ride turned into a raucous affair, with the doughboys trying to court every French girl they saw, and one Fighting Illini continued to sing the University of Illinois alma mater every chance he got.[7] Once they arrived at Lunéville, the troops of the 149th, like those of the other two artillery regiments, were parceled out to the French.[8]

The Alabamians arrived at Lunéville and were preparing to go into the trenches when they became the first of the Rainbows to experience an aerial bombardment. Joe Romano was with his buddies when a German aircraft appeared overhead. Some of the troops were still not used to aircraft, especially not in a combat zone, and began to wave at the plane. Sergeant "Buttermilk" Niles recognized the distinctive markings of the enemy and began to scream at his troops to scatter, "You Goddamned fools! That's a German spotting for artillery."

Romano and one friend did not need to be told twice, and they dove for cover while other 167th soldiers, who either did not hear the warning or moved too slowly, were caught in a barrage. When the firing ended, Romano and some other lucky soldiers carried the wounded, many of them unconscious, to the medics. As Romano and his friends learned to their horror, many of the men believed to be unconscious were dead, without a mark on them; their necks had been snapped by the concussion of the German shells. As the smoke cleared, among the dead was Sergeant "Buttermilk" Niles, who, without regard for his own safety, had tried to move the troops out of harm's way.[9]

On 18 February, the regimental headquarters at Glonville had a visit from a German bomber who dropped one bomb that nearly hit Colonel William Screw's headquarters building. The next morning, another bomber returned just as the 167th's chaplain, Captain Emmett P. Smith, and the regimental adjutant, Captain Robert Joerg, were sitting down to breakfast. Other officers of the headquarters, smelling fresh hot coffee, were about to join them when a bomb dropped in an orchard only seventy-five yards away. In the rush to get out of the building to the safety of a ditch, the table was turned over and the precious, wonderful-smelling coffee went all over the floor. In the ditch, the devout chaplain heard more cursing over the bomb and the spilled coffee than he cared to.[10]

Pershing's staff had worked out a plan with the French, who by this time realized that although America had tremendous industrial potential and seemingly unlimited manpower, the North American giant was terribly short of critical equipment. Industry had not yet caught up with the requirements of a modern war. The French would supply artillery ammunition, which had been in very short supply for the Americans in France, but small-arms ammunition would be supplied by the American Service of Supply (SOS). It was the duty of the 42nd Division to ensure that the required thirty days' supply go with the division to Lunéville. The estimates prepared by AEF Headquarters proved to be woefully inadequate for the type of combat the Rainbows were about to embark upon. For example, it was estimated that a trench mortar battery needed 600 rounds per Stokes Mortar for thirty days.[11] The 117th Trench Mortar Battery (twenty-four three-inch Stokes mortars) would use four times that amount in a one-month period.[12]

The French also would make food available if needed, but the AEF would be required to replace what was taken from French stocks. Gas masks would be of American manufacture, but horse masks had to come from the French stocks.

Medical supplies would come with the 117th Sanitary Train, and various levels of medical units, from dressing stations to field hospitals, would be established with French help. The French had much more experience placing the various stations, which promised to be very busy.[13]

Pershing was not a commander to neglect logistics. He recalled in March 1918, "Each combat division required the equivalent of twenty-five carloads of supplies daily, and these supplies had to be delivered promptly and regularly to points within short truck-haul of the location of the troops."[14] In the case of the 42nd Division, the French would assist in measurable ways to supply food, ammunition, and other items. However, if Pershing was to make his AEF a maneuver army, he would have to straighten out what was becoming a logistics nightmare.

While the combat infantry, machine gunners, and artillery were moving into the trenches around Lunéville, MacArthur began to construct what he hoped would be the Rainbow's permanent combat staff.

Someone once wrote that no carefully prepared plan ever survived the first actual contact with the enemy. This might be true, but it was and is the careful writing of the initial order that gets the troops to the point where they can engage the enemy in combat. Staff orders add coherence to that movement by giving subordinate commanders an idea of what the commanding general intended. Orders must take into consideration several vitally important items: first, the mission; second, the enemy situation; third, the troops, including attached troops, the commander has at his disposal to conduct the battle; fourth, the execution of the order, or how units arrive on the battlefield and how they array to battle the foe; fifth, specific items such as communications, presence of command posts, resupply and medical activities, and the like.

In December 1917, Pershing directed that a general staff school be established at Langres, France, under the direction of Brigadier General James W. McAndrew, a well-schooled Regular who eventually became Pershing's chief of staff in May, 1918. The school was to be three months in length, but few of the early arrival officers could spend that long away from their divisions. Pershing's problem was that "we were confronted with the task of building up an army of millions that would require as many trained staff officers as we had officers in the whole Regular Army at the beginning of the war."[15]

Functions of a complete staff must be divided into primary and special areas. The primary staff includes the G1, or Personnel Officer, who deals with questions of casualties, replacements, orders, decorations, deaths, and emergencies. If he does not function, the unit does not have an accurate picture of manpower available for duty. The G2, or Intelligence Officer, is a critical person in that he informs the commander and subordinate units about what force is opposing the division. He assigns patrols and analyzes reports from observation posts and all observers. If he fails, the results could be disastrous. The G3, or Operations Officer, formulates the plans based on the higher missions, the status of manpower, the force opposing the unit, and the supplies available to support the operation. Telling the commander and the G3 what supplies are at hand is the G4, the logistics officer. No commander wants to commit his force to combat, especially maneuver warfare, if there are shortages in food, equipment, and ammunition. The G4 takes the mission, analyzes it, and orders what supplies are needed to sustain combat.

The staff is tied together by the chief of staff, who coordinates the efforts of the primary staff officers, oversees the writing of orders, and ensures that those orders are passed to subordinate commands in a timely manner. In addition to those duties, General Menoher saw MacArthur as a "battle captain" who would oversee the execution of plans by being close to the troops. World War I divisions did not have assistant divisional commanders, as found in modern combat formations, and the chief of staff had to perform a multitude of functions with few staff officers serving under him.

As his special staff, MacArthur had a good group of Regular Army and National Guard officers. At the Rainbow headquarters, the special staff (a modern term) consisted of the chief surgeon, the senior judge advocate general, signals officer, gas officer, air service liaison officer, and other officers who advised the commander or the chief of staff in very specialized areas. But it would be the primary staff, usually four key officers, who would bear the greatest burden for orders and work when the division was in combat. When an American liaison officer queried the French as to why an American division was not committed to battle, the response was, "It was not individual American courage or valor which was deficient...The staff work was simply not adequate yet."

There was another problem associated with rank and positions in the American divisional staff. The brigade commanders were brigadier generals, while the chief of staff was a full colonel. The chief of staff could be at a very definite disadvantage when dealing with matters of orders, discipline, and administration with the subordinate brigades. Nine months earlier, MacArthur had been a major on the General Staff in Washington, and overnight he was a colonel. Consequently, MacArthur had youth, rank, and the source of his colonelcy acting as a barrier in getting his job done. Menoher was a first-rate commander who gave his chief of staff a good deal of latitude, but MacArthur had yet to prove himself as a chief of staff or as a battle captain.[16]

MacArthur began organizing his primary staff officers, and he made good, solid selections. As the G1, MacArthur obtained the service of Lieutenant Colonel Frank Lawton, a Regular from the Quartermaster Corps. As the G2, MacArthur selected Major Noble Brandon Judah from the Illinois 149th Field Artillery. Judah, a lawyer from the Chicago area, was reputed to be one of the most brilliant men in the Rainbow Division. Judah had Captain Oscar W. Underwood, Jr., of the Alabama National Guard, as an assistant. MacArthur had considered William Donovan for the G2 position, but he recognized that as commander of the 1st Battalion, 165th Infantry, Donovan was probably where he could render the best service. At any rate, Wild Bill Donovan would have resisted being brought to staff, and it was best to leave the Irishman alone for the time being.

For the critical post of G3, MacArthur selected his old childhood friend, Lieutenant Colonel William N. Hughes, Regular Army. To assist Hughes, First Lieutenant Walter B. Wolf of the 149th Field Artillery was brought to the staff. Normally, staffs had a G5, who dealt strictly with training matters, and AEF Headquarters was organized this way. MacArthur decided to combine the G3 and G5 into one staff area, avoiding duplication and conflict. Training, however, was in the hands of the French, and a G5 would have been superfluous at that point. MacArthur also merged the positions of G1 and G4 (supply) when he issued General Order No. 8. Lawton, who was a member of the Regular Army's Quartermaster Corps, would do both jobs. As a trained supply practitioner, Lawton would certainly have the expertise to get the job done, and perhaps MacArthur felt that once fighting began G1 duties would be seriously reduced (which was not the case). A plausible explanation rested with MacArthur's difficult time in dealing with AEF Headquarters in late November and December 1917, when many supplies were diverted from the Rainbow Division for the Regular Army's 1st and 2nd Divisions. MacArthur recalled that "50,000 pairs of heavy marching shoes were promptly taken over by GHQ to supply deficiencies in other divisions. We suffered greatly later on from a lack of replacement equipment and supplies."[17]   A reasonable explanation for MacArthur's failure to appoint a G4 was simply that not doing so kept supplies in his hands, and he could counter moves by AEF Headquarters. If there were a fight over supplies, Colonel MacArthur could fight it better than a lieutenant colonel not well known at Chaumont.

MacArthur finally got permission to accompany a French raiding party on 26 February, but by that time he was no stranger to No Man's Land. On 20 February, Menoher, MacArthur, and Captain Thomas T. Handy were scheduled to observe a French raid against the German trenches. MacArthur became separated from Menoher; the General returned to divisional headquarters late in the afternoon, but his aide and MacArthur were nowhere to be found. Within the staff there was concern that something had happened to the two soldiers, who were just as fresh at the front as any other Rainbow soldier. Major Hugh Ogden and the staff were at breakfast, still worried about MacArthur and Handy, when the colonel came into the mess and, "planted in the middle of the table a German steel helmet he had peaceably acquired from a prisoner on the border of No Man's Land."[18] Ogden and the other staff officers were not thrilled with their chief of staff's exploits, and Ogden confided, "He ought to stay here and not do such crazy stunts. He is too valuable to risk dodging barrages."[19]

MacArthur constantly wore a soft cap with all stiffeners removed, looking more like the jaunty aviators of World War II than a doughboy. He neither carried nor wore the steel helmet, even though it was required of all soldiers at the front. Seldom, if ever, did MacArthur carry the required gas mask, and indeed he would become a gas casualty in a few weeks. As chief of staff, he constantly admonished all soldiers to keep their steel helmets and gas masks near them and to keep them maintained and cleaned. Clean and usable weapons were also a consistent theme for MacArthur's memoranda to the troops, but he did not carry one himself.[20]

If a chief of staff who issued such orders did not see fit to obey them, why should a doughboy in the trenches wear the uncomfortable steel helmet and carry the cumbersome gas mask? Pershing and most other AEF officers were raised on the old army adage, "lead by your example." After the Armistice on 11 November 1918, MacArthur became very ill due to the amount of gas he had inhaled from Lunéville to the Meuse-Argonne.[21]

The work of the division was being carried on by the battalions under the control of French teachers and subject to French orders, since they were in the line held by the French VII Corps. Usually, the French formed several *Groupe de Combat* (GC) in the first line of trenches. If the tactical situation required it, a *Poste d'Appui* (PA) was to the rear of the GCs and could support the groups by rifle, machine-gun or mortar fire. Two or more PAs were supported by a *Centre de Resistance* (CR). Normally, a GC was considered a self-contained combat unit, surrounded by wire, covered with machine-gun fire, and supported by artillery. In theory, if one GC was engaged, it could be supported by another; or if a general attack took place, the *Group de Combat* could fight independently if surrounded or cut off completely from other GCs. The fall of one GC did not, then, mean that the whole line caved in, and the PAs or CRs could concentrate on a particular crisis without interfering with the rest of the line.

The French 128th Infantry Division prepared a detailed and precise three-part order to bring the first battalions of the 167th and 168th American regiments into their own CRs. Between 28 February and 1 March, all six battalions would be placed in the trench rotation sequence so that each battalion spent time in each of the three trenches. Elements of the 117th Engineer Regiment were assigned tasks to support those two regiments. To ensure that everyone understood what was to occur, General Segone, commanding the French 128th Division, made certain that an annex to the Operation Order was published detailing the movement of the battalion trenches, step by step.

This French attention to detail came from their long, bloody experience in the trenches and the knowledge that one of the most critical times for soldiers in the trenches came when one unit replaced another. That would be a perfect time for artillery or gas to be used, causing heavy casualties and great confusion, something General Segone did not want.[22]

The movement into the trenches filled the doughboys with apprehension. Hugh S. Thompson lead his platoon of Company K, 168th Infantry, into the French-held trenches and reported to the captain. The first view was a shock for Thompson, who remembered: "A muddy officer poured over papers on a candle-lit table. A chorus of snores came from a dark tier of bunks. The underground shelter was heavy with sewer-like odors."[23] After being told about distribution of rations and water, gas alarms, and artillery barrages, Thompson was taken to his portion of the line, GC 9. His feeling of isolation increased as he saw GC 9. The untried lieutenant recalled:

The sight that greeted us brought an immediate and positive reaction. "Desolate" was the only name for it. A mass of rusty barbed wire was strung on crisscrosses of posts that seemed to grow from the ground. Ghost-like trees to the right were splattered with shell scars. Some had fallen into the mass of twisted wire and upturned earth. Others were broken off at various heights, like so many match sticks. The expanse of desolation sloped up a gentle rise. The German trenches were hidden behind the crest some 200 yards away.[24]

As he toured the line, Thompson was overpowered by a sickening stench. French intelligence was examining the body of a dead German soldier to find documents and to confirm the dead man's unit for order of battle information. The young officer became so violently ill that he staggered back to the dugout, where he was still overwhelmed by the smells of death, unwashed bodies, human excrement, rotting equipment, and spoiling food.

He watched as the ever-present "Slum" was served to the troops, who had no rags to clean their mess tins. An old wad of newspaper or a crust of bread was used to wipe the greasy mess-plate that a few minutes before had held stew. All the lessons on military hygiene that Thompson had learned were invalid once in GC 9. A few minutes later, he looked at his wooden bunk, one of many in a tier, and underneath the bottom bunk stood ankle-deep water. On a small field table a single flickering candle illuminated the dugout, and all Thompson could feel was a sense of isolation and desolation.

The Irish of the 165th believed that their renowned luck was with them as they moved into their trench system. It had been a quiet part of the line, and the reserve trench, right behind the CR, was in a woods they immediately named Camp New York. The ground was muddy and the weather damp and cold, but they had a good military road running through the Forest of Parroy to Haute Arbre woods, where the regiment made its headquarters. The main GCs and PAs in the trenches were at Rouge Bouquet. The name, meaning red bouquet, appealed to those Irishmen who liked to see themselves as a race of poets, and conjured up peaceful scenes. Father Duffy, accompanying Major Donovan and the 1st Battalion to Rouge Bouquet, noticed, "Off duty men live in mean little dugouts thinly roofed, poorly floored, wet and cold. But they are happy at being at the front at last, and look on the discomforts as part of the game."[25] And Martin Hogan recalled:

There is a strange transformation that the soldier undergoes. The report of any gun, at first, makes him jumpy, but the report of his own guns—these being nearer usually—make him jumpiest of all. But when he becomes acclimated, becomes accustomed to the work at the front, there is nothing that adds to his peace of mind and contentment like the crack of his own guns near at hand. When your own guns are belching a heavy torrent of steel over your heads, you, if you are a seasoned campaigner, sleep a sweet sleep that knows no dreams.[26]

Al Ettinger was with the first contingent of the 165th to go into the forward trench on 22 February. Being in the Pioneer Platoon, Ettinger and his buddies moved into a dank, smelly dugout at night. As they emerged the next morning to see their new surroundings, they found a souvenir left by the Germans, a large white sheet saying "Welcome, Rainbow Division." It was all too obvious to Ettinger and the New Yorkers that their careful movement into the forward trench had certainly not fooled the combat-wise Germans.[27] The Germans did the same thing to the Alabama regiment, but the Southerners saw the banner as a challenge and as an affront to Alabama's honor.

Before going into the trenches, Colonel Screws' Alabamians had their heads shaved again to ward off the ever-present cooties. It did no good. The dugouts were breeding places for them, and soon the Alabamians were infested as badly as before. The Germans greeted them with a tremendous artillery barrage that cost no lives but was an introduction to life in the trenches. Their trenches ran through a totally destroyed village named Ancerviller, where the stone walls of the former town formed parts of several GCs. Private John B. Hayes of Company I, who had experienced the welcoming artillery bombardment, was on guard duty, sensibly, as he saw it, staying very close to the walls. A new lieutenant saw Hayes and took umbrage at his failure to walk his post in a military manner, as had been taught in the three-months officers' school. While he was in the process of dressing Hayes down for such an egregious breach of front-line discipline, the Germans fired a Whiz-bang (an 88mm shell) into the ruins. The young officer brushed the mud from his uniform and quickly departed. Hayes went back to "hugging the wall."[28]

Almost as soon as the Alabamians were in the trenches, firing at the Germans began. Patrolling and crossing No Man's Land became a specialty of the 167th; in fact, the regiment was tasked to make the first raid to bring back German prisoners. On 4 March, a patrol led by Sergeant Varner Hall of Birmingham, Alabama, captured two Germans from the 77th Bavarian Infantry Regiment after a particularly sharp hand-to-hand fight that merited the French Croix de Guerre for each member of the patrol. Because of the nature of the combat, a few days later Hall and his soldiers also received the Distinguished Service Cross for heroism. This patrol was unusual in that every man was a non-commissioned officer, men determined to prove their bravery in battle.[29]

The 167th Infantry Regiment was quickly developing into the most aggressive and combat-proficient unit in the Rainbow Division. There had been great worry over the indiscipline within this regiment at Camp Mills, and the continual bouts of disease also concerned divisional headquarters, but once in the trenches the 167th manifested a desire to fight unmatched by any other regiment. The Alabamians also found Slum to be "an appetizing and nourishing concoction of meat and vegetables."[30] Many of the Alabama troops were from rural and impoverished areas where life was hard, food was not abundant, and they lived "near to the ground," as the Southern expression goes. Perhaps it was natural for them to take to hard campaigning.

Medic Lawrence Stewart went into the trenches with the 3rd Battalion of the 168th Infantry. In the same Iowa regiment as Hugh Thompson, Stewart found the trenches unpleasant, to be sure, but was impressed with the French troops they relieved. They were from Algeria, "gaunt, somber, beak-nosed men, uniformed in a combination of khaki and horizon blue, with their heads swathed in gorgeous turbans and wrappings of cloth." Stewart's main concern was with life in the trenches and the casualties that combat would produce. This area had a sort of live-and-let-live policy, and the French and Germans had developed a tacit agreement not to fire on one another. Washing hung out on the wire, and men moved freely about on both sides. But that changed, as Stewart recalled, when "Yankees, craving excitement and following out their own program of thoroughness and speed at all costs, disregarded the reigning state of affairs and shot at everything in sight." The unofficial truce ended.[31]

The Germans answered with some shelling and sniping, and began planning to really welcome the Americans to the Western Front. Second Lieutenant Paul H. Jarrett of Company M, 166th Infantry, recalled that the brigade commander informed his soldiers, "There is no No Man's land in front of our division, it is Rainbow land up to the German trench."[32]

Very quickly, casualties began to appear at the various first-aid stations as a result of this change in conditions. Providing medical care for the troops in the trenches was extraordinarily difficult. The muddy, twisting trenches made transporting any litter case very difficult. Also, most of the litter cases were moved during combat, when the danger was at its height. Medics stood an equal chance of being felled by shot, shell, or gas, but caring for the wounded had to take precedence over their own safety. Once out of the trench, the wounded man was probably even more in harm's way because there was no protection from shrapnel and bullets.

Near the trenches was an aid station where the wounded received their first real treatment. Walking wounded were looked at quickly and sent to the dressing station, usually about a mile to the rear. Ambulances, both motor and horse-drawn, were close to the aid station to take litter cases to the dressing station as quickly as possible. This station rendered more treatment and could keep patients with less severe wounds under their care. Severely wounded were sent from the dressing station to the field hospital, which had a higher level of care and a triage unit to assess the severity of the injuries. Patients with the best chance of survival were given priority, while those who would not survive were made as comfortable as possible. Many were sent to evacuation points, then to base hospitals that had been established all over France.

Often, field hospitals came under artillery fire, air, and gas attacks due to their proximity to the battlefield, and the nature of World War I fighting made the movement of the wounded to the rear difficult at best. Most of the doctors, like Major Frew of the Wisconsin Guard and Lieutenant van Dolsen of the

District of Columbia National Guard, had never faced the severity of the cases brought to them. Van Dolsen had been given command of the 166th Field Hospital on 24 January 1918, and he had never seen a combat casualty before.

The French had the Rainbow troops begin an active program of patrolling. Usually these patrols went into No Man's Land to gather information on German defenses, noting new wire entanglements, listening for German work parties improving old trenches or building new ones, trying to locate minefields in front of the enemy trench, and finding German trench mortar locations. The intelligence officer of the battalion, who normally initiated and wrote the order, briefed the entire patrol on what was known about the enemy. The sentinels and friendly outposts had to be alerted as to the times of departure and return of the patrol.[33] The combat patrol and air reconnaissance (balloon and aircraft) were the two primary sources for the intelligence officers, and when German prisoners were taken they were usually questioned at length. American intelligence was in its infancy in France, and the French taught U.S. intelligence personnel a great deal based on their four years of practical experience.

While each one of the regiments had patrols, the first raid on an enemy trench was conducted by the 168th Iowa Infantry. Then the Ohio and the New York regiments had their schooling in raids. But the Alabama regiment excelled in the art of patrolling and raiding, and it fell to them to take the first German prisoners.[34]

By 1 March, the Germans were well aware of the aggressive nature of the Americans facing them. The Alabama troops had crossed No Man's Land one night and put signs in the German wire facing their trenches which read, "Germans, give your soul to God because your ass belongs to Alabam." On 5 March the Germans staged a raid on the Iowa trenches and were repulsed, with bloody losses. During a particularly heavy barrage at the same time, First Lieutenant Edmund P. Glover, the intelligence officer of the 2nd Battalion, 167th Infantry, was working in his dugout when a shell struck the trench and severely wounded him. A month later, after infection and diphtheria set in, Glover became the first Alabama officer to die in France from a combat wound.[35]

The growing reports of enemy contact and American casualties brought Pershing to the 42nd Division on 6 March to see Menoher and his two brigade commanders, Generals Lenihan and Brown. Pershing heard a glowing report from the French about the progress of the Rainbows, and he was pleased with his visits to the 165th, 167th, and 168th Infantry Regiments. Next, Black Jack went to visit the wounded and was deeply moved by Indiana Artillery Lieutenant A. W. Terrell, who had lost a leg when the German guns engaged the 151st Field Artillery Regiment. Terrell told Pershing that he did not want to leave the AEF until the war was over and asked if Pershing might have a job for him as a clerk at Chaumont or some place in the AEF.[36]

Life in the trenches, while certainly unpleasant, had taken on an air of "business as usual," with routine broken only by German shelling, by patrolling, and by the occasional raid. The French advisers and teachers were growing more apprehensive as they watched the tendency of the Americans to become complacent and fall into bad habits. The French also noted a heavy usage of the telephone, even though that had been expressly regulated by the intelligence section of the French responsible for American training. The Americans tended to talk too long and include important tactical information; consequently, a six-minute time limit on all calls was instituted, and the French urged that messengers be utilized. The telegraph, while not all that secure, was the second-preferred method of communicating with higher headquarters.[37]

French advisers were also disturbed over the American tendency to show themselves carelessly in the trenches, providing German observers with opportunities to record the routine of the troops and, worse, to ascertain American schedules such as time and method of feeding and the relief of outposts and guards. Disregarding French warnings, the doughboys would often stand on top of the trenches or walk on top of the trench lines. Donovan was also growing aggravated with his troops' disregard of operational security. On 4 March, his patience reached its limit when a lieutenant from Company C came to battalion headquarters to inform Donovan and his intelligence officer that he and "a group" of sergeants were moving into the first line of trenches to observe procedures. Since Donovan's battalion was scheduled to move into those trenches in two days, the request seemed natural. A reconnaissance by an officer and three or four NCOs was good military procedure, but in a few hours Donovan found out that the small party actually numbered over a dozen men. The presence of such a large number of newly arrived men had attracted the attention of German observers, and a heavy barrage of artillery hit the front trench. Donovan, furious, raked the company commander over the coals, saying, "We are not conducting a Cook's Tourist Agency, and such parties as were sent up today must not be sent again."[38]

The dawn of March 7 brought with it the promise of a warm and sunny day, a welcome relief for the damp and muddy soldiers of the Rainbow Division. If the sun continued, it would be a day to dry clothing and air out the wet, lice-infested straw bedding that had been in the dugouts for weeks. There was little shelling or small-arms fire throughout the morning, and more mattresses were brought out into the sunlight. The lunch meal was served hot, as it was now possible to bring the cans containing the stew into the trenches quickly due to the lack of firing. Soldiers climbed out of the trenches to dry clothes, smoke, eat, and enjoy the early spring afternoon. About 2 P.M., a few German shells landed near the trenches; and the French adviser in the forward trenches, Lieutenant Colonel André Dussauge, warned that he believed the Germans were registering targets. He was ignored.[39]

Ettinger, of the 165th's Pioneer platoon, was also enjoying the sunny day, and there was little work scheduled for the afternoon. Martin Hogan was preparing his gear, since the Shamrocks would move into the forward trenches the next day. Donovan was working in his dugout when, at 2:50 P.M., the ground began to shake as from an earthquake. German artillery pounded the forward trenches for two hours. There was pandemonium as soldiers of the 165th who had been smoking and enjoying the warm afternoon sun were rushing about trying to find gas masks, stumbling over wounded comrades, and trying to organize themselves for a possible German infantry assault. Rouge Bouquet dugouts began to collapse as they were hit by shell after shell. Parts of the trench caved in, making it almost impossible for men to get from one part of the line to the next. Two dugouts containing over thirty Irish regiment soldiers sustained direct hits, burying the troops alive in the mud and debris.[40]

A high explosive shell struck the dugout containing the signal section under Lieutenant John Norman, collapsing the beams and burying the men inside. Norman managed to get the two shaken enlisted men out, then rushed into the trench to organize rescue attempts for the nearly thirty men in the other collapsed dugout. Lieutenant Norman and the Irish soldiers immediately began digging, as they could hear the cries of the men. A few soldiers had been brought out when, under the strain of the bombardment, the rest of the dugout collapsed. Norman was pinned beneath a felled beam, his chest crushed, and died immediately.[41]

Donovan was now on the scene, where military discipline had begun to crack under the strain. He knew that this heavy cannonade might well be the prelude to an infantry attack by the enemy and began to organize a defense. He quickly ordered men into the outposts in front of the destroyed trenches. Private Eddie Kelly, a small lad of seventeen, volunteered to go in front of the trench, and Donovan quickly sent the young man to hold an outpost.[42] One soldier had totally lost control of himself and was screaming and running up and down the trench. Donovan, noticing that other soldiers were becoming unnerved by the distraught man, hit him solidly on the jaw. The soldier fell into a heap, and Donovan quickly ordered NCOs to get hold of their men and prepare for an attack or work in the rescue attempts.[43]

Rushing from the rear came Ettinger and the Pioneer platoon, elements of the 117th Engineers, Father Duffy, and Joyce Kilmer. Under heavy artillery fire, Ettinger and the engineers went to work trying to extract the buried men. Work in the trench had to be stopped throughout that night and the morning of 8 March because of the severity of the bombardment, and by the afternoon it was clear that almost two dozen 165th soldiers were dead, entombed in their collapsed dugout. While ministering to the dead and wounded that morning, Duffy came across the body of Eddie Kelly, from whom he had heard confession only the day before. Kelly, the volunteer, had been killed by enemy shrapnel during the night.

The confusion that had reigned during the day increased at night, and one company commander lost control of himself. Ordering his men to prepare to repulse a German attack, the officer issued no less than five separate gas alarms and requested that the machine-gun company supporting his position begin firing into No Man's Land. The commander of the machine-gun unit refused, pointing out that there were American and French patrols out there. The company commander had contributed so to the chaos that a general panic gripped his unit, and during the night a nervous sentry fired at what he thought to be Germans. At dawn it was discovered that the "Germans" were really another American sentry post, and one American had been killed by mistake.[44] Donovan relieved the company commander on 8 March.

On 9 March the Germans continued to shell the Rainbow lines with a growing intensity. While pounding the New Yorkers, enemy artillery began to fall on the 168th Iowa Infantry. Company M and Company F were sent with two French companies each to raid the German trenches at 1:00 P.M. Once in the German trenches, they trapped a number of the enemy in their dugouts and threw grenades on them. Company M found two prisoners and returned to its lines. During the day, the Iowans had five soldiers killed, twenty-seven wounded, and one missing. Among the wounded that day was Everett Scott, who had had to carry a dispatch back to higher headquarters. During his trip through the trenches a shell exploded and Scott fell, a searing pain from a shrapnel wound in his thigh.[45] Scott found out that casualty lists were sent back to the United States very quickly, and he realized that his mother and family would soon know of his wound. As soon as he could, he wrote telling them that he had been wounded "going over the top." They were not to worry about him, as it was only a minor wound and he would rejoin his company soon.[46]

Enemy shelling subsided after 9 March, and it was time to take stock of what had happened during the three bloody days of combat. Donovan was, along with a number of other New Yorkers, awarded the French Croix de Guerre for valor. The body of Eddie Kelly, who had been almost too young to join the Fighting 69th, was laid to rest in a grove of trees called Croix de l'Arbre Vert (Cross of the Green Tree). Father Duffy, who had heard the boy's last confession, presided over the service. Engineers were still working to find the bodies of the men who were buried in the collapsed Rouge Bouquet trench, but sporadic enemy fire made the work painfully slow and dangerous.

Joyce Kilmer suggested that the bodies remain where they had fallen. They were dead, Kilmer argued; why risk more casualties trying to extricate those whose souls were already far from this earth? It was agreed that the collapsed dugout would remain sealed, and later a marble tablet was placed on the site at Rouge Bouquet stating, "Here on the Field of honor rest..." followed by the inscribed names.[47] In honor of his fallen comrades Kilmer wrote possibly his best war poem, simply titled "Rouge Bouquet," which Duffy used in a memorial service for the dead a few days later.

The 67th Field Artillery Brigade was serving with the French, supporting its Rainbow comrades in the line, and Charles MacArthur found Lunéville to be a mixed blessing. His battery position was in a sea of mud, made worse by rain and then snow, but very close to the guns was a French canteen which dispensed a very harsh, potent red wine. Soon the Illinois men were playing dice, drinking, and had built a fire over which to heat the ever-present Corned Willie. The Germans observed the Americans moving into the area and fired a short salvo to greet the new arrivals. The next morning, the artillerymen began to dig deep gun pits into the mud.[48]

Leslie Langille found that his battery was not scheduled to move up soon, and he and his Battery B mates explored Lunéville. Here he found numerous bars, not unlike those at Camp Coetquidan, with cheap, free-flowing liquor and women of negotiable virtue. However, the prostitutes associated with the bars charged more than those who were "lone wolves," or acting on their own without benefit of saloon keeper. Langille recalled seeing outside of a lone wolves' room

long lines of Poilus, Tommies, Scots, Chinks, Japs, Algerians etc. waiting to take their turn at the old home plate. A few of the Americans less inclined to spend freely can be found in this line. None, however, of our Southern brethren can be seen on these lines; in fact, the old Southern spirit of chivalry, aided and abetted by a few shots, causes those boys to go out trouble bent, and gives us no end of concern when they meet up with such lines of waiting "gents," as it is no easy matter to keep our Alabamians, Georgians etc., from cleaning up the assembled mob, very often not even overlooking the "babes" themselves.[49]

The troops of the 117th Engineer Regiment, numbering about 1,000, found their lives complicated by the fact that the infantry regiments were in four different locations. In his monthly report, Colonel William Kelly, commanding the engineers, simply listed the ongoing tasks for the unit as "digging trenches, constructing concrete dugouts, building roads in and around trenches, constructing barbed wire entanglements and building barracks." In addition, the regiment did considerable electrical work to provide lights to the bunkers and dugouts in the trenches.[50]

Each and every engagement, from the smallest amount of rifle and mortar fire in the trenches to the bloody days of 7-9 March 1918, produced casualties. After a sharp fight involving the Iowa soldiers, medic Stewart recalled:

Somehow we got the men back to the dressing station at Badonviller. It wasn't ours to reason why just then. The trenches were narrow and so twisted that four men carrying a stretcher could scarcely pass through. The mud was up to our knees, the communication trench destroyed and under heavy shell-fire. At the dressing station we bathed and stanched wounds, splinting broken arms and legs, for by then casualties were coming thick and fast. During all this time shells varying in size from three to eight inches were raining like hail upon our trenches."[51]

In his field hospital well within range of German observation and artillery, van Dolsen was no longer the callow youth he had been at Rolampont. His stints in the operating room ran over eight hours, and still the wounded kept coming. Two 165th soldiers were brought in, victims of shrapnel wounds. One had over thirteen wounds, the other four, and van Dolsen spent over four hours trying to save them from immediate death or subsequent infection. He wrote to his mother:

Shrapnel wounds are queer things. When you see the men undressed you would think that they had been hit by a charge from a shotgun. Just small holes here and there but you see they have great power of penetration and go way down deep and are apt to carry lots of clothing and gas forming bacillus. You have to cut way down deep and open them wide taking out all of the damaged tissue.[52]

Once out of the trenches, those soldiers who were able to get into Lunéville found themselves confronted by the bars and houses offering wares in spirits and in human flesh. Of course, the venereal disease rate spiralled upward, much to the distress of divisional officers and AEF Headquarters. Pershing, as a professional soldier, was well aware of the problems of VD among soldiers, and he was not unrealistic in his attitude toward troops away from home for the first time. But this was not just a Regular Army war. There were National Guard and draftees in the Army from the small towns of America, and venereal infections and immorality would not be acceptable at all. The popular song of the day, "How You Gonna Keep them Down on the Farm After They've Seen Paree" was more than just a funny song. Pershing stated that venereal disease "was destined to give us considerable concern because of the difference between the French attitude and our own regarding the suppression of the source of infection."[53]

Contracting venereal disease was a court-martial offense, and many AEF soldiers were tried for the infection. VD went up during the Lunéville period because of access to the town where the unregulated "lone wolves" abounded. Captain H. L. Sanford, the 42nd Division's urologist, stated in a lecture to the AEF Sanitary School at Langres, France, in late February 1918:

The soldier...owes his maximum physical efficiency to the service, and any deliberate interference with that efficiency, such as may follow the incident to a venereal infection, is rightly held as an offense slightly below a self-inflicted wound or mutilation in gravity... At each sexual exposure he voluntarily places himself in an environment where an infection becomes possible."[54]

In his lecture, Captain Sanford listed a number of possible remedies for the dangers of infection, including lectures, regulation of prostitution (to include the arrest of infected women), and the establishment of stations offering prophylaxis, which soldiers would be obliged to use. Another lecturer dealt with the question of giving soldiers condoms, which had been shown to be effective in reducing venereal diseases. The doctor expressed the prevailing view in the AEF when he said, "I don't think you should hand them out a license to cohabit, and the condom pretends to represent an absolute guarantee against infection."[55]

In January 1918, there were 107 cases of venereal disease in the Rainbow Division, but by the end of March, the Lunéville period, the cases doubled. Gonorrhea led the list of infections, and the highest rate of overall infection was in the Ohio and Alabama regiments.[56] Lieutenant Colonel Jay W. Grissinger recognized that while the men were at Lunéville, given the nature of the seamy establishments there, prophylaxis stations had to be available. Chief Surgeon Grissinger issued a directive to all regimental surgeons to open stations providing the materials for prophylaxis in clearly marked and accessible buildings. Areas within the buildings would have privacy and hot water. Most importantly, medical personnel were required to oversee the proper administration of the prophylaxis.[57]

Lieutenant van Dolsen would remember Lunéville because of the arrival of nurses for his hospital, and for the moment at least, he was happy to have the help as casualties continued to mount from the shelling and small-arms fire. One of his newly arrived nurses, a veteran weighing only about 98 pounds, was walking to the main hospital tent when a German shell landed near her and lifted her, tossing her into a recently vacated garden. Van Dolsen was sure she was dead, but the nurse came walking out of the garden brushing dirt from her uniform and saying that she should eat more and gain weight so she "would be too big to be blown into the salad bowl." The young doctor needed comic relief, having just performed an amputatation. As the soldier came out from under the anesthesia he had grasped van Dolsen's arm, asking, "Did you have to take my leg off?"

The young doctor, choked with emotion, could only lie, "I don't know, I wasn't there."[58]

Rumors had begun to circulate that by 21 March, the 42nd Division would be out of the Lunéville trenches and would be sent to a quiet area to evaluate its performance and to train for the next phase of combat experience. Pershing and his staff had decided that after one month's practice training with the French, the Rainbow Division would be sent back to Rolampont. There shortages in equipment and manpower could be made up, the men would be allowed to train using the lessons learned while at Lunéville, and the divisional, brigade, and regimental staffs could again exercise control over their men, which was not possible while at Lunéville. But on 21 March, the Germans launched a major spring offensive, and the allies were hard-pressed. Every British and French soldier would be needed to stop the Germans who had punched through the British lines. There could be no rest and rehabilitation at Rolampont for a full American combat division fresh from realistic trench training.[59]

Donovan and his battalion would be leaving the trenches, and he had every reason to be pleased with his performance as a commander. On his khaki wool tunic he wore the red and green ribbon of the French Croix de Guerre. As a going-away gesture, Wild Bill Donovan went into the front trenches to see off a French raiding party, then went with them into the German trenches. During the raid the Germans opened up with artillery and killed three of Donovan's men, but Donovan returned to his dugout safely. It would be his last action at Lunéville.[60]

On 21 March, a German observation plane was seen taking photographs of the trench system. Every New Yorker opened fire on the German observer, but missed, and an hour later the German artillery, with terrific accuracy, pounded the Shamrocks with a storm of shot and shell. By the morning of 22 March, only thirty men stood uninjured. Martin Hogan was not among them; he had been felled by mustard gas. He was blind, and his knees were badly burned from the deadly vapor. "The pain in my eyes and head had grown intolerable...The water flowed in such a stream down my cheeks that I began to fear that my eyes themselves were running out." Sightless, Hogan was led back to the dressing station, where the painful process of healing began.[61] Donovan recorded that 410 soldiers of the 165th Infantry had been gassed, and the equivalent of one full company was *hors de combat*.[62] This would be the worst single set of casualties the Rainbow suffered while at Lunéville.

What were the lessons learned for the Lunéville period? The division learned who could or could not function under fire in combat. This was vitally important, because no training, regardless of how realistic, can approximate the fear of real battle.

Also, the troops learned to live in a combat environment where artillery, gas, and small-arms fire could snuff out a life very quickly. It is possible to train soldiers to exist in a field environment, to be sure, and conditions can be made as miserable as possible. But the gut-wrenching fear, felt when the first artillery shell comes in, cannot be reproduced. The Rainbow soldiers never became blasé about it, but they learned to cope with it.

Once Lunéville was over and the division moved to the Baccarat sector, the soldiers realized that they had officers, NCOs, and buddies that they could trust in a deadly situation. This was not only true for the Joe Romanos, Al Ettingers, Martin Hogans in the ranks; it also applied to the officers like Thompson of the Iowa regiment and van Dolsen of the medical corps.

Squads, platoons, companies, and battalions learned to rely on each other. Patrolling, calling for artillery, hand-to-hand combat, first aid, and so on were all skills sharpened in the trenches. The higher staffs, however, received less real combat training, and that was a weak spot for the Rainbows. The regimental, brigade, and divisional staffs were almost bystanders, since the French had control of the training within the trenches. The staffs had little to do but to read the orders and react as best they could, since they had no role to play in the drama unfolding in the three trench systems.

The division was in motion toward Rolampont when MacArthur received an order from AEF Headquarters that the movement back to the old training area was to be halted. The order arrived on 23 March and gave the troops four days to rest, clean equipment, and prepare to move to the Baccarat area.[63] MacArthur, after a hurried conference with Menoher, changed the direction of march to Baccarat, about fifty kilometers to the south of Lunéville.[64] Baccarat was considered to be a quiet sector, as was Lunéville, but it was a section of the line that would be turned over to Americans completely. If Pershing had any doubts about the wisdom of the move—and indeed staffs at the regimental, brigade, and divisional levels were untested—he had no choice. The great German offensive, which had been expected for months, was on, and the French divisions holding that Baccarat sector had to be shifted as rapidly as possible to stem the German tide. There would be no more training, and the Rainbows would not leave the line for anything but a little rest and refitting until the end of the war.

NOTES

1. A. Churchill Ettinger, (ed.), *A Doughboy with the Fighting 69th* (Shippensburg, PA: White Main Publishing, 1992), 58-59.

2. Martin J. Hogan, *The Shamrock Battalion of the Rainbow: A Story of the Fighting 69th* (New York: D. Appleton and Co., 1919), 59-60.

3. John B. Hayes, *Heroes Among the Brave* (Loachapoka, Ala.: Lee County Historical Society, 1973), 12.

4. Lawrence Stewart, *Rainbow Bright* (Philadelphia: Dorrance, 1923), 45.

5. Douglas MacArthur, *Reminiscences* (New York: McGraw-Hill, 1964), 54.

6. Leslie Langille, *Men of the Rainbow* (Chicago: O'Sullivan Co., 1933), 58-59.

7. Charles MacArthur, *War Bugs* (Garden City, N.Y.: Doubleday, Doran and Co., 1929), 26-28.

8. Walter B. Wolf, *Brief Story of the Rainbow Division* (New York: Rand McNally Co., 1919), 11.

9. Notes provided by Joseph O. Romano, Jr., Birmingham, Alabama, based on his conversations with his father, Corporal Joseph O. Romano, 167th Infantry (hereinafter, Romano Notes).

10. William B. Amerine, *Alabama's Own in France* (New York: Eaton and Gettinger, 1919), 93-94.

11. AEF GHQ (Coordination Division) to Commanding General I Corps, 12 February 1918, in National Archives, Washington, D.C., *Records Group 120 Records of the AEF, 42nd Division*, carton 1 (hereinafter, RG 120).

12. Peter H. Ottosen, *Trench Artillery AEF* (Boston: Lothrop, Lee, and Shepard, 1931), 97-100. By the end of the war, the Trench Mortarmen had their own special specialty insignia—a three-inch winged bomb, named by the mortarmen a "pig."

13. Memorandum from G4, AEF GHQ to Chief, French Mission to the AEF, 12 February 1918, in RG 120, Carton 1.

14. John J. Pershing, *My Experiences in the World War*, Vol. 1 (New York: Frederick A. Stokes Co., 1931), 349.

15. Ibid., 259.

16. There are differences of opinion among scholars about how much Menoher commanded and how much MacArthur actually did. Menoher was an artillery officer with little experience with infantry, but he learned quickly, and from the documents it is clear that he commanded with MacArthur as his energetic chief of staff. See D. Clayton James, *The Years of MacArthur, 1880-1941* (Boston: Houghton-Mifflin, 1970), 166-67.

17. MacArthur, *Reminiscences*, 53. The document that set up the staff was General Order No. 8, HQ, 42nd Division, 23 February 1918, in RG 120, carton 3.

18. Letter from Ogden to his wife, np, 21 February 1918, in Ogden Letters, in U.S. Army Military History Institute Archives, Carlisle Barracks, Pennsylvania, 42nd Division AEF Collection (hereinafter, MHIA).

19. Ibid.

20. See James, *Years of MacArthur*, 156. MacArthur, because of his unorthodox dress, which was distinctly non-regulation, was once captured as a German. See Donald Smythe, *Pershing: General of the Armies* (Bloomington, Ind.: Indiana University Press, 1986), 228. MacArthur himself makes reference to his attire, but he puts a very different light on the matter. See MacArthur, *Reminiscences*, 70.

21. Ibid., 71.

22. Ordre Général, No. 94, et mesures et detail en execution de l'Ordre Général No. 94, 27 February 1918, in RG 120, carton B12. For more on the organization of the French trenches see Henry J. Reilly, *Americans All: The Rainbow at War* (Columbus, Ohio: F.J. Heer Printing Co., 1936), 166.

23. Thompson, Hugh S., "Following the Rainbow," *The Chattanooga Times*, 27 January 1934.

24. Ibid.

25. Frances P. Duffy, *Father Duffy's Story* (New York: George H. Doran Co., 1919), 60.

26. Hogan, *Shamrock Battalion*, 68-70.

27. Ettinger, *Doughboy*, 63.

28. Hayes, *Heroes Among the Brave*, 13.

29. Amerine, *Alabama's Own*, 97-98.

30. Hayes, *Heroes Among the Brave*, 15.

31. Lawrence Stewart, *Rainbow Bright* (Philadelphia: Dorrance, 1923), 44-46.

32. Statement by Paul H. Jarrett, formerly of Company M, 166th Infantry and a member of the Nebraska National Guard, on 22 March 1989, in Military History Institute WWI Questionnaires, MHIA.

33. From the personal notebook of Wagoner Edgar Lowe, HQ, 168th Infantry, MHIA.

34. Wolf, *Story of the Rainbow*, 12.

35. Amerine, *Alabama's Own*, 16.

36. Pershing, *Experiences*, Vol. 1, 339.

37. HQ, 42nd Division Memorandum No. 62, 27 February 1918, in RG 120, carton 1.

38. Memorandum by Donovan, 4 March 1918, in ibid., carton 26.

39. "Report on the Events Which Took Place in C.R. Rouge Bouguet, Held by 2nd Bn, 165th Infantry, on 7-8 March 1918," by Lieutenant Colonel André Dussauge, 8 March 1918, in ibid., carton 78.

40. Ibid. See also Duffy, *Story*, 61-63; and Ettinger, *Doughboy*, 67.

41. Dussauge report, RG 120, carton 78.

42. Duffy, *Story*, 63-64.

43. Entry Donovan Diary, 7 March 1918, MHIA.

44. Dussauge report. RG 120, carton 78.

45. "Return of Casualties, near Badonvillers, 9 March 1918, 168th Infantry," RG 120, carton 33.

46. Scott to his brother, np, 18 March 1918, in Scott Letters, manuscripts in the author's collection.

47. Duffy, *Story*, 64; Ettinger, *Doughboy*, 70-72.

48. MacArthur, *War Bugs*, 33-35.

49. Langille, *Men of the Rainbow*, 62.

50. Monthly Report for March 1918, 117th Engineer Regiment, RG 120, carton

40.

51. Stewart, *Rainbow Bright*, 47.

52. Van Dolsen to his mother, np, 28 February 1918, MHIA.

53. Pershing, *Experiences*, Vol. 1, 177.

54. Lecture by Captain Sanford, in U.S. Office of the Surgeon General, *The Medical Department of the United States Army in the World War. Vol. 6: Training*, (Washington: Government Printing Office, 1926), 670-72.

55. Lecture by Colonel Edward L. Keyes, U.S. Army Medical Corps, ibid., 1908.

56. Monthly VD Report by Lieutenant J.W. Grissinger to Chief Surgeon, AEF GHQ, 16 January 1918, in RG 120, carton 66.

57. Memorandum No. 73, from Grissinger to all Surgeons, 25 February 1918, ibid., carton 9.

58. Van Dolsen to his sister, np, 17 March 1918, and Van Dolsen to his mother, np, 19 March 1918, MHIA.

59. General Orders No. 10., AEF GHQ 20 March 1918, in Center of Military History, *United States Army in the World War. Vol. 3: Training and Use of American Units with the British and the French* (Washington: Government Printing Office, 1989), 682.

60. Entry 20 March 1919, Donovan Diary, MHIA.

61. Hogan, *Shamrock Battalion*, 87-88; Duffy, *Story*, 74-78.

62. Entry 23 March 1918, Donovan Diary, MHIA.

63. HQ, 42nd Division, General Orders No. 11, 23 March 1918, in CMH, *United States Army in the World War*, Vol. 3, 682-83.

64. HQ, 42nd Division, General Order No. 11 (a different order clarifying points in the original General Order No. 11), 23 March 1918, RG 120, carton 129.

4

From Baccarat to Champagne

The movement from the Lunéville area to Baccarat showed just how far the Rainbow Division had come since the poorly ordered, uncoordinated road march from Vaucoleurs to Rolampont. General Order No. 10, which put the 42nd on the road to Baccarat, was a well-thought-out and professionally written field order issued on 20 March 1918, specifying the start of the movement at 7:30 A.M., 25 March. The organization of the march was delineated in a separate column for each of the two infantry regiments, each under command of the two infantry brigade commanders. With the 83rd Brigade, under Brigadier General Lenihan, there was the 149th Illinois Field Artillery Regiment, a battalion of the 117th Engineers, the 166th Field Hospital, the 165th Ambulance Company, and elements of the 117th Ammunition Train. The 84th Brigade, under Brigadier General Brown, had the remaining two artillery regiments and the other elements of the division. Brown's brigade, considered the better of the two, had more troops (including the Missouri Signal men) and more engineers, medical, and ammunition units. The staff had created two self-contained fighting units, capable of sustaining themselves in combat.

Liaison teams from each major unit were to move forward to each stopping place to prepare billets and have hot food and drink ready as the soldiers arrived from their march. Daily reports to division headquarters informed the division as to the state of animals, rations, and troops.

Of course, there were major differences between the Rolampont march and this one moving the division to Baccarat. The weather was certainly more moderate, even though spring rains made the marching difficult. By late March, the staffs of all the elements of the Rainbow had gained great experience. Once at Baccarat, the regiments would move directly into the trenches, with the artillery and other parts of the Rainbow occupying preselected positions. There would be liaison officers from AEF Headquarters at Chaumont watching the occupation of the Baccarat sector, and everyone was aware of the historic nature of the 42nd Division's having responsibility for the first totally American section of the line.

The front occupied by the Rainbow Division was sixteen kilometers long and relieved two French divisions, enabling them to be sent to help stem the German tide on the Somme. The operational plan drawn up by the divisional staff was a good one that took advantage of key terrain, fields of fire, good firing positions for the artillery, and roads and trails for resupply. Wisely, G3 Hughes made it very clear which unit had responsibility for what area. The foward trench was divided into Centre of Resistance (CRs), corresponding to the French tactical organization. From left to right (Northwest to Southeast), the CRs were named Ancerville (3rd Battalion, 165th Infantry), Champois and Village Negre (3rd Battalion, 168th Infantry). The 166th Infantry Regiment was retained in general support of the front line units, with one battalion dedicated to each of the regiments. The remaining battalions of the 165th, 167th, and 168th were located in the trenches and positions behind the front battalions, close enough (one to three miles) to come to the assistance of their sister units should combat require it.

The 83rd Brigade headquarters occupied the town of Merveiller, or rather what was left of it, while the 84th Brigade took over the few remaining buildings in Nuefmaison. Division headquarters, about six miles from the CRs, was located in farm houses near the crossroads town of Deneuvre, on the Meurthe River. The 84th Brigade was familiar with this area and occupied trenches in which it had already operated.[1]

There was throughout the Rainbow a good deal of confusion as to what lay ahead for the division. For Charles MacArthur and his Illinois gunners, the rumor was that the entire unit was to be pulled back to a rest camp after leaving Lunéville, and indeed they marched to a town named Haudonville, where they camped for a few days. Haudonville quickly became "Hoodlumville" for the cannoneers of the 149th Artillery. Since most of MacArthur's battery had not been paid in some time, they traded equipment for food and drink, and one enterprising soldier managed to steal a large sack of real flour, which he traded to one of the Hoodlumville prostitutes. It looked as if the artillerymen were about to begin another of their drinking and carousing episodes, when word reached the unit to move, in a driving rainstorm, to the Baccarat area.[2] Leslie Langille had also been sure that a rest was in order after Lunéville, but instead of heading toward Rolampont the guns lumbered on in the mud to Baccarat. Langille and his buddies were upset because, anticipating a period of rest and relaxation, they had sent their barracks bags, with all their extra clean clothes, back to Rolampont.[3]

On 27 March, Father Duffy paid a visit to Donovan's battalion and arrived just in time to see Wild Bill leading his troops off on a cross-country run, which Donovan won. Duffy said Mass for the troops and celebrated Holy Communion before they began their march to Baccarat. As Donovan's first battalion swung out onto the road to the trenches, Colonel Barker, mounted on a fine horse, situated himself where he could watch the 165th march by. Seeing Duffy

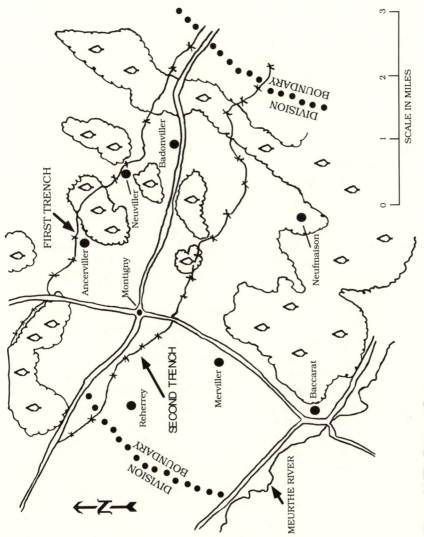

Figure 4.1 The Baccarat Sector

marching at the head of the Irish regiment beside Donovan, he offered the priest a ride on his newly acquired horse. Duffy thanked the colonel, but stated that he preferred to march with his parishioners to Baccarat—which he did, in fine form.[4]

General Menoher left the Lunéville headquarters on his way to Baccarat and, looking up into the sky, saw a beautiful rainbow on the horizon. What a harbinger of good things to come, the general mused.[5]

Lieutenant Hugh Thompson arrived at Baccarat with only fifty soldiers left from his original platoon of seventy, and they were to go immediately into the forward trenches. It was to be a night relief, and as they started forward, the Germans began firing into the ruins of the town behind them. This was not such a quiet sector for the Iowa troops, who immediately fell back into a trench routine. Just as in Lunéville, there were difficulties in maintaining telephone communications with higher headquarters, and runners were continually being wounded because they had to expose themselves to enemy fire. Food details had to cross nearly three miles from kitchens in the rear, and, "chow details labored manfully up the winding ditches. Slum was often spilled in route due to Boche shelling. Picturesque language followed from the hungry men at the front."[6]

Thompson had been informed that Company M of the 168th Infantry was to conduct a raid on the German trenches in a few days. Obviously, higher headquarters did not see Baccarat as any sort of quiet sector. Thompson, who was in Company K, was ordered to set up ambush patrols in No Man's Land near sections of the wire that had been cut to allow Company M to pass through on its raid to the German lines.

The Alabama troops remembered their time in the Baccarat sector as very uneventful, but for some reason the Germans took great exception to the Iowa troops occupying a sector of the line. Corporal Archie M. Simpson, of Company A, 168th, had been in the trenches only two days when the Germans raided his CR. Engaging the enemy at close quarters, Company A had two men wounded in the sharp, short fight, but it was clear that the enemy was not going to allow the Rainbow Division to rest and enjoy the spring weather in Baccarat.[7]

Medic Lawrence Stewart knew from the start that their section of the line would not be peaceful. Soldiers' humor, however, was a part of the dangerous duty so close to the Germans. As green replacements filled the units, old-timers waited until nightfall and then, with night exaggerating the terrors of combat, they would scream, "Pas de gaz [no gas] coming over!"[8] The veterans had a good laugh as terrified rookies tried to get their gas masks on. Not all soldiers conducted themselves well. Stewart was disgusted with one Iowa souvenir hunter who knocked out a dead German's gold teeth with the butt of his rifle.[9]

One of the happiest soldiers in the Irish 165th was Al Ettinger, who had become a dispatch rider with a new motorcycle. No matter that he could not ride the machine. Back at Camp Mills he had bragged, as young men will do with no regard for the truth, that he had been a pretty fair motorcycle racer. Now, in mid-March, he stood before Colonel Barker and, worse, the regimental sergeant major. There was a motorcycle outside, a dispatch from Colonel Barker to higher headquarters, and little time to get it delivered. Off roared Ettinger, and, out of sight of his commander, he rode straightaway into a muddy ditch.

Ettinger was undaunted, and he learned to ride the machine. When he took messages to the French he would always wait around for mealtime. Of course, "they had better cooks. If you were a French chef as a civilian, you'd be a chef in the French Army. Hell, in our company, we had an undertaker as mess sergeant, a wall street runner as chief cook, and a couple of section hands as assistant cooks."[10] From a 168th Iowa dispatch rider Ettinger had learned a major secret—where the best bordello was in the Baccarat sector. The house was near the town of Deneuvre, and his first sojourn there would be free if he gave the madame's business cards to his buddies.[11] Dispatch riding had its rewards, of sorts.

The Rainbow slowly got settled into the trenches at Baccarat. The rotation of troops in one trench system was set up on an eight-day basis, with a complete rotation taking place every twenty-four days. After being in the rear trenches for eight days, the soldiers could go into the local towns, such as Baccarat, that had all the dubious attractions of any French town so near the front. When the 42nd was alerted to move to Lunéville, AEF Headquarters had informed the headquarters of the YMCA to have its representatives to the Rainbow ready to move with the division.[12] Wherever the Rainbow went, there the "Y men" were supposed to go also. When the United States went to war, Pershing convinced the YMCA to take over the running of Post Exchanges in the field for the AEF, and unwisely, in a fit of patriotism, the YMCA authorities agreed to undertake the task. Pershing and the AEF simply did not have the manpower to staff small exchanges where soldiers could buy tobacco, candies, and the like. The problem for the YMCA was that it remained chronically short-handed, and it also had commodities from Army exchange stocks that it was expected to sell rather than give away to the soldiers. The soldiers believed the YMCA was selling goods that had been sent as presents, and that YMCA representatives really preferred their plush recreation areas on the French Riviera to the mud of the front. Often YMCA workers, men and women, tended to be particularly pious folk who were indeed not ready for service with hard-bitten veteran combat troops.[13]

Charles MacArthur recalled that his comrades, when they were off the line and in their cups, would

visit the YMCA canteen, a second-hand stable operated by a human scantling with a bad temper. This bozo passed out paper and envelopes but never had both at the same time; what's more he didn't want any remarks about the shortage....After two weeks of sound teasing he quit his job.[14]

However, some units liked their YMCA man. During an advance, the Alabama regiment captured several sturdy horses from the retreating Germans and turned them over to the Y representative so that he could have a wagon capable of keeping up with the Alabamians.[15] Usually, the doughboys of the Rainbow came out of their wartime experience with a very low opinion of the YMCA. Much of it was unmerited, but the organization made an error in taking on the task of being an exchange for the AEF.

Breaking the routine of life at Baccarat was a visit to the trenches by Secretary of War Newton Baker. Pershing's relationship with Baker was not a warm one, but he was the ultimate civilian authority for the AEF (except, of course, President Wilson), and his visit generated great interest in the Rainbow Division. James Harbord, Pershing's chief of staff, accompanied Baker to the Rainbow's positions, where Baker greeted Douglas MacArthur and others whom he had known in Washington. Then the entourage went forward into the trenches. During an inspection of Donovan's battalion, some comment was made by General Menoher about Donovan's wearing his Croix de Guerre ribbon on his tunic. Baker intervened and gave Donovan "executive permission" to wear the decoration.[16]

The actual date of relief of the French units in the area was 1 April 1918, even though Rainbow troops had been in the trenches or on the firing line well before that. In normal times, the Baccarat sector would be a tourist's dream. The countryside was predominately agricultural, with small towns and villages. The main city of Baccarat was world-famous for its glass works. The River Meurthe, which formed the rear boundary of the 42nd Division, was a slow-moving, picture-postcard scene. The key terrain feature was a large, surfaced road that ran through the city of Baccarat, a French main supply route into Alsace. In fact, the Germans had briefly cut the road in August 1914, but were driven back at the battle of Grand Couronne.

But the city of Baccarat and the large town of Badonviller had attracted the seamier side of war—cheap bars, prostitutes, and speculators. Venereal disease rates went up again, and the staff became concerned for the overall health, physical and moral, of the troops. Several officers, off the line for a short time, secured rooms in the towns and were caught with either prostitutes or willing local girls in their lodgings. They were quickly court-martialed, receiving a stiff formal reprimand, a lecture on morals from MacArthur, and a forfeiture of pay for several months.

Of all the units of the Rainbow at Baccarat it was the 167th that seemed to be the most aggressive. William Donovan was amazed at the willingness to engage the Germans at every opportunity.[17] Even when wounded they seemed to bear the pain better than others, but Lieutenant van Dolsen ventured, "I do not know if they would make good parlor pets or proper chaperons for young ladies at the movies, but they sure are wonderful fighters."[18] The French soldiers had begun calling them tigers, *les tigres*. The Alabama regiment began an active program of patrolling, usually with two men rather than with larger groups. If they expected a fight or wished to pick one, the number would then be increased to meet the situation.[19] There were good reasons for this program—with fighting raging to the north, no one wanted to be surprised by the Germans. As the combat starting on 21 March had shown, the Germans were far from defeated, and "caution and conservatism" became the order of the day.[20]

Joe Romano believed that he was a permanent fixture in No Man's Land. It seemed to the Alabamian that the 167th did more patrolling than anyone else; as early as the Mexican Border Operation, the Alabama troops had done a great deal of reconnaissance and observation. Romano and his young comrades decided to liven up their chore of gathering information. During a two-man patrol, Romano and his friend observed German outpost personnel in the process of doing laundry on a warm April day. They could hear the Germans laughing and joking while they washed cootie-infested clothes. For some reason known only to the minds of foolish youths, the two-man patrol opened fire. Two Germans fell, and the washers abandoned their washtub and grabbed weapons. What began as a lark for the two Alabamians now turned sour, because the men washing clothes also manned a machine-gun position. Soon the machine gun was firing, and Romano and friend found themselves in a tight spot. They were crawling through the mud for dear life, when suddenly Romano felt something slam into his hip and then a warm, wet spot on his side. "I'm hit, I'm hit!" he called out to his laughing buddy, who pointed out that all the enemy damaged was his canteen. After they were back among their fellow Southerners, they had a good laugh, but Romano never again engaged the Germans unless a lot of the Company D men were around.[21]

As artillery fire and sniping increased all along the line, most troops were not inclined to show themselves. One morning, an Alabama sergeant was looking after his men when he saw a dejected Corporal Floyd Hughes, of Company K, sitting in the muddy trench. What was wrong? the NCO asked. Hughes replied that he was "fine, but I was just thinking of what a fool I was to let a man hold me up with just a 32-caliber pistol back in Birmingham."

The Germans were firing more gas shells into the Rainbow lines, also. Private William Gaffney, a cook, heard the Klaxon sounding and looked for his gas mask, which was nowhere near his cookstove. As the alarms grew louder, he could see the gas shells exploding and promptly stuck his face into a discarded rubber boot. He emerged from that gas attack unharmed; the rubber hip-boot kept the gas from injuring him.[22]

When German observation balloons went into the sky, artillery began firing at the American trenches with greater accuracy, and the number of wounded increased. The continual patrolling against the German trenches and for control of No Man's Land was bound to trigger some sort of reaction from the enemy. Lieutenant Thompson was constantly engaged in this deadly business, as were many other Rainbow lieutenants. Usually, a raiding party would move through the wire toward the German trenches and create some havoc with whatever they found there. Once the raiding party cleared the friendly wire and moved into the darkness of No Man's Land, Lieutenant Thompson would move an ambush patrol into selected positions near the lanes in the wire where the raiding party would pass. The hope was that the Germans would be foolish enough to follow the raiding party and stumble headlong into Thompson's waiting Iowans.

By mid-April, the intelligence sections at regimental level and at division ordered a raid to find out what enemy units occupied the German trench. It was to be an unusual daylight raid, conducted by troops from Companies I, K, and M of the 168th after a short barrage. Once the raiders moved off, Thompson and his troops would occupy ambush positions. The Germans, who had the unchallenged advantage of superior aerial observation, suspected that preparation for a massive raid was in progress and opened up with their artillery, taking a fearful toll of the exposed attackers. All of No Man's Land erupted. "We sought the trench bottom in a panic," Thompson recalled, "There was a deadening explosion in a nearby bayou. Shells screamed and whistled, filling me with a fear that I had never known before. An angry express train flashed above us. Suddenly all became quiet."[23] The raiding party staggered back, having been caught in the fearsome bombardment, and Thompson found that a man in a hole next to him had been blown to bits, with not a piece to be found.

The constant patrolling had a definite military purpose. The intelligence sections of the regiments, brigades, and division needed information to complete the picture of what enemy was before them, in what strength, and the state of morale and discipline. The concept of tactical intelligence was basically new, but as with so many war-fighting skills, the doughboys learned much from the French. The French, on the other hand, had learned the hard way from August and September 1914 on about the need for battlefield information that could be processed into tactical intelligence.

At AEF Headquarters, the "Second Section" produced a daily summary of events, the Intelligence Summary, that painted the big picture for the corps and division Second Sections. While telling what was going on in a given area, almost every summary contained some useful information about enemy troops and equipment, a new tactic that had been observed, or a new piece of technology that the enemy had employed on the Western Front. The summaries also contained drawings, charts, and maps that illustrated these new innovations or changes. GHQ Second Section encapsulated information that was, in part, general, but also included items of very real importance to the tactical commanders.[24]

Corps also produced a summary of intelligence that was a compilation of the information the divisions sent to them and that which could be gleaned from the GHQ's Second Section summary. The real production of information, however, came from the division level that was closest to the enemy. At the division, reports from patrols and raids were analyzed and published for the division and for higher headquarters. It was at brigade, regimental, and battalion level that the most basic of all tactical intelligence tasks were performed. The companies had no intelligence section per se, but the requirements for patrolling, taking of prisoners, and reporting anything and everything was heaviest on these units.

The patrols and the taking of prisoners provided the main source of information. Usually, the regimental intelligence section designated the areas to be covered by patrols or ordered the mission to take prisoners and bring them back into the American trenches. The battalion intelligence officers, usually holding the rank of captain, would go forward into the front trenches to debrief a patrol or to take charge of captured enemy soldiers. Lieutenant Thompson remembered, "Lieut. Ery, the intelligence officer, handed me a sketch of the trenches. I was to trace the path we were supposed to have taken."[25] Thompson then wrote down everything that happened on the patrol and gave his information to the officer, who in turn consolidated all of his patrol reports from the regiment. This was standard procedure throughout all of the infantry regiments. Joe Romano recalled being surprised at the number of day and night information-gathering patrols he went on while in combat.[26]

Prisoners remained important for intelligence. At divisional headquarters, Lieutenant Colonels Judah (G2) and Hughes (G3) worked with Douglas MacArthur on a standard procedure for handling captured enemy soldiers. Regimental commanders were required to establish a single location for a "prisoner post," to which all enemy POWs would be brought. Strict silence was to be imposed on the prisoner and on the guards. Once at the post, only the intelligence officer would be allowed to speak to prisoners while they were searched.

A time limit of two hours was imposed on the capturing unit to get the POWs to the divisional prisoner-collecting station. Upon arrival at the divisional station, the prisoners were separated into two groups. The first group included all officers, all specialists (especially in gas and communications), and an arbitrary 60 percent of all NCOs and rank and file. The remaining 40 percent, considered to be of little intelligence value, constituted the second group. The first group would then be dispatched quickly to the Corps Collecting Station, where intelligence officers from the G2 would interrogate and examine the prisoners. All documents, letters, diaries, and so on were confiscated from the prisoners for examination by both divisional and Corps G2 personnel, and often excerpts from prisoners' letters (minus name and rank) would be published in the summaries from division and Corps to illustrate the state of morale, unit information, and conditions at its front.

Wounded POWs would be, depending on severity of wound, searched at the lowest unit prisoner post. Then the wounded enemy would be sped to Caserne Ladmirault, Hospital No. 226, for treatment. The regimental intelligence officer had the duty to inform the divisional G2 of the evacuation of POWs to Hospital No. 226. When the condition of the patient allowed, and if the POW was of sufficient rank or specialty, the divisional G2 or one of his staff would visit the hospital to interrogate. Information such as the division needed was perishable, and the G2 did not need old information.[27]

The acquisition of information to be processed into combat tactical intelligence showed a level of sophistication acquired by the Rainbows while in France. In the fall of 1917, when the 42nd Division was formed, there was not an intelligence officer so designated. MacArthur named the brilliant Lieutenant Colonel Noble Brandon Judah only after the division arrived at Lunéville.

Security, which went hand-in-hand with tactical and operational intelligence, was of great concern to all. For example, telephone conversations were limited, and the use of messengers became a normal method of communications. Prior to moving into the trenches at Lunéville, in fact, the troops had been instructed to keep all conversations at a minimum. Diaries were prohibited as a matter of policy, and there was a very strict censorship of outgoing letters. Every letter written had to have an officer's signature, rank, and date on it to verify that he had read the letter and censored all material that might refer to location of troops, names of senior officers, operations, rumors, and unit designations. The rules were strictly applied to all ranks, and any violation was sternly dealt with. Of course, there were those who kept diaries when they could. Major Wild Bill Donovan did so for a while, and so did Father Duffy, but usually these diaries were devoid of immediate tactical information. As the 42nd occupied trenches, first at Lunéville, then at Baccarat, the fears of enemy subversion grew. G2 at AEF Headquarters continually bombarded all American units with stories about attempts "to weaken American morale." These included, particularly, sending enemy agents into the American lines to spread rumors and to gain information.

During the month of April, the division planned and carried out a series of important raids. A major raid was planned for the middle of April involving the 166th Ohio Infantry on a salient in the Bois de Chien woods across from the Ohio trenches. The mission was simple: Two companies of infantry would destroy the salient. The attack would be preceded by a massive artillery barrage, and the units, supported by engineers, would rush the trenches, destroying everything there, rendering them useless, forcing the Germans to abandon that part of the line.[28] The 167th Infantry and the 168th would also carry out supporting attacks to divert German attention.[29]

While the raid itself accomplished very little, it was a significant milestone for the Rainbow Division. The operational plan for the Bois de Chien raid included some very sophisticated attaching of troops and assigning of command authority. The actual tactical plans, standard signals, and training for the mission fell to Brigadier General Lenihan of the 83rd Brigade. He was given the general plan, and then divisional staff stepped back and allowed him to do the rest.

In addition to allowing Lenihan to function as the on-the-spot tactical commander, the Rainbow staff had to integrate into the fire plan French heavy artillery that had been allocated to it by the French Corps. The three artilleries—trench (also supplemented by French batteries), the 67th Field Artillery Brigade, and the heavier guns of the French—would be coordinated under the command of American Brigadier General Charles H. McKinstry, a solid Regular Army artilleryman who had just taken command of the Rainbow's artillery brigade. The instructions to McKinstry were just as general as those for Lenihan, and McKinstry, the professional, planned the details for fire support for the upcoming Bois de Chien raid.

Added to the Rainbow's impressive display of combat power were aircraft and balloons. This was the first time that the 42nd had worked with air assets, and while its association with this new battlefield phenomenon would grow, the concept of air support was new. A French Escadrille furnished a command plane for "the observation of fire upon moving objects." A French company of two balloons was to observe and adjust artillery fire. Two French airplanes would also be used by the artillery as spotters. While of more importance to the cannoneers, the addition of aircraft and balloons to the Rainbows presented to the staff a learning situation.

The Germans were not, in April, a defeated enemy, and they responded rapidly. However, with the great attacks taking place to the north of Baccarat, the Germans had few options at their disposal other than artillery and gas. Throughout April and into May, the 42nd Division came under constant gas attacks, some of them extremely heavy and very lethal. Lieutenant van Dolsen, now a young man bitter about his socialite friends who had avoided military service, saw the mounting gas casualties. Nothing in medical school or at Lunéville had trained him to operate on wounded soldiers whose clothes and skin were so covered with gas that he had to wear a gas mask while cutting.[30]

Shrapnel and gas were taking a daily toll of the troops in the trenches, and it was clear that the medical plan for treatment was not adequate for the task. Father Duffy noted that more and more of his time was spent at the various hospitals nearby, and usually those wounded men were back in the line within a few weeks.[31] With this situation becoming serious, the medical staff of the Rainbow reorganized their plan for treating the wounded and sent some doctors, including van Dolsen, off to school to learn new life-saving techniques like blood transfusion.[32]

Menoher finally approved a plan submitted by Lieutenant Colonel Grissinger that placed emphasis on life-saving first aid at the company level. Immediate first aid—stopping the flow of blood, covering the wound, and treating for shock—would be emphasized for those forward posts that were established very near the companies in the front trenches. This placed medical personnel, as well as the company medics and stretcher bearers, closer to the front than ever before. Grissinger's plan emphasized speeding the suffering to the battalion aid post, where the wounded would be examined, given anti-tetanus injections, and then moved even farther to the rear. The field hospital would be where the patient was treated for his wound, and if possible, he would then be kept there. Truly serious cases would be sent to Hospital No. 226 at Ladmirault.[33]

The plan addressed another serious problem. Some well-meaning regimental surgeons were doing more than basic life-saving first aid in the trenches, and any sort of operation in the forward trenches was very dangerous. Men who were wounded in combat lay in extraordinary filth. Human excrement, rotting bodies, decaying food, and mud made it imperative that a soldier be removed as quickly as possible for fear of gangrene and tetanus. No matter how careful he was, a surgeon performing even minor surgery increased the dangers of infection.

As the Germans increased their gas attacks, it became vital for the Rainbow staff to enforce stern measures to protect the men in all the trenches. Once out of the first two lines of trenches, the troops had the tendency to disregard gas discipline. To counter this, the entire division had to wear the mask at all times. Shaving was required every day, except for a mustache, because for any gas mask to be effective the mask must seal airtight to the face, and facial hair other than a mustache would interfere with that sealing process.

Rainbow soldiers were required to wear the mask in the "alert position," hung from the neck and resting on the chest. The World War I gas mask, or respirator, was a facial mask with a hose hanging down into a square canvas bag that contained the metal canister which filtered the air. Wearing the mask was extremely uncomfortable because a clothespin apparatus clamped down on the doughboy's nose so that the only air inhaled came directly from the canister into the mouth. The men were required to sleep with the mask in the alert position, and after a while many found it possible to sleep with the mask on. Training in gas mask drills and gas alarms was stepped up as the danger of enemy chemical attack increased.[34]

The use of chemical weapons was on the increase throughout April, and most officers expected a major gas attack from the enemy at any time. Their concerns translated into stepped-up training and increased security, and their vigilance and concern certainly paid off in late May when massive attacks were launched against the 42nd Division. The doughboys still wore their heavy wool uniforms, which offered some protection for the arms, neck, and body against gas, but the Division gas officer argued that any soldier who had his clothing permeated by even the smallest amount of mustard gas had to be evacuated and given new clothes. His old clothes would be then boiled in water to which was added a chloride solution. Many soldiers did not consider gas inhalation to be a real wound, since blood was not drawn, but AEF Headquarters made a gas victim eligible for the right-sleeve V-shaped wound stripe.[35]

The Germans opposing the Rainbow Division were too experienced to limit their response simply to gas and high-explosive shelling of the lines. They mounted their own patrols, some of which penetrated into the rear of the American trenches. One such patrol of three Germans got into the ruins of Ancerville, which was held by the 166th Ohio Regiment. The Germans intended to take prisoners, and they happened upon Private Red Smith of Company B, 1st Battalion. When Smith felt a pistol in his back and was told that he was a prisoner, he spun, hitting the German in the jaw. As the German fell he shot Smith in the stomach, but the alarm had been raised. Ohio soldiers rushed into the street to answer the call, and in the fight one German was killed and two 166th soldiers were wounded.[36] Smith survived his wound. On 23 April, the 165th Infantry relieved the Ohio men and took over the Ancerville sector, and the Irish casualties began to mount.[37]

The Alabama troops spent more time in the line than any other 42nd Division regiment, and their reputation as indomitable fighters continued to grow. The Alabamians became masters at the "go-and-come" raid—a raid not to seize and hold terrain, but, as the name implies, to occupy a trench, take prisoners, and destroy whatever possible. During one raid in April, a lieutenant noticed a lanky Alabamian crawling out of the trench fifteen minutes early. The officer hollered out, "Here, where in hell are you going?"

The lean Southerner replied, "Oh, I cannot run as fast as the other fellows, and I thought I would start fifteen minutes early, so as to get there on time."[38]

Not every unit taking casualties was infantry. The 117th Trench Mortars served continually on the line in support of every unit rotating in and out of the front trenches. During artillery bombardments, the Germans tried to knock out the Trench Mortars because they offered excellent and quick support for any CR under attack. On 17 April, the 117th assisted in a massive bombardment of the woods in front of the Ohio regiment, which saw over 400 gas shells fired at the Germans. In a retaliation raid by the enemy on 18 April, the Trench Mortarmen were instrumental in breaking up the assault, but at heavy cost each time.[39] The Maryland Trench Mortar Battery was growing dangerously small.

Colonel Kelly's 117th Engineers remained constantly busy throughout April and May repairing damage caused by the increasing German shelling of the trenches. They did everything from selecting and constructing new machine-gun positions to repairing blown-away wire and combat outposts beyond the first trench. Perhaps the strangest task was to construct a horse fumigation facility behind the lines. Horses and mules, like humans, were susceptible to gas attack, and there had to be a central location where the animals could receive treatment and be cleansed of the lethal mustard gas. Since animals also had respirators, the engineers constructed a facility for the repair, maintenance, and issue of that vital piece of equipment. During go-and-come raids, squads and even platoons of engineers accompanied the attacking infantry, adding their expertise in the destruction of German positions by explosives. As in every other combat unit, casualties continued to mount for the 117th Engineers. In May, Company F, 21st Engineer Regiment, was attached to the 117th to assist in building a small rail line to bring supplies closer to the combat units. A little later, Company L of the highly respected 23rd Engineers arrived to help maintain and construct roads. The 117th Ammunition Train and the 117th Sanitary Train were having severe difficulties moving to the front because of the damage to the roads caused by German shelling. The Engineers had to keep those roads open.[40]

The three regiments of the 67th Field Artillery Brigade supported all operations, but by the end of April the cannoneers were in real danger of wearing out their guns. Artillery pieces are sturdy, but continual firing will render the rifled barrels of the guns inaccurate. The American brigade was firing between 500 and 1,000 rounds per day into the German lines. Between 1 and 21 May, German artillery fired between 800 and 1,500 per day into American positions, a goodly portion fired as counter-battery fire against the 67th Field Artillery Brigade.[41]

Leslie Langille wrote: "Hot damn!...Shells are popping with regularity on the road to the right of the Battery. The wide ones land in front and to the rear of our position....They are falling too close for comfort." And they were.

Langille, while serving his guns, felt something wet and warm run down his neck. He thought it was sweat; it was not. Leslie Langille of the Illinois 149th Artillery Regiment had been wounded.[42]

In the midst of the German response and mounting casualties, the infantry and artillery regiments had few things to smile about. Once off the line, there was some escape from the shrapnel, gas, and infantry raids in the nearby towns where dubious pleasures awaited for a price. However, on 23 April the infantry units were to select two men per battalion and two men per artillery regiment to attend a pigeon-handling school to be held in Baccarat. These men and their birds would then always be on duty with their battalion or regiment, as part of Pigeon Liaison Service under the divisional signal officer. While the hard-bitten combat soldiers had a good laugh about being a "bird man," there was good reason to have a back-up for radio and telephone communications, which could well be disrupted during combat. Sixteen posts were established with trained Rainbow soldiers as handlers.[43]

During April, the Rainbow reported intercepting dogs that were used, or so it was thought, to carry messages from the German lines into towns where the Germans had agents. This story of courier dogs runs through the AEF and was reported by numerous units. The 166th Ohio reported killing one such dog in April. Joe Romano recalled hearing such stories while in the Baccarat sector.[44]

When Major Walter B. Wolf wrote his short history of the Rainbow Division, he included a grisly photograph of a dead black dog with a small dispatch case around his neck.[45] There seems to be little doubt that the Germans were using canine couriers to communicate with someone behind American lines. With the apparent laxity of the French concerning the bars and prostitutes in Baccarat and surrounding towns, it is little wonder that the Germans had agents there to discover information. The reaction of the G2 and the rest of the staff was to deal with the immediate tactical and operational consequences by altering schedules, changing passwords and codes, and increasing emphasis on security patrols.

It was a prudent thing to step up security in the Rainbow sector because intelligence estimates indicated that, with fighting slowing down to the north, the Germans were reinforcing their lines in the Baccarat area. Reports of a German buildup were correct. On 1 and 2 May, the enemy artillery opened up with a massive gas attack all along the 42nd's first two trenches. Phosgene and mustard gases drenched the positions for almost two days, and Rainbow artillery estimated that an extraordinary 50,000 rounds of all types (excluding small arms by the infantry) were exchanged.[46] The 117th Trench Mortar battery estimated that in the 48-hour period, its troops fired nearly 1,000 rounds of all sizes of trench mortar rounds. Of course, the 117th Battery sustained more casualties,[47] and eventually the Rainbow had to be reinforced by several French trench mortar units.

Charles MacArthur was deaf for a week after the tremendous exchange of artillery. He lost his hearing during the first ten minutes of the firing, but he was lucky; some of his comrades were permanently deafened.[48] While artillery continued to crash down after dark on the night of 2 May, the Ohio troops launched a major raid into the German trenches. There twenty-one Germans were found dead, and their uniforms confirmed that new enemy units were in the area. The 166th and 117th Engineer raiders set about destroying a large section of the German trench, and they were so successful that the enemy did not try to occupy it again. The Ohio men had two killed and nineteen wounded during the raid.[49]

On 3 May, the Alabama regiment's patrol came back bloodied, with Second Lieutenant Alton P. Woods of Company F and other members of the patrol wounded; Woods would die while being evacuated.[50] Everett Scott was slightly gassed while performing his duties as a dispatch runner, his second wound in three months.[51] By the third week of May, the patrols and the observers in their aircraft and balloons indicated that the enemy was engaged in some sort of buildup on their side of the line. On 21, 22, and 23 May, there seemed to be a lull in activity for the artillery. German fire slackened, and for every one enemy shell counted, the Americans and French fired two.[52]

During the morning of 23 May, observers noted a considerable increase in activity behind German lines but were unable to ascertain what the enemy was doing. The 24th passed quietly, with a significant lack of artillery. That night there were patrols, but no noticeable activity, and the day of the 25th seemed to be passing without incident. About 5:30 P.M., with food carriers bringing the ever-present Slum up to the front trenches, the Germans opened fire with gas and high explosives. Adding to the deadly exchange were German projectors, which threw large canisters of gas into the American lines. The barrage continued for four hours, the majority of the shells falling on the Iowa 168th Infantry.

Medic Lawrence Stewart was caught in the middle of the storm of shell and gas.

Below us in the valley hung low clouds of gas. They settled right there, and those of us on higher ground were safe. But we wore masks for three hours straight....A large percentage of officers and men of the sanitary detachment died or suffered severely from the gas....Little help could be given the gas victims. We placed them on stretchers, kept them quiet as possible and hurried them to the hospital.[53]

Major Wolf recalled, "The fumes from the bombs turned the leaves of such trees as were still able to show foliage from their spring green to an ashen white. The gas was so intense that when liberated near a man, the explosion blew his mask off and the man was suffocated."[54]

Lieutenant Thompson was relaxing in a dugout with fellow officers, ready to begin censoring mail, when the fierce bombardment started: "We were showered with falling mud. Shells ca-rumped all around us. For minutes, hours we huddled, cringing together on our bellies."[55] A large German raiding party assaulted the Iowa wire but was driven off with heavy losses, and the artillery continued to fall all along the line, particularly on the 168th Infantry. The Alabamians, brigaded with the Iowa soldiers, watched as their comrades rushed to the parapets of the trenches and inflicted a serious defeat on the enemy, despite having just had nearly 100 men killed and wounded.[56]

Of all the war experiences for the men of the 168th Infantry, the night of 25-26 May remained in their memories decades after the war. Corporal Archie Simpson, Company A, 168th Infantry, knew that some sort of attack was coming, but "although we were expecting it, ...it came so suddenly that we were hard hit. We [his platoon] lost 18 men including our First Lieutenant. The rest of the company were gassed more or less and the most of them were taken to the hospital. I received my share."[57]

Private Ray E. Laberten of Company B saw several of his comrades gassed, and then on 26 May he also fell victim to mustard gas: "I was sent to Baccarat to the hospital where I stayed four days when they sent 400 of us to Vittel on a hospital train."[58]

Lieutenant Thompson had never experienced anything like the ferocity of this attack. He was aware suddenly that another officer had a mask on. It was a gas attack.

I was conscious of the shelling outside and of a sickening sweet odor. Unseen hands pushed me onto a bunk. I vomited violently and tried to rip my mask off....Someone was strangling me. Now rough hands were holding me down. While I vomited into the mask and bit into the rubber mouth piece I felt like a cornered rat.

Thompson, who had survived so many ambush patrols, was blind, a ghastly mess. As the shelling slackened, medics carried him from the trench, and he became one of those Iowa soldiers on the way to the hospital at Vittel. Just before they carried him from the dugout, his sight slightly returning, he saw the bloody legs of a friend. There was no torso, only familiar boots.[59]

On 6 June the Germans again fired massive amounts of mustard and phosgene into the Ohio lines. On 7 June the Germans launched a major attack against the French division to the left of the Rainbows and then assaulted the American lines, with no success. The Americans, rallying from the bombardment, gas, and sustained rifle and machine-gun fire, halted the enemy 200 meters in front of the Rainbow wire.[60] It had been a tense time for the Ohio men when the bombardment began. Two patrols were out in No Man's Land and remained in shellholes for the duration of the barrage. When the enemy assault came, it was not in the area where the two patrols were sheltered, and the men survived with only slight wounds.[61]

The Ohio troops bore the brunt of the attack, and the 166th sustained forty-four casualties from gas alone. The adjacent 167th Infantry sustained one, the 149th Field Artillery Regiment reported three gas injuries, and the 150th Indiana Artillery regiment had five men gassed. It was a day of heavy loss to gas, and an inspecting officer found out that in the excitement to repulse the German assault many had removed their masks to see better and to more accurately site their rifles. This cost them dearly as the gas drifted in on them.[62]

It had become necessary to find a way to counter the German's ability to launch such devastating artillery and gas attacks. Patrolling certainly yielded a great deal of information, and often Americans penetrated into the second and third German trench lines. But artillery had firing ranges of many miles, and there was simply a need to look deeper into enemy-held territory. This was easier said than done, since horse cavalry, the traditional eyes of the ground force commanders, was of little or no use in this type of warfare. There was available, however, the airplane and the balloon, which the French had used sparingly in the Baccarat area. While most of the experienced French air assets were needed elsewhere, those of the Americans were available for service, though the fliers had limited experience.

On 8 June 1918, First U.S. Army assigned the 12th Aero Squadron (Observation) and the 2nd Balloon Company to the 42nd Division.[63] The attachment was very important, for the Rainbows now could use the air to look deep into enemy territory. A balloon, while stationary, could see well over fifteen kilometers, and air observers could fly even farther. The Germans had employed both observation aircraft and balloons along the Baccarat sector for a while. Their presence, everyone knew, meant that the Germans were getting valuable information, making their artillery more accurate. For Rainbow planners, the battlefield now took on a three-dimensional aspect, a development which would affect the issuance of orders and the assignment of missions. Ground artillery received from the stationary balloons immediate targeting information by way of a telephone hook-up between the artillery and the balloon. Intelligence personnel found that the air observation added to their understanding of enemy movements and gave the division vital time to react to German activity.

An air liaison officer came to divisional headquarters to establish face-to-face coordination and to assist in such matters as training for the ground forces. Pershing decided to adopt the French model for handling all questions of liaison between units and higher headquarters and between attached units and the gaining headquarters. As with many things, published French doctrine was adopted in toto by Pershing and his staff. A French manual was translated quickly, and *Instruction for Liaison for Troops of All Arms* (Paris: Imprimèrie Nationale, 1918) became American doctrine for this new dimension of the battlefield.

The 12th Aero Squadron, consisting of eighteen two-seater observation aircraft (normally, observation squadrons had twenty-four aircraft), arrived in the Baccarat area with a five-fold mission: visual and photographic reconnaissance of the enemy, adjustment of artillery fire, cooperation with the infantry and artillery, training with the infantry and artillery, and air coordination.[64] No pursuit aircraft would be available to protect either the observers or the balloons, and once aloft they would have to rely on their own weapons for air-to-air defense.

The American Air Service was a new part of the army, and the 12th Aero Squadron was less than a year old when it was attached to the 42nd Division for combat operations. Its members had seen action with the 1st Infantry Division at Toul, prior to their arrival in the Baccarat sector, and they already knew many of the pitfalls of working with ground troops.[65] No matter how well-trained the staff, the 42nd had no real experience with aircraft as an integral part of the division. Notes, documents, and pamphlets had been sent from AEF Headquarters, but there had been little practical training. The ground forces, those infantrymen in the field, had even less training, and they had a tendency to fire on anything that flew in the air. They did this simply because they had been the victims of German air observation and bombing. Billy Mitchell noted that troops that were not used to aircraft usually refused to lay out markers or panels, believing that if the American airmen could see them, the Germans could also. As Mitchell also noted, training of ground forces in working with aircraft was spotty, and most soldiers had forgotten what they had learned weeks or months before.[66]

From the historical summary of the Rainbow artillery, it is clear that the addition of observation aircraft and balloons made targeting more exact deep behind enemy lines. A vital part of artillery spotting, a balloon company had one balloon and a number of men to make it operate. Its key elements were the observers and the radio men who kept the officers in the basket in touch with the artillery PC.[67]

It was often misunderstood when the air service liaison officer stated that the aircraft could not fly or the balloon observers could not see because of bad weather conditions. Because air fields were well behind the lines and usually near towns, the front-line troops usually felt that the air service men, be they fliers or balloonists, had life easy. But once in the air the combat was very real, and there were no parachutes in the planes. Many a flier was incinerated alive as his airplane was hit. The balloon personnel did have parachutes, but they sometimes failed when the men in baskets had to jump.

Now that the 12th Aero Squadron and 2nd Balloon Company were formally attached to the Rainbow Division, it became General Menoher's responsibility to use them properly. Menoher would become chief of the Air Service after World War I, but in June 1918 his exposure to air power was extremely limited. As General Billy Mitchell saw it, it was the divisional commander's duty to issue orders to both elements of the Air Service, just as he would command his infantry, artillery, or other elements within the division. Air Service personnel referred to their aircraft in these circumstances as "infantry planes" or "artillery planes." Official orders and texts also use these terms; the designation meant that those aircraft were under the orders of the division commander. The division had the responsibility of ensuring that there were designated areas, well-marked, for observer aircraft to drop messages. The Air Service provided to the unit an immediate and far-reaching method of seeing battlefield areas unaccessible to couriers or runners.[68] Another definite advantage for the divisional commander and his staff was that in the heat of battle, with regiments and brigades hotly engaged, the tendency could very well be to ignore or forget reporting vital information to higher headquarters. The Rainbow troops became so used to their attached Aero Squadrons that by the St. Mihiel offensive in the fall of 1918, they were called a part of the "Rainbow Family."[69]

Throughout the rest of June, the drudgery of trench warfare continued as regiments rotated their battalions in and out of the trenches. On the night of 18 June, the Germans bombarded the Alabama forward battalions with high explosive and gas shells. With shells hitting the 1st Battalion, Captain James Y. Hamil, a doctor in the 167th, rushed into the forward trench to assist those hit by shrapnel. Before he realized that the bombardment was a mix of explosive and phosgene, he was gassed. Despite his serious condition, Hamil continued to give first aid and oversaw the evacuation of the wounded. When the last Alabamian was removed, Hamil collapsed and was carried to the hospital, severely affected by the gas.[70]

Father Duffy had heard rumors that the Rainbows were soon to be relieved by the 77th Division of the National Army. The 77th, Statue of Liberty, Division was made up mainly of men from New York, and the chaplain knew that he had a number of former pupils and parishioners with that unit.[71] Donovan would be happy to get out of the trenches, too. Just recently he had observed one of his lieutenants who had fallen asleep while trying to eat Slum from his mess kit. Donovan recoiled in disgust when "a huge rat came along and dragged away the piece of bread he was eating."[72]

Heavy fighting was again raging to the north, with another German offensive underway. This offensive involved American troops in maneuver warfare, and by the time the Rainbows were out of their trenches, the names of Chateau-Thierry, Belleau Wood, and Cantigny were well-known. The AEF's 1st and 2nd Divisions had been heavily involved in the fighting, and Pershing had decided to commit other AEF units to the series of battles shaping up. The Rainbow Division was off for Champagne, even though the troops had been in the Baccarat trenches for 140 days, and the division was jaded.

Leslie Langille was now back with his fellow Illinois artilleryman, his wound healing and his lower right sleeve sporting the V, the wound stripe. In talking to his comrades he described the cleaning of the wound and the anti-tetanus shot given in the stomach. He really earned the stripe for the shot, which was much more painful than the shrapnel.

Soon the Rainbows were off to Champagne, leaving Baccarat to the new fellows from the 77th. What visions Champagne conjured up for the raucous gunners! As they hauled their muddy, scarred guns away, Langille would have been less enthusiastic if he had known that within one month, all of the Rainbow men would be referring to "Lousy Champagne!" Baccarat had been a long, trying, and bloody experience for the 42nd Division, but as the troops marched away for new battlefields, almost to a man they felt that they had emerged from the trenches as "first-class combat troops."

NOTES

1. The information about the tactical array of the Rainbow Division in the Baccarat sector is taken from Henry J. Reilly, *Americans All: The Rainbow at War* (Columbus, Ohio: F.J. Heer Printing Co., 1936), 189-91, and map following p. 228.

2. Francis P. Duffy, *Father Duffy's Story* (New York: George H. Doran Co., 1919), 81-83.

3. *New York Times*, 27 April 1919. Walter B. Wolf, *Brief Story of the Rainbow Division* (New York: Rand McNally Co., 1919), 14.

4. Hugh S. Thompson, "Following the Rainbow," *The Chattanooga Times* 18 February 1934.

5. Statement by Corporal A. M. Simpson, formerly of Company A, 168th Infantry, undated, in Military History Institute WWI Questionnaires, Military History Institute Archives (hereinafter MHIA).

6. Lawrence Stewart, *Rainbow Bright* (Philadelphia: Dorrance, 1923), 49-50.

7. Ibid., 91.

8. A. Churchill Ettinger (ed.), *A Doughboy with the Fighting 69th* (Shippensburg, PA: White Main Publishing, 1992), 85-87.

9. Ibid., 91.

10. Telegram from Colonel Fox Connor to YMCA headquarters, Paris, 12 February 1918, in the National Archives, Washington, *Records Group 120 Records of the AEF, 42nd Division*, carton 1 (hereinafter, RG 120).

11. An avalanche of complaints reached the United States via soldier's letters, and there was great criticism of the YMCA at home. To counter this flood of bitterness, YMCA workers rose to defend the organization. In 1920 Katherine Mayo published *That Damned Y* (New York: Houghton-Mifflin), which was a syrupy defense of the YMCA. Regardless of the defenders, the YMCA's reputation suffered. Interestingly enough, when one reads the CMH's questionnaires completed by doughboys in the 1980s, the harsh criticism of the YMCA continued, well after fifty years. Not every doughboy complained about the YMCA. Kansan Sergeant Calvin Lambert, while in the hospital, was well treated by the local YMCA representative when he was out of money and needed things the YMCA was selling. "The boys knock the Y but I have nothing but admiration and gratitude for the organization," he wrote. Calvin Lambert Diary (entry for 15 April 1918), manuscript, Emporia Public Library, Emporia, Kansas, 128.

12. Charles MacArthur, *War Bugs* (Garden City, N.Y.: Doubleday, Doran and Co., 1929), 60-62.

13. John B. Hayes, *Heroes Among the Brave* (Loachapoka, Ala.: Lee County Historical Society, 1973), 34.

14. Donovan to his wife, np, 28 March 1918, in the Donovan Papers, MHIA.

15. Donovan to his wife, 13 May 1918, ibid.

16. Van Dolsen to his aunt, np, 19 February 1919, in U.S. Army Military History Institute Archives, Carlisle Barracks, Pennsylvania, 42nd Division AEF Collection, MHIA.

17. Notes provided by Joseph O. Romano, Jr., Birmingham, Alabama, based on his conversations with his father, Corporal Joseph O. Romano, 167th Infantry (hereinafter, Romano Notes).

18. Walter B. Wolf, *Brief History of the Rainbow Division* (New York: Rand

McNally Co., 1919), 15.

19. Romano Notes.

20. William H. Amerine, *Alabama's Own in France:* (New York: Eaton and Gettinger, 1919), 314.

21. Thompson, "Following the Rainbow," 18 February 1934.

22. The Second Section at AEF Headquarters is well-recorded in Department of the Army, Historical Division, *The United States Army in the World War, 1917-1919: Reports of the Commander-in-Chief AEF, Staff Sections and Services, Part II* (Washington: Government Printing Office, 1948). This is a very detailed summary of the many and varied activities of the G2 of AEF.

23. Thompson, "Following the Rainbow," 18 February 1934.

24. Romano Notes.

25. HQ, 42nd Division, Memorandum No. 134, 12 April 1918, in RG 120, carton 3. This memorandum is of critical importance because of the increasing demands of the regiments to obtain prisoners for intelligence purposes and because it spells out a very modern method for handling POWs in a tactical environment.

26. HQ, 42nd Division, "Plan for Raid upon the Bois De Chien," 8 April 1918 in RG 120, carton 9.

27. Wolf, *Brief Story of the Rainbow*, 16.

28. Van Dolsen to his mother, np, 24 and 28 March 1918, MHIA.

29. Duffy, *Story*, 90-91.

30. Van Dolsen to his mother, np, 19 April 1918, MHIA.

31. HQ, 42nd Division, Memorandum No. 130, 10 April 1918, in RG 120, carton 9.

32. HQ, 42nd Division, "Standing Orders on Defense Against Gas," 18 April, in ibid.

33. Romano Notes. Corporal Joe Romano was gassed several times, but he wore only wound stripes for wounds that drew blood. Douglas MacArthur, on the other hand, did wear the wound stripe for gas, and he was gassed a number of times.

34. R.M. Cheseldine, *Ohio in the Rainbow: Official Story of the 166th Infantry, 42nd Division in the World War* (Columbus, Ohio: F.J. Heer Printing Co., 1924), 126-27.

35. Duffy, *Story*, 90-91.

36. Major Hugh Ogden to his wife, np, 7 June 1918, in Ogden Letters, MHIA.

37. Peter H. Ottosen, *Trench Artillery AEF* (Boston: Lothrop, Lee and Shepard, 1931), 100-01.

38. Monthly reports for April and May, 1918, 117th Engineer Regiment, RG 120, carton 40.

39. 67th Field Artillery Brigade Historical Summary of Engagements, nd, ibid., carton 2.

40. Leslie Langille, *Men of the Rainbow* (Chicago: O'Sullivan Co., 1933), 74-76.

41. HQ, 42nd Division, Memorandum No. 30, 8 April 1918, RG 120, carton 10.

42. Romano Notes.

43. Wolf, *Brief Story of the Rainbow*, 35.

44. 67th Field Artillery Brigade Historical Summary of Engagements, nd, RG 120, carton 2.

45. Ottosen, *Trench Artillery*, 100.

46. MacArthur, *War Bugs*, 68-69.

47. Cheseldine, *Ohio in the Rainbow*, 133-34.

48. Amerine, *Alabama's Own*, 105-06.

49. Scott to his brother, np, 7 May 1918, in Scott Letters, manuscripts in the author's collection.

50. Entries 1-22 May 1918, in 67th Field Artillery Brigade Historical Summary, as cited in Note 49.

51. Stewart, *Rainbow Bright*, 58-59.

52. Wolf, *Brief Story of the Rainbow*, 18.

53. Thompson, "Following the Rainbow," 11 March 1934.

54. Hayes, *Heroes Among the Brave*, 16.

55. Statement by Corporal A. M. Simpson, formerly of Company A, 168th Infantry, undated, in Military History Institute WWI Questionnaires, MHIA.

56. Statement by Private Ray E. Laberten, formerly of Company B, 168th Infantry, undated, ibid.

57. Thompson, "Following the Rainbow," 18 March 1934.

58. Entry 5-6 June 1918, in 67th Field Artillery Brigade, Military History Institute WWI Questionnaires, MHIA.

59. Cheseldine, *Ohio in the Rainbow*, 140-45.

60. Gas Casualty Report, by Captain Charles H. Gorrill, 42nd Division Gas Officer, to HQ, 42nd Division, 8 June 1918, in RG 120, carton 57.

61. HQ, I Corps, Special Orders No. 131, 8 June 1918, in ibid., carton 58.

62. Office of Air Force History, *The U.S. Air Service in World War I*, Vol. 1 (Washington: Government Printing Office, 1978), 185-86 (hereinafter, *The U.S. Air Service*, with appropriate volume).

63. "History of the Twelfth Aero Squadron," in U.S. Air Force Historical Agency Archives, Maxwell Air Force Base, Alabama, File SQ-RCU-12-HI (hereinafter, AFHA).

64. Brigadier General William "Billy" Mitchell, "Tactical Application of Military Aeronautics," 5 January 1919, ibid., File 167. 4-1.

65. *The U.S. Air Service, Vol. I*, 379-88. First Lieutenant S.W. Ovitt, *The Balloon Section of the American Expeditionary Force* (1919), 56-57, in AFHA, File 167. 401-22.

66. *The U.S. Air Service*, Vol. 2, 205-11.

67. Ibid., Vol. 4, 100.

68. Amerine, *Alabama's Own*, 106-07.

69. Duffy, *Story*, 114-15.

70. Entry, 12 June 1918, Donovan Diary, MHIA.

71. Langille, *Men of the Rainbow*, 77-79.

72. "The Lorraine Mission Paid Off," *The Rainbow Reveille*, (April 1950), 4-5.

5

FROM CHAMPAGNE TO THE MARNE

For the 167th Alabama, the very name Champagne conjured up visions of rolling hills, vineyards, and bottles of the bubbly fruit of the vine. Joe Romano, Ashton Croft, and John Hayes were glad enough to be out of the Baccarat trenches and looked forward to moving into the open country. Spring was in full bloom, and in areas not touched by the war the countryside was beautiful.[1] Charles MacArthur had some doubts about the move, however. The Illinois artillery rumor mill had it that the Rainbow was going to Chateau Thierry to fight alongside the U.S. Marines. The Rainbow and the leathernecks had developed a mutual dislike, and whenever possible the two would wade into each other with fists flying.

It seems that at some point Rainbow soldiers had run afoul of the Marine Military Police, and after 140 days in the trenches, the men of the 42nd were tired of reading and hearing about the exploits of the "Fighting Few."[2] Whenever the Marines of the 2nd Division would pass the Rainbow, verbal taunts and abuse flew. "What's the brightest color in the Rainbow?" some Marine would holler.

"Yellow!" another would respond, and the fight was on.[3]

By June, the Rainbows had become veteran fighters with a very high reputation among the French. Only the 1st Division, the Big Red One, and the National Guard's 26th Yankee Division would spend more time in Europe than the Rainbow, with the 2nd Division coming in a close fourth.[4] After so many days in the trenches, the spring weather and the resiliance of youth took over. Only veteran fighters like the Rainbow and the Marines of the 2nd Indianhead Division could go after each other with such gusto.

This move took well over four days by 40-and-8s, and then there was time to rest before beginning a new assignment. The mission for the 42nd Division was a defensive one in Champagne, the Rainbow coming under the 4th French Army, commanded by one of the most colorful characters and experienced soldiers France produced during the war—General Henri Joseph Eugène

Gouraud. He immediately took a liking to the men of the Rainbow and they to him. The one-armed general with flamboyant style and bushy beard would serve as honorary president of the Rainbow Veterans Association until his death in 1946.

Gouraud was a colonial soldier who had served in West Africa, and in 1912 he was named deputy to General (later Marshall) Lyautey in Morocco. In 1915 Gouraud lost an arm in the fighting at Gallipoli, and by 1918 he was a full general in charge of defending the Champagne area. Hearing that his American troops were arriving at Chalons, the army commander decided to see them up close. He and his driver left his headquarters and sped, as only the French can drive, toward where *La Rainbow* was moving to its assigned position in the center of 4th Army's lines. Rounding a corner in the village of Tilloy, Gouraud's car hit something. He had found the Rainbow, running over the first 42nd Division doughboy he had come across.

"This is a fine kettle of fish," General Gouraud thought, sitting in the back of his car, "General Pershing assigns me the Rainbow Division for reinforcements, and voilà, the first man to fall is knocked senseless by my own automobile."[5] It certainly was not a fine beginning for Private C.W. Burnett of the Georgia 151st Machine Gun Battalion. He was lying in the street with a number of his fellow Georgians standing over him, his leg badly hurt. Much to Gouraud's relief, however, Burnett survived the war to return to Macon, Georgia.[6]

Colonel Henry J. Reilly was determined that his Illinois gunners present a smart and soldierly appearance moving up to the front. They had been transported by 40-and-8s, but the weather was warm and stops were numerous. Unknown to Reilly, however, the soldiers staying on the open, windy flatcars with the guns had been well-fortified with rum provided by their comrades, who felt sorry for them. As the guns were moved to the front, Reilly and several French colonels decided to review the big parade. Much to Reilly's horror, strapped to a gun and singing lustily was a very drunk Illinois artilleryman. Reilly stopped the procession and had the inebriate unstrapped and brought to him for a severe tongue-lashing. The soldier, now in tears, made a less than coherent speech about his undying committment to Franco-American friendship and vowed he was ready to march to the front to die for France, whereupon a deeply moved French colonel kissed him on both cheeks and prevailed upon Reilly to allow the man to die nobly for France. Reilly, suppressing a smile, buttoned the soldier's tunic, adjusted his helmet, and turned him over to his ashen-faced lieutenant.[7]

Happily for Gouraud and the Rainbow, the meeting between Chief of Staff MacArthur and the legendary Gouraud was productive and amicable. MacArthur, who could probably recognize a kindred soul, was awestruck by the hero of Gallipoli. He was, MacArthur remembered, "without a weakness."[8] The French general believed that the Germans would strike in force through Champagne, with its primary objective the city of Chalons. Once Chalons was

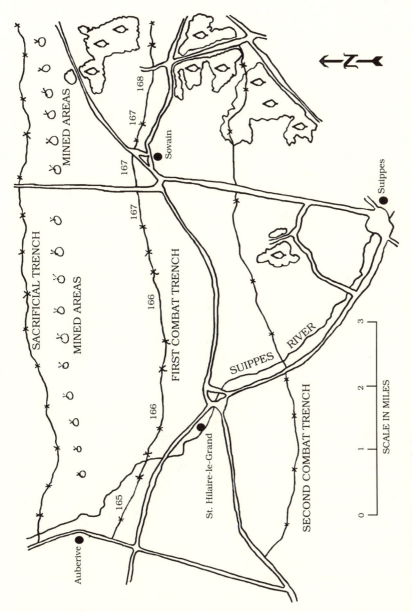

Figure 5.1 The Champagne Defense

taken, the Germans would then launch a major, possibly war-ending, attack on Paris. Gouraud told MacArthur that he had no intention of allowing this, even if every Frenchman and American perished at his post.

Pershing, like many French generals, believed that the next full-scale attack would come in the Champagne, and that the troops were needed there. Pershing had available the 1st, 2nd, 3rd, 4th (all Regulars), the 26th, 28th Keystone, and 42nd (National Guard) to repulse the coming attack. There were also five inexperienced divisions in training in France. Black Jack Pershing still did not have his totally American army, but seven divisions stood ready to help stem the German offensive.[9]

As the 166th Infantry marched through Chalons toward its place in the line, the troops noticed that the ground was a chalky white. Looking back at the lights from Chalons, which had not yet been torn asunder by war, the Ohio soldiers regretted that they could not stop and see the town. As they got closer to the place they would defend, they learned that Gouraud intended to leave the first trench lightly manned, a "sacrifice trench" it was called, so that the Germans would reveal their assault plans before striking the main line of defense. Who, the Ohio men wondered, would be sent forward to be in the sacrificial trench?[10]

On came the Alabamians into their place in the line. They pitched their tents in wheat fields, and at night they could see the lightning-like flashes of the guns to the north and west near the city of Rheims, where a battle raged. The Southerners lounged in the grass, smoked, and enjoyed the very strange sensation of not being in a cootie-infested, gas-drenched trench.[11]

Gouraud planned to place the Rainbow in line tightly sandwiched between two experienced French divisions, expecting that the Americans would hold their sector as well as any French combat unit—even his veterans of the Marne and Verdun. He saw, with more clarity than did Chaumont, that they were ready to meet the enemy, and Gouraud had confidence in General Menoher's leadership.[12]

The battle-wise Gouraud, however, would leave nothing to chance in placing an American division into the line. The Rainbows were assigned to the 21st Army Corps under General Pierre Naulin, a respected combat veteran who devised the defensive plan for his sector. Naulin took a risk and placed the Rainbows directly in the path of the German advance. In looking at the terrain, it appeared to the French that the Germans would launch two major attacks into the area held by the 21st Corps. Directly in front of the first trench line, five miles away, were two key terrain features: to the left, the ridge of Notre Dame des Champs (about four miles long) and to the right the Souain butte (about five miles long). These two pieces of high ground were tall enough to mask enemy movements when one looked to the front from ground level. Air observation was critical, because aircraft and balloons would be able to look beyond those two ridge lines. Between the ridges, about five miles of flat land offered a rapid avenue of approach into the French defenses. To the immediate left of the Notre Dame des Champs ridge lay about four miles of flat land, bordered on the Germans' right flank by the River Suippes. This was the second high-speed avenue of approach. The river also offered to the Germans a secure right flank because it was a natural obstacle denying the French the possibility of a counter-attack on the flank.

Naulin already had three good combat infantry divisions in his corps: the 43rd, 13th, and the 170th. Now he had the Rainbows and attached artillery. On 2 July Naulin and General André Pretelat, his chief of staff, placed the 42nd in the center of the line and assigned a portion of it to the divisions on each side, the 170th and the 13th, for guidance and coordination. This was certainly wise, because the Rainbows had not faced combat as violent and decisive as Gouraud and Naulin believed this would be. The order from Naulin and Pretelat specified that the 42nd would be in the second line of defensive trenches, where Gouraud knew the main battle would take place.[13]

Assigning the Rainbows to the second line caused a good bit of confusion later, when Americans wrote about the Champagne Defensive action of July 1918. The tendency was to dismiss the Rainbow's fight on 15 and 16 July as less important than it actually was. Naulin's order stated, "The 42nd Division, U.S. is destined only for the defense of the second line." When American Army writers read this in the 1920s, they did not undestand what Gouraud planned. Despite what is found in dispatches from the 42nd and from the French, the Rainbow's record was ignored by Regular Army historians later.[14]

The French offered advice, which was usually gladly accepted by the Rainbow staff. Members of the 21st Corps, as an experienced unit, knew that they had time before the German attack was launched. While poilu (French soldier) and doughboy alike enjoyed the respite from mortal combat, the staff of the French Corps were busy. Of special concern to Naulin was the American artillery, which had had little real experience as part of a complex artillery support operation. Gouraud fully expected the guns to be instrumental in breaking up German formations before they closed with the infantry, and the Americans had never actually dealt with that. Naulin dispatched Colonel François Broussaud, commander of the 21st Corps Artillery, to the 67th Field Artillery brigade. He found that previous training had left the gunners woefully ignorant of infantry tactics, and Broussaud's first recommendation was that the officers of the 67th Brigade study what infantry had to do.

The most devastating round the gunners had in their stocks was not gas or high explosive, but shrapnel-producing rounds which could be detonated effectively among enemy troops. The Americans planned to use shrapnel at about 5,000 meters in front of the first trench, the sacrificial trench. Absurd, commented Broussaud; at long ranges one employed high explosive to break up enemy formations, but at 3,000 meters or less, shrapnel should be employed. Indeed, as the artillery lessened the ranges, the French and American infantry would be in increasing danger; but, as Broussaud indicated, mounting enemy casualities would be worth it.[15] Brigadier General Charles McKinstry studied Broussaud's observations and recognized their importance to his brigade. Each regiment got a translated copy for information, and, more important, "for guidance."[16]

The French and the Americans had the luxury of having some time to iron out problems and to get to know each other well. Pershing, however, always remained skeptical of French training, believing that the French had become too wedded to the trench. In this case, however, in preparing for what could well be termed the decisive battle of 1918, the French showed a definite willingness to fight. An aggressiveness and a solid spirit of cooperation developed between the 42nd and the French 4th Army and 21st Corps.

Preparing for the coming battle occupied Lieutenant van Dolsen's time. Besides being the newly appointed gas officer for the hospital,[17] he was still the mess officer. He was in a state of complete frustration, as the hospital had not received rations for several days, and on 8 July he traveled twenty miles to Chalons-sur-Marne to obtain food. With what money he had, he procured roast beef, potatoes, bread, butter, salad, wine, and coffee. Upon returning with his groceries, van Dolsen found that the cooks and the KPs were almost ready to fight each other, and someone had lost a very large griddle that had been used for making hot cakes. Van Dolsen had straightened that out as well as he could, when he discovered that carefully hoarded condensed milk had been taken by the nurses back to their tents, for tea. Standing in the middle of ruin, van Dolsen muttered, "I hope that they sit down in a mustard gas cloud." As he emerged from the mess tent van Dolsen saw a French artillery battery digging in its guns only a few yards from the hospital.[18]

Martin Hogan had been released from the hospital, his gas wound healed, his eyesight restored. He found the 3rd Shamrock Battalion in the line at Champagne, where his fellow soldiers were sleeping, enjoying the sun and the quiet. There had been a tobacco issue, a gift from New Yorkers. Hogan, now a jaded veteran, knew the respite could not last.[19]

Iowa medic Stewart's buddies received mail, the first delivery in several weeks. There was at least some peace and quiet in which to read the papers and the letters from home, but one Iowa doughboy suddenly crumpled up his letter, complaining that his girlfriend back home had just married a naval officer. "If I'd a sprouted fins and gold braid I supposed she'd have fallen for me instead. Well, its me for the first French girl I see," he said.[20] Everett Scott had heard nothing from Louise back in Primgahar, Iowa, and he was sure that he had lost his best girl, too.[21] At least Scott felt good to be out of the trenches of Baccarat.

It sure seems good to be where one knows when he goes to bed that he can stay there until morning without having the buildings blown down around your ears or else having to sit up half of the night with a gas mask on....I suppose the boch get just as tired of it as we do....I don't know what I would have done without my old pipe.[22]

The Iowa 2nd Battalion was situated near a small wood. Like other Rainbow troops, they had pitched pup tents and were enjoying the calm of Champagne. Off in the distance the soldiers of L Company's 4th Platoon saw a heavily laden doughboy walking toward them. As he grew closer, the veterans of Lunéville and Baccarat recognized Lieutenant Hugh Thompson. Thompson, guant after his treatment for the severe gassing he took at Baccarat, was back with the Iowa 168th Infantry. There were new faces, men in clean uniforms. Here and there sat the old veterans, many "reading their shirts," or holding their shirts close to their faces so they could pick off the unmerciful cooties. Thompson had a strange thought: "By golly, I was home!"[23]

Father Duffy knew that soon the Champagne front would erupt in a violence that his Irishmen had not seen before. He wanted to go to the forward battalions and tend to the souls of his doughboy parishoners, but Colonel Frank McCoy, the new commander of the regiment, wanted Duffy to rest.[24] The good priest would have none of that. Duffy had just refused a chance to become chief chaplain of the Rainbows because he wanted to stay with the Irishmen, and besides, he had the pleasant company of Sergeant Joyce Kilmer. Kilmer became more devout every day, and his lengthy discussions with Duffy over religion and the church allowed Duffy to use the full powers of his great intellect. Yet Duffy had a depressing feeling that one or the other would not survive the war.[25]

One Rainbow soldier who had no worries about surviving the impending battle was Al Ettinger, now a dispatch rider behind the lines. He was sitting in a small apartment in Chalons, as drunk as a lord. On 12 July, Ettinger was carrying a dispatch when a German shell hit near him, killing two artillerymen and slicing open his left knee. The doctors dispatched him to a hospital in Chalons, but before he entered he met an old friend. They proceeded to go to a nearby apartment and drink themselves into silliness. When the bombardment started on 15 July, Ettinger was finally in a hospital ward waiting for an operation. He would miss the fight in Lousy Champagne.[26]

All of the Rainbow men who had seen Lunéville and Baccarat knew that the peace and quiet was only a respite. General Gouraud issued an order on 7 July informing his troops that soon the battle would begin, "In a cloud of smoke, dust and gas." No one, Gouraud stated, would take a step to the rear. In other words, Frenchmen and Rainbows alike were told to die in place. This was to be a desperate struggle: "Each will have but one thought: to kill, to kill a-plenty, until they have had their fill."[27]

Here was a general who meant business and who appeared to have more confidence in his Americans than did AEF Headquarters. The 42nd Division was well arrayed for a defense in depth. The Rainbows had the French 170th Infantry Division on their left and the 13th French Infantry Division on their right. They had a rectangular piece of Champagne to defend that was about five miles wide and ten miles deep. Running through the middle was the blasted macadam road to Chalons-sur-Marne. On either side of the road, Gouraud placed battle-tested French battalions. These experienced veterans, he correctly believed, would help the Americans. Gouraud trusted his National Guard doughboys; they held a critical piece of terrain that most believed would be a major German objective.

Gouraud's battle plan called for the normal front-line trench to be abandoned, except for a few platoons of French soldiers who would deceive enemy observers into reporting that the trench was occupied as normal. The first German artillery barrage would then fall on nearly empty trenches. As the Germans moved forward, they would pass over the blasted trenches into a killing zone between the front trench (the sacrificial trench) and the second line, where unscathed infantry, heavily supported by machine guns and artillery, would be waiting. Between the sacrificial trench and the second line there would be anti-personnel mines to slow up the Germans. Once beyond the first trench, approaching the second trench line, the artillery would then pour a deadly fire onto the attackers, by that time mired down in the mines, wire, and other obstacles.

The second trench, and then a third trench, would be ready to break the battered assault waves. There were the normal wire and other obstacles, and the second and third trenches were fairly shallow, not the elaborate labyrinth the doughboys were used to at Lunéville or Baccarat. This fight would be more open, but that meant less cover for the defenders.

The 42nd's own battle plan was sound. The two brigades occupied equal pieces of ground, with the New York and Ohio troops on the left of the Chalons road, and the Alabama and Iowa soldiers on the right of the road. No one single regiment occupied a line. On the left, in the second trench line, from left to right, were the 2nd and 3rd Battalions of the 165th, then the 3rd Battalion of Ohio's 166th. The three battalions were supported by the Wisconsin 150th Machine Gun Battalion. Two miles behind was the third trench. From left to right one found elements of the 117th Engineers ready to fight as infantry, then Donovan's 1st Battalion, then the 2nd and the 1st of the 166th Infantry.

Crossing the road in the second line was the 2nd Battalion of Alabamians, then the 2nd Battalion of Iowans. Both battalions were supported by the Georgia 151st Machine Gun Battalion. There were good reasons to have only two battalions in the front line. First, it was a shorter distance from the Chalons road to the boundary between the Rainbows and the French 13th Division, and second, directly in front of the Alabama and the Iowa battalions was what was left of a small wood of shot-down trees and scrub pines. The Germans could very well use this small copse as cover and concealment as they advanced, falling on the doughboys quickly. They did just that, and it was better that the preponderance of rifles was in the third trench line. To even the odds a little, the small Maryland 117th Trench Mortar Battery, commanded by Captain Robert Gill, was slightly forward of the second trench battalions. The 117th would pour fire into the Germans in the small woods as they advanced toward the Iowa and Alabama troops.

Two miles behind the two battalions was the remainder of General Brown's brigade. From left to right, Brown had placed the 1st and 3rd Battalions of Screws' "Alabama Wildmen," then the 1st and 3rd Battalions of the Iowa 168th. About five miles behind this last line of infantry was the Rainbow's steady 67th Field Artillery Brigade, with the Illinois 149th on the left, the Indiana 150th in the center, and the Minnesota 151st on the right. Gouraud also added a fair number of French batteries to the artillery line, with some heavier guns at Bussy-le-Chateau, about ten miles behind the 67th Field Artillery Brigade. It was these French guns that disturbed Lieutenant van Dolsen so. His hospital and the main supply base for the Rainbows were on the critical crossroads at Bussy-le-Chateau.

Up went French observation balloons, and targets were plotted by all of the artillery. Since General McKinistry had been assigned to the railroad section of the Service of Supply in Pershing's attempts to strengthen the AEF's transportation and supply system, the 67th was now under Brigadier General George Gatley. The troops remained under camouflage netting, waiting for the order to rain destruction onto the advancing German infantry. This was a well-conceived, well-coordinated artillery support plan by the staff of Gouraud's 4th French Army.

There is some luck in war, but usually success smiles on the general who plans well, understands his troops and those of the enemy, has a good, aggressive, independent-minded staff, and is never content to "await events." In Gouraud's service to France, he never waited for anything. Those Germans closest to the Allied lines would most probably be in the first assault waves, and if all went well, a prisoner might be of sufficient rank and knowledge to tell Gouraud's intelligence personnel what they wanted to know. On the night before 14 July, the French national holiday, a French patrol brought back a German prisoner who knew precisely what Gouraud needed to know—the exact time of the start of the German offensive! It would start a few minutes after midnight on 15 July.[28]

Gouraud's major subordinate commanders knew that the attack was coming, and a code, François 570, would be flashed to the waiting divisions just prior to the attack to tell the soldiers of the coming maelstrom of shot, shell, steel, and gas. Late in the afternoon of the 14th, the telephone in the PC of the Rainbows rang, and the operator picking up the phone heard, "François cing-sept-zéro." He verified the message, then ended his message with "Bon chance"—Good luck.[29]

The alert went down to the battalions, and troops prepared the best they could for the onslaught. Gas masks were checked, rifles and ammunition were closely inspected, Corned Willie, cooked in the same old slum, was eaten, and men then waited. On the artillery gun line, the gunners checked their ammunition again to make sure that when the assault came, the cannons would be able to do their work. Sergeant Lawrence Quigley, Battery D, 151st Gopher Gunners, checked his gun one last time. It was clean and ready. Quigley, from Minneapolis, had named his 75mm howitzer Mary Ann, after the girl he planned to marry. Tonight Mary Ann, he hoped, would be a part of the artillery support that would break the backs of the Germans and bring him closer to home, to the real flesh-and-blood Mary Ann.

At a few minutes after midnight on 15 July, German guns opened up on a forty-two-mile front. The Rainbow soldiers had never seen anything like it. High explosives and gas swept the front, but in Gouraud's sector, most of the shot and shell fell on the very lightly held sacrificial trench. Doughboys and

French infantry alike were awestruck by the sights and sounds of one of the great artillery displays of the war.[30]

Father Duffy looked at his watch. It was 12:04 A.M. when the shelling began. As he watched the sight, he was reminded of the aurora borealis in its dazzling intensity. He knew that many of his beloved 69th men would not survive another twenty-four hours. That afternoon, Private Hunt of Company E, 165th, had received a cablegram announcing the birth of his first-born child. Hunt now lay in death, struck by shrapnel, his blood staining the cablegram.[31] Wisconsin National Guardsmen of the 150th Machine Gun battalion took a terrible pounding, Private Walter Melchior's machine gun was destroyed and his comrades were all dead or wounded. He grabbed a rifle and rushed to a company of the 165th to fight as an infantryman. He never survived the day.[32]

In the second line, the Alabamians were swept by artillery. Sergeant Percy L. Atkinson had a few men and a small 37mm cannon. His gas mask failed him, and other soldiers tried to carry him to the rear. Atkinson refused to leave his men or the small gun, which helped repulse several German attacks. Two days after he had been so severely wounded he finally allowed his gun crew to carry him to the rear.[33]

The Minnesota artillery were not immune from the bombardment. As the Gopher Gunners ran to their guns, a German shell landed on one of the cannons, and Corporal Malcolm had an arm torn off. As he lay on the ground, the eighteen-year-old Malcolm hollered to his comrades, "Give 'em hell, boys. I guess I can't help anymore."[34]

The bombardment continued until dawn, and then the fire slackened. The German infantry, mainly Prussians, were advancing toward the sacrificial trench where, miraculously, some Frenchmen were still alive. As the Germans crossed the trench and advanced into the mines, the poilus came out of their holes and opened fire, confusing the Germans, who had expected to find the first trench filled with the enemy rather than almost empty. On into the minefield the gray ranks went, and then the artillery opened fire on them. From the sacrificial trench to the second line where Americans and Frenchmen stood were nearly two miles of bursting artillery shells and deadly gas.

The slaughter was the worst the doughboys had seen. The main force of the German infantry was heading directly for the small, shattered wood directly in front of the French troops, the 2nd Battalion of the Alabama 167th, and the 2nd Battalion of the Iowa 168th Infantry. As expected, the Germans drifted toward the small amount of cover offered by what was left of the little wood. The Alabams knew that they would bear the brunt of this first attack, and, with their French comrades shouting encouragement, they fixed bayonets and prepared to meet the Prussian charge. Shells smashed into the woods, and gray-clad bodies piled high. A Rainbow veteran, the sight fresh in his mind, recalled, "Direct hits from high explosive shells began piling into the attackers. But still they kept on, thousands more climbing over heaps of bodies to fill the gaps. And finally, by sheer disregard of losses, they came to the intermediate second lines—the allies' first real line of defense."

If any Alabamian had ever dreamed of being in one desperate battle, he had his wish on 15 July 1918. The Iowans knew that they, too, would have to fight for their lives as the Germans surged forward. The French, placed in the line to bolster these war novices, were shouting, and the Alabamians and the Iowans began to shout also. What was left of two German divisions was in the destroyed woods, advancing rapidly toward the waiting Allies. And then the second line opened fire. The 151st Machine Gun Battalion raked the Germans with lead. Small cannon fired directly in their ranks. Sergeant Atkinson, of Birmingham, Alabama, lying in the bottom of the trench, lungs scorched, hoarsely encouraged his gunners to keep up the rate of fire. German infantry was only a half mile from the defenders, taking fearful losses.

That 15 July 1918 was a St. Crispin's Day for the Baltimoreans of the 117th Trench Mortar Battery. Captain Gill had selected the exposed position for the battery because the troops could fire where other artillery would be least effective. For three hours as the Germans came forward, the 117th Battery poured its devastating fire into the advancing infantry. Finally the battery's guns were either destroyed or buried, and the survivors of the 117th fell back to the next position.[35]

John B. Hayes of 2nd Battalion, 167th, believed that the bombardment against the forward Alabama battalion was the worst he had experienced. He was in a dugout as large shells exploded all around, literally taking the breath away from the men nearby. The dugout door was blasted to small pieces by shrapnel, and an officer sitting near Hayes said that this was the longest day he had ever seen.[36] Joe Romano was in the second line, his Company D being pounded just as hard as the first-line units.

The Alabamians knew that soon it would be man against man, bayonet against bayonet. Corporal M. D. Riley of Company G saw that the Germans had set up a machine gun in front of his company and had begun to fire into the poilus and doughboys. Heedless of the dangers, Riley climbed to the top of the trench and shot five German gunners before he himself fell back into the trench, killed by a bullet to the head.[37] All along the line, it was hand-to-hand fighting of the worst type, the first of its kind for the Americans, and the Alabamians held. Captain Julien M. Strassberger, commanding an Alabama machine-gun company supporting Companies E and F in the forward line, hastily sent a field message to regimental headquarters, "Boche dead are piled around here sky-high. Ils ne passeront pas!"[38]

Without formal orders, the French and the 167th counter-attacked over the ground littered by German and American dead. By platoons the troops went forward, retaking positions lost when the tidal wave of gray smashed the sacrificial trench and fell upon the first line. The German assault on the Rainbow's center right had failed to move that "impregnable....human Gibraltar."[39]

Seven waves hit the second line, and each time the Americans and the French threw them back. While the most vicious fighting of the day occurred first with the 167th and then with the Irish 165th, no part of the line was immune. Second Lieutenant Hugh Thompson found himself caught up in the hurricane of gas, shot and shell. He had new men in his fourth platoon and found them huddling in a dugout with a candle burning. As he checked on these men, who had never before experienced a bombardment, the dugout was hit. A searing pain shot through Thompson's right side and arm. In a daze, he heard the alarm for gas, and he found that the only hand that would respond to his growing panic was his left one. He somehow got his mask on as he slipped into oblivion. When he awoke he found his right arm, torn by a shell, strapped to his side, and his bloody trouser leg split open.[40]

Ohio's men of the 166th were also raked by fire. As they huddled in the trenches watching the great weight of German artillery firing into the sacrificial trench, they heard familiar voices announcing that the ration wagons had arrived with the usual Corned Willie Slum. Before the "François 570" warning had been announced, the ration wagons had left for the trenches. Caught in the bombardment, they pushed forward. As the troops hurriedly took their Slum and bread and rushed back to safety, they noted that seventeen-year-old Private Wilber Jones, who was dishing out the Corned Willie, had the body of another supply company private lying on the front seat of the wagon. Private Walter Phillips, the only supply company man to die in battle in France, had been killed by shrapnel. Jones refused to leave the body of his comrade on the road, and when the serving was over he left to take his buddy's corpse to those who would give it a decent burial.[41]

Martin Hogan could sense the lessening of shell fire, and he knew that the German infantry was advancing toward the 165th. A few minutes before, Father Duffy and the battalion commander had spoken to each man, telling them that they would hold this section of the line to the last man. About 9 A.M. the shells stopped, and the New Yorkers could see the mass of gray infantry coming directly at them. Hogan recalled,

They broke furiously upon our line and the line of the Sixty-ninth became a dizzy whirl of hand-to-hand combats....Clubbed rifles were splintered against skulls and shoulder bone; bayonets were plunged home, withdrawn and plunged home again; automatics spit here and there in the line; grenades exploded; while a man occasionally shot his dripping bayonet free from his enemies' body. Our front line became a gruesome mess.[42]

Father Duffy was in the thick of the fighting on the second line. He saw Private Joe Daly, an ammunition carrier, confront a German who had just dropped into the trench. Daly had no weapon of his own, but he quickly grabbed a rifle lying near the body of a 69th man, smashed in the helmet of the German, and rushed into the fight. Duffy was sickened at the sight of so many of his beloved Irishmen now dead or wounded in the melée in the trench.[43]

Even the clearly marked field hospitals were not immune. Major Frew, the Wisconsin National Guard doctor, had spent most of the night in a trench. The shelling grew in intensity in the rear as the Germans closed with the Rainbows and the French to the front. Frew was infuriated. Many of the wounded who could not be moved were now dead, lying in tents that had been shredded by hot steel.[44] Lieutenant van Dolsen had worried about the ability of his nurses to withstand the bombardment, but now he had no such concerns. They remained stoic throughout the onslaught and performed excellent service. He ordered the nurses in one tent to the trench for safety, but they refused, remaining at their posts to comfort the wounded.[45]

By late afternoon the German tide had receded, and American and French troops moved into the first, sacrificial trench. The Alabams had repulsed seven major assaults, the New Yorkers five, and every unit in the Rainbow had suffered from the fighting that day. The Kansas Ammunition Train had left the main supply base at Bussy when the shelling started. Calvin Lambert watched in horror as an artillery round smashed into a hospital. The YMCA building was left a smoldering ruin. Lambert looked into the sky and saw a German airplane spotting for the artillery as the gunners shifted their fire and the gray infantry assaulted the front trenches. The Kansas journalist-turned-sergeant felt the ground roll under him.[46]

German aircraft were in the air as night began to fall, and the 67th Field Artillery Brigade recorded that over twenty German observation balloons were aloft. It was obvious that the next day, 16 July, would see a renewal of the severe fighting.[47] Through the night, ammunition, supply, and food wagons braved the heavy German high-explosive and gas rounds to bring needed supplies to the front trenches and to evacuate the wounded.

During the night of 15 July, 42nd Divison headquarters was able to report that the lines had held. Gouraud was delighted at the performance of his 4th Army, because at no point in the line did the enemy gain a foothold. The fighting had produced horrendous casualities, especially among the German infantry. As dawn began to break the sky at about 4:30 A.M. on 16 July, Rainbow headquarters informed AEF Headquarters that it was quiet and the division was optomistic about the forthcoming combat. At noon, the Germans again opened up a terrific barrage against the 4th Army, and the troops braced for another major assault.

From captured German documents Gouraud and the 42nd knew that the number and first-class quality of the divisions in the attack make it clear that the enemy expected great results....Chalons....was expected to be taken at 4 A.M. on the morning of the 16th. However, the battle has so far resulted in a complete check for the enemy at all points. The three divisions of the XXI Corps aided by elements of the 42nd Division and a Polish regiment broke the attack of seven divisions of the best German troops.[48]

The major assault of the day fell on the left of the Rainbow and French lines with sharp hand-to-hand fighting. Majors Donovan and Alexander Anderson, commanding the 3rd and 2nd Battalions of New York's 165th Infantry, took the brunt of the massive infantry assault. To the right of the Irishmen, a battalion of Ohio infantry held the line and poured a flanking fire into the oncoming Germans. Lieutenant Kenneth C. Ogle of Anderson's Company G saw the Germans coming for the sixth time. Ogle personally led "thirty-eight wild sons of Erin, yelling and rushing....with long, bare bayonets."[49] The Germans could not retreat quickly enough, and Ogle and his men were on them, killing twenty-eight in hand-to-hand fighting.

As night began to fall, it was obvious that the Germans had spent their force in the last day of their last offensive. The line had not been broken, but the Rainbows had suffered terribly. Sixteen hundred Rainbow soldiers were either killed or wounded in the two-day battle for "Lousy Champagne."[50]

The night of 16 July belonged to German aircraft, which bombed and strafed facilities and troops alike. Artillery continued to fire, but to the gunners from the Midwest it seemed that the great infantry assaults were over. Indiana artilleryman Elmer Sherwood noticed that there was an overwhelming stench of death in the air. One could not escape it.[51] Charles MacArthur recalled that as the firing slackened, the rumors started that the Rainbows were to be pulled out to rest. Immediately, the Illinois gunners packed up their tents, rolls, and knapsacks in anticipation of the move. True to form, the skies opened up and rain poured down.[52]

The Gopher Gunners heard that they were being taken out of the line on 18 July. While there was general rejoicing, Sergeant Lawrence Quigley sat by his gun, tears rolling down his cheeks. His gun, Mary Ann, had started the Champagne defensive cleaned and well-oiled. Now the 75mm gun was mud-spattered, scratched, and gouged from German shrapnel. After firing for seventy-two consecutive hours, Mary Ann just died, worn out, and would be left behind. Quigley was saying good-bye to an old friend.[53]

Leslie Langille, who had delighted in singing in his church choir, was appalled at the horrible slaughter before his eyes. He was in prayer to God "to look down upon these bleeding, mangled, dying and dead heaps of humanity." And then Langille asked Heaven, "Why?" During the fierce German counter-battery fire, Langille saw Private Einer Johnson, a company cook who had been sent forward to serve up Slum, suddenly scream that he was hit. His tunic and trousers were a mass of red, for a shell had hit near him and a very large can of whole tomatoes had spilled over the frightened cook. The last the Illinois gunners saw of Johnson was his form disappearing down the road as quickly as he could run.[54]

On 18 July the Rainbows began to leave the line. Everett Scott was happy to leave. He placed his helmet on his head, and it looked odd. During the first day, a large part of the rim had been cut away by a piece of shrapnel. After the shock had worn off, Scott had found a dugout where he shook for five hours as the artillery continued to pound away.[55]

The Rainbows came out of the Champagne Defensive with a new sense of confidence and a healthy relationship with the French under whom they fought so well. Gouraud stated, "We repulsed his offensive, we broke his morale, we made it impossible for him to attack again."[56] Naulin was no less effusive in his praise for the Rainbow's part in the 21st Corps. The Alabama defense and decisive counter-attack on 15 July was praised by all, and established the 167th as the best fighting regiment within the division.

The Rainbows also had developed a very real hatred for the Germans. During the bombardment, the doctors and nurses moved what wounded they could to a dugout, and the once-callow Lieutenant van Dolsen recoiled in horror at what he saw:

Well we got down into the dug out and my dear mother such a shamble I never hope to see again. A long black tunnel lighted just a little by candles, our poor wounded shocked boys there on litters in the dark, eight of them half under ether just as they had come off the tables their legs only half amputated, surgeons trying to finish and check blood in the dark, the floor soaked with blood, the hospital above us a wreck, three patients killed and one blown out of bed with his head off. Believe me I will never forgive the bastards as long as I live.[57]

One Alabama private who was in the thickest of the fighting on 15 July wrote to his mother, "All of you can cheer up and wear a smile for I'm a little hero now. I got two of the rascals and finished killing a wounded with my bayonet that might have gotten well had I not finished him....I couldn't be satisfied at killing them, how could I have mercy on such low life rascals as they are?"[58] A good bit of this hatred resulted from Germans approaching American lines dressed in French uniforms taken from the dead in the sacrifice trench.[59]

The hand-to-hand fighting was especially severe for the Alabamians and New Yorkers, and many of their comrades were killed or wounded in the fighting for the second line and in the counter-attacks that followed. Adding to the confusion was the occasional round of friendly artillery that fell short and hit the Americans as they repulsed the enemy.[60]

Shortly after the Champagne defensive operation, and while the Rainbows were fighting in the campaign to reduce the Marne salient in July and August, German newspapers carried accounts of atrocities committed against helpless prisoners and wounded on 15 July. The G2 of AEF Headquarters, Brigadier General Dennis E. Nolan, directed Menoher to undertake an immediate investigation of the charges. The focus of the investigation fell on the 2nd Battalion, 165th; 3rd Battalion, 168th; 2nd Battalion, 167th; and Companies E and F of the 168th.

There had always been rumors of units taking no prisoners. Donovan, in May, described to his wife the possibility of the Alabamians' capturing and killing two Germans, and he ended his letter stating, "They [the 167th] wander all over the landscape shooting at everything."[61]

Elmer Sherwood, the Hoosier gunner, reported the story that the Alabamians attacked a German trench with Bowie knives. "They cleaned up on the enemy," Sherwood recalled, "but it is no surprise to any of us, because they are a wild bunch, not knowing what fear is."[62]

While in Germany on occupation duty with the Rainbow, Lieutenant van Dolsen wrote to his aunt back in Washington, D.C., that the Alabams "did not take many prisoners, but I do not blame them much for that."[63]

The New York regiment was also known for fierce fighting and taking few prisoners on the battlefield. Most probably, the nature of the hand-to-hand fighting and the fog and friction of war caused a great number of deaths that could very well be questionable. The issue would again surface after the severe fighting at the Croix Rouge Farm, where the Alabamians and Iowans were heavily engaged at close quarters with a determined enemy.

A formal inquiry was held into the events of 15 July, with twenty-three officers testifying and fifteen company-grade officers required to give depositions. The testimony was uniformly a denial that atrocities were committed during the fighting that day. The findings were forwarded to AEF Headquarters and there the matter was dropped.[64]

Gouraud bade good-bye to his Rainbow troops, and rumors ran through the ranks that the division was to be rested for a while before being sent to another front. Martin Hogan's Shamrocks were halted after a day's march, and pup tents were pitched. A small river offered the tired and filthy troops an opportunity to wash and attack the merciless lice that had plagued them so in Champagne. Perhaps a long rest really was in order, the Irishmen thought as they cleaned themselves and their equipment.[65]

Father Duffy was delighted to be in Vadenay, by the river that had afforded Martin Hogan so much pleasure. While making the rounds of the battalions, however, Duffy saw that the ranks had grown thin. Colonel McCoy, now commanding the 165th, had told Duffy that time for the Irish regiment at Vadenay was short and that probably within two weeks the Rainbow would be back in battle, possibly one worse than the Champagne fight. With an urgency that he kept from the troops, Duffy organized four Masses in one Sunday to see to the souls of his men. Also, Duffy found a new chaplain, Father James M. Hanley of Ohio, waiting for him. The news that Hanley would join the 165th delighted Duffy, who continued to have premonitions of death.[66]

As the Rainbow soldiers enjoyed a good wash and some rest, they were joined by French soldiers from the old 21st Corps who invited many to have a drink in honor of France's national holiday, 14 July, belatedly celebrated on 19 and 20 July. On the 14th the troops, American and French, were bracing for the storm of shot and shell they knew was coming. The celebration was put off, and the champagne and wine now flowed like water.[67] The Rainbows and the French had developed a healthy respect for each other, from general down to private.[68] The 42nd Division had spent more time directly associated with the French than had any other AEF combat division, and the troops had become used to how the French operated. The French, in turn, knew the Rainbow Division well, their respect reaching a high point with the Champagne defensive operation.

While the doughboys were in Champagne resting and cleaning, the first of the great Allied offensives of 1918 had begun on 18 July. Maréchal Ferdinand Foch had decided that the first Allied blow would fall against a German salient formed by the Aisne River on the west and the Marne River on the east. Foch attacked first toward the town of Soissons on the western flank of the salient, and in taking the town he cut the Germans' main supply and communication route. The Germans then decided to withdraw from the entire salient. However, the German army was not defeated, and the professional soldiers who guided her tactical and operational destiny had no intention of seeing the Ainse-Marine operation by the Allies result in a German rout.

Pershing had eight battle-ready divisions to throw into the fight: 1st, 2nd, 3rd, 4th (Regular Army), and 26th, 28th, 32nd, and 42nd (National Guard). In typical Pershing fashion, he fretted about the lack of training of his divisions, but the time had come to commit American forces en masse.[69] Certainly the 1st, 2nd, 26th, 28th, and 42nd were no strangers to combat, but it was clear that Pershing still distrusted all but his Regular Army units. At any rate, American forces were going to play a major role in the reduction of this German salient so close to Paris.

On 20 July, Menoher received an order attaching the 42nd Division to the French 6th Army for operations in the Marne. Orders went out to subordinate units to prepare to move by train on 21 July, with a terminus at Chateau Thierry.[70] At that time the French 6th Army was under the command of General Jean Degoutte, a competent fighter who had a mixed group of French and American troops, including the 26th Yankee Division, under his command. All that was known to G2, 42nd Division, was that the land was deceptively attractive, pastoral, dotted with picture-postcard stone farms. It was also known that the New England Guardsmen of the Yankee Division were being bled to death in the rich wheat fields of the Marne.

The Rainbows had been scratched at Baccarat, bloodied in the Champagne, but now they were about to enter into a fight that Douglas MacArthur called "six of the bitterest days and nights of the war for the Rainbow."[71] As the trains pulled out, French civilians came down to cheer the 42nd doughboys, but that send-off was tempered by the name Chateau Thierry, a beautiful name but a frightening one because of the blood that had been spilled there. The Rainbow was off to the Marne.

NOTES

1. John B. Hayes, *Heroes Among the Brave* (Loachapoka, Ala.: Lee County Historical Society, 1973), 16-17.

2. Statement by Second Lieutenant Paul H. Jarrett, formerly of Company M, 166th Infantry, 22 March 1989, WWI Questionnaires, Military History Institute Archives (hereinafter, MHIA).

3. Charles MacArthur, *War Bugs* (Garden City, N.Y.: Doubleday, Doran and Co., 1929), 75-77.

4. U.S. War Department, *The Official Record of the Great War* (New York: Parke, Austin and Lipscomb, 1923), 124-28.

5. General Henri J. E. Gouraud, "My Memories of the Rainbow Division," *The American Legion Monthly* (November 1933), 26.

6. Ibid., 27.

7. MacArthur, *War Bugs*, 76-78.

8. Douglas MacArthur, *Reminiscences* (New York: McGraw-Hill, 1964), 56-57.

9. John J. Pershing, *My Experiences in the World War* (New York: Frederick A. Stokes Co., 1931), Vol. 2, 152-53.

10. R.M. Cheseldine, *Ohio in the Rainbow: Official Story of the 166th Infantry, 42nd Division in the World War* (Columbus, Ohio: F.J. Heer Printing Co., 1924), 151-53.

11. Hayes, *Heroes Among the Brave*, 17.

12. Gouraud, "My Memories," 56.

13. Etat Major, 21 Corps d'Armée, Ordre No. 2.289.3, 2 July 1918, in the National Archives, Washington, *Records Group 120 Records of the AEF, 42nd Division*, carton 13 (hereinafter, RG 120).

14. See Captain J.S. Switzer, "The Champagne-Marne Defensive," *Infantry Journal* 20 (January-June, 1922): 1-6. Appearing in the respected and widely read *Infantry Journal*, this lengthy, and in the main accurate, analysis is simply misleading as to the Rainbow role because the author had an imperfect understanding of what Gouraud and Naulin did with the Rainbow Division. As one might imagine, there was a storm of letters trying to correct Switzer's article. The authoritative work done by the General Services Schools at Fort Leavenworth, Kansas, in 1923, titled *The German Offensive of July 15, 1918: Marne Source Book*, does very little to put the 42nd's role in proper perspective.

15. Colonel François Broussaud, Report No. 5.040.3, 9 July 1918, in RG 120, carton 10.

16. Endorsement by Brigadier Charles McKinistry to the English-language translation of Report No. 5.040.3, 9 July 1918, ibid.

17. Van Dolsen to his mother, np, 2 July 1918, in U.S. Army Military History Institute Archives, Carlisle Barracks, Pennsylvania, 42nd Division AEF Collection (hereinafter, MHIA).

18. Van Dolsen to his mother, np, 8 July 1918, ibid.

19. Martin J. Hogan, *The Shamrock Battalion of the Rainbow: A Story of the Fighting 69th* (New York: D. Appleton and Co., 1919), 118-20.

20. Lawrence Stewart, *Rainbow Bright* (Philadelphia: Dorrance, 1923), 63.

21. Scott to his mother, np, 7 July 1918, Scott Letters, manuscripts in the author's collection.

22. Scott to his mother, np, 26 June 1918, ibid.

23. Hugh S. Thompson, "Following the Rainbow," *The Chattanooga Times*, 25 March 1934, and 1 April 1934.

24. Francis P. Duffy, *Father Duffy's Story* (New York: George H. Doran Co., 1919), 130, 132-33.

25. Ibid., 97.

26. A. Churchill Ettinger (ed.), *A Doughboy with the Fighting 69th* (Shippensburg, PA: White Main Publishing, 1929), 124-25.

27. Walter B. Wolf, *Brief History of the Rainbow Division* (New York: Rand McNally Co., 1919), 25-26.

28. MacArthur, *Reminiscences*, 56-57. Pershing, *Experiences*, Vol. 2, 152-53.

29. Wolf, *Brief History of the Rainbow*, 25-26.

30. Raymond S. Thompkins, *The Story of the Rainbow Division* (New York: Boni and Liveright, 1919), 54-55.

31. Duffy, *Story*, 130, 132-33.

32. Ibid., 133.

33. William B. Amerine, *Alabama's Own in France* (New York: Eaton and Gettinger, 1919), 332-33.

34. Elmer W. Sherwood, *Diary of a Rainbow Veteran: Written at the Front* (Terre Haute, Ind.: Moore-Langen, 1929), 19.

35. Peter H. Ottosen, *Trench Artillery AEF* (Boston: Lothrop, Lee and Shepard, 1931), 102-04. Gouraud, "My Memories," 58.

36. Hayes, *Heroes Among the Brave*, 20.

37. Amerine, *Alabama's Own*, 125.

38. Thompkins, *Story*, 60.

39. Gouraud, "My Memories," 58.

40. Thompson, "Following the Rainbow," 1 April 1934.

41. Cheseldine, *Ohio in the Rainbow*, 164.

42. Hogan, *Shamrock Battalion*, 127-28.

43. Duffy, *Story*, 136-37.

44. Major Frew to Norbert Frew, np, 16 July 1918, Frew Papers, MHIA.

45. Van Dolsen to his mother, np, 17 July 1918, ibid.

46. Calvin Lambert Diary, manuscript, Emporia Public Library, Emporia, Kansas, 175-76.

47. G2, 42nd Division headquarters, "Summary of Events," in U.S. Army, Center of Military History, *The United States Army in the World War* (Washington: Government Printing Office, 1989), Vol. 5, 166 (hereinafter, CMH).

48. G3, GHQ, 42nd Division headquarters, "Summary of Events," in ibid., 166.

49. Thompkins, *Story*, 64-65.

50. American Battle Monuments Commission, *42 Division, Summary of Operations in the World War* (Washington: Government Printing Office, 1944), 15-16.

51. Sherwood, *Diary*, 25-26.

52. MacArthur, *War Bugs*, 94.

53. Thompkins, *Story*, 69.

54. Leslie Langille, *Men of the Rainbow* (Chicago: O'Sullivan Co., 1933), 94.

55. Scott to his mother, and from Scott to his brother, np, 20 July 1918, Scott Letters.

56. Gouraud, "My Memories," 58.

57. Van Dolsen to his mother, np, 17 July 1918, MHIA.

58. Corporal Gary Roberts, Company B, 167th Infantry, to his mother, np, 28 July 1918, in Alabama State Historical Archives, Montgomery, Alabama, 167th Infantry Collection.

59. Thompkins, *Story*, 65-66. Many of the Rainbow unit histories and personal memoirs recount these stories of the Germans using such a ruse.

60. Cheseldine, *Ohio in the Rainbow*, 170.

61. Donovan to his wife, np, 13 May 1918, in the William J. Donovan Papers, MHIA.

62. Sherwood, *Diary*, 22.

63. Van Dolsen to his aunt, Occupation Forces, Germany, 19 February 1919, MHIA. See also Stewart, *Rainbow Bright*, 70-71.

64. 42nd Division headquarters, "Report of Investigation of Reported Killing of German Prisoners of War," 22 August 1918, RG 120, carton 59.

65. Hogan, *Shamrock Battalion*, 136-37.

66. Duffy, *Story*, 146-47.

67. Thompkins, *Story*, 59.

68. Sherwood, *Diary*, 28.

69. See Pershing, *Experiences*, Vol. 2, Chap. 37.

70. 42nd Division headquarters, General Order No. 48, 20 July 1918, in CMH, *United States Army in the World War*, Vol. 5, 518.

71. MacArthur, *Reminiscences*, 59.

165th Infantry on the "Valley Forge" march, December, 1918. Courtesy of US Army Military History Institute.

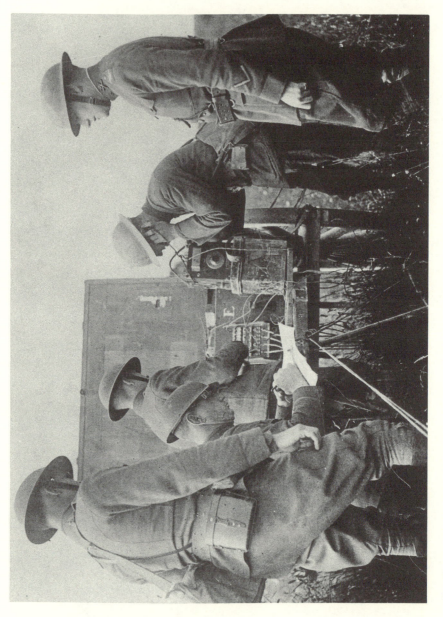

Col. Henry J. Reilly (left), May, 1918. Courtesy of US Army Military History Institute.

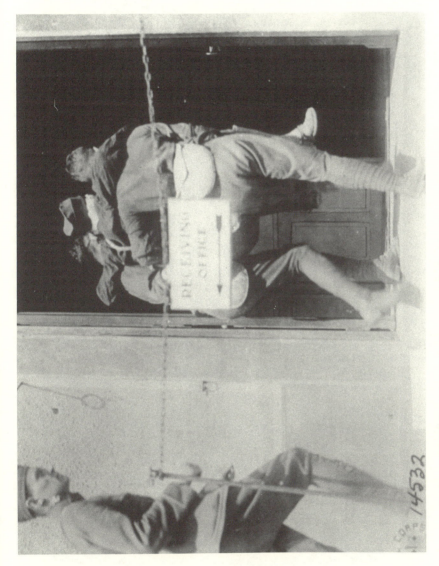

Rainbow Soldier, Gas Casualty, May, 1918. Courtesy of US Army Military History Institute.

165th Field Hospital, Washington, D.C., National Guard, Meuse-Argonne, October, 1918. Courtesy of US Army Military History Institute.

167th Infantry Baseball Team, (note gas masks), May, 1918. Courtesy of National Archives.

Stokes Mortar, 117th Trench Mortar Battery, January, 1918. Courtesy of National Archives.

General Michael J. Lenihan, March, 1918. Courtesy of National Archives.

General Charles Menoher (left), Col. Douglas MacArthur (right). Courtesy of National Archives.

LTC William J. Donovan, September, 1918. Courtesy of National Archives.

LTC George S. Patton, July, 1918. Courtesy of National Archives.

Col. Benson Hough and Staff, April, 1919. Courtesy of US Army Military History Institute.

Col. William Screws, April, 1919. Courtesy of Alabama State Archives.

167th Dead at Fére-en-Tardenois, August, 1918. Courtesy of National Archives.

Chatillion Hill, October, 1918. Courtesy of National Archives.

General Clement Flagler, Germany, 1919. Courtesy of National Archives.

Rainbow Soldiers Window Shopping, Neuenahr, Germany, 1919. Courtesy of US Army Military History Institute.

Headquarters Battery, 150th Artillery, Altenahr, Germany, 1919.

Headquarters Battery, 150th Artillery, Christmas Dinner, Altenahr, Germany, 1918.

Typical Rainbow Veteran with Rainbow Patch, Germany, 1919.

6

CROSSING THE OURCQ RIVER

By 17 July 1918, the German offensives on the Western Front died out. The next day, Marshall Foch decided the time had come to counterattack the heavily attrited German armies. Pershing first sent into battle his two best Regular Army divisions, the 1st under Charles P. Summerall and the 2nd under James Harbord. In a few days the two American divisions were spent, having advanced farther than any other units save an extremely tough division of Moroccans and Foreign Legionnaires. The French and Americans had cut the vital Soissons-Château Thierry road, denying the Germans their main supply route into the Marne salient. The Germans began to pull back now that their position had become untenable, but they were too well-trained, their officers too professional, to allow a disorderly retreat from the large Marne salient.

The momentum of the attack, however, had to be maintained, and Pershing pushed more American troops into the battle on the Marne. The AEF deployed eight good combat divisions—the 1st, 2nd, 3rd, 4th, 26th, 28th, 32nd, and 42nd Divisions representing the Regular and National Guard forces. The 26th Yankee was already in the line and fighting with the 6th French Army as the Rainbows began their move toward the Marne.

While the Germans were withdrawing the mass of their infantry and needed supplies from the Marne salient, they left behind a well conducted defense, centered on an excellent disposition of their machine-gun units. The 42nd's area of operation was dotted with large farms made up of massive stone buildings, barns, and enclosed courtyards. These were turned into forts that would have to be taken one by one. The farms were usually situated in clearings, and the Germans hid machine guns in the woods to cover the open fields around the farm-forts. The Rainbows had trained in trenches, where a living tree was a rarity. The Marne area had green forests, picturesque stone farmhouses, and rich wheat fields. It was a deadly deception for those who had to attack the salient. The power of artillery, so useful in the Champagne defensive, would be less helpful because of German tactical dispositions. The forests of the Marne salient became a slaughter pen for the Rainbows.

One of the first units to arrive on the Marne River was the 117th Kansas Ammunition Train. Since the troops had their own vehicles, they departed for this new operation as quickly as possible to prepare for combat. The soldiers pitched their pup tents, and immediately brought out the cards, with games of black jack and stud poker occupying the time. Calvin Lambert, however, was in no mood to play cards; he decided to walk by the Marne River. "The Marne," he mused, "was so bright and silvery, and it was difficult to picture it as the bloody Marne." The moon was so bright that night that Lambert found it difficult to sleep.[1]

John Hayes and Joe Romano were only too happy to leave Champagne for the Marne. The Alabamians had been hit almost every night by German air bombardment. Most of the troops were sleeping in an open field, and only a few miles away were German observation balloons. Where there were sausage-shaped balloons, the enemy bomber aircraft and artillery would not be far behind.[2]

Father Duffy was delighted to know that the Irish regiment was going to the Marne. He had always wanted to see that river because of his study of history. As the trains pulled out from Chalons, on a beautiful day, French women, children, and a number of questionable ladies turned out to wave good-bye to the doughboys who had just fought such a vicious battle.[3]

Small clusters of 84th Brigade officers discussed their concerns over Brigadier General Robert Brown, commander of the brigade, who seemed overly tired. During the Champagne defensive battles, Brown was unable to sleep and become more and more agitated as the fight progressed. They questioned Brown's physical and mental health and how he would respond to the strain of the great battle shaping up on the Marne.

The Rainbow arrived at its staging areas at Epieds, about ten miles from where the battle was in progress. At Epieds, the troops received ammunition and extra rations, and officers and NCOs counted their men and briefed them about what was known of the fighting ahead. The 42nd Division was finally out of the trenches, preparing for a stand-up fight that relied on maneuver.

It is much harder to maneuver troops in an attack than to plan and execute a defense. At Lunéville, Baccarat, and then in the Champagne, the Rainbows fought a basically defensive action with little or no large-scale maneuvering. Now it would be different. Unit commanders, especially above the battalion level, had little experience with the attack, and very few had real working knowledge of how to conduct a successful maneuver-based operation. There would be serious errors made during the upcoming Marne attack, to be sure, because the staffs and higher commanders were basically novices at this type of war-fighting.

The terrain over which the 42nd was to advance was not slashed with trenches or wire obstacles. Troop formations would have to react to the configuration of the terrain, including woods, gullies, rivers, and the like, as well

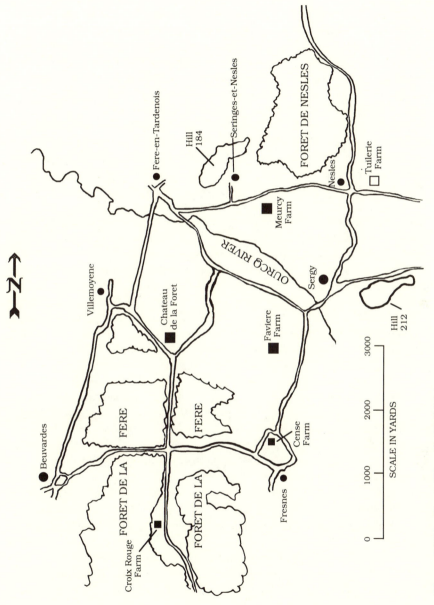

Figure 6.1 The Ourcq River Battlefield

as to enemy defenses. Communication with the troops on the ground and with the aircraft and balloons in the air would present numerous problems. Those dealing with supplies would also have to react to a different set of circumstances that would, before this operation was over, try everyone's patience.

The area of operations for the Rainbow Division was about four miles wide and six to seven miles long. The division was in contact with the enemy from 26 July to 3 August and sustained 6,500 casualties, a high number indicative of the nature of close and violent combat. While artillery was of critical importance and air observation vital, the Aisne-Marne offensive, as it was officially called, was an infantryman's fight.

The rectangle in which the Rainbow fought was a mixture of woods, open fields, heavily defended stone farms, small towns, and the Ourcq River. North of the Ourcq there was high ground, Hills 184 to the east and 220 to the west. (Hills with no particular name were designated by their height in meters.) Observation and concealment went to the enemy, who used the hills to cover the approaches to the Ourcq River with machine-gun and artillery fire. North of the Ourcq and the hills were more woods, ridges, stone farm complexes, and three towns: from west to east, Seringes-et-Nesles, Nesles, and Sergy. These small, built-up areas were directly in the Rainbow's area of responsibility and had to be cleared of Germans. Each one of the towns was on a main east-west road that linked with Fére-en-Tardenois, a large town in the west that was in the area of operations assigned to the French 62nd Infantry Division, with Château Thierry to the south. On the Rainbow's right flank was Hill Mass 212, which was half in the Rainbow's sector and half in the sector belonging to the U.S. 28th Infantry Division.

The most complex movement the Rainbows would make going into the Aisne-Marne would be the relief of French and American combat units. The Iowans and Alabamians of Brown's brigade relieved elements of the battered 26th Yankee Division, then moved into attack positions on the early afternoon of 26 July. While this was taking place, the 83rd Brigade, under Brigadier General Lenihan, replaced the 170th Infantry Regiment of the French 167th Division. This division was no stranger to the Rainbows, since they had worked together while training in the trenches at Lunéville. The entire maneuver was tightly controlled by a series of orders issued by the French 6th Army and the 38th Corps to all subordinate units.[4]

About a mile and a half from the spot where the 84th Brigade relieved the elements of the Yankee Division was a farm complex known as Croix Rouge Farm, and the Iowans and Alabamians were ordered to take the farm and move to occupy the crossroads a little over a mile north of the buildings. Facing the farm on the left were the soldiers of the 168th's 2nd Battalion; next to them were two battalions of the 167th, the 1st and the 3rd. The movements of the three assaulting battalions were hidden by a thick woods known as the Fôret de Fére. Once out of the woods, the troops had to advance over several hundred yards of cultivated fields to the farm, which had been turned into a veritable fortress bristling with enemy machine guns.

When the Iowa and Alabama veterans of the Rainbow met after the war, the name Croix Rouge Farm stirred up memories of the most intense battle they ever had. It eclipsed the Champagne defensive and the Meuse-Argonne offensive. Throughout the night of 25 July, German artillery kept up continual fire on the Fôret de Fére, where the two regiments were assembling to assault the farm and the crossroads beyond.

The Iowans moved up within 200 yards of the woods. It was a cloudy day with threats of rain, and observation was not good. It would not have mattered much if it were a bright, sunny day, for the German defenders of the farm and woods were dug in and well-camouflaged. German artillery fired into the Fôret de Fére blindly, but the troops were so tightly packed into the assault lines that casualties began to mount. Colonel Bennett of the 168th set 2 P.M. as the time for the attack to begin.[5]

There was no information about the enemy, ammunition was very slow in coming up, and a French battalion from the 409th Regiment, which was to be in the assault, arrived late. The attack was rescheduled for 4:50 P.M., with artillery preparation to begin two hours prior to the attack. A steady rain began to fall. There could be no more waiting, and at 4:50 P.M. Companies E and F, 168th, emerged from the woods with fixed bayonets, moving with a steady tred. Companies D and G followed by about 200 yards. The French and Alabamians were out of the woods into the open fields, bearing down on the farm and the woods and crossroads beyond. Suddenly the field was swept by German machine guns, and the tempo of the enemy artillery increased, tearing holes in the ranks of the assaulting units. One Iowa lieutenant passed by two of his men who were dying, both beseeching him to write to their mothers that they had done their duty.[6]

The Alabamians were in equally dire straits. When they came out of the woods and met the same withering fire as had the Iowans, the assaulting troops of the 1st Battalion broke into a run, screaming what the Iowans knew as the Rebel yell. Men fell by the score.[7] Joe Romano of Company D was in the first assault wave, and he found himself on the ground with the rest of his company, pinned down by the deadly machine-gun and artillery fire. John Hayes' Company I sprang from the woods, and only went a few feet before Lieutenant John Powell, commanding the company, was killed.[8]

Captain Julian Strassburger, commanding the 167th's machine gun company, saw the serious situation of his Alabama comrades and brought his gunners out of the woods. He got as far as Lieutenant Powell and was struck dead by a burst of machine-gun fire. In the thick of the fight, the Alabamians heard the sound of a small cannon firing into the enemy lines. This gun had been brought up by newly commissioned Second Lieutenant Edward R. Wren, recently an Auburn University football hero, now of Company B. Standing exposed in the open field, he and his men fired into the German machine-gun nests.[9]

The slaughter in the fields at Croix Rouge Farm went on for nearly an hour, with American and French casualties mounting every minute. The French battalion, which entered the fight with about thirty men per company, was no longer a factor. Officers, where there were any left standing, had little or no control over their men. The chances of any reinforcements were slim, due to the heavy rains that made movement difficult. Ammunition was in short supply, and the ammunition trucks were bogged down on the muddy roads.

Sometime around 6 P.M., Lieutenant Ernest Bell of Company D and Lieutenant Robert Espy of Company B, 167th, led their Alabams in a headlong bayonet charge against the farm.[10] The Iowans, seeing Alabama go forward, also moved. Bell started his charge with fifty-eight men; when they took the farm, there were only twenty-five left. Espy began his dash with fifty-two soldiers, but counted eighteen when the fight was over. Joe Romano of Company D was one of those left standing. The soldiers of Companies I and K had managed to get into the woods to the left of Croix Rouge Farm, and had silenced the machine-gun positions one by one. The Germans began to retreat as what was left of the Iowa-Alabama assault force swept the field. Once inside the stone walls that had protected the Germans, the Alabamians kept up a deadly fire. Counterattacks died out by 8 P.M. Croix Rouge Farm and a major portion of the Fôret de Fére was in Americans hands, but at a terrible price.[11]

Over a thousand Americans were either killed or wounded in the fight for Croix Rouge Farm. The night of 26 July was marked by heavy rains, constant shelling by the German artillery, and the shrieks and cries of both American and German wounded, many still in the woods. Men had not been fed in over twenty-four hours, and worse, it was nearly impossible to move the wounded back to the aid stations due to the muddy roads and constant shelling.

The fight at the Croix Rouge Farm was necessary, but the battalion, regimental, and brigade commanders were clumsy in handling their troops. First, from all sources it appears that there was little ground or air reconnaissance of the area the Iowans and Alabamians were to attack. The Iowans were hampered by the lack of maps and information, and Colonel Bennett had only a crude sketch of the area with which to brief his assaulting units. There was little attention paid to the question of logistics. Ammunition was in very short supply, and food did not arrive until the early morning of 27 July. The troops went over a day and a half without food. From Sergeant Calvin Lambert's diary it is possible to deduce that there was no real sense of urgency in the 117th Kansas Ammunition Train.[12] There is every reason to believe that Lieutenant Colonel Frank Travis, commander of the 117th Ammunition Train, did not exert sufficient influence on the movement of his men. In fact, Travis was relieved later, with a comment from the divisional commander that "he was unfit to command the Ammunition Train [due to] a lack of interest and appearance of timidity for his personal safety."[13] There is also evidence that the division had earlier been unhappy with Travis' performance during both static trench or defensive fighting. At any rate, when fighting began again on the morning of 27 July, some of the Alabamians and Iowans were short of ammunition for rifles and machine guns, and there was a lack of grenades, a piece of ordnance vital to close infantry fighting.

Division headquarters also seemed to be unaware of the magnitude of losses in the two combat regiments. Sometime after 1 A.M., the Rainbow Division received an attack order to cross the Ourcq and seize the high ground on the north side of the river. The 6th French Army knew that the Germans were withdrawing rapidly from the Marne salient, and the fighting on 26 July prompted the enemy to move his forces quickly.[14]

The French Army commander and his French and American corps commanders seemed to be just as ignorant of the condition of the enemy and their own troops as were divisional commanders on the ground. While the infantry was struggling forward, the 67th Field Artillery brigade was in the process of trying to move heavy artillery pieces along the muddy mess that passed for roads (with the attached 51st Field Artillery Brigade of the 26th Yankee Division). The 28,000-man division of World War I was woefully short of artillery. Four infantry regiments simply could not be supported by only three regiments of field guns. The trench mortars in the 117th Battery, and the trench mortars in each regiment, could not hope to provide the artillery needed, especially during offensive operations. The 67th Brigade would add artillery muscle to the Ohio and New York troops, while the Yankee gunners of the 51st Brigade would fire for the 84th Brigade. The French also added heavier guns to the operation. Given that the Germans had the time to dig in and camouflage their machine-gun nests and took advantage of every stone-enclosed farm, the need for more guns was obvious.

Hoosier Elmer Sherwood was surprised to see many of the Rainbow infantry being moved to the front in trucks driven by Indochinese. Having never seen such a large contingent of Asians, Sherwood was constantly amazed by the expert way they handled their trucks on shell-pocked roads. Soon, however, Sherwood's attention was turned to the evidence of wanton German looting and destruction of civilian property as the enemy retreated from Château Thierry.[15]

The field artillery brigades, as good as they were, learned some valuable lessons during the first two days of the Aisne-Marne operation. There were few recriminations from the Iowa and Alabama soldiers about the lack of artillery fire at Croix Farm, but the lack of those powerful weapons was noticeable. Artillery had to realize that infantry cannot always advance in exactly the way planned in the operations order. Terrain, weather, and the enemy determine to a large extent how the foot soldiers move. Artillery liaison personnel had to be forward with the advancing elements.[16] Another group that had a hard time getting into position was the 117th Sanitary Train, "the gasoline and iodine gang," as the men called themselves. Their basic plan was good, but getting to their appointed places over muddy, congested roads was another thing entirely. The main field hospital was located at Epieds, about five kilometers from the 25-26 July jumping-off point for the 84th Brigade. Epieds was on a main road, but that road did not go directly to the area of combat. Consequently, wounded had to be carried, often under heavy shelling, over forest trails that were littered with broken trees and the debris of battle. Other field hospitals and the main evacuation hospital were located at Château Thierry, about ten kilometers from Epieds over a battered road. The Epieds field hospital was within range of German artillery, while the hospitals at Château Thierry were not.[17] Lieutenant van Dolsen felt he was going to lose his mind after five days of combat, having remained on his feet for thirty-six hours before he could rest. The chief surgeon had put him in charge of the gas and the shock wards, and for the first time he came into contact with hundreds of cases of shell-shock. As the fighting continued, the wounded poured into Epieds, where van Dolsen was stationed, and the caseload became so heavy that the division surgeon asked for surgical teams to be sent to assist in operating. In a few days, Navy operating teams arrived to help the hard-pressed and exhausted Rainbow doctors.[18]

Van Dolsen and the other weary doctors would see a lot more in the next few days. During the early hours of 27 July, orders were issued to both brigades to prepare to attack across the Ourcq river. The divisional order was basically simple. The heaviest fighting that day would fall on the Irish 165th and on the tired Iowa 168th. The two brigades would advance in column of regiments moving swiftly to the river, force a crossing, and seize the high ground directly north of the river. The action was to begin with a heavy artillery bombardment once both artillery brigades were in place to offer support to the attacking infantry regiments. Facing the river, the 83rd Brigade would assault with the 165th leading the way, backed up by the 166th and the 150th Machine Gun Battalion. On the right, the Iowans would first hit the river with the weary Alabamians, still short of ammunition, and the 151st Machine Gun Battalion following. The operation was scheduled to begin at 9:40 A.M., but was delayed until 1 P.M. General Lenihan established his headquarters at a stone house known as the Château de la Fôret, on a crossroads at the end of the Fôret de Fére, about two miles from the river. Lenihan's decision was a solid, professional one in that he had a good view of the battlefield.[19]

The Ohio troops moved just north of the Fôret de Fére and arrayed their battalions in echelon, with the 1st in the front, followed by the 2nd, then the 3rd. They were not to move any farther that day.[20] The Germans were not making things easy for the Americans, and at about 1 P.M. their artillery began to hit the assault regiments. Company B, 166th Infantry, for example, had seventeen men killed and fifty-five wounded from these storms of high explosive and shrapnel rounds.[21]

The heaviest engagement of the day came when Donovan and his 1st Battalion reached the Ourcq sometime after 1 P.M., but the German artillery and machine-gun fire was such that the men had to fall back to the safety of the stone walls of Faviére Farm, less than a mile from the river.[22]

Two Iowa battalions, the 1st and the 3rd, also reached the Ourcq, but they too were beaten back. The Ourcq River would not be crossed on 27 July. Curiously, the Alabama 167th was quiet that day; in fact, the whole of the 84th

Brigade, under the now-suspect General Robert Brown, seemed hesitant, unresponsive to the battle.

The 42nd Division was basically fighting blind in trying to force its way across the Ourcq River. To help remedy this, Liggett's U.S. I Corps attached the experienced 12th Aero Squadron to the division during the early morning of 27 July 1918. If the weather held, at least the divisional intelligence officers, planning section, and the artillery would have eyes across the Ourcq. The 12th Aero was a good organization that had moved to the Aisne-Marne area on 18 July to support I Corps operations.[23] However, there were problems encountered by both the squadron, which now received missions from division, and the Rainbow staff. One of the critical missions for the 12th Aero was to keep Menoher and the G3 informed as to where the troops were on the battlefield. In two days this was accomplished only three times, due to the failure of ground troops to use proper procedures in marking their positions. Often pilots flew dangerously close to the ground, 300 down to fifty meters, while the air was filled with German and American artillery and machine-gun fire. The pilots were more successful in the area of coordination with artillery.[24] The Rainbow gunners had much more success supporting the infantry with the 12th Areo Squadron in the air.

A proposed night assault was planned, then canceled, and preparations were made for another try at getting troops across the Ourcq in daylight on the morrow. This was imperative, because on 28 July, the U.S. 28th Division was to occupy positions on the Rainbow's right flank. The overall French commander wanted to push the enemy hard, as there was every indication that the Germans were ready to abandon the Ourcq positions and fall back even farther.[25]

At 4:50 A.M. the 3rd Battalion, 168th, crossed the Ourcq River under heavy fire. Within two hours the remainder of the Iowa regiment was across. By 9 A.M., under very heavy fire, the Alabamians crossed the river to take the small town of Sergy, where German machine gunners ripped holes in the attacking 2nd Battalion ranks. During the fight for Sergy, Private Julius Grogan of Talladega, serving in Company F, was hit eight times. As Company F began to fall back to better positions, the bleeding Grogan called for his comrades to carry him to safety, but due to the hail of machine-gun bullets no one could reach him. Suddenly, the blood-soaked Grogan jumped up and hollered, "All right, damn it. I'll take myself," and in the storm of lead he limped to the rear. Miraculously, Grogan was not hit again.[26]

Large numbers of German aircraft were busy bombing and strafing the Rainbows during the afternoon of 28 July. Enemy artillery was accurate due to air observation and inflicted heavy casualties on the assaulting units.[27] Around 5 P.M. the 2nd Battalion, 168th, launched a general attack against the ruins of Sergy. The 84th Brigade soldiers paid a heavy price for the attack, but they took the town and held on to it throughout the night as German artillery pounded the area.

The New York 165th had assaulted across the Ourcq about the same time as had the Iowans. Company K, under the command of Captain John Hurley, and I Company, under Boer War veteran Captain Richard J. Ryan, were the first across the river. Their objective was the stone complex known as Meurcy Farm, less than a mile from the river. In Company K there were five Kelleys and five Sullivans, all related to each other. At the end of the day two Kelleys were dead and one wounded, and one Sullivan was critically wounded. Father Henley, whom Duffy was so happy to see only a short time ago, lay severely wounded on the field. Both Ryan and Hurley were wounded. The Old Shamrock Battalion was melting away.[28] Martin Hogan's lieutenant lay not far away, with a machine-gun bullet through the heart. Major James A. McKenna, battalion commander, was dead, and it looked as if the 3rd Battalion would cease to exist. Donovan brought up his 1st Battalion, and Major Alexander Anderson threw his 2nd Battalion men into the fight, finally bringing out what was left of the Shamrocks.[29] The 83rd Brigade was spent.

How much infantry was left to do the fighting? Menoher had begun to receive frantic messages from General Brown telling of the great possibility that the 84th Brigade, once the division's best, might soon be incapable of any offensive activity. Brown appeared to be in a near panic, even though his men had accomplished their missions so far and held their main objective by their fingernails. I Corps realized, too, the situation in the 42nd Division, and took steps to help when it placed two battalions of the 47th Infantry Regiment, 4th Infantry Division, with the Rainbows. These two battalions would bolster the divisional attack on 29 July.

Early in the morning of 29 July, the Germans counterattacked Sergy and drove the Rainbows out of the ruins, back to the river. Again the Germans set up machine-gun positions, and the sky was dotted with German observation and bombardment aircraft. According to the operational reports of the day, the weather was partly cloudy, with fair visibility. The Americans' report concluded at the end of the day, "The enemy had complete possession of the air."[30]

Douglas MacArthur decided that the 1st and 3rd Battalions of the 47th Infantry would make the main attack to retake Sergy. There also came a realization that mass attacks, such as the ones at Croix Rouge Farm and then at Sergy on 28 July, did nothing but use up the infantry. It became necessary to go after machine-gun positions one by one with small groups—one group firing to keep the gunners down while the other group of Americans rapidly bounded to another position. Once in place, they in turn began firing, occupying the German machine gunners while the other group moved. In modern terms, the infantry now used fire and maneuver to silence those deadly guns. As one veteran recalled, "Rushing through the open up to the concealed German machine guns in the hope of frightening the gunners into surrender, or of catching them off guard, was sheer suicide. That was now certain."[31]

At divisional headquarters it was clear that something was not right. Since the fight at Croix Rouge Farm on 26 July, the Rainbows had moved forward only about two kilometers at best. MacArthur went forward to see the battle as closely as possible. What he saw was that the greatest possibility for a successful attack rested with the Ohio and Iowa troops because the New Yorkers and Alabamians were pinned down by heavy machine-gun fire, and it would take time to take those well-positioned, dug-in German gunners out of the fight.[32]

At 8:30 A.M., the Iowans, with the 3rd Battalion of the 47th leading the charge, swept the Germans from Sergy. Company L of the 47th routed the Germans, after hand-to-hand combat, from the ruins of the town. Donovan's 1st battalion slowly took the Meurcy Farm, and 2nd Battalion moved up to help Donovan's men hold the stone structure. During the fight for the farm, the French, fighting now for Fére-en-Tardenois, brought up 75mm artillery to help silence some machine-gun nests contesting the 165th's advance.[33]

The Ohio regiment started the day badly when the 1st Battalion became pinned down near the shattered village of La Fontaine Sous Pierre at 8 A.M. Slowly, the 166th began to fire and maneuver against the dug-in Germans, and by 4 P.M. the 2nd Battalion was able to assault Serenges-et-Nesles and attack the eastern slopes of Hill 184 in conjunction with the French 62nd Infantry Division.[34]

By the end of the 29th, the Rainbows had finally taken the towns and heights that overlooked the Ourcq River. But beyond that, a new set of obstacles, the Fôret de Nesles and two stone farms known locally as Château de Nesles and Tuilerie Farm—greeted the doughboys. Scouts and air observers noticed that the Germans were rapidly installing barbed-wire barriers, and there was every reason to believe that machine guns were as well-placed in the woods and in those farms as they were anywhere.

MacArthur, who was moving from regimental command post to command post, heard the unmistakable sounds of the Germans blowing up munitions and positions to the north. The Germans were in the process of abandoning the Marne salient, and believed that the slow but inexorable advance of the French and Americans made a more rapid retreat advisable. MacArthur now wanted to push on to gain control of the Fôret de Nesles and Tuilerie Farm. If pressed, MacArthur reasoned, the Germans would not be able to regroup or dig in until they reached the Vesle River, about eight miles to the north. He sent, on his own, a message to the two artillery brigades to move forward "with audacity," and prepare to cross the Ourcq to support an attack.[35]

Early in the morning of 30 July, MacArthur reached the command post of the 165th and found Colonel Frank McCoy in a somber mood. Father Duffy, usually the epitome of morale and encouragement, was in tears. They had just buried the poet-scholar Sergeant Joyce Kilmer.[36] Kilmer had volunteered to go with Donovan on a reconnaissance forward of the 165th's positions. Donovan had left Kilmer waiting by a tree, and when Wild Bill returned, he saw Kilmer lying under the tree, seemingly asleep. But Kilmer had been shot through the head by a German sniper.[37] Donovan returned the body to the PC of the 165th, where Duffy presided over the burial under one of the few trees remaining on the battlefield.

Air observers and 165th scouts reported that the Germans were placing more wire and obstacles near the Château de Nesles, and this information was forwarded to Colonel McCoy's PC.[38] In the afternoon, the 165th reported to Reilly that it was taking flanking fire on its left from German machine gunners. Could McCoy's Illinois gunners silence those positions? They did, and the Irish inched forward. By 8:45 P.M. Reilly was certain that McCoy's men had taken their basic objectives. He ordered his gunners to replenish their ammunition to prepare for the next day's fight, which promised to be a harder one.[39]

Menoher had not allowed the two artillery brigades to cross the river, but they were moved up to the far edge of the Fôret de Fére and began a heavy bombardment of one and a half hours. Spearheaded by the strong 1st and 3rd Battalions, 47th Infantry, the 168th and 167th attacked the Tuilerie Farm and the town of Nesles. Not everyone believed that an attack could succeed. In a meeting with his three battalion commanders, Colonel Bennett heard their protests. Scouts had seen German machine gunners preparing to receive any attack. In a destroyed farmhouse lighted by only a single flickering candle, Bennett told his commanders. "[This] is an army order. The Corps orders the attack. I have no choice. We shall make it."[40] The lead battalion commander went so far as to lodge a protest in writing against the assault. At 9 A.M. the Iowans moved forward toward the farm and Nesles, and they were greeted by a solid sheet of machine-gun and artillery fire. American artillery support, promised by Brigadier General Dwight Aultman of the 51st Artillery Brigade, failed to materialize. The 3rd of the 47th was taking very heavy casualties while the Iowans painfully reduced each machine-gun position by fire and maneuver. "We had to crawl from the start," remembered one Iowa captain, "The bullets were just skipping over the top of the ground, in a seemingly solid wave."[41] Everett Scott, the messenger, was certain he would die. Other runners were down, but somehow he survived the day without a scratch.

What had happened to the 51st Artillery Brigade of the Yankee Division? That question arose after the fighting. It appears that the confusion rested with Robert Brown's orders as 84th Brigade commander. Brown was located in a farmhouse where he had communications with his regiments. He received a report from the 167th that the trenches that the 168th was heading toward were filled with Americans, not Germans. The 84th Brigade commander then called Colonel Bennett, who assured him that the trenches in question were manned by German machine gunners. Unsure of himself, Brown then called on the 167th for confirmation of the presence of Americans, and from their position on the battlefield they restated that Americans were present in the trenches. Brown preferred to believe the report of the 167th regiment, and ordered Aultman to cease firing. Aultman protested the order, but Brown was adamant, and the artillery fell silent. Lieutenant Colonel Willard B. Luther, Aultman's second in command, witnessed this extraordinary behavior on Brown's part.[42]

The 167th Regiment continually received support from the artillery, however.

Whatever Aultman's orders to his brigade, the 101st Field Artillery of the Massachusetts National Guard continued to fire as Colonel Screws used them to reduce one machine-gun position after another. The 101st had established a solid working relationship with the Alabamians after the Croix Rouge fight.[43] Whether they received the order to cease fire, or whether Aultman's order extended only to the 102nd Field Artillery, is not known. Regardless of the confusion, the Alabams continued to make good use of the Massachusetts gunners' 75mm howitzers, while the bloodied Iowans received no assistance.

Regardless of the good working relationship between the 167th and the 101st, a basic problem rested with Brigadier General Robert Brown's decision making. Rather than believe Bennett, the Iowa commander on the spot, who was looking directly at the fight, Brown rested his decision on the reports of the 167th, viewing a smoky fight at an angle. This was another critical error on Brown's part and figured into his removal the next day.

Medic Lawrence Stewart was at a dressing station in a farmhouse where, surprisingly, he and his comrades found a terrified French family huddled in a loft. During the fighting, Stewart watched as three Iowa stretcher-bearers struggled to bring a wounded man to the dressing station. They were only a few hundred yards away when a German shell exploded, killing two bearers and their patient. The third bearer, his head bloody from a shrapnel cut, examined the three lifeless forms, then grasped the blood-soaked stretcher and staggered back to the fight. In the farmyard, the Iowans discovered a deep well full of clear water, and they distributed water to the infantry men as best as they could.[44]

With the 1st Battalion of the 47th in the lead, the Alabams attacked in tandem with the 168th, but they got no farther than did their Iowa comrades. The 167th had learned its lessons well. It moved slowly using fire and maneuver, but to little avail, against the concentration of German machine-gun and artillery fire.[45] By noon, the 167th and 168th had to conclude that they could make no further progress, and the attacks came to an end.

On the right of the Rainbows, the 28th Division continued to attack in its sector, and on the left the 62nd French Division also pushed north. This would eventually have the effect of weakening German resistance against the 42nd, because Germans generals could very well see the possibility of their troops being caught in a pocket. That was of little comfort to the infantrymen bogged down slightly north of the Ourcq River, however.

I Corps commander General Hunter Liggett, who had been with Menoher on the night of 29 July, placed the entire 7th Infantry Brigade, 4th Division (39th Infantry and 47th Infantry regiments and the 11th Machine Gun Battalion), under the operational control of the Rainbow Division. The casualties among Rainbow infantrymen had been severe, and something had to be done to strengthen the division if it was to keep fighting. The plan was for the 4th Infantry Division, the Ivy Division, to relieve the Rainbow in early August. Liggett informed Menoher that the 32nd Red Arrow Division (Michigan and Wisconsin National Guard) would relieve the worn-down 28th Division on the Rainbow's right flank.

While this was good news for the soldiers of Pennsylvania's Iron Division, it caused problems for Menoher and his staff planners. Probably, the Red Arrows would be slow the first day or so in coordinating attacks with the 42nd Division.

This would also be the 32nd's first real contact with the enemy, and while the division had every prospect of being one of the AEF's best, it was new to shot, shell, and gas. It is also highly probable that Menoher discussed with Liggett, at this time, the relief of General Brown and his replacement by Douglas MacArthur as 84th Brigade commander. Liggett's I Corps issued another order to attack just east of Meurcy Farm at 4:30 A.M., but the 84th Brigade failed to make any headway. The after-action report written by Colonel Hughes after the war simply said that the brigade "failed to make any appreciable progress due to the inability of the troops on our right to progress."[46]

While it seems that the 32nd Division did not get into the fight as planned, it is also true that General Brown had to be constantly prodded to move his two regiments. Brown bombarded Menoher with descriptions of the condition of his troops, while Menoher was growing very concerned with reports of low morale and confusion in what had once been his best infantry brigade. During the afternoon, Menoher informed Liggett that he had had enough of Brown, who was, in Menoher's words, now unfit to command. MacArthur would take over the brigade as soon as possible, and Lieutenant Colonel Hughes would become chief of staff. MacArthur went immediately to brigade headquarters.[47]

The night of 31 July was filled with frustration for the Rainbows, who were just barely holding on to what they had gained. The regiments had been in continual combat, and the troops were physically tired and mentally exhausted. The divisional surgeon reported that 3,276 men had been processed through the various stations, and this number represented the wounded only. There was no way to know the number of men killed or missing at that time, but it was clear that the Rainbows were approaching a crisis. The German forces arrayed before them consisted of elements of four German divisions—the 201st, the 4th Prussian Guards, the 10th Landwehr, and the 6th Bavarian Reserve.[48] Conventional military thinking says that an attacker must have a three-to-one ratio for an assault to succeed. The weakened Rainbow Division had nowhere near that.

In the Irish 165th, the leadership was fast melting away. Company C of Donovan's battalion was commanded by Captain Hermann "Papa" Bootz, a German immigrant, veteran of the Regular Army and much beloved by his men. During the fight on 31 July, Bootz went down. A bullet pierced him from side to side, and sorrowing Irishmen believed this good officer was dying. As they carried him from the field, Bootz threw his old battered pipe to one of the surviving officers of Company C. Whenever Company C went into a fight Bootz had led it, pipe clenched in his teeth. He survived the war, won a Distinguished Service Cross, and retired from the Regular Army as a colonel. But when he went down with such a severe wound, a great deal of combat leadership was gone.[49] Disease was becoming a problem for the Rainbow as well. The water supply was often polluted from the debris of battle. Corpses floated in the Ourcq River, and small pools left by the rain were often befouled by the dead or by human refuse.[50] The 168th had its small well near the aid station, but that was hardly productive or close enough to assist the entire division. Rations, which had to take second place to ammunition and medical supplies, were slow in arriving, and the wagons and supplymen were just as subject to artillery and air attack as were the infantrymen. German snipers and gunners waited until they could hit those carrying supplies, and the men in the front lines simply went hungry and thirsty as the flow of supplies dwindled to a trickle.

On the evening of 31 July, Benson Hough of the Ohio regiment could report that his 2nd Battalion was in firm control of the town of Seringes-et-Nesles. His much-reduced 1st Battalion, 166th, which had fought across the river to the northern end of the Fôret de Fére, was now a regimental reserve. The 3rd Battalion, which had also suffered heavy losses, held onto positions near the 2nd Battalion. The fighting to take Seringes-et-Nesles had been vicious—hand-to-hand, clubbed rifle, and bayonet.[51]

The Iowa 168th secured the right flank of the division when it fought its way up Hill 212, north of the village of Sergy. With the French in Fére-en-Tardenois on the left and the 168th in contact with the hesitant 32nd on the right, the high ground north of the Ourcq River was finally in Allied hands. That small piece of Marne real estate had been bought at a terrible price. The Alabamians also anchored the entire line with positions in and around Nesles under their control. Two questions, however, were not answered. What could happen if the Germans decided to counterattack in great force? And was there infantry enough to mount any sort of effective pursuit of the Germans?

The 4th Division would soon relieve the Rainbows, but when this relatively untried division would be able to assume the offensive was another matter entirely. Division headquarters had a short-term answer for the infantry problem. On 28 July, the G3 of the Rainbow had ordered the 117th Engineers to assume the role of divisional infantry reserve, to be used if needed. Now it was needed, and on 1 August the regiment, minus two companies that had to continue working on bridges and roads, moved into the line as combat infantrymen.[52] Colonel William Kelly, commanding the regiment, was informed that his 117th Engineers would participate in a general attack at 4:15 A.M. on 2 August. In fact, the 117th Engineers had the critical task of securing the left flank of the 32nd Division as it also attacked to the north.[53]

Menoher's eyes that morning were on the attack of the Engineers and the 168th Infantry. As they moved forward, they encountered very slight resistance from the enemy. Where once there had been masses of German machine guns, now there were abandoned positions. The enemy had broken contact and was in the process of moving back to the Vesle River in good order. German artillery was still active, and about 11 A.M. the enemy laid down a continual, heavy barrage to slow up the doughboys of the Rainbow and the Red Arrows. By the end of the day, the Americans were in the Fôret de Nesles.

As the 117th Engineers pressed on, with the 167th and 168th following, they encountered scattered machine-gun fire, and the advance on 2 August was described as a slow one.[54]   This was Douglas MacArthur's first real day as commander of the 84th, and he was euphoric and overly dramatic in his reports to Menoher and the new chief of staff. He informed Menoher:

I am advancing my whole line with the utmost speed. If he [the enemy] has not already a prepared position in the Fôret de Nesles, I intend to throw him into the Vesle. I am using small patrols acting with great speed and continually flanking him so that he can not form a line of resistance. I am handling the columns myself and my losses are extraordinarily light.[55]

MacArthur did have good reason to believe things were going well, but despite his optimism, a real pursuit at that time was not possible. The Rainbow Division was used up, tired, and incapable of any sustained operation such as a pursuit.

The 4th Division relieved the 42nd Division on the night of 3 August, with the 67th Field Artillery Brigade being attached to the Ivys for the pursuit to the Vesle River. Early in the morning of 4 August, General Menoher wrote to Hunter Liggett requesting that the Rainbow be sent "to a rest area in order to recuperate, reconstitute, re-equip, and amalgamate the replacements it is to receive."[56] Menoher pointed out that the division had lost 6,000 men (another 2,000 had been lost in the Champagne defensive), had lost a large number of officers and NCOs killed and wounded, and had little rest. The Rainbow would need from four to six weeks to accomplish the rebuilding it so urgently needed.

Liggett was well aware of the dire condition of the Rainbow, and he agreed that Menoher's request should be granted as soon as the 77th Infantry Division was available for operations. The Rainbows would pull back to an assembly area in the Fôret de Fére-Epieds area to begin the process of cleaning equipment and resting.[57] Liggett knew, however, that there was no possible way to grant the Rainbows six weeks to recover from the Aisne-Marne offensive. Plans were being made for the St. Mihiel offensive, and the 42nd would be needed for that.

One of the first items of business for Menoher was to issue the necessary orders to formalize the relief of Robert Brown as 84th Brigade commander, a task easier said than done. When Menoher strongly urged Brown's removal, the request was quickly granted by Major General James W. McAndrew, chief of staff at Chaumont, but McAndrew required that a full report be made as soon as possible to clarify why Brown was removed. Brown was sent from the field to Blois "to await instructions." MacArthur, according to McAndrew, was to relinquish command once the fight was over and return to the United States to command an infantry brigade in the newly formed 11th Division. MacArthur and Menoher were dismayed over the prospect of Douglas MacArthur's leaving the AEF.[58]

Brown was already in Blois when the actual order, dated 8 August, was issued. A West Point graduate, class of 1884, he had served as an officer in a number of cavalry regiments, including the famous 7th Regiment in 1891. As a Regular Army colonel, Brown was temporarily promoted to brigadier general in the National Army on 5 August 1917. With his removal came a reduction in rank to the rank of colonel. In a Regular Army, such as the one controlling the AEF, this was a drastic move, a career-stopper, but Pershing had no qualms whatsoever about removing an inefficient or physically worn-out officer.

On 8 August, at Blois, Brown officially contested his removal, arguing that he was indeed capable of commanding an infantry brigade. A lengthy hearing was set in motion. Eighteen officers were interviewed, from Menoher, MacArthur, Judah, and Hughes to captains and majors within the 84th Brigade, and they all told the same story. Brown had cracked under the strain, could not sleep, became incoherent at times, contested orders, and constantly asked Menoher to pull the 84th off the line. Certainly the stress of the Aisne-Marne operation was considerable, but Lenihan, commanding the equally hard-pressed and bloodied 83rd Brigade, did not manifest such behavior. The issue was decided by Pershing, AEF Headquarters, with Brown's removal. On 20 August, Major General James G. Harbord, commanding the Service of Supply, stated that Brown's services were not needed there either, and on 5 September Pershing had Brown officially reduced to colonel and sent back to the United States.[59] No Regular Army officer liked to see another, especially one so associated with the AEF from an early date, meet this end, but to the credit of Menoher, Harbord, and ultimately Pershing, an officer deemed unfit to command men and safeguard their lives in combat was relieved.

Douglas MacArthur took over the brigade and received his first general's star. William Hughes was elevated to the rank of colonel and became chief of staff of the Rainbow Division. The 42nd also got a new G3, Major Grayson M.P. Murphy, a West Point graduate who had left the army to pursue a very successful career in finance and banking. Murphy had come to France as head of the American Red Cross, and in June 1917, went with Pershing to Chaumont as a part of the permanent staff of AEF Headquarters. While on Pershing's staff, Murphy coordinated Red Cross activities with the army's medical service in the field. His West Point background and good service in the infantry in the Philippines impressed Pershing enough to send him to the 42nd Division in the critical position of G3.[60]

While the staff of the division was undergoing command changes, the troops languished in the Fôret de Fére for a week. Lawrence Stewart and his Iowa buddies hated the place because "the ground was spongy, oozing with mud; the woods reeked with explosive fumes, gas and decay; pup tents failed to provide adequate protection from unhealthful dampness."[61]

Even Father Duffy, normally a soldier who bore the heaviest burdens cheerfully, looked around him and did not like what he saw. "This is a dirty, dank, unwholesome spot and the daily rains are making it more intolerable," Duffy wrote.[62] The Rainbows would not leave the forest until 11 August, when the 77th Division was in the area.

The Rainbow Division had lost heavily in the fight to cross the Ourcq River and secure positions on the north bank. The 165th Infantry, for example, had 1,571 soldiers killed, wounded, or missing—nearly half the strength of the regiment. Some officers in the division would return to service, like Lieutenant Hugh Thompson of the 168th and Captain Hermann Bootz of the 165th, but many had to leave active service for good and would not see their comrades until the units came home. The loss in company grade officers and NCOs was extraordinarily heavy, with, in a few cases, senior corporals in command of platoons where lieutenants should be. A number of battalion commanders, like Major James A. McKenna of the 165th, were dead or wounded.

When Al Ettinger rejoined his units in the Fôret de Fére, he found that some companies that originally had 250 soldiers now had 30 effective fighters left.[63] Martin Hogan had been gassed for the second time near the end of the struggle near Château Thierry, and he would not rejoin the Shamrocks until the Meuse-Argonne offensive in October.[64]

The Rainbow received replacements from the troops arriving in France, but many of those had very little training. Some had been in the army less than four months, and much to the horror of some veterans, a few had never even assembled or disassembled their rifles. Part of any combat force is unit cohesion, men knowing and trusting each other when the shooting starts. This mutual trust and dependence begins with basic training and builds through shared experience. Troops of a particular unit, for example, will have funny stories that are uniquely their own and could very well be incomprehensible to a person from another company or battalion. Integrating large numbers of green replacements becomes very hard to do, and often those replacements suffer the highest casualties in the next fight.

The veteran troops were in terrible shape physically. Almost everyone had lost great amounts of weight due to the monotonous Slum diet. Oftentimes the troops would go over a day and a half without any meal except for reserve rations, which were more of the same cold Corned Willie. The Rainbow men also looked like ragamuffins in torn and incredibly filthy, cootie-infested uniforms. Equipment had been damaged or lost during the intense fighting. Duffy believed that he had never seen a sorrier-looking lot of men in his life.

On the other hand, the Rainbows had learned a lot in the Aisne-Marne operation. The infantry learned the value of fire and maneuver. No longer would the troops rush machine-gun positions with a cheer and a bayonet, and in the upcoming battles in the Argonne forest this would certainly save lives. The need for accurate artillery spotting by air and ground observers was another valuable lesson learned by the Doughboys.

Some of the command changes were needed. The most outstanding change was, of course, within the 84th Brigade, where Douglas MacArthur assumed command in place of the tired and shattered Brown. MacArthur became a very competent brigade commander, even though he tended to continually overdramatize his role in battle. Very quickly the 84th Brigade, with its regiments of Alabamians and Iowans, became again the best in the Rainbow, as the Argonne fighting would demonstrate.

The Rainbow Division did not come to grips with the potential of air power in the Aisne-Marne operation. It had the services of the highly competent 12th Areo Squadron, but that was an observation unit badly outnumbered by the German observation and fighter aircraft, which maintained almost complete air superiority. Rainbow doughboys recalled long after the fight how the German aircraft bombed, strafed, and observed at will, with nothing to impede their progress. There was no balloon company assigned to the Rainbows; neither did the division ask for one. Artillery, intelligence, and operational planners usually profited from the presence of a balloon company, but those long-range eyes were not there during the Aisne-Marne battles. Of course, the 12th Areo pilots reported back to Colonel Billy Mitchell that the Rainbow troops had almost no training in liaison, or air-ground coordination. What little the 12th Areo did was lost because of poor training and ignorance on the part of the infantry. This would change in the upcoming St. Mihiel and Argonne battles.

When the Rainbows began to depart the Fôret de Fére on 11 August, they were tired, dirty, hungry, cootie infested, and ready for a change. But this division had learned a lot from the terrible fighting, which had been so costly. Those National Guardsmen who had left Camp Mills in the late fall of 1917 were not callow youths any longer. It would not take long for the 42nd Division to be ready to participate in the next great battle of the war, St. Mihiel.

NOTES

1. Calvin Lambert Diary, manuscript, Emporia Public Library, Emporia, Kansas, 181-82.

2. John B. Hayes, *Heroes Among the Brave* (Loachapoka, Ala.: Lee County Historical Society, 1973).

3. Francis P. Duffy, *Father Duffy's Story* (New York: George H. Doran Co., 1919), 152-53.

4. 6th French Army, 18th Corps, General Operations Order No. 160 and 133.3, 25 July 1918, and Special Order No. 134.3 and 1902.3, 26 July 1918, in the National Archives, Washington, D.C., *Records Group 120 Records of the AEF*, 42nd Division, carton 13 (hereinafter, RG 120). (These are English translations of the French orders, prepared at 38th Corps Headquarters for the 42nd Division headquarters.)

5. John H. Taber, *The Story of the 168th Infantry* (Iowa City: State Historical Society of Iowa, 1925), 322-23.

6. Ibid., 330.

7. Ibid., 331.

8. Manuscript prepared by First Lieutenant Edmund F. Hackett, "The Fight at Croix Rouge Farm," in the Alabama State Historical Archives, Montgomery, Alabama, 167th Infantry Collection. See also William B. Amerine, *Alabama's Own in France* (New York: Eaton and Gettinger, 1919), 150.

9. Hackett manuscript, 4.

10. Ibid., 4-5.

11. Amerine, *Alabama's Own*, 153-54. Hayes, *Heroes Among the Brave*, 26.

Taber, *168th Infantry*, 340-41.

12. Calvin Lambert Diary, 182-84. These entries reflect no sense of an impending battle. The troops do not give any appearance of preparing to resupply in heavy combat.

13. "The Relief and Discharge of LTC Frank L. Travis, 117 Ammunition Train," 17 May 1919, in the National Archives, Washington, D.C., Records Group 200, Pershing Files, carton 12 (hereinafter, RG 200).

14. 7th French Army Corps, Special Order No. 449, 26 July 1918, RG 120, carton 13.

15. Elmer W. Sherwood, *Diary of a Rainbow Veteran: Written at the Front* (Terre Haute, Ind.: Moore-Langen, 1929), 34-35.

16. Henry J. Reilly, *Americans All: The Rainbow at War* (Columbus, Ohio: F.J. Heer Printing Co., 1936), 508-10.

17. U.S. Office of the Surgeon General, *Medial Department in the World War. Vol. 7: Field Operation* (Washington: Government Printing Office, 1926), 394-98.

18. Van Dolsen to his mother, np, 30 July 1918, in U.S. Army Military History Institute Archives, Carlisle Barracks, Pennsylvania, 42nd Division AEF Collection (hereinafter, MHIA).

19. Duffy, *Story*, 160-61.

20. R.M. Cheseldine, *Ohio in the Rainbow: Official Story of the 166th Infantry, 42nd Division in the World War* (Columbus, Ohio: F.J. Heer Printing Co., 1924), 192-93.

21. Alison Reppy, *Rainbow Memories: Character Sketches and History of the First Battalion, 166th Infantry* (Np: Private printing, 1919), 14.

22. Duffy, *Story*, 160-61.

23. 42nd Division headquarters, General Orders No. 51, 27 July 1918, in U.S. Army, Center of Military History, *The United States Army in the World War, 1917-1919* (Washington: Government Printing Office, 1989), Vol. 5, 521 (hereinafter, CMH). U.S. War Department, Chief of Air Services, "Battle Participation of the Air Service, A.E.F., U.S. Squadrons, 1918" (1923) in U.S. Air Force Historical Agency Archives, File 167. 401-19. (hereinafter AFHA).

24. Office of Air Force History, *The U.S. Air Service in World War I* (Washington: Government Printing Office, 1928), Vol. 1, 213-19.

25. French 6th Army, 38th Corps, General Order No. 165, 27 July 1918, RG 120, carton 13.

26. Amerine, *Alabama's Own*, 159.

27. Thompson, *Story*, 82-83.

28. Duffy, *Story*, 164-76. Duffy relates that there was great confusion over General Lenihan's orders to Colonel McCoy, commander of the 165th. According to Duffy, Lenihan wanted to suspend the attack, but it appears that McCoy went ahead anyway (164). The results were tragic.

29. Martin J. Hogan, *The Shamrock Battalion of the Rainbow: A Story of the Fighting 69th* (New York: D. Appleton and Co., 1919), 171-73.

30. 42nd Division headquarters, Operations Report, 29 July 1918, in CMH, *United States Army in the World War*, Vol. 5, 525.

31. Thompson, *Story*, 84-85.

32. Douglas MacArthur, *Reminiscences* (New York: McGraw-Hill, 1964), 59-60.

33. Duffy, *Story*, 177.

34. Cheseldine, *Ohio in the Rainbow*, 199-202.

35. MacArthur, *Reminiscences*, 60.

36. Ibid., 61.

37. Duffy, *Story*, 192-93.

38. Entry 30 July 1918, 10:00 A.M. in HQ, 149th Field Artillery Regiment's Record of Events, Book No. 1, in the Henry J. Reilly Papers, MHIA.

39. Entry 30 July 1918, 8:45 P.M. in ibid.

40. Taber, *168th Infantry*, Vol. 2, 2-3.

41. Ibid., 8-9.

42. Ibid., 19-20.

43. Russell Gordon Carter, *The 101st Field Artillery, A.E.F., 1917-191* (Boston: Houghton-Mifflin, 1940), 166-68.

44. Lawrence Stewart, *Rainbow Bright* (Philadelphia: Dorrance, 1923), 83-84.

45. Amerine, *Alabama's Own*, 161. Hayes, *Heroes Among the Brave*, 26-27.

46. Operations Report, July 25-August 3 1918, HQ, 42nd Division (written while in Germany, 1919, by Colonel Hughes). Found in D. Clayton James Papers, Special Collections, Mississippi State University Library, Starkville, Mississippi.

47. D. Clayton James, *Years of MacArthur, Vol. 1: 1880-1941* (Boston: Houghton-Mifflin, 1970), 187-88.

48. Thompson, *Story*, 90; MacArthur, *Reminiscences*, 60.

49. Duffy, *Story*, 187; A. Churchill Ettinger (ed.), *A Doughboy with the Fighting 69th* (Shippensburg, PA: White Main Publishing, 1992), 140-41.

50. Walter B. Wolf, *Brief Story of the Rainbow Division* (New York: Rand McNally Co., 1919), 33.

51. Cheseldine, *Ohio in the Rainbow*, 208.

52. E.J. Sadler (ed.), *California Rainbow Memories* (Np: Private printing, 1925), 37.

53. HQ, 42nd Division, Memorandum, 117th Engineers to Combat Service, 1 August 1918, in CMH, *United States Army in the World War*, Vol. 5, 527. See also Monthly report for August 1918, 117th Enginner Regiment, RG 120, carton 40.

54. 67th Field Artillery Brigade Historical Summary of Engagements, nd, ibid., carton 2.

55. Field Message from MacArthur to Menoher, 2 August 1918, ibid., carton 10.

56. Memorandum from Menoher to Liggett, 4 August 1918, ibid., carton 1.

57. I Corps internal memorandum by Liggett, 4 August 1918, ibid.

58. "The Relief and Reduction of Brigadier General R.A. Brown." 84th Infantry Brigade, 5 May 1919, RG 200, carton 8.

59. Memorandum by Pershing, 5 September 1918, cited in ibid.

60. John J. Pershing, *My Experiences in the World War* (New York: Frederick A. Stokes Co., 1931), Vol. 1, 71, 108, 280.

61. Stewart, *Rainbow Bright*, 87.

62. Duffy, *Story*, 207. See also Cheseldine, *Ohio in the Rainbow*, 217.

63. Ettinger, *Doughboy*, 136.

64. Hogan, *Shamrock Battalion*, 177-79.

7

THE ST. MIHIEL OFFENSIVE

When the doughboys of the Rainbow pulled back to the assembly area in the Fôret de Fére, they found a distressing sight. The dead of the 42nd still lay where they fell. Since the 117th Engineers had been put into the battle as infantry, there was no one to bury the fallen. But strange things occur in war, and in the midst of the Rainbows' misery, the troops in the Fôret de Fére were visited by the popular American entertainer Elsie Janice, who sang for the soldiers from a broken-down old wagon. One Rainbow fighter remembered her visit: "And into the middle of this filthy backyard of war with its sickening smells and sights and its unkempt, lousy men there bounded Elsie Janice—fluffy, beautiful, piquant—not at all unlike a goddess just stepping out of the clouds for a bit to see what it was all about here below."[1]

There were no diversions for the 67th Field Artillery Brigade, however. Elmer Sherwood would be more than happy to get away from this assignment of supporting the 4th Infantry Division during its attack north toward the Vesle River. The Hoosier artillerymen were losing about a man per day, but the greatest problem was food. "The food we get is punk," Sherwood wrote, "All we had to eat today [10 August] is dried peaches, bacon, and coffee which has been boiled so many times it had lost its original flavor, and worse still, we don't even have enough of this plain bill of fare to satisfy rugged appetites."[2]

Leslie Langille watched as new recruits came into Battery B. Sergeant George Rogers looked over the large number of new, untrained men. One was from Louisiana, a rustic in every sense of the term. Another was an eager lad who had been in the army only six weeks. Ten minutes after Sergeant Rogers welcomed this new man to the unit, the Germans shelled the battery position, and he, so new to the army, so eager to please Rogers, was in an ambulance, critically wounded and on his way to the rear.[3]

The National Guardsmen did not think much of the green 4th Division. The newcomers were not wise to the battlefield, made many mistakes, and seemed unwilling to seek advice from the veteran Rainbow fighters attached to them.

Much to the distress of the Rainbows, the 4th Division decided to quarter its horses and mules directly in back of the artillery positions. The Regular Army lieutenant in charge of horses ignored warnings that German observation balloons would soon see the draft animals and begin firing on them. Not only would a major source of transportation be wiped out, but some enemy artillery shells would invariably fall short, hitting the men of the 149th. Very quickly, enemy artillery opened up, and the Illinois men had had enough of the unexperienced young officer, his horses, and German shells. They dispersed the horses and chased the officer through the woods.[4]

On 11 August, the artillery of the 77th Division began to relieve the 67th Field Artillery Brigade. The Rainbows had heard enough from the men of the Ivy Division, who had taken every opportunity to inform the National Guardsmen that, despite having almost no combat experience, they were the Regulars. The 77th soldiers, on the other hand, were veterans of the trenches and heavy fighting, and since they were almost all New York City men, they felt a kinship to the Rainbow because of the 165th Infantry. Brigadier General Gatley moved his brigade about thirty kilometers south to the Epieds area, where bathing and cleanup took place. Wool uniforms had to be boiled in huge vats to kill the vermin and to clean them of the dirt of a month's bitter campaigning. Very few soldiers got back their original uniforms after they had all been boiled and dried together. Once dry, the uniforms were arranged in piles by sizes, and each doughboy picked one as close to his size as possible. Size labels meant little, because the wool shrunk in the boiling process; consequently fitting was by chance. Underwear, socks, caps and the like went through the same process, although every effort was made to get new or at least clean socks and underwear to the doughboys. Men were fumigated en masse. Hair was cropped very short. Mail, which had not been delivered in over thirty days, was passed out, while officers began the sad duty of informing parents, wives, or loved ones that a soldier had been killed or wounded in the recent battle. Being good artillerymen, they procured a large quantity of liquor, and the exuberance of youth began to replace the fatigue of continual combat.

Calvin Lambert and a few of his 117th Ammunition Train buddies decided to visit some of the small towns on the Marne river on 14 August. When they returned to camp, they found that they had missed a chance to visit Paris on a two-day pass, but it did not matter much. The next day was payday, and Lambert and his friends were destitute. Paris could not be much fun when you are broke, he reasoned.[5]

The division was centered on a chateau and village known as La Ferte-sous-Jourre, where most of the men were content to wash and get clean clothes, a haircut, some hot food, mail, and contraband alcohol. Rations were slow in coming up for the first day, but eating anything without the smell of the battlefield was sheer joy. One early meal consisted of hot coffee, bread, and heavy molasses syrup. An Ohio soldier, Private Jawbone Osborne of the supply

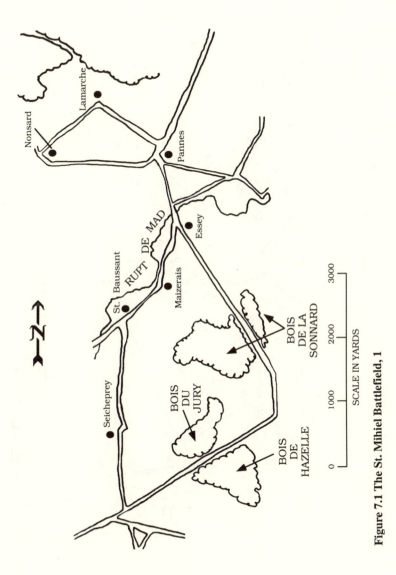

Figure 7.1 The St. Mihiel Battlefield, 1

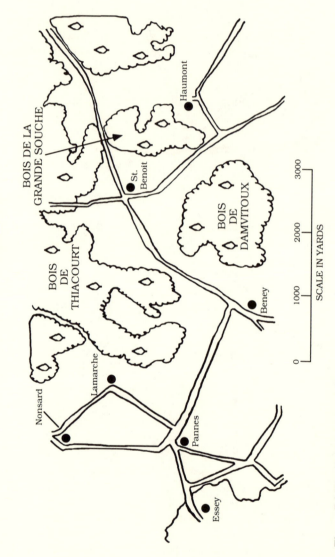

Figure 7.2 The St. Mihiel Battlefield, 2

company, took to the bread and sweet syrup immediately. Unfortunately, bees and flies also like the sweet smell of the syrup, and soon he was surrounded by the buzzing insects. Unable to eat, Jawbone abandoned his mess plate to the flying nuisances, crying out, "Take it, take it, you bastards. You've lived on German deadmen so long your just like the Dutch—dirty, stinking, low down thieves....Take it....damn you."[6]

The Alabamians, who had suffered such fearful losses at the Croix Rouge Farm, began to receive new replacements. Those men who had come from the Western 41st Division a month before were now integrated into the unit or were dead. These new men, however, were poorly trained and had little idea of the rudiments of soldiering, let alone fighting in a major battle. John Hayes of Company I, who had sustained a slight wound, was resting with his comrades when they were approached by soldiers of a quartermaster company stationed nearby to help in the Rainbow wash-up. A number of the supply men wanted to trade positions with Alabamians in the combat regiment. The soldiers of the 167th told the SOS troops they were fools, but when the offer of the trade was made again, no Alabama soldier took advantage of it.[7]

There was a rumor running through the Alabama camp that every soldier would receive a seven-day furlough during his stay of six weeks in the rest area. The enlisted men of the regiment laughed at such a thought, and even though about twenty officers from the 167th visited Paris, most just swam, ate, and prepared for the next fight.[8]

Everett Scott wanted to go to Paris, but he had no money. There were rumors that the 168th would be paid while they were in the rest area, and Scott did want to see the fabled French capital. He spent most of his time resting like the other soldiers, and he wrote to his family a good bit. "I hope," he wrote, "that we never have to go through such a hot time again. I heard a boche prisoner say the other day that the war would be over this fall, but I don't know. I sometimes think it will last forever."[9]

Over half of what was left of the Iowa regiment had diarrhea, contracted while in the unhealthy Fôret de Fére, and there was a critical need to restore those infantrymen to some state of health. Once the 168th was paid, the troops scoured the countryside for fresh vegetables, fruits, bread, and good wine.[10]

Al Ettinger and his New Yorkers also suffered from the lack of funds with which to visit Paris. One of Ettinger's buddies had distant relatives in the French capital, and he prevailed upon his captain for a pass, which was granted. As the soldier explained to Ettinger, he had not the wildest idea where those cousins were in the city. He just wanted to go to Paris to find female company, and would Ettinger join him? Since the paymaster had failed to visit the 165th, a sorrowing Ettinger had to say no and content himself with swims in the Marne River.[11]

Duffy, despite his legendary constitution, was worn out from his continual labors. General Michael Lenihan offered the chaplain a bed, which Duffy accepted, and he slept long into the next morning. Of concern to Duffy, McCoy, and others were the new replacements coming into the Irish 165th. They were mainly from the newly arrived National Army and National Guard divisions, which had been designated as replacement divisions, and few were adequately trained to do the job. Consequently, a four-week program was drawn up to instruct these new arrivals, but time did not allow them to be adequately trained. Immediately, Duffy began to prepare a rigorous religious program, but he was prevailed upon by McCoy and Donovan to rest for a week at the Army hospital at Vittel. Duffy did not protest, and for a week he recuperated, preparing for the next great battle.[12]

Lieutenant Hugh Thompson, once out of the hospital, had a chance to transfer to an Aero Squadron, but something—he really could not describe what—brought him back to the 168th Infantry. Once back with his company, he found that his closest friend had been killed on the Ourcq. He had, in doughboy slang, "gone west." In the last minutes of his life, before starting on the road west, Thompson's friend had had a last message scribbled on a rumpled, stained envelope: "Tell Hughie to tell the folks I died game." Hugh Thompson could no longer see the scrawl; it was a blur from his tears, and he wondered off to be alone with his sorrow.[13]

On 10 August, the 1st American Army was formed with Pershing in command, and on that day a dispatch arrived at Chaumont authorizing Pershing to prepare for the reduction of the St. Mihiel salient. For Pershing, this document was a personal triumph, culminating months of demanding that an American Army be committed to battle as an American force. There had been severe opposition, but the commanding general stuck to his guns and had finally won.[14]

There was good reason to reduce the St. Mihiel salient. It was a huge bulge that protruded into the Allied lines. Donald Smythe noted: "It cut the Paris-Nancy railway and served as a jump-off line for a possible German flanking attack against Verdun to the west or Nancy to the east. It also served as an effective German bulwark against any allied advance against Metz or the vital Briey iron mines."[15] The French had smashed against the St. Mihiel triangle several times during the war, but to little avail. Pershing believed he could take it, straighten out the line, and have American troops ready to participate in the great Meuse-Argonne offensive, which would begin on 26 September. The St. Mihiel salient was twenty-five miles wide and fifteen miles deep, with the town of St. Mihiel only a scant two miles from the line of departure. French troops that participated in the offensive would liberate this town, which had been under German control since 1914. That, the Americans reasoned, was only right and just, but the bulk of the fighting would fall to the U.S. divisions assaulting from the east into the salient.

The 42nd Division became part of the newly organized IV Corps under Lieutenant General Joseph T. Dickman. Dickman, a hard-driving professional, had commanded the 3rd Division, as solid a group of fighters as Pershing had. The corps commander had been an honors graduate from every school he attended and had translated a number of major German military works into English, which marked him as a rare combination of soldier and scholar. The 3rd Division, the "Rock of the Marne," and Dickman had risen to glory during the German's Marne offensive in the summer of 1918, and his leadership marked Dickman for higher command and a third star. In IV Corps was the 1st Division under Charles P. Summerall and the 89th under Major General William M. Wright. Dickman's old 3rd was the Corps Reserve, commanded by Beaumont B. Buck, a solid Regular who had been with Pershing since September 1917.

AEF Headquarters was determined that, when battle was joined on 12 September at 5 A.M., those corps and divisions would have everything they needed to fight. James G. Harbord, now commanding the SOS, worked at a fever pitch to see that supplies and rail lines were ready to support combat operations. In the air, Colonel Billy Mitchell would have 1,476 aircraft, including those observation squadrons dedicated to the divisions.[16]

In military doctrine, the rifleman and the machine gunner, backed up by artillery, were still the heart and soul of victory. Pershing had never changed his mind about that, but as the war went on he saw the need, as did his G3 subordinates Fox Connor and George C. Marshall, for divisions to be tailored for combat missions. Units with specialties had to be attached directly to the division, coming under divisional control to enhance the combat power of the unit. Colonel Fox Connor prepared a list of all troops assigned to 1st U.S. Army on 16 August. These units were parceled out to the Corps, and they enlarged the divisions considerably for the upcoming operation.[17]

The Rainbows received the 90th Aero Squadron and the 3rd Balloon Company as their air assets. The 90th was a respected observation squadron that, when used with the balloonists, could extend the vision of the battlefield many kilometers for the artillery, intelligence, and operational planners. The Rainbow had worked with the highly proficient 12th Aero Squadron before, but had recently had some bad experiences with a French flying unit in the Ourcq fighting. The 90th was well trained and professional, and the 3rd Balloon Company came with a reputation for sustaining continuous days on the line under fire.[18]

AEF Headquarters also assigned to the Rainbows the U.S. 327th Tank Battalion and two battalions of heavy French tanks. They would be under the operational command of a flamboyant tank officer by the name of George S. Patton, who promptly brought himself to Rainbow headquarters and irritated everyone there. The 42nd Division had never worked with any type of tanks before, and the St. Mihiel operation would be a learning experience.

Company A, the first of the 1st Gas and Flame Regiment to reach France in late 1917, was attached to the Rainbow Division for the St. Mihiel operation, adding expertise in smoke and gas offensive capabilities. The company was broken into platoons, and a platoon assigned to each of the brigades for combat, with a platoon held in reserve.

To bolster the artillery capabilities of the Rainbow, the 3rd Division sent two regiments, the 10th and 18th, as well as the 3rd Trench Mortar Battery, which was assigned to Douglas MacArthur's 84th Brigade.[19] The 117th Trench Mortar Battery had never really recovered from the pounding it took in the Champagne defensive, and it was assigned to maintaining ammunition dumps during opening phases of the St. Mihiel offensive.[20] The French 228th Field Artillery Regiment, consisting of nine batteries (twenty-seven pieces) of the light but deadly 75mm howitzers, came to the Rainbows. For all practical purposes, the 42nd Division had just been augmented with another brigade of first-class artillery and could actually assign one brigade to each infantry brigade.

The enlarged 42nd Division moved to a staging area near the town of Bourmont, then shifted about fifteen kilometers north to Neufchâteau on 31 August. Artillery continued to move toward the division's place in the line, but AEF Headquarters had orchestrated the infantry and support moves to avoid congestion on the roads and detection by enemy air observation. Pershing's G3 planners estimated that, once in Neufchâteau, it would take the Rainbow seven days of solid marching to be in attack positions for 12 September. This detailed planning, much of it done by George C. Marshall at AEF Headquarters, applied to all of the AEF units.[21]

The Rainbow would go into the St. Mihiel operation with two new regimental commanders. Colonel Frank McCoy of the 165th was promoted to brigadier general and left the division. His place was taken by Colonel Harry D. Mitchell. Donovan was considered for the promotion, but he argued against his elevation, prevailing upon the outgoing McCoy to secure the command for Mitchell.[22] The other change was far less happy for everyone concerned. Colonel Edward R. Bennett, commander of the Iowa 168th Infantry, left for the United States in early September, turning command over to the reliable Lieutenant Colonel Mathew A. Tinley.

Bennett had been associated with the old 3rd Iowa from the time of the Spanish-American War. Both he and Tinley were subalterns in the 51st Iowa Regiment when it went to the Philippines in 1898. The regiment had a good combat record, and upon returning to Iowa both Bennett and Tinley remained in the National Guard. When the 3rd Iowa, now 168th, was called to the colors in the summer of 1917, Bennett was selected to command it, with Tinley as second-in-command.

Bennett's attitude toward the Regular Army soured in February 1918, when he obtained a copy of an inspection report filed by Major General A. W. Brewster stating that Bennett and Benson Hough of the 166th Ohio were of "doubtful ability" and should be replaced by competent Regular officers. From then on, the situation festered.

Contrary to censorship and operational security directives, Bennett kept an extensive personal diary that detailed the service of his regiment and his very personal feelings, especially about the Regulars at AEF Headquarters in Chaumont. On 15 June, Bennett gave his diary, letters, and other papers to First Lieutenant Charles Tillotson of the 168th, who was returning to the United

States.   While on board the USS *Henderson*, the documents came into the possession of U.S. Naval Intelligence, which sent them to G2, AEF, at Chaumont. Pershing was furious, and ordered that an investigation be held.

Bennett was scathing in his remarks about the Regulars. He wrote:

There is one regular division over here officered mostly by reserve officers; there will be no more regular troops in France so long as there are other troops in the US to come. They will remain at training camps and at bases in France, but not at the front. The N.G. which the army is seeking to destroy will all be sent and the volunteer soldier as in past wars will bear it all. How long will the people stand for the regular army with all its inefficiency, cheap aristocracy and arrogance.[23]

Menoher was a Regular Army officer, but returned the report without taking disciplinary action. The Rainbow commanding general pointed out that Bennett's regiment had been one of the best within the division, and he never manifested any sense of criticism in his regiment or at divisional headquarters.[23]   At any rate, there were elements of truth in Bennett's criticisms of the Regular Army's treatment of Guard units in the AEF. Bennett had been suffering from severe influenza for some time, and in early September he turned over command of the 168th to Tinley.[24]

On 4 September, the division moved north again, arriving at Colombey-les-Belles on 6 September. Two days later, the troops moved north of Toul, where they waited until 10 September. On the night of 10 September, the division moved into the Fôret de la Reine. While getting into position, the Rainbows saw other troops moving into the woods. A Rainbow soldier asked, "What outfit do you belong to?"

The response came back, "First Division, Regulars."

There was a brief silence, and then the Rainbow soldier called out, "I asked what your number was, not your handicap."[25]

While moving the division to the start point of the attack, the staff had to wrestle with some monumental problems. Lieutenant Colonel Murphy, while a West Point graduate and a veteran soldier, had just recently been a Red Cross official. Now he was dealing with operational matters, and while he did it well, his concerns were magnified by his time away from the army. To complicate his situation, he had to deal with an aggravating George S. Patton. Patton, who had arrived in France with Pershing in the fall of 1917, had a plan to present to Murphy and to Hughes concerning the deployment of his machines. It was well thought out, and would have helped the hard-pressed staff if Patton had stopped there.

Patton had been in command of the 1st Brigade of Tanks since 20 August, and he had worked hard to put the plan together.[26]   Mainly, the 84th Infantry Brigade would get the U.S. 327th Tank Battalion of forty-nine light Renault tanks. The 83rd Brigade would get the two groups of thirty-three heavy French tanks, operated by Frenchmen. The tanks would lead the assault because, as Patton stated, they could cut wire and take out obstacles. The light Renaults would cover about 1,000 meters of frontage and advance in two wedge formations. In a second echelon would be two tank companies, with two more tank companies in reserve.[27]

There were few complaints or questions from either Menoher, Murphy, or Hughes, since they had never worked with tanks before. They seemed content to adopt Patton's plan of 7 September. Hughes issued a template for study to Lenihan and MacArthur, who were also inexperienced with tanks.[28] Murphy, who was deeply involved in planning, appeared to Patton to be inattentive and unsympathetic to some of his requests. Patton requested special engineer support if the tanks were to cross the Rupt de Mad River and continue operations. He also stated that he needed one airplane to hunt for anti-tank guns. In addition, the tank commander asked for a battery of 75mm guns, "whose sole duty is to get the range of probable localities of anti-tank guns." To cap this off, he asked for special smoke requirements to be added to the divisional fire and smoke plans.[29]

Now it was the older Murphy's turn to take exception to Patton. Murphy stated that under no circumstances could Patton's smoke request be included in the fire support plan for the division's attack. The large number of stencils required to publish the orders had been finished, and frankly, Murphy was now tired of these special requests. The problems associated with putting out a divisional order in World War I were tremendous. Stencil machines were new, and in comparison to later, sophisticated reproduction machines, they were primitive and difficult to maintain in a combat field environment. Murphy had to reproduce an entire division order, with all its annexes, and get them to the subordinate units in a timely manner for the brigades to study the order and then issue their orders to the battalions. Battalions, in turn, had to repeat the process for their companies. Patton, in his zeal to push his special requests, had overstepped himself. By his own count, he had eighty-two tanks plus his tank repair unit and supply. Murphy was working on detailed plans, with a definite time limit, for a division of 28,000 troops plus attachments.

Since the 83rd Brigade would be the first to encounter the Rupt de Mad, Patton sought out Brigadier Lenihan, who listened politely but could do nothing to help. Patton was still fuming over Murphy's rejection, and he confided to his diary: "Maj [sic] Murphy told me he could not put smoke in plan as stencil was already cut. The biggest fool remark I ever heard showing just what an S.O.B. the late chief of Red Cross is."[30]

But Patton was not through. He sent another memo to Murphy stating that, in his opinion, the practice maneuver of some troops with tanks was unsatisfactory. To remedy this, Patton wrote, "recomend that Tank Officers of 327 Bn with 42 Div. be allowed to give brief lectures to platoon and company officers of the assault Bns. 42 div. No other means of training is available. This will be better than nothing."[31] Evidently, Murphy ignored this missive as well and went on with his detailed planning.

The Rainbow's plan of attack was predicated on the linear nature of the section of the battl_field allocated to it by IV Corps. It was just about two miles wide, a very long rectangle. The most critical natural terrain feature was the Rupt de Mad River, which normally was not wide, but rain was now constantly falling. The Rainbow's mission was basically a simple one on paper. The division was to cross the line of departure at 5 A.M., reach the high ground just north of the Rupt de Mad within six hours, and then strike north to a line running from the towns of Thiaucourt on the right to Nonsard on the left. While both towns were outside the Rainbow's area of operation, a key road junction at the town of Pannes, about three and a half miles from the line of departure, had to be taken. From Pannes to the objective line for the day was another two miles.

From observation and prisoner interrogation, the G2 of AEF had a good picture of what faced the doughboys as they attacked. An analysis of the area showed that the German defenses were in three belts, with the strongest wire and obstacles forward, closest to the line of departure. Once through those initial defenses, the Americans could expect to find a series of continually weaker wire obstacles and trenches. G2 of AEF expected the town of Pannes to be defended because it was a German supply and communications center. Once through the initial defenses and past Pannes, the Woëvre Plain offered rapid advance and good fields of fire. On the reverse, once past Pannes, cover and concealment became less available for the attacking Americans. Throughout the area were heavy woods, lakes, streams, and of course, the Rupt de Mad River.[32] The task for the Rainbow, then, was not simple, but the possibility of a bloodbath such as the one on the Ourcq was less. No one could tell what condition roads and fields would be in, since the rains were falling heavily as the hour for the attack to begin (5 A.M., 12 September) drew near and there appeared to be no real let-up in sight. What effect that would have on aircraft, balloons, or Patton's tanks remained to be seen.

In another report on the enemy situation, the AEF G2 was on target in assessing German capabilities in the St. Mihiel salient. Just before the start of the action, the analysts believed that the Germans were not making an attempt to reinforce in the salient; neither did they appear to have any intention of doing so. However, the G2 estimated that the Germans could fight a stiff delaying action with only machine guns and artillery.[33]

The basic operational plan for the Rainbows was a good one, taking advantage of the attachments while being very much aware of the narrow frontage assigned to the division. The rectangle was divided between brigades, with MacArthur's 84th on the right and Lenihan's 83rd on the left as the division faced the line of departure. The terrain and frontage dictated that the division attack in a column of battalions, each brigade having two battalions in the first echelon, two in the second, and a single battalion in the third echelon or brigade reserve. The division would assault, then, with four battalions on line. Each brigade got a part of the 117th Engineers, a battery of 75mm guns, and a platoon of Company A, 1st Gas and Flame. Probably one of Murphy's irritations with

Patton was that 75mm guns and smoke, through the gas and flame platoons, were already assigned to the brigades. Patton's battalion of light Renault tanks would be with MacArthur, and would assist the 84th in the woods directly to his front.[34] The heavier French tanks, under the capable command of Major Charles M. Chanoine, would be with Lenihan. In fact, Chanoine, who arrived just before start time, made very detailed liaison with Lenihan and his staff. His battle plan was just as detailed as Patton's, but was more specific as to the teamwork between his heavy tanks and the 83rd Brigade.[35]

Within the brigades, the battle array was well thought out. In the 84th Brigade, the 1st Battalion of the 167th would be on the left and the 1st Battalion of the 168th would be on the right. They would advance, with tanks, on line with each other. The second echelon consisted of the 2nd Battalion of the 167th on the left and the 2nd of the 168th on the right. The reserve, or third echelon battalion, was the 3rd of the 167th. The 3rd of the 168th became the divisional reserve.

Lenihan's dispositions were a mirror of MacArthur's. In the first echelon, from left to right, was the 3rd Battalion of the 166th, and next to it was Donovan's 1st Battalion of the 165th. On line with the second echelon Lenihan arrayed, left to right, the 1st of the 166th and the 2nd of the 165th. The badly battered 3rd Battalion, still not fully recovered from the Ourcq bloodletting, was the brigade reserve. The 2nd Ohio Battalion went to the divisional reserve.[36]

Medic Stewart remembered the final night march, starting on the evening of 11 September, that brought them to the start point. The only guide he had to find the first aid station was a wire strung in the trees. The night was pitch black, and a steady rain fell, turning the ground into soupy mud.[37] The 117th Engineers had run tape to every battalion position, and despite the weather, troops got into line. But even more serious work was awaiting the engineers. Companies D and F would precede the attack, cutting the enemy wire to open lanes through which the attacking Alabamians and Iowans would surge.[38] Two other companies would do the same for the New Yorkers and the Ohioans.

Father Duffy was concerned that the leg wound Father Hanley sustained on the Ourcq had not healed, and, over Hanley's serious and loud protests, he assigned the recuperating priest to the triage unit in the rear. When Duffy returned to the 165th's PC just hours before the attack began, he found two chaplains waiting for him. One was an Irish priest, another a Methodist minister, and Duffy was glad to see them. The move, accomplished without serious injuries in the black of night and in a torrential downpour, seemed to Duffy to be a miracle.[39]

For Iowa's 168th, the confusion of the night led to near tragedy. Scouts and guides of the lead companies had overshot their assault trenches and crossed into No Man's Land. They had almost reached German outposts in the Bois de Jury, a thick woods that would soon be engulfed by the American's four-hour-long barrage. Quietly and quickly the lost units found their way back to the 168th's start point, just in time. The bombardment began at 1 A.M.[40]

While the artillery swept the front, Charles MacArthur and his fellow gunners were right behind Bill Donovan's Irishmen on the front line. He was in the battery of three 75mm guns that were to support the infantry with point-blank fire. They would go "over the top" with the doughboys of the 83rd Brigade, manhandling their guns across No Man's Land in support of the attack. MacArthur was in this situation because he had volunteered. When his battery commander received the order to support the assault battalion, he called for volunteers. Every man in the unit stepped forward. MacArthur recalled, "The response was unanimous. That's the worst part of a call for volunteers. It takes more courage to say No than Yes." Consequently, he was sitting in a muddy hole, rain falling in torrents, watching the Irishmen begin preparations to advance.[41]

Leslie Langille was in the rear, his guns joining in with the terrific Allied bombardment of German positions. His mind, however, was on the doughnuts, hot coffee, and pancakes handed out to his battery by the stalwart women of the Salvation Army. When the doughboys offered to pay for those small comforts, the women refused, and the hot coffee and cakes were deeply appreciated.[42]

While the guns roared into the night, problems were developing for the Rainbow Division. Over 25 percent of the vehicles of the Texas 117th Supply Train and the 117th Kansas Ammunition Train were hopelessly stuck in the sea of mud that several days of relentless rain had created. A vast number of men were engaged in digging those wagons and trucks out, and as soon as one vehicle got out another stuck.[43]

Calvin Lambert was having a hard time keeping his trucks on the road, but he felt truly sorry for "the mule drivers these black nights. We hear them along the corduroy road, swearing, slipping and floundering among the branches of the trees and in the deep mud holes. Our truck drivers have a tough time but the horse section catches real hell."[44]

Lieutenant van Dolsen and the other medical personnel of the 117th Sanitary Train were also in position on that rainy night, and they were located on a decent road network. There were two roads running from the hospital area at Ansauville, a town about seven kilometers from the divisional line of departure. These two roads ran as far as the town of Maizerais, just south of the critical objective of Pannes. At least, it was believed, the wounded could be evacuated with more facility than during the Marne fight.[45] It turned out, however, that the roads so depended upon by the ambulances were obliterated by the heavy artillery barrage of 12 September. It was indeed fortunate that casualties were light on 12 September, and the advance was so rapid that the field hospitals and triage section were able to move to the towns of Essey and Maizerais on 13 September.

Everything that could be done had been done. Lieutenant Colonel Murphy had been informed in writing that, prior to the start of the artillery fire, all units were in their attack positions and liaison, via wire or messenger, had been established.[46] Douglas MacArthur, true to form, was in the front trench, ready to lead his men over the top into the Bois de Jury and then into the larger Bois de la Sonnard.[47] Everyone remembered the attacks through the Fôret de Fére and Fôret de Nesles, and these woods looked equally formidable.

At 5 A.M. the artillery stopped and the Rainbow surged forward with its wire cutters in the lead. Patton's tanks, under the command of Captain Ranulf Compton and French Major Chanoine, were having a very difficult time. The severe rains of the past five days and the heavy artillery bombardment left the terrain in No Main's Land a mass of water-filled shell-holes and seas of mud. The tanks were getting stuck and the majority of the iron monsters were of little value to the advancing doughboys. Several French tanks were assisting the advance of Lenihan's 83rd Brigade, and twelve of the light Renaults with MacArthur's 84th Brigade were firing at machine gun nests in the woods. Probably in an ill humor, Patton informed Murphy, "Smoke screen excellent."[48]

Company A of the 1st Gas and Flame Regiment, under the command of Captain Walter F. Pond, had planned its first day's operation quite well. The company had eight four-inch Stokes Mortars to deliver the smoke rounds. Pond divided them equally, and his men were firing with great effect. The heavy, moist air kept the smoke low to the ground, and since there was little wind that day, Pond's Gas and Flame gunners could work effectively. When Captain Pond submitted his support plan to Murphy, he stated that as soon as infantry had moved beyond the range of the Stokes Mortars, his men would dismantle the guns and go forward as well. Pond did not envision the problem presented by the weight of the mortars in such muddy, torn-up ground as they had before them. There was no transportation to move quantities of ammunition, and after the first hours of fighting the company was of very little use to the Rainbows. Pond's troops would get into the fight again, but their effect was minimal.[49]

The heaviest fighting that morning was in the devastated Bois de la Sonnard in front of MacArthur's Alabamians and Iowans. The Alabamians looked out over the field, and First Lieutenant John M. Bryan of the 167th's Mortar Platoon remarked, "An attack under the existing circumstances would certainly be a failure unless the High Command used submarines for tanks, ducks for carrier-pigeons, and alligators for soldiers."[50] Since there were no alligators available, the 1st Battalion, 167th, moved into No Man's Land, followed by Joe Romano and John Hayes with the 2nd Battalion. Major Robert Joerg, Jr. brought his men into No Man's Land, following an artillery barrage, moving at the prescribed 100 yards every three minutes. The wire cutters found an agreeable surprise. The Germans had not noticed that their barbed wire had grown rusty and brittle during the years of being in a quiet zone. Much of the wire had already been broken when the cutters and the 1st Battalion reached it.[51]

Hugh Thompson was in the second line with the 2nd Battalion, about a thousand yards behind the lead battalion. Through the forward trenches where the 1st Battalion had been only a few minutes before, and then out into No Man's Land, "the line took up its march behind a curtain of smoke and flame....On, on I floated, hardly conscious of the woodpeckers whose rat-tat-tat hammered duly above the terrifying shells. The barrage crept down the hill. I floated on in a fantastic trance unmindful of the angry wasps that droned past my ears."[52]

The rolling barrage swept the Bois de la Sonnard as the Iowans came on, but many Germans had survived the maelstrom of shot and shell. Once the storm of hot steel and iron had passed, the remaining Germans rushed to their posts and poured heavy fire into the advancing Americans. Wire-cutters had the first men through the remaining German barbed obstacles. The 2nd Battalion was in the wire. Almost every officer in Company M was hit and down. Thompson, with Company L, came through the wire and ran at the German positions. Second Lieutenant Karl Wheeler, a newcomer to Company L, went down with a mortal wound.[53] Thompson knew that his men were in a very hot spot, but they had to move through the German wire. He rushed into the broken wire with an automatic rifleman firing as they advanced. Suddenly he saw the soldier fall face down in the wire, his helmet riddled with machine-gun rounds. The Germans were firing rapidly now, and Thompson felt an unbelievable pain in his legs. He had also been hit by a German machine-gun round, and his right hip was shattered. Thompson had received his third wound, and would never return to the Rainbow Division.[54]

Major Guy Brewer, commanding 2nd Battalion of the 168th, was wounded about mid-morning, and Company M had no officers left. In Company K, Sergeant Leo McHugh stepped forward to command the second platoon, but he was killed and a corporal assumed control. Lieutenant William D. Doty, newly commissioned and in his first fight, led his fourth platoon out of the wire and into the woods. He was killed instantly when struck by shrapnel. The 168th was bleeding itself to death as it had done on the Ourcq.[55]

Fate had put the 168th in the worst possible place in the woods, but the Germans were reaching the end of their rope as well. Germans began to surrender, some after a fight, some with no fight at all. Private Terry Shafer of Company M entered a dugout and saw what he believed to be fellow Iowans. He asked out loud if anyone had a cigarette, and to his surprise five German soldiers surrendered. Iowa's haul in prisoners that day was probably over 900. Escorting prisoners from the field was Private William J. Grenlauch of the headquarters company. He saw a German soldier wearing a belt buckle with his family name engraved on it, took him aside, and found that he was face to face with a first cousin he had never met.[56]

On the left of the line, Wild Bill Donovan led his men with panache. All during the bombardment he moved from group to group, reassuring his soldiers that this fight would be easy, not like the Ourcq. The rush of the 165th into the Bois de Remières was rapid. When machine guns began to fire, the Irishmen, who had learned their lessons well on the Ourcq, flopped to the ground, began to crawl, and dispatched the guns one by one. Once the deadly guns were silent, Donovan and his men were up again. He was going at break-neck speed for the Rupt de Mad River. The Germans now tried to organize a defense in the little town of Maizerais, on the high ground just north of the river. Donovan could not wait and give the enemy time to set up more of the deadly machine guns. Leading thirty men into the small river, they dashed across and came up the hill on the German flanks. At that point the Germans began "Kamerading," giving up to the Irishmen. Maizerais was now in American hands, and Donovan was prepared to push on to the village of Essey before the enemy could put together a resistance there.[57]

Al Ettinger came face to face with what war meant in Maizerais. French families who had lived under the German occupation since 1914 poured into the streets to joyously welcome their liberators. Many of the families brought out what meager provisions they had and tried to share it with the Americans, who were more intent on looting German beer supplies. Officers had a difficult time with the souvenir-hunting doughboys caught up with the euphoria of the moment.[58]

The battered Shamrock Battalion was in the third wave, and Martin Hogan was more than happy that this advance seemed less like a major offensive than a cake walk, with a steady stream of German prisoners going to the rear.[59]

Douglas MacArthur was also astonished at the rapidity of the American attack. In Essey he saw the unmistakable signs of a retreat in panic. An officer's horse was fully saddled in a barn, a complete battery of artillery was abandoned, and members of a German regimental band had fled without their instruments.[60] Colonel Benson Hough's Ohio soldiers experienced as easy an advance as did Donovan's battalion. The opposition was almost nonexistent on the extreme left. What little opposition there was to the Ohio advance was quickly dispatched by Chanoine's tanks and Ohio's 3rd Battalion.[61] With the cumbersome tanks moving in support, Hough's Ohioans almost felt that they were on a Sunday stroll. Directly in front of them was the village of St. Baussant, about two kilometers from the 166th's line of departure. There was a trench just outside of the town, and as the doughboys approached, several German machine guns began to fire, contesting their advance. Rather than pit man against machine gun, the 2nd Battalion commander brought up the mortars of the regiment, which went into action, lobbing eight shells into the trench. The Germans, in an uncharacteristic move, abandoned their positions and fled to the north, leaving their machine guns. Company I captured the three German machine guns with few casualties. St. Baussant appeared also to be deserted by the enemy, and the 166th bypassed it, leaving only Company M to secure the town.[62]

Colonel Hough had a present. Company I had sent a patrol in the direction of Pannes that came upon a German major and his orderly ready to mount two fine-looking horses. They did not escape the Ohio doughboys, who took them prisoner, confiscated the horses and equipment, marched the two prisoners away, and presented the steeds to Colonel Hough as a memento of the day's advance.[63]

By 2 P.M. the doughboys entered Pannes and moved quickly to the line that marked the first day's advance. Three units converged on Pannes at once, and elements of the 167th and 166th enveloped the town, while Donovan led his men into it.[64] Donovan's men, while being kissed and cheered by the French, made a dash for the German billets to find souvenirs of any sort. Even Donovan grabbed a handful of letters from a German officers' military post box.[65] Lieutenant Colonel Alexander Anderson, commanding the 2nd Battalion of the 165th, found that his men had liberated a large barrel of German beer and were about to break into it. Anderson smashed the barrel, much to the consternation of his thirsty Irishmen.

By 3 P.M. Patton's tankers were on the scene, having moved with difficulty over the shell-pocked roads and fields. General Lenihan was ready to push on, as was MacArthur. After a brief discussion with the infantry brigade commanders, the French tanks again moved with the 83rd Brigade, and the American Renaults pushed on with the 84th Brigade beyond the objective line of the day.[66] When the tanks entered Pannes, they found thirty Germans and took them prisoner. Lenihan was anxious to press the advantage, and late in the afternoon the 83rd Brigade, with tank support, moved on the town of La Marche, which was beyond the objective line.[67]

There were problems, however, with such a pell-mell advance. The brigades were short of ammunition, and they had outrun much of their artillery support. It would take time to move the guns forward in the rain, over such terrain. The 89th Division had found its movement to be slowed because of terrain and enemy resistance. While the "Rolling Ws" were moving and taking prisoners, they had not been able to maintain contact with the 42nd Division. A gap was beginning to open up between the two divisions, and that could invite disaster. There had been disorganization as the doughboys looted German billets and warehouses. Consequently, the division halted, ready to attack north on the morning of 13 September. It had been a good day. A number of Rainbow doughboys sported brand-new German officers' boots that night.

The morning of 13 September was misty and wet, but the Rainbows moved on through La March and then cautiously through the woods to the north, the Bois de Thiaucourt. The objective was St. Benôit-en-Woëvre and then the woods bordering a main road from St. Benôit to Woël, a critical rail junction.

Moving across the fields that morning in a horse-drawn cart was Ohio medic Private George A. Dennis. He had been ordered to bring up critical medical supplies on the possibility that the 13th could produce sharp fighting and casualties. Cautiously, Dennis entered St. Benôit and set up shop in a wine cellar, hanging out his Red Cross flag. Thirty minutes or so later, he saw doughboys in the town and reported to Lieutenant Frank Radcliff of the battalion machine gun company. Radcliff was astounded to find out that an Ohio medic had preceded the infantry into the town.[68] St. Benôit-en-Woëvre had initially been taken by an unarmed medic advancing in a one-horse cart.

Colonel George Leach, commanding the Gopher Gunners, watched in sorrow as the civilians vacated Pannes and Essey for safety in the rear. "Men, women, and children," the Minnesota officer recalled, "plodded along in the mud up to their knees, carrying what little household effects they could, and they presented the most forlorn sight I have ever seen."[69]

By the end of 13 September, the Americans had taken all of their objectives before the scheduled time and were north of the woods, which they had discovered was full of German equipment and weapons, but no infantry or machine gunners. Casualties for that day were minimal. The Rainbows had driven to the end of the salient, and the possibilities were glittering. Only twenty miles away was the city of Metz. With the Germans in such confusion, reeling from the rapid American advance, which was being pressed on several fronts, the question was raised: Why not march on and take this major French city, which had been under German occupation since 1914? Certainly, MacArthur believed that this was a golden opportunity for the AEF. According to MacArthur, he and his brigade adjutant Major Walter B. Wolf, made a reconnaissance near the city and felt that it could be taken from the confused enemy rather quickly. He urged that the 84th Brigade be put on the road to move against the city.[70]

IV Corps and 1st Army flatly rejected any move on Metz, and with good reason. The St. Mihiel operation had proceeded so rapidly that American planners were surprised. As professional soldiers they knew from their training that the best time to counter-attack an enemy was when he was flush with victory, but still disorganized after the assault. In hindsight, both Dickman and Pershing had second thoughts about their decision not to drive on Metz.[71] But at that point, to put one division on the road piecemeal while ignoring the need to orchestrate such a move with all available forces would have been irresponsible, especially in an army so new to conducting an offensive operation.

On 14 September, the 67th Artillery Brigade and attached artillery began shifting forward and had a very difficult time moving in the mud- and water-filled shell holes. The guns would be slow in joining the infantry.[72] The sun broke through on the morning of 14 September, but the fields remained swamps. Metz faded from the mind, and the Rainbow settled into a routine of relative inaction from 14 September to 1 October, just prior to the Meuse-Argonne operation. This period was known as the Essay-Pannes sector, and it gave the Rainbows time to prepare for their last great battle.

MacArthur's 84th Brigade became responsible for the line just north of the Bois de la Grand Souché, with the 167th taking the furthermost positions. The 83rd Brigade moved back into a reserve position, while the 1st Battalion of the 150th and the entire 151st Field Artillery Regiment were assigned to the 89th Division for continued operations.[73] MacArthur moved into the Chateau de Saint Benôit, where he enjoyed life until German artillery totally destroyed it on 23 September.[74] The Iowans and the Alabamians conducted a series of very aggressive patrols and raids while in this relatively quiet sector. The 3rd Balloon Company was moved up to Maizerais, where it remained for several days. Since the weather had changed for the better on 14 September, the balloon observers were able to keep a close eye on the Germans and rendered important service to the artillery. On 16 September, for example, the 3rd Balloon Company adjusted fire for the artillery 118 times. The G2 of the division was also a direct beneficiary of this long-range observation, and balloon information helped confirm an enemy presence in several areas in front of the Rainbow.[75] This information led to a highly successful raid carried out by the 167th Infantry on the village of Haumont on 16 September, and a raid on the night of 21 September when the Iowans hit the Germans in the fortified Marimbois Farm just south of the town of Dampvitoux, two miles from the 84th Brigade lines.

The relationship of the Rainbow and the 90th Aero Squadron was also generally good. However, every Aero Squadron assigned to IV Corps for observation and artillery spotting during the St. Mihiel offensive reported having grave difficulty establishing communications with the artillery. They complained that when messages were communicated or dropped near artillery PCs, they were ignored. Major L. H. Bereton, commanding the 1st Army's Observation Wing, felt that much of the responsibility rested with partially trained crews on observation aircraft and a lack of training on the part of ground forces to respond to aircraft.[76]

Menoher was basically unsympathetic to the Air Service's complaints. Menoher, who would become chief of the Air Service, believed that the infantryman was "the real hero, the real ace of aces in this war game. So in the air game the observer is the one for whom all others in the Air Service are but servants....He is the one who fulfills the primary function of the Air Service—to be the eyes of the Army."[77] The relationship, then, of the Rainbow's commander to the Balloon Service observers was basically more cordial than that of the Air Service flier. It is interesting that when Menoher's after-action report was written for Dickman's staff, the general never mentioned air or balloon support during the St. Mihiel operation.[78]

The one officer who appreciated and cited the Air Service was Lieutenant Colonel Ruby Garnett, the Rainbow signal officer, the man responsible for communications and for the work of the Missouri 117th Field Signal Battalion. Like the Air Service, the signals represented new and far-reaching battlefield technology. His observations, made to Menoher, Hughes, and Murphy, cover some of the achievements and difficulties in employing signal equipment. The initial plan, which was implemented, called for the establishment of telephone wire and hookups between division and the combat brigades. The regiments were linked into the brigade PC by telephone. The regimental signal men went into action with the regimental commander, carrying heavy amounts of wire on their backs. Before World War I, commanders had never had such communications with units in combat, and this new technology had the potential of giving to divisional, corps, and army commanders immediate information covering areas unheard of before, and rapid decision-disseminating capabilities.

There were problems involved in keeping the signals operational. Most heavy, large spools of wire, equipment, and tools had to be conveyed in hand-drawn or horse-drawn carts. Priority of road movement went to artillery, ambulances, and ammunition resupply. The signals' carts were forced off the road into fields where movement was slow, and often carts got stuck. In any future operation, the signals would have to be able to use the roads as an equal partner with the infantry and the artillery. Also, the tanks, once they were able to get into the fight, rolled over and tore out large sections of telephone lines.

When the initial signal plan was submitted to Murphy, it was envisioned that brigade commanders would be in their PCs, close to telephones linking them with their regiments and to the divisional PC. MacArthur went forward with the initial assaulting battalions, and he had no way of knowing what messages were coming into the 84th Brigade PC. As the battle and advance progressed, the signal troops rigged a telephone for MacArthur by splicing into the main line, which ran through the 167th Regiment's sector. It was not ideal, but at least the brigade commander could know what was going on in all of his brigade rather than just a very small portion of the lead assaulting battalion.

The original plan, submitted by Garnett, established radio communications with "regiments, brigades, and division, and from division to corps and to air service." The radio sets following the regiments and brigades got bogged down in mud and traffic jams and did not catch up with their units for several days. The use of radio was ignored at times by the division headquarters. Since signals had the primary responsibility of maintaining contact with the air, Garnett wrote that the relationship was good, and messages dropped from the 90th Aero Squadron were communicated quickly. All in all, the division signal officer believed that much was learned about the integration of signals with an infantry division during a rapid advance in a war of maneuver.[79]

When one looks at the after-action report filed by Lieutenant Colonel Garnett, and a similar report filed by the 90th Aero Squadron, it becomes difficult to understand Menoher's ambivalent feelings toward the contribution of the Air Service. On 12 September, the 90th flew twenty four sorties, often at only 200-meters above the ground. Between 13 and 16 September, an equal number of sorties were flown, and, according to the report by the 90th, many of these resulted in good information being relayed to Rainbow headquarters, where the 90th had established an Air Service liaison officer from the squadron.[80]

The St. Mihiel offensive had not been costly for the Rainbows. The division had suffered 1,214 casualties, with the highest number coming in the 168th Iowa. The losses in equipment, weapons, and supplies were minimal, and the time between 16 and 30 September gave the men a chance to rest, refit, and prepare for the next operation. When the Rainbows left the Essey-Pannes sector, they could count 26,792 soldiers present for duty.[81]

On 29 September 1918, a messenger from AEF Headquarters delivered a secret set of orders to Menoher. The Rainbow division was to begin moving from the Essey-Pannes sector toward the Argonne, where it would temporarily become the 1st Army Reserve Division.[82] The 89th Division would assume responsibility for the sector by 1 October. That day the infantry was to board trucks and vehicles and begin moving toward the town of Souilly, where it would pass from the IV Corps to the operational control of the V Corps. As soldiers boarded the vehicles, driven by the exotic-looking Indochinese, many sensed that they were on their way to what would be, perhaps, the last battle of the war. They had seen the first real evidence of breaks in German morale and the results of war-weariness. They saw the large number of young Germans, many only boys, that simply surrendered in the wake of the relentless American attack. The Rainbows faced the future, not with anticipation, but with a fatalism and a hope that this might be the last great struggle.

NOTES

1. Raymond S. Thompkins, *The Story of the Rainbow Division* (New York: Boni and Liveright, 1919), 95.

2. Elmer W. Sherwood, *Diary of a Rainbow Veteran: Written at the Front* (Terre Haute, Ind.: Moore-Langen, 1929), 65.

3. Leslie Langille, *Men of the Rainbow* (Chicago: O'Sullivan Co., 1933), 119.

4. Charles MacArthur, *War Bugs* (Garden City, N.Y.: Doubleday, Doran and Co., 1929), 116.

5. Calvin Lambert Diary, manuscript, Emporia Public Library, Emporia, Kansas, 190.

6. R.M. Cheseldine, *Ohio in the Rainbow: Official Story of the 166th Infantry, 42nd Division in the World War* (Columbia, Ohio: F.J. Heer Printing Co., 1924), 220.

7. John B. Hayes, *Heroes Among the Brave* (Loachapoka, Ala.: Lee County Historical Society, 1973), 32-33.

8. William B. Amerine, *Alabama's Own in France* (New York: Eaton and Gettinger, 1919), 165-66.

9. Scott to his mother and brother, np, 7 August and 21 August 1918, Scott Letters, manuscripts in the author's collection.

10. John H. Taber, *The Story of the 168th Infantry* (Iowa City: State Historical Society of Iowa, 1925), 43, 51-52.

11. A. Churchill Ettinger, *A Doughboy with the Fighting 69th* (Shippensburg, PA: White Main Publishing, 1992), 141-42.

12. Francis P. Duffy, *Father Duffy's Story* (New York: George H. Doran Co., 1919), 228-29.

13. Hugh S. Thompson, "Following the Rainbow," *The Chattanooga Times*, 22 April 1934.

14. John J. Pershing, *My Experiences in the World War* (New York: Frederick A. Stokes Co., 1931), Vol. 2, 225-32. James G. Harbord, *The American Army in France, 1917-1919* (Boston: Little, Brown and Co., 1936), 416-20.

15. Donald Smythe, *Pershing: General of the Armies* (Bloomington, Ind.: Indiana University Press, 1986), 179.

16. William "Billy" Mitchell, *Memoirs of World War One* (New York: Random House, 1960), 238-39.

17. AEF Headquarters, G3, Memorandum by Colonel Fox Connor, 16 August 1918, in U.S. Army, Center for Military History, *The United States Army in the World War* (Washington: Government Printing Office, 1989), Vol. 8, 131-41 (hereinafter, CMH).

18. Air Service, AEF, "Battle Participation of the Air Service," AEF, U.S.

Squadrons (1918) in U.S. Air Force Historical Agency Archives, Maxwell AFB, Ala., File 167.401-19, (hereinafter, AFHA). First Lieutenant S.W. Ovitt, *The Balloon Section of the American Expeditionary Force* (1919), 66-67, ibid., File 167.401-22.

19. Peter H. Ottosen, *Trench Artillery AEF* (Boston: Lothrop, Lee and Shepard, 1931), 126.

20. Ibid., 104-5.

21. 1st Army, AEF, "Plan of Concentration," 29 August 1918, in CMH, *The United States Army in the World War*, Vol. 8, 169-71.

22. Duffy, *Story*, 228-29.

23. Papers relating to "Report of Investigation of Field Censorship Regulations Violations by Colonel E.R. Bennett, 166th Infantry," 31 August 1918, in the National Archives, Washington, D.C., *Records Group 120 Records of the AEF, 42nd Division*, carton 57, (hereinafter, RG 120).

24. Chaplain Winifred E. Robb, *The Price of Our Heritage: In Memory of the Heroic Dead of the 168th Infantry* (Des Moines, Iowa: American Lithographing and Printing Co., 1919), 20-25. The official history of the 168th is silent about the change of command. Taber's *The Story of the 168th Infantry*, Vol. 2, indicates that Bennett left the regiment after the protests over the "tragic thirtieth," but this does not appear to be the case (20-21). It does seem more likely that the bloodshed on the Ourcq, coupled with continual influenza and the incident over the diary and letters, brought about the change in the Iowa regiment.

25. Ogden to his wife, np, 15 September 1918, in Major Hugh W. Ogden Letters, U.S. Army Military History Institute Archives, Carlisle Barracks, Pennsylvania, 42nd Division AEF Collection (hereinafter, MHIA).

26. General Headquarters, Tank Corps, Special Orders No. 13, 20 August 1918, in RG 120, Entry 1298 Tank Corps, carton 15A.

27. Rough draft by Patton of a Memorandum to Chief of Staff, IV Corps, 5 September 1918, ibid., carton 11.

28. Headquarters, 42nd Division, undated memorandum by Hughes, ibid., carton 10.

29. Memorandum from Patton to Hughes, 7 September 1918, ibid., carton 11.

30. Cited in Martin Bluenson (ed.), *The Patton Papers, 1885-1940*, Vol. 2 (Boston: Houghton-Mifflin Co., 1972), 628.

31. Memorandum from Patton to Murphy, 7 September 1918, in RG 120, Entry 1298, carton 9.

32. G2, 1st U.S. Army, "Analysis of German Defensive System in St. Mihiel Sector," 18 August 1918, in CMH, *The United States Army in the World War*, Vol. 8, 142-45.

33. G3, 1st U.S. Army, "Estimate of Situation with Respect to Hindenburg Line," 12 September 1918, ibid., 257.

34. Douglas MacArthur, *Reminiscences* (New York: McGraw-Hill, 1964), 62.

35. Groupement Chanoine, "Ordre préparatoire d'Opération, No. 550," 10 September 1918; "Plan d'Engagement, No. 552," 11 September 1918, in RG 120, carton 13.

36. Brigadier General Michael Lenihan, "After Action Report: Tactical Lessons Derived from St. Mihiel Operation (83rd Brigade)," 22 September 1918, in RG 120, carton 23.

37. Lawrence Stewart, *Rainbow Bright* (Philadelphia: Dorrance, 1923), 110-11.

38. E.J. Sadler (ed.), *California Rainbow Memories* (Np: Private printing, 1925), 43. See also, headquarters, 117th Engineer Regiment, Memorandum to G3, 42nd Division, 7 September 1918, in RG 120, carton 20. This document is a rough draft from Colonel Kelly.

39. Duffy, *Story*, 233-34.

40. Taber, *168th Infantry*, Vol. 2, 88.

41. MacArthur, *War Bugs*, 135-36.

42. Langille, *Men of the Rainbow*, 134-35.

43. Tompkins, *Story*, 109-10.

44. Calvin lambert Diary, 179.

45. U.S. Office of the Surgeon General, *The Medical Department of the United States Army in the World War* (Washington: Government Printing Office, 1926), Vol. 8, 492-94.

46. G2, 42nd Division Headquarters, Memorandum for Lieutenant Colonel Murphy, 11 September 1918, in the Lieutenant Colonel Harry S. Grier Papers, MHIA.

47. MacArthur, *Reminiscences*, 62.

48. Field message from Patton to Murphy, 9:30 A.M., 12 September 1918, in RG 120, Entry 1298, carton 11. See also Blumenson, *Patton Papers*, Vol. 2, 633-34; Dale E. Wilson, *Treat 'Em Rough: The Birth of American Armor* (Novato, Calif.: Presidio Press, 1989), 107-8.

49. Memorandum from Pond, "Function of the Gas and Flame Troops," 8 September 1918, in RG 120, carton 20. See also, "After-Action Report," submitted by Menoher to Dickman, 26 September 1918, ibid., carton 14.

50. Amerine, *Alabama's Own*, 173.

51. Ibid., 175-77.

52. Thompson, "Following the Rainbow," 6 May 1934.

53. Taber, *168th Infantry*, Vol. 2, 94.

54. Thompson, "Following the Rainbow," 6 May 1934.

55. Taber, *168th Infantry*, Vol. 2, 95.

56. Ibid., 98. Also see: Major Claude M. Stanley, Commanding 2nd Battalion, 168th Infantry, "After-Action Report," 22 September 1918, in RG 120, carton 33.

57. Duffy, *Story*, 236-37. Also see: Colonel H. D. Mitchell, "After-Action Report: Tactical Lessons Derived from the St. Mihiel Operation," 21 September 1918, in RG 120, carton 14.

58. Ettinger, *Doughboy*, 143.

59. Martin J. Hogan, *The Shamrock Battalion of the Rainbow: A Story of the Fighting 69th* (New York: D. Appleton and Co., 1919), 210-12.

60. MacArthur, *Reminiscences*, 63.

61. Field messages from Patton to Murphy, 6:45 A.M. and 9:30 A.M., 12 September 1918, in RG 120, Entry 1298, carton 11. Captain Ranulf Compton, who commanded the 345th Tank Battalion that fought with the Rainbows, has an interesting account of the action that day. See also: Captain Ranulf Compton, "War Diary of the 345th Battalion, Tank Corps," found in the World War I Surveys, Carton Tank Corps, MHIA.

62. Cheseldine, *Ohio in the Rainbow*, 232-33. Also see: Colonel Benson Hough, "After-Action Report: Tactical Lessons Derived from St. Mihiel Operations," 21 September 1918 in RG 120, carton 23.

63. Cheseldine, *Ohio in the Rainbow*, 235.

64. Duffy, *Story*, 238-39.

65. Donovan to his wife, np, 21 September 1918 in Donovan Papers, MHIA.

66. Field message from Patton to Menoher, 4:45 P.M., 12 September 1918, in RG 120, Entry 1298, carton 11. The date on this message is in error given the locations and the time of advance toward the town of St. Benôit-en-Woëvre.

67. Patton to Murphy, field message, 7:40 P.M., 12 September 1918, ibid.

68. Henry J. Reilly, *Americans All*: The Rainbow at War *(Columbus, Ohio: F.J. Heer Printing Co., 1936), 569.*

69. Ibid., 572-73.

70. MacArthur, *Reminiscences*, 63-64.

71. D. Clayton James, *The Years of MacArthur. Vol. 1, 1880-1941* (Boston: Houghton-Mifflin, 1970), 208-10.

72. Sherwood, *Diary*, 122.

73. American Battle Monuments Commission, *42nd Division, Summary of Operations in the World War* (Washington: Government Printing Office, 1944), 48.

74. James, *MacArthur*, 211-12.

75. Major John A. Pagelow, Commander, Army Balloons, "After-Action Report: Operations of Allied Balloons in the Saint Mihiel Offensive." 28 September 1918, in AFHA, File 167.601-4, 1917-1918.

76. Major L. H. Bereton, Commander, 1st Army Observation Wing, "After-Action Report: Lack of Cooperation between Artillery and Air Service, Operations of September 12th to 17th," 19 September 1918, ibid., File 167.601-7. For the Air Service view of the entire war, including the St. Mihiel offensive, see: AEF History Division, "Brief History of the Air Service, American Expeditionary Forces, 1 July 1920" (typed manuscript), ibid., File 167.401-4. The Air Force Historical Agency Archives has an interesting insight into life in the 90th Aero Squadron at this time. It is an unsigned manuscript titled "Experiences of an Infantry officer from the Front with an Aero Squadron (90th) in Action," 1918, ibid., File SQ-Bomb-90-SU-PE.

77. Major General Charles T. Menoher, "Problems of American Aeronautics," *Air Power* (April 1919), 457.

78. "After-Action Report," submitted by Menoher to Dickman, 26 September 1918, RG 120, carton 14.

79. 42nd Division Headquarters, Division Signal Office, "Report on the Work of the Signal Troops of the 42nd Division in Action Near St. Mihiel, Sept. 12 and 13," signed by Lieutenant Colonel Garnett, 23 September 1918, ibid.

80. Office of Air Force History, *The U.S. Air Service in World War I* (Washington: Government Printing Office, 1978), Vol. 3, 691-92.

81. Monuments Commission, *42nd Division, Summary*, 50, 94.

82. G3, AEF Headquarters, Special Orders No. 314, 29 September 1918, in RG 120, carton 3.

8

The Meuse-Argonne Campaign

In late September, AEF corps began to disengage from their locations and move rapidly to the Argonne area. Within a week, three AEF corps (I under Hunter Liggett, III under Robert Lee Bullard, and V under George H. Cameron) were in line and ready to attack in coordination with the French on 26 September. Lieutenant General Hunter Ligget's Corps, consisting of the 1st, 28th, and 77th in the line with the 82nd and the French 5th Cavalry Division in reserve, made the move in four days.[1] Pershing counted on sheer weight of numbers and the element of surprise to smash into a series of formidable German defenses. Pershing later recalled, "On the afternoon of the day before the attack I visited the headquarters of corps and divisions to give a word of encouragement here and there to leaders upon whom our success on the following day would depend. They were all alert and confident and I returned feeling that all would go as planned."[2]

As Donald Smythe, Pershing's biographer, wrote, "No judgement was ever more wrong."[3] The bombardment, falling mainly on empty German trenches, began at 11:30 P.M., and at 5:30 A.M. the doughboys climbed out of their trenches expecting a "stroll" such as they had experienced at St. Mihiel.

Remember that no plan, no matter how well conceived, survives the first contact with the enemy. This is what happened to Pershing and the AEF. An official report written in 1923 said about the Meuse-Argonne offensive, "Every available American division was thrown against the enemy. Every available German division was thrown in to meet them. At the end of 47 days of continuous battle our divisions had consumed the German divisions."[4] It took forty-seven days and 120,000 American casualties to advance thirty-four miles into enemy-held territory. A tremendous amount of supplies and equipment were brought forward, creating the greatest traffic jams the world had seen to that date. Everywhere there was optimism, exuberance, and a can-do attitude, and as James Harbord later wrote, "To doubt audibly was to be a traitor."[5]

The battlefield dictated how the Americans would attack—straight ahead, with more mass than finesse, more battering ram than maneuver. From left to right, Pershing arrayed the 77th, 28th, 35th, 91st, 37th, 79th, 4th, 80th, and 33rd. Of the nine, four were National Guard, four were National Army, and one was Regular Army. The 28th Pennsylvania Keystone Division first saw combat in the Champagne-Marne operation in July. The 35th Kansas-Missouri had no combat experience, the 91st from the West and Northwest had no previous battle time, and the 37th Ohio Buckeyes also had seen little fighting. The 80th and the 33rd were equally new to the Western Front. Only the 77th, 4th, and 28th, or less than half of the attacking divisions, were veterans. To be sure, these divisions attacking at dawn on 26 September were made of good stock, with very capable commanders, but the price for such a novice assault force became tragically evident.[6]

The terrain was filled with thickets, heavy woods, deep ravines, very strong German defensive positions, key high ground, and road networks that the Germans had no intention of giving up without a bloodletting. A key objective for the first day was the high ground and major crossroads at Montfaucon, in the area assigned to V Corps, commanded by Lieutenant General George H. Cameron. He attacked with the 91st, 37th, and 79th Divisions, all green to combat. The 77th and the 35th Divisions in the other corps became totally lost and almost incapable of sustained battle. On 29 September, the Rainbow received marching orders to leave the St. Mihiel area and proceed by three routes, at night, to the Argonne. The move was to be completed by dawn of 2 October, and the 42nd would form the reserve for the V Corps.[7] Al Ettinger, the 165th dispatch rider, watched as the Irish regiment filed out of the St. Mihiel. Duffy climbed onto a piece of high ground and blessed the troops as they marched by. While poor, sorely tried Duffy called down the protection of God, the veterans of the 165th were lustily singing an obscene barracks song, "Banging Away on LuLu."[8] If ever any troops needed the eternal patience of the Almighty, it was those of the Rainbow.

Wild Bill Donovan left the rolling hills of the St. Mihiel an irritated man. Colonel Hughes had tried to have him transferred to divisional staff, where a lawyer with an excellent knowledge of French was needed. Douglas MacArthur intervened, citing the Argonne fight now looming large in the future, and he won Menoher's agreement to put any thought of a transfer on hold until after the completion of the next operation.[9]

John Hayes had been assigned to the 167th's kitchens in the village of Pannes, where he thought he would be free of the constant, lethal activity of the front areas. However, he found out that as the AEF began to consolidate air assets under Billy Mitchell, the German aircraft could raid at will. During one raid, American anti-aircraft searchlights and guns concentrated on German planes. The enemy fliers took immediate umbrage at being so singled out and swept down on the searchlights, guns, and rear area men. An immediate howl went up, with machine-gun bullets spraying the area, to turn the lights off. They were turned off, and the enemy aircraft flew away. Kitchen duty, for Hayes, was

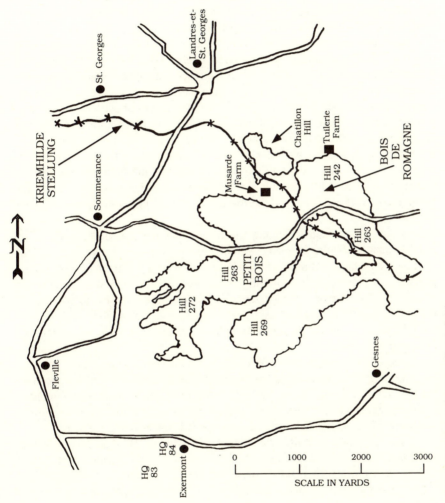

Figure 8.1 Meuse-Argonne Battlefield

not the soft job he thought it would be.[10]

Before the 168th left St. Mihiel, the regiment gathered for a memorial service preached by Chaplain Winifred Robb, who had just recovered from a wound received in July. His voice choked with emotion, an American flag draped over a crude altar, Robb prayed with his men for the war's end and for the memory of the Iowa men who would not go home again. The service concluded when the 168th band struck up "Onward Christian Soldiers," as the depleted ranks marched back to their bivouac to prepare to leave.[11]

There were no bands playing when the troops of 168th marched from their camps on 30 September. They covered twelve kilometers to the destroyed village of Apremont, which the Germans had earlier defended against the French. From the ghost town, they marched into a dark and dank Fôret d'Apremont, where on either side of the road were the unburied dead of battles years before. The whitened skeletons shrouded with rotted rags of French horizon blue could be seen all through the grass and newly sprouted trees. Once out of the woods, the troops were greeted by miles of French trucks driven by the ever-present Indochinese. On they went through Bar-le-Duc, with the flashes of the guns in the Argonne looking like late summer lightening on the horizon. At a crossroads a sign read, "vers Verdun," and the Iowans knew that they were on the road into a cauldron.[12]

Rumors had circulated among the troops that the Americans were being roughly handled by the Germans, who obviously were not through fighting "für Gott und Vaterland." Running through the record books of the AEF G2 was the phrase, "Our troops....encountering stubborn resistance from a reinforced enemy."[13] On 3 October the 1st Army G3 ordered the Rainbow to continue to move into the V Corps' area. On three different roads, the 42nd moved through the village of Brocourt into the Bois de Montfaucon, where it assumed the role of V Corps' reserve division.[14]

When the first attack was launched on 26 September, the 79th "Lorraine" Division had the mission of taking the heights and crossroads at Montfaucon on the first day. This was accomplished on the 27th, but the cost to the untested division was frightful. The human debris of that battle was all around the Rainbow. The unmistakable stench of unburied bodies hung in the air.

Leslie Langille found life tolerable after St. Mihiel. He shared a shack with some men from the 41st Division who had been sent as replacements earlier and who were now accepted as full-fledged members of his battery. They had found a French army canteen only a few kilometers away, and the supply of red and white wine seemed inexhaustible. The Catholic Knights of Columbus came to the 67th Field Artillery Brigade and distributed cookies and candy bars. Much to the surprise of the artillerymen, the YMCA showed up selling candies, cookies, and smokes. Langille recalled, "Those two birds had apparently gone broke in Paris and were out on a selling campaign to recoup their fortunes. After picking up a few francs, they would then be able to return to Paris and their harems, and live like kings again."[15] Much to the 67th Field Artillery

Brigade's surprise and dismay, as the soldiers prepared to leave the St. Mihiel area they found that they were to go into the Argonne fight ahead of the infantry, in support of the hard-pressed 32nd Division.

Once into the Bois de Montfaucon, Charles MacArthur saw scenes that would forever burn in his memory:

The woods were splintered into small bits, green with mustard gas. There wasn't a live leaf in twenty miles. Thousands of dead men sprawled in the ulcerated fields. Horses, their legs awkwardly pointing up, and general litter of junk. Wagons, rifles, socks, rations, love letters....One of the kids [of the 79th Division] lay on the ground dying with a bullet in his guts. He had been yanked from a stenographer's job in New York, trained (as they say) and exposed to his first fire—all in thirty-seven days. He was slightly bewildered by it all.[16]

Martin Hogan and the Shamrock Battalion entered the Argonne full of élan and espirit de corps. He was sure that the Irish 165th and the Rainbow could crack any position the Germans decided to man, but he was also aware of the horrible costs of this battle. While marching to the Bois de Montfaucon, they had seen the wagons loaded with American and German wounded. Hogan saw the "acres of graves," some old, many freshly dug, and knew that he was entering what had to be an absolute hell.[17]

The Rainbow remained in the Bois de Montfaucon for well over a week while the AEF pounded against German defenses. In the Argonne, the Germans had prepared a series of defensive belts that had to be taken one by one, at great cost. The key to the campaign was a series of exceptionally well-constructed fortifications known as the Kriemhilde Stellung, which was on high ground, bristling with machine-gun nests and infantry fighting positions. The area was dominated by two high hills, No. 288 and the Côte de Chatillion. Beyond those two hills were the towns of St. Georges and Landres-et-St. Georges, which had been heavily fortified with wire, obstacles, machine-gun positions, and mines. If the Kriemhilde Stellung could be taken and the two towns overrun, there was a valley beyond where German defenses were not as extensive. Into that meat grinder went the Big Red One, the pride of Pershing's regulars, battering against the defenses of the Kriemhilde Stellung.

The 1st Division, despite the rivalry between it and the 42nd, was a fine group of soldiers commanded by Major General Charles P. Summerall, a ruthless, relentless fighter who in 1917 had been the Rainbow's 67th Field Artillery Brigade commander. He had graduated from West Point in 1888 and served with Pershing in the Philippines, where his battery commander had been Captain Henry J. Reilly. Reilly had cited the younger Summerall for gallantry and recommended his promotion several times. During the Boxer Rebellion in China, Summerall won glory for taking his section of guns and blasting open four successive walls and the gate of the imperial Forbidden City. In May 1917, he went to Europe to observe the training of French and British troops, and then commanded the Rainbow's artillery in France until early 1918, when he took a similar position in the Big Red One. On 11 October Summerall became commander of the U.S. V Corps, rising from colonel to lieutenant general in a year and a half.

The weather had turned nasty, with heavy rain and cold temperatures. Hoosier Elmer Sherwood found it hard to sleep on the cold, damp, frost-covered ground with only three blankets. Sherwood did not have an overcoat—no one did—and he wanted the SOS to get some winter underwear up to the Bois de Montfaucon soon.[18] Influenza had made its presence known to the AEF early this year, and the wet, cold, poor rations, and loss of sleep made many an American soldier prey to the dreaded disease.

The order that would send the Rainbows into battle also attached an Aero Squadron (observation) and the 2nd Balloon Company for the now-commonplace observation missions. One of the major problems in the Meuse-Argonne was the terrible weather. It continued to be overcast or rain, with poor aerial visibility. Company C of the 1st Gas and Flame Regiment reported to the division, but it faced the same problems as it had in the St. Mihiel drive. The ground was difficult to traverse with the heavy four-inch Stokes Mortars. Once the infantry went "over the top," the weighed-down Gas and Flame troops would have a difficult time. Tanks also presented difficulties because of the marshy terrain.

The Rainbow was scheduled to relieve the battered Big Red One on 11 October and continue the mission of attacking to the north. Had it not been for the superhuman efforts of the 1st Division, the Rainbow would have stood little chance of overcoming the Kriemhilde Stellung. The 1st had taken the outskirts of the town of Sommerance on the left of the division boundary, and it had fought for control of the Côte de Maldah, a hill 247 meters high. The Big Red One had driven into the Bois de Romagne on the right of the division boundary and had kicked the Germans out of the critical woods, which could offer some cover and concealment to the Rainbows as they massed to attack Hill 288 and then the Côte de Chatillion, the key to the German defensive positions.

The Rainbows were to participate in the fourth phase of the Meuse-Argonne offensive, which would start on 12 October and last until 16 October. No one, at any level, believed that the task would be easy. The operations report of the G3 for 1st Army cited specifically German combat effectiveness in the 42nd Division's area of operations when he wrote on 12 October, "The resistance of the enemy was very obstinate....A strong line of resistance ran from Granpré to Landres-et-St. Georges."[19]

The objectives assigned to the Rainbow were first to take Hill 288 and the Côte de Chatillion on 14 October, and then drive the enemy from the St. Georges and Landres-et-St. Georges area, establishing a line on the high ground north of the two towns. To do this the division placed, from left to right, the 83rd Brigade and the 84th Brigade. Douglas MacArthur's 84th would bear the responsibility of taking the two critical hills, while Lenihan's 83rd Brigade would attack toward St. Georges and Landres-et-St. Georges. While this looked like an equal division of combat power, MacArthur's 84th would have the benefit of fighting almost constantly in the woods. When the 83rd broke toward the two towns, it would be in the open, advancing against formidable wire and obstacles, and it would be subjected to severe flanking machine-gun fire from the Côte de Chatillion. Over a mile of ground was open, and this meant that the Irish and the Ohioans of Lenihan's command would be visible to German artillery spotters.

Neither Lenihan nor MacArthur were second-rate soldiers, and they both took the opportunity to move forward to see the terrain over which they would fight on 14 October. MacArthur recognized that the Côte de Chatillion was the key to the entire attack. If his brigade failed to take it, the rest of the plan was just worthless paper. General Summerall, commanding the V Corps, also understood this and, after examining the divisional attack plans, went directly to MacArthur's PC. Summerall looked worn and tired, and MacArthur got him a near-scalding cup of coffee. "Give me Chatillion, MacArthur," Summerall said. "Give me Chatillion or a list of five thousand casualties." From Summerall, this was not pre-battle rhetoric, and MacArthur knew it. He responded that Chatillion would be taken or his name would head the list of those 5,000 fallen.[20]

At the PC for the 1st Battalion, 165th, Donovan had cleaned his uniform and had polished his insignia as best he could under the circumstances. He then carefully sewed on his ribbons, the Croix de Guerre and the Distinguished Service Cross, and polished his boots and Sam Browne Belt. Tomorrow he would look the part of a dashing officer leading his troops, and he knew that his men would respond to the image and follow him.[21]

Father Duffy was filled with a sense of foreboding. He had gone to as many positions as he could, in darkness and driving rain, to hear confessions. Duffy had said a special blessing for the men of the 117th Engineers, who would be in the first wave as wire cutters. Many of them would be the first soldiers of the Rainbow to "go west" on 14 October.[22]

All of the regiments sent out patrols to scout enemy positions and learn more about the terrain. The Alabamians patrolled on the night of 12 October and learned that in front of the 84th Brigade was the German 41st Division. A short time later, another German from the 11th Regiment, 52nd Division, fell into Alabam hands. The Irish patrolled and captured soldiers from the 147th Regiment, 37th Division. All along the line, patrols reported the Germans to be very active in either repairing or emplacing new wire. The weather was abominable, with fog, mists, and chilly rain. Nothing could fly, and there was no aerial observation by either side.[23]

By the afternoon of 13 October, less than a day before the attack, the Germans stepped up their machine-gun and artillery fire on Rainbow patrols and trenches. Patrols did confirm that the Germans had occupied La Tuiliere Farm and La Musarde Farm, typical stone farm complexes less than a mile from where the 168th Infantry would go into the fight. Since the Ourcq, the doughboys had come to dread these fortified farms.[24]

Lieutenant Ralph G. Knowles, Intelligence Officer, 3rd Battalion, 165th, remained concerned about the terrain in front of him. The divisional G2 had constantly warned that the Germans had strong machine-gun and infantry positions all along the front. He led a patrol that did not get over 200 yards in front of its position before the German machine guns began to fire. At least, everyone knew that there would be stiff resistance as little as 200 yards from the starting point.[25]

The 83rd Brigade order, like that of the 84th, was a well-prepared document. The actual first assault to get through the American wire would begin at 6:30 A.M. This would be the 166th's 2nd Battalion, which was to strike north of Sommerance toward objectives at St. Georges and to the east. The Shamrocks of the 165th would go forward at 8:30 A.M. and aim toward Landres-et-St. Georges.[26] The 84th Brigade would drive toward Hill 288 and the Côte de Chatillion, taking the critical hill masses one after another.

V Corps envisioned that the attack on the third critical objective, the high ground just north of St. Georges and Landres-et-St. Georges, would begin the first day. In fact, Corps estimated that the 84th Brigade would have taken Chatillion Hill within six hours and would then move with the 83rd to take the high ground north of the objective.[27] Corps transmitted a speed-up in the times for the various phases of the attack to begin, and Murphy and Hughes had to transmit the changes via telephone. One must wonder if the Corps G3 was reading the patrol reports and the Rainbow's "Summary of Intelligence," which since 10 October had been issued twice daily by Lieutenant Colonel Judah.

The assault waves, from left to right, 2nd Battalion of the 166th Infantry, 3rd Battalion of the 165th, 3rd Battalion of the 167th and 1st Battalion of the 168th Infantry, were prepared. Machine guns from the two machine-gun battalions went forward, as did platoons from Company C, 1st Gas and Flame, and the 117th Engineers. All was in readiness, waiting for the Allied gunners to begin the preparatory fires at midnight of 14 Oct.

Elmer Sherwood stood by his artillery piece before midnight, waiting for the order to begin the barrage that would open the fight for the Rainbows. He was sick to his stomach, the result of inhaled gas. He had eaten little except for a loaf of slightly moldy white bread he found on the ground. A German shell had hit a supply dump, scattering Corned Willie, hardtack and bread. Sherwood grabbed a loaf from the ground, wiped it off, and ate part of it.[28] A little after midnight on 14 October, the 67th Field Artillery Brigade, the 1st Field Artillery Brigade from the Big Red One, nine batteries of 75mms from the French 219th Field Artillery Brigade, nine batteries from I Corps artillery, and three battalions of huge eight-inch guns from the 59th Coastal Artillery opened fire on German positions in preparation for the infantry assault to begin a little after dawn. The ground rolled from the crash of so many guns pouring shot and shell into the German positions, from St. Georges on the left to Chatillion and Hill 288 on the right. The Germans responded, but they were saving most of their ammunition for what they knew was coming at them. The woods just north of the Bois de Romagne were turned into a hell of flying pieces of steel, sharp, heavy pieces of wood, dismembered bodies, and churned equipment and animals.

Telephone checks were made with all the assault battalions about an hour after the artillery bombardment began, and brigade PCs received an "All set" from the regiments. As the American and French bombardment lifted, the Ohio troops moved forward. At the same time, the Iowa and Alabama regiments assaulted Hill 288, which was very steep, covered with underbrush, and heavily defended by the Germans. Major Lloyd Ross was commanding 1st Battalion, 168th, that morning. It was his men who would assault the tangled, deadly slopes of Hill 288. Douglas MacArthur told Colonel Tinley, "Ross is the absolute key to the whole situation." The plan, as outlined by brigade, was unrealistic. Ross was to sweep Hill 288, take La Tuiliere Farm, and then establish a foothold on the base of the Côte de Chatillion, all within an hour and a half to two hours.[29]

The Germans had come alive and, despite the terrific barrage, rushed to their guns and poured a deadly fire into Ross' Iowans and into the Alabama 167th trying to advance with them. Sergeant George A. Wilkinson of Company A saw his men begin to fall from the hail of machine-gun bullets. Iowan Wilkinson rushed three machine-gun nests in order and silenced them. Immediately he reorganized his platoon and began to attack again, when a fourth gun blazed away at the Iowa men. Wilkinson dashed forward and silenced the deadly gun, but when the smoke cleared he lay dead near the machine gun he had just put out of action.[30]

By noon, Second Lieutenant Daniel Fox led his platoon from Company C onto the crest of Hill 288 and established a permanent foothold on the crest. In a few minutes Fox would be carried from the field severely gassed, but his troops held on as more Iowa men came to secure the hill and prepare to assault north toward the prize of the day, Côte de Chatillion.

Alabama troops were pinned down as they attacked toward La Musarde Farm and the base of Chatillion Hill. The machine-gun fire from the hill, the farm, and from Hill 242 just south of Côte de Chatillion halted them. Artillery, well directed from Chatillion and Hill 242, raked the 167th's front. For one of the few times in the war, the Alabama 167th was simply stopped.

Wild Bill Donovan had been detailed as the officer in charge of the entire advance of the 165th, while he still retained command of his own 1st Battalion. Donovan had geared the Irish advance to that of the 167th, but when the Alabams could not move Donovan decided to go it alone around 8:30 A.M., regardless of what was happening on his right flank.

The Germans reacted to the advance of the Ohio troops by pouring gas shells into Sommerance and onto the 2nd Battalion, 166th, attacking north from the town. Colonel Hough reported that the 82nd Division, on his left flank, had seized Hill 230 and was moving on line with the Ohioans. Gatley's 67th Field Artillery brigade began to fire a massive rolling barrage so that the 166th could continue forward.[31]

By noon, however, problems began to surface all along the line. The 83rd Brigade, which had made early progress, became bogged down north of

Sommerance and could not advance. The 165th had lost all contact with the Alabamians on the right, who were totally immobilized by German machine-gun and artillery fire. Donovan had made the decision to press on without maintaining contact with the 167th, and by noon the New Yorkers were being hit on the exposed flank by a heavy German fire. A heavy artillery bombardment of the wire and trenches in front of the 83rd Brigade was scheduled from 3:30 P.M. until 5:30 P.M. Once the bombardment was completed, the gunners would begin a rolling barrage so that the infantry could resume the advance.[32]

The Rainbow began to pay the price for Donovan's decision to move forward without the 167th. By the time the artillery bombardment began, Donovan discovered that the Alabama lines were a full kilometer behind his lead battalion, and that the Alabama advance had shifted to the northeast so as to better assault the Côte de Chatillion when its troops could get through the Germans defenses. A gap had begun to appear between the two brigades as they moved in different directions. In the confusion, word reached the PC of the 166th that the 165th had taken positions to the left of Landres-et-St. Georges, which would have meant that the New York regiment was far in advance of all other Rainbow regiments and could very well be cut off if the lines were not adjusted. The 166th found out that the report of the 165th was in error. The 165th Irish were nowhere near the wire and trenches running from St. Georges to Landres-et-St. Georges, which was by 4 P.M. blasted by the 67th Field Artillery.[33]

That afternoon division headquarters reported to the 83rd Brigade, "The 84th Brigade are now mopping [up] Côte de Chatillion and Tuiliere farm." Nothing could have been further from the truth. The 84th Brigade was fighting for a hill mass between Côte de Chatillion, the Musarde and Tuiliere farms in the north, and Hill 288, about where it had been at 9 A.M.[34]

Sometime in the early afternoon (MacArthur placed it at noon), Hill 288 was finally in American hands. Douglas MacArthur telephoned to divisional headquarters;

Have taken Hill 288. The fighting has been of the most desperate character. The battalion [1-168] which took the hill is very badly shattered and I am making replacements. The position was splendidly entrenched, heavily wired and strongly manned. It had to be taken inch by inch in the most sanguinary fighting. It was superbly defended and heroically won.[35]

Ross' battalion of Iowa troops was not just badly shattered, it was combat-ineffective at the end of the fight. Only six officers and 300 soldiers were left standing; well over two-thirds were down. Companies B and C were amalgamated under the command of a lieutenant. Those companies had gone into the fight with about 500 men, but now they could count only seventy men together.[36]

Around 5 P.M. MacArthur telephoned Menoher, who could not have been happy with the lack of progress that day. He told Menoher that, unless ordered to do otherwise, the 84th Brigade would fight throughout the night to sweep toward the Côte de Chatillion. What he envisioned was a two-pronged assault, with the 167th attacking from its positions to the west of the hill and the Iowa 168th attacking straight north. They would take the base of the hill, at least, and they would do it with the bayonet, no rifle fire being allowed. MacArthur's orders to attack with only the bayonet had merit, given the circumstances. To advance without firing meant that enemy machine gunners could not sight in on advancing doughboys by watching the flashes of their rifles as they fired. At night, in wooded terrain, with poor visibility due to rain and fog, it would be difficult for the Germans to see targets. Also, by advancing with the bayonet only, the possibility of the Americans' losing their night vision due to nearby muzzle flashes was decreased. Menoher initially agreed, and MacArthur issued the orders for the night attack by his brigade.[37]

MacArthur was also concerned that when the attack started, the gap between the 167th and the 165th would become even wider. The 165th was bogged down only a few hundred meters in front of its line of departure and would be unable to stretch its lines to cover the opening. The fight for the Côte de Chatillion would require almost every man MacArthur could throw into the battle. His description of the hill was very accurate: "[The hill's defense] comprises a series of trenches with dug-outs and new wire with steel posts. It is strongly manned by both machine guns and infantry. One estimate puts the number of machine guns at 200."[38]

When the historian of the 168th Infantry wrote the story of the Iowa regiment, he compared the fight for the hills to a bad dream. Iowa medic Stewart recalled being knocked senseless while working with the wounded:

The next thing I knew, my head was looking around for the rest of me and couldn't find it. I wiggled my neck and it still seemed to be attached to something. Some earth gave way and as I shook myself hard I freed my hands and dug myself out of the ground, where the exploding shell had buried me up to my neck.

A little while later, Stewart saw an officer who had had his left arm blown off. With his good arm, he was taking his West Point graduation ring off the finger of the severed hand.[39]

Somehow, messenger Everett Scott had survived so far without a scratch, even though he had carried messages through some of the hardest of the fighting. By now he believed that with this type of fighting, the war could go until the spring. However, he was happy to have made it so far in this fight for the hills.[40]

Menoher was particularly disturbed because it seemed that the whole New York effort had died out in front of the German wire and trenches protecting St. Georges and Landres-et-St. Georges. As a professional soldier, he recognized that as long as the Germans held Chatillion hill, they could continue to rake the entire 83rd line with devastating machine-gun fire and accurate artillery. Rather than waste any more life, Menoher canceled MacArthur's night attack and ordered the artillery to pound the Côte de Chatillion all night in preparation for a new dawn attack. Menoher was certain of his decision when at 8:39 P.M., a message reached division headquarters from Lenihan's PC to the effect that Donovan remained pinned down by machine-gun fire from the towns and from the hills.[41]

Lieutenant Colonel Judah officially described the enemy when he wrote in the "Summary of Intelligence," "Throughout the period [14-15 October] the enemy has continued his resistance with undiminished fury and has at no time showed any tendency to withdraw or surrender."[42] In the 24-hour period, the Rainbow artillery, with its attachments, fired an extraordinary 23,000 75mm rounds and 2,600 155mm shells.[43] Throughout the night, Lenihan worked to strengthen his line to resume the attack at dawn. The Irish Shamrocks, now reduced to a shell, had led the attack. When the 1st and 2nd Battalions relieved the weary Irishmen, the 3rd became a small brigade reserve. The 2nd Battalion of the Ohio 166th was also incapable of offensive action, and it was relieved by the 3rd. The 1st Battalion remained in place to support the new attack.[44] All of these changes were made under a heavy artillery barrage. MacArthur, however, did not relieve his units, feeling that the losses in dark and rain would be too confusing. If there was any rest to be had, it had best be done in place, with little movement.

During the night there was a tremendous amount of support activity. Wounded had to be removed, and somehow food had to be gotten to the troops. This was obviously difficult under fire, and losses in men and equipment ensured that some units got nothing to eat at all. The most pressing need was for ammunition, and it was again very slow in coming up. It appears that there was little sense of urgency in the 117th Ammunition Train to prepare for a resupply operation. Sergeant Calvin Lambert recalls that on the night of 14 October, a large number of 117th troops were in the YMCA dugout getting newspapers and buying what the YMCA had to offer.[45]

Martin Hogan and his fellow Shamrocks were spent as they pulled back to let other 165th soldiers take their place. They were exhausted, as,

each man was putting into the fight all of his strength, all of his skill as a marksman, all of his acuteness of vision, and all he had learned about fighting against men in cover. The paths that led to the enemy machine gun nests were unthinkably bad, yet they were rushed, front-on, again and again....These were taken one at a time, in headlong charge, by encircling, by being stumbled upon accidently, fallen into, and captured after silent arguments with blood dripping bayonets.[46]

Al Ettinger stayed close to Donovan and the PC throughout the first day, to do whatever was ordered. He had a package of tobacco and a roll of cigarette papers, but found he did not have any matches. He crawled to a nearby foxhole, where he found Sergeant William Sheahan, one of the colorbearers for the 165th. Sheahan had extra matches, and Ettinger crawled back to his hole. Then a large German shell exploded, burying Ettinger and his buddy in the mud. After freeing himself and his comrade, he saw that the foxhole where Sheahan and the other man had been was gone. It was now a large crater. They found the other man dying, his legs blown off. At dawn they found a charred torso, with a web belt on which was written in ink "W.S.," the only earthly remains of Sheahan.[47]

Donovan had spent a good bit of the night trying to realign forces for the attack the next morning. It was a superhuman task in the bad weather; it was still misty and very dark. To add to Wild Bill's irritation, the ammunition and grenades were very late in arriving. Finally, about dawn, the 117th arrived, but distribution slowed the timing of the assault.[48] From brigade headquarters, he learned that the 83rd Brigade was to be supported by sixteen tanks with a mission of preceding the infantry to cut wire and reduce enemy positions, but they were nowhere to be seen.[49] Sometime before dawn, Donovan received the morning's operation order, which specified that the artillery would begin firing at 7:15 A.M. and the infantry would attack fifteen minutes later. The objective given was the high ground several hundred meters north of the St. Georges to Landres-et-St. Georges line, which the brigade expected to be reached around noon.[50]

The tanks promised by brigade headquarters failed to materialize at the appointed hour, and Donovan could not waste any more time. The artillery preparation was due to lift at 7:30 A.M. and then shift into a rolling barrage. The infantry would then advance behind the barrage, through the wire, and on into the two towns. General Menoher became involved in the problem within the 83rd Brigade. His decision was, like Donovan's, to begin the infantry attack without the tanks. To have lost the benefits of the artillery barrage was probably far worse than waiting for the tanks, which might not show up. Menoher also seemed to be losing patience with the slow progress of the 84th Brigade and the nonexistent progress of Lenihan's brigade.[51] Even with telephone communication, Donovan did not want to chance anything. At 7:30, without the tanks, the 83rd Brigade's force went forward.[52]

About 7:45 the tanks finally reached Sommerance, and it had already been a day of frustration for the tankers. The constant rain and continual artillery bombardment had made the roads and fields quagmires of shell holes and mud. It was slow going for the iron tanks, which could muster a few miles per hour at best. Finally, by 8:30 A.M., the tanks and infantry were moving together against the German wire and obstacles south of the St. Georges and Landres-et-St. Georges line, where they encountered heavy German bombardment. The tanks were taking hits; a number were put out of action, and others began to experience mechanical difficulties. While the 165th and 166th made a heroic effort to penetrate the German defenses, a hail of machine-gun and small arms fire poured onto their flanks from the Côte de Chatillion and the two towns. By 9:00 A.M., the attack had stalled again.[53]

Every unit in the 165th was absorbed in the fight for the wire. As Martin Hogan led a group of Shamrock soldiers forward, a German sniper fired at him, shattering his left hand. His comrades dispatched the enemy rifleman, but Hogan had to remain on the field until darkness could hide his movements. An officer finally ordered Hogan to get to a dressing station where he could get help. "On the way back," Hogan recalled, "I saw men being carried with legs shattered, with blood-drenched clothes from the flow of ghastly body wounds, and I passed one man sitting against a tree with half of his head torn away....He must have seated himself here after the first shock to rest and have died moments later." Once in the dressing station Hogan was operated on. As he slipped under the merciful spell of the ether, he felt ashamed to be among those badly maimed men with such a minor wound.[54]

In all fairness to Lenihan and the attacking force, the terrain dictated that the 83rd Brigade would have the hardest task because of the several kilometers of open area they had to cross. While Lenihan's New Yorkers and Iowans were stalled in front of the wire, MacArthur's 84th Brigade was making slow progress against La Musarde Farm and Tuiliere Farm, as well as against the base of Chatillion Hill. During the morning of 15 October, a frustrated General Summerall ordered that the tanks, which had left the battle a little after 10 A.M., be assembled near the front for maintenance and repairs, not in the rear. He was aggravated that there was a shortage of wire-breaching bangalore torpedoes for the infantry. They were to be brought up by the ammunition train and made ready for a major assault on 16 October. Summerall had written the 15th off as far as the 83rd Brigade was concerned. That spelled serious problems for Lenihan as brigade commander.[55] To trouble the 83rd Brigade commander even more, word reached his PC before noon that Wild Bill Donovan had been seriously wounded.

Al Ettinger was with Donovan before he was wounded, and he knew that the attack against the wire was not going well. In fact, to Ettinger it was a "slaughter at the wire."[56] Duffy was also concerned that Donovan was exposing himself too much while trying to get the 165th to move forward. At the wire Duffy saw Irish infantry and men from the 117th Engineers desperately cutting through the well-placed, well-prepared wire. The storm of machine-gun rounds from several directions and very accurate enemy artillery fire made the task nearly impossible. No infantryman or engineer could stand long enough to cut the wire. Bodies littered the ground and corpses were hanging on the wire. Donovan was still urging the troops forward when, about 10 A.M., he was hit in the lower left leg by a machine-gun round. Donovan went down and was carried from the forward position to a small dugout, where he continued to direct the futile efforts of his infantry and engineers.[57]

At 10:30 A.M. Colonel Mitchell received another attack order, to be executed at noon. The message went forward, but reached the wounded Donovan little before the time for the attack to begin. Donovan, who had been at the wire until his leg was shattered, knew first-hand the impossible conditions at the front. Mitchell included with the order a note of his own stating that it was imperative the assault take place, since the order originated with Summerall's corps headquarters. Donovan, who adamantly refused to leave the field, was carried back to his 1st Battalion PC. He was aghast at the order, and when Major

Anderson arrived at his PC, Donovan informed him that he would take full responsibility for countermanding it.[58]

Donovan knew that his decision would have serious repercussions, possibly leading to his own court-martial, but he remained determined. He sent a message to Mitchell at 12:40 P.M. stating simply that the slaughter at the wire was too great, the artillery had not knocked out the machine gunners, and the attack was impossible.[59]

On the right, the fight for the Côte de Chatillion was going as slowly as ever, with the 168th slugging its way up the base of the hill and the Alabamians hitting against a brilliant defense at La Musarde Farm. Within the 168th, some companies were down to fewer than 50 men, and the cost in officers continued to rise, but progress was being made. The lessons of the Ourcq and St. Mihiel paid off for the Iowans on the Côte de Chatillion. Using fire and maneuver, and taking advantage of cover and concealment, the machine guns were being silenced one by one.[60]

The situation in front of the 83rd Brigade grew worse as the afternoon wore on. The reserve battalions for the 165th and 166th were pushed to the front, as were cooks, mechanics, and anyone else capable of carrying a rifle.[61] By 2:30 P.M., units were intermingled, and the situation at the enemy wire was chaotic. The troops could go no farther until the Côte de Chatillion was in American hands.[62] At 6:25 P.M. Menoher called Lenihan and ordered him to bring his regimental commanders to the divisional PC at 7 P.M.

When Lenihan, Hough, and Mitchell arrived at the Rainbow PC, Menoher was not there. He would arrive later, since he was in conference with Summerall over the day's fighting. At 9 P.M. MacArthur reported that his Alabamians and Iowans had taken La Tuiliere Farm, thus flanking the Musarde Farm and paving the way for its capture.[63] There was no question now that the 165th had to attack and succeed on 16 October.

Throughout the night, the 117th Engineers moved troops up to support both brigades. On the left of the Rainbow line, the 82nd Division began to move forward and reached the St. Georges area with elements of Hough's 166th on line with them. Things seemed to be finally moving slowly on the left of the divisional line. On the right, the 84th continued to inch up the Côte de Chatillion, but in the center the 165th was again pinned down by heavy fire.

The 82nd Division, known as the All Americans, maintained a fairly good liaison and coordinated well with the 166th through the morning. Both were able to make headway, but the All Americans were also wearing down. Major General George B. Duncan, commanding the 82nd, had gone forward on the morning of the 16th and was appalled at the condition of his troops.[64] The Rainbow and the All Americans were just about at the end of their rope, and still the St. Georges to Landres-et-St. Georges line held firm. What they did not know was that the Germans had just about reached their limit as well. The 165th reported at 4:16 P.M. that the 1st Battalion had only 186 soldiers, the 2nd Battalion had 480 men, and the 3rd Battalion, which had been a reserve unit after the first day, counted 496 effective soldiers. The Machine Gun Company had four functioning guns.[65] This regiment had a little over 40 percent of its combat troops left with which to fight.

At 1:43 P.M., Colonel Hughes telephoned Lenihan to report to the 42nd's PC as soon as possible. Mitchell, Reilly, and Hough were to attend this meeting. In addition to the four officers, Lieutenant Colonel Charles A. Dravo, the division's machine-gun officer, also was present. The meeting was short and to the point. Lenihan was relieved of command, and Colonel Henry J. Reilly assumed charge of the 83rd Brigade. Colonel Harry Mitchell met a similar fate, and his place was taken by Dravo.[66]

There was some real soul-searching in the relief of Lenihan, who had recently been strongly recommended by Menoher for divisional command. Not willing to acquiesce in this decision, Lenihan demanded a hearing. Summerall later sent Colonel S. Field Dallam, the V Corp's Inspector General, to investigate the matter. Dallam felt that Lenihan was a victim of circumstances and recommended that he be restored to duty. Summerall disapproved Dallam's report, and the question went to General Hunter Liggett, who overrode Summerall's decision and sent Lenihan to the 77th Division to command a brigade.[67]

Mitchell remained with the division for a while, then he, too, found another position. Given the terrain, weather, fog, and friction of war, there was little more that the 83rd Brigade could do before the very strong defenses of the Kriemhilde Stellung. The brigade was at 40 percent rifle strength, and what was left was worn out. For three days, with very little food and water, the 166th and 165th battered themselves against the wire and defenses from St. Georges to Landres-et-St. Georges, where there was almost no cover or concealment for the assaulting units.

Benson Hough's 166th Ohio had made fair progress. Linked up with the hard-fighting 82nd Division, they were moving from Sommerance to St. Georges because there was some cover and flanking fires from the 82nd Division. Consequently, Hough remained in command of his regiment, or rather what was left of it. General Summerall was not convinced that Lenihan had done all he could and ordered an investigation to be held, especially dealing with the events of noon on 15 October. It was fairly clear that Donovan had countermanded the order to attack, but he did so as the senior officer present, appointed by Mitchell to be a "battle captain" at the front. Regardless, Summerall wanted results, and he would not forget the failure of the 83rd Brigade.

The selection of Henry J. Reilly, an artilleryman, to command an infantry brigade surprised some Rainbow officers, but Reilly and Summerall had served together in the Philippines and the Far East and knew each other well. Reilly also had a solid reputation as a fighter and a good disciplinarian. Summerall's choice, with Menoher's agreement, was a good one, but Summerall's subsequent treatment of the 83rd Brigade was indeed shabby.

The morning of the 16th was a time for reorganization and resupply in preparation for the final assault on the hill. Companies E, M, and I, including parts of Companies F and K of the Alabama 167th, moved about 500 yards to their right where the Iowans had opened up sections of the wire at the base of the hill. Once through the wire, the Alabamians encountered heavy machine-gun fire, which threatened to stop the entire advance again. Captain Thomas H. Fallaw, of Opelika, Alabama, would not be deterred from his mission, and he led a wild, mass charge of screaming Alabamians into the woods. The Germans began to retreat in the face of the reckless assault.

In the ranks of Company M was Private Thomas C. Neibaur of Sugar City, Idaho, a National Guardsman from the 41st Division. Neibaur had joined the 167th several months earlier and was an automatic rifleman. As the Alabams pushed up the hill toward the crest, Neibaur and some other men were sent out to enfilade enemy positions. He was severely wounded in both legs, all of his comrades were killed, and he came face to face with a German counterattack. He opened fire alone and drove the enemy back. At one point he was rushed by four Germans, whom he killed, and he ended the day by capturing eleven Germans despite his painful wounds. He was awarded the Congressional Medal of Honor.[68]

Sergeant Ralph Atkinson, who had been badly gassed during the Champagne defensive, was in charge of the regiment's Stokes Mortar platoon that day. With many of his men out of action and all of his guns destroyed, Atkinson placed a mortar between his legs and fired and loaded by himself, helping to repulse another enemy counter-attack. For his courage, Atkinson won the Distinguished Service Cross for valor.[69]

By late afternoon, the situation on the Côte de Chatillon had reached the boiling point. Near the summit, Company E, 168th, was in sight of the prize, but the German fire was withering, and there was evidence that the Germans were massing for a counterattack. Captain Glenn C. Haynes had been forward with the 1st Battalion intelligence officer to survey the critical situation. As they were returning to the tired Major Ross's PC, a shell severely wounded the intelligence officer, and shrapnel sliced into Haynes' heel and foot. Painfully limping and losing blood, Haynes described the situation and was overheard by a liaison officer from the 1st Division Artillery Brigade, which had been attached to the Rainbow. This officer ordered a devastating barrage placed on the summit of the hill, and the Germans broke. The Iowans charged forward on the right and the Alabamians on the left, and they finally took Chatillion Hill.[70]

The Kriemhilde Stellung had finally been broken, after bloody combat first by the Big Red One and then the Rainbow. The military significance of the fight for the Côte de Chatillion was apparent. Henry J. Reilly wrote:

The capture of the Côte de Chatillion also meant that instead of the Germans looking down into the American position the Americans now looked down into German lines. Thus, the American artillery observers were able to make the whole valley of the Rap de St. George, which formerly had been hidden entirely from them unsafe for the Germans.[71]

Why did they not immediately follow up the taking of the Kriemhilde Stellung with an assault to the north? First, the Rainbows were fought out. Second, there were still very strong enemy positions along the line from St. Georges to Landres-et-St. Georges, and, except for the 166th, there was little hope that the battered 83rd Brigade, now under new command, could push forward. Third, directly in front of MacArthur's 84th Brigade was a woods known as the Bois de Hazois, on high ground, directly north of Landres-et-St. Georges. That woods had a high observation hill; while not as tall as the Côte de Chatillion, still it was 270 meters high. The woods and the hill were part of a new line known as the Freya Stellung. This position was not as formidable as the Kriemhilde Stellung, but it was insurmountable for the exhausted Rainbows. From 167th patrols it was known that the Germans had both machine guns and artillery in the Bois de Hazois and all along the Freya Stellung.[72]

The condition of the entire American 1st Army was serious, as many of its best units had been reduced to dangerously low levels of manpower. Artillery and machine guns were reaching a point where they would soon be worn out, inoperable in battle. Despite superhuman efforts, the Service of Supply was unable to keep the necessary sinews of war flowing forward. Transportation was in critically short supply.[73] If the AEF was to continue the offensive, replacements had to be brought forward, new uniforms and weapons issued to replace those now nearly useless, and stockpiles of ammunition replenished. Of concern to Liggett was the unusual number of stragglers separated from their units, many by their own decision, who were now wondering over the rear of the area of operations.[74] Pershing reluctantly agreed to the halt in the operations.[75]

In the Ohio 166th, the process of rehabilitation started on 18 October with the issue of new underwear and socks and the cleaning and drying of the wool uniforms. Food remained a problem, however, even during this respite. "The food was still inadequate," Captain Raymond Cheseldine, commander of the 166th's supply company, recalled. "Canned meat, dehydrated potatoes and onions, and hard bread were staple articles for two weeks."[76]

In the 165th, conditions were worse due to the heavy loss of officers and NCOs during the recent fighting. Duffy was heartsick as he saw the physical condition of the 165th deteriorate. Many of the doctors had to be restrained from sending almost every man examined to the hospitals in the rear. The soldiers of the regiment, Father Duffy recalled, "had one blanket apiece, and were without overcoats, underwear or socks, in the unpleasant climate of a French autumn. They were dirty, lousy, thirsty, often hungry; and nearly every last man was sick."[77]

Not all of the devastation was in the infantry. The 117th Engineer Regiment had fought as infantry, and more often than not the regiment's soldiers were first to the wire to cut lanes for the advancing riflemen. Colonel James Johnson of South Carolina, now commanding the 117th (Colonel Kelly had been promoted in September), requested that all engineers be released from infantry duty so that the 117th could perform its role as road repairers, dug-out builders, burial details, or whatever might be required.[78]   In the artillery there were changes, but Brigadier George Gatley, the steady Regular, continued to command the brigade. When Henry J. Reilly left the Illinois 149th to command the 83rd Brigade, Major Curtis Redden became the new regimental commander.

The troops of the division rested as best they could, given the continual rain and cold.   There were constant exchanges of artillery, and patrols were aggressive and often deadly.   On 20 and 21 October, the troops of MacArthur's 84th Brigade were relieved by the 83rd Brigade, allowing them some rest and cleanup in the rear. Most of the 84th moved back to the town of Exermont, five miles south of the Côte de Chatillion. Lieutenant Colonel Judah's "Summaries of Intelligence" reflected a lessening of German will, even though the Germans could indeed mount artillery bombardments, their machine-guns were still formidable, and their patrols were active.

Toward the end of the month, rumors began to circulate that the Rainbow would again take to the offensive on 1 November. This proved to be untrue, as orders were published stating that the 2nd Division would pass through the Rainbow and continue the attack to the north. Reilly argued with Menoher to allow his 83rd Brigade to make the lead assault, followed by the 2nd Division. It would be a way for the 83rd to retrieve some of its tarnished reputation. Summerall declined, since the orders were already issued for the Indianhead Division to attack.[79]

In 1929, Summerall told Reilly that General Liggett had made a decision to use only relatively fresh divisions to commence the assaults of 1 November. There must be some question as to how much trust Summerall placed in the 83rd Brigade. On 26 October, Summerall, in his capacity as V Corps commander, issued a statement of appreciation for the efforts of the 84th Brigade and the 67th Field Artillery during the assaults on the Kriemhilde Stellung. Nowhere did he mention the 83rd Brigade, shabby treatment of a unit that had sustained very heavy casualties in its brave but futile efforts to breach the wire on the St. Georges to Landres-et-St. Georges line. Summerall's statement of appreciation was printed so that every Rainbow soldier, except those in the 165th and 166th, would get one for a souvenir. There were still irretrievable bodies from the 165th Infantry hanging on wire, riddled by machine-gun fire.

Statements and letters meant very little to the doughboys engaged in the deadly business of holding the front, and the Rainbow continued to lose a small number of men daily. On 23 October, Corporal Joe Romano took a patrol out into No Man's Land to gather information. A few hundred yards beyond the 167th's defensive positions, the patrol came under heavy fire, and Romano felt a sharp pain rip into his stomach. The Germans had caught them in a deadly fire, and the seriously wounded Romano lay in a shellhole, his patrol dispersed. During the night Germans found him and made him as comfortable as possible, then left him for the next Alabama patrol, which discovered him the next day. Romano had been severely hit, a bullet lodged near his spine. Joe Romano of Company D would recover, but for him the war was over.[80]

In preparing the groundwork for the advance by the 2nd Division, veteran Al Ettinger went with an officer of the 165th to locate mortar positions. With Ettinger and the lieutenant was a new replacement with almost no training. They were caught in a gas attack, and the new man had no idea how to put on his gas mask. Ettinger removed his to show the new man how to save himself, but in doing so exposed himself to the the gas. Once back in their PC, both Ettinger and the replacement became violently ill and were sent to the hospital. The replacement, poorly trained and in France only a few days, died. Ettinger survived, but his stay in the hospital was a long one.[81]

The 166th continued aggressive patrolling in front of its positions, gathering important information. On the night of 21 October, Second Lieutenant Joseph Enfield led a thirteen-man patrol all the way to St. Georges, where it was discovered by the enemy. The Germans opened a heavy fire and sent up flares, illuminating the battlefield, but Enfield's men remained hidden and observed German dispositions at St. Georges through the night. At dawn, Enfield led his patrol safely back through the 166th's wire. Immediately, Enfield and his men were questioned by Second Lieutenant Allison Reppy, the 1st Battalion intelligence officer, and information and maps were sent to Judah's G2 section at division.[82] On 1 November, after a furious barrage, the entire 1st American and 4th French armies, under the command of General Gouraud, smashed through German defenses. By the end of the day, Colonel George C. Marshall could write: "A successful attack [has] penetrated well into the enemy lines."[83] The Rainbows received orders that they were to be transferred to I Corps under the command of Lieutenant General Joseph T. Dickman and would participate in the pursuit of the collapsing German army. The Meuse-Argonne operation, which had been so very costly in American lives, now turned into a race against time. Rumors of an armistice could be heard from every quarter. A prize beckoned Pershing and the AEF on. That prize was the famed, historic city of Sedan, and Pershing wanted the Americans to take it. His urge to capture the city, which had been the scene of France's military humiliation in 1870, would propel the Rainbows into the last great action of the war.

NOTES

    1. Hunter Liggett, *Commanding an American Army: Recollections of the World War* (Boston: Houghton-Mifflin, 1925), 74-75.

    2. John J. Pershing, *My Experiences in the World War* (New York: Frederick A. Stokes Co., 1931), Vol. 2, 294.

    3. Donald Smythe, *Pershing: General of the Armies* (Bloomington, Ind.: Indiana University Press, 1986), 195.

    4. U.S. War Department, *The Official Record of the Great War* (New York: Parke, Austin and Lipscomb, 1923), 124.

    5. James G. Harbord, *The American Army in France* (Boston: Little, Brown, 1936), 436.

    6. G3 of AEF Headquarters, Memorandum for General Pershing, "Proposed

Concept for Meuse-Argonne offensive," 4 September 1918, in Center of Military History, *United States Army in World War, 1917-1919* (Washington: Government Printing Office, 1989), Vol. 9, 3-4 (hereinafter, CMH); G3 of AEF Headquarters, "Initial Outline of Concentration," ibid., 4-6; G3 of 1st U.S. Army, "Concentration of First Army, AEF, for Meuse-Argonne Operation," 19 November 1918, ibid., 64-66 (this document was prepared by Colonel George C. Marshall).

7. G3 of AEF Headquarters, Special Orders No. 314, 29 September 1918, in the National Archives, Washington, D.C., *Records Group 120 Records of the AEF, 42nd Division*, carton 3 (hereinafter, RG 120).

8. A. Churchill Ettinger (ed.), *A Doughboy with the Fighting 69th* (Shippensburg, PA: White Main Publishing, 1929), 150.

9. Francis P. Duffy, *Father Duffy's Story* (New York: George H. Doran Co., 1919), 255-56.

10. John B. Hayes, *Heroes Among the Brave* (Loachapoka, Ala.: Lee County Historical Society, 1973), 35.

11. Lawrence Stewart, *Rainbow Bright* (Philadelphia: Dorrance, 1923), 117.

12. John H. Taber, *The Story of the 168th Infantry* (Iowa City: State Historical Society of Iowa, 1925), Vol. 2, 151-53.

13. CMH, *United States Army in the World War: Reports G2*, 349.

14. G3 of AEF Headquarters, Special Orders No. 348, 3 October 1918, RG 120, carton 3.

15. Leslie Langille, *Men of the Rainbow* (Chicago: O'Sullivan Co., 1933), 145.

16. Charles MacArthur, *War Bugs* (Garden City, N.Y.: Doubleday, Doran and Co., 1929), 173.

17. Martin J. Hogan, *The Shamrock Battalion of the Rainbow: A Story of the Fighting 69th* (New York: D. Appleton and Co., 1919), 230-31.

18. Elmer W. Sherwood, *Diary of a Rainbow Veteran: Written at the Front* (Terre Haute, Ind.: Moore-Langen, 1929), 158.

19. G3, 1st Army, Operation Report, 12 October 1918, in CMH, *United States Army in the World War*, Vol. 9, 252.

20. Douglas MacArthur, *Reminiscences* (New York: McGraw-Hill, 1964), 66. D. Clayton James, *The Years of MacArthur. Vol. 1: 1880-1941* (Boston: Houghton-Mifflin, 1970), 216-17.

21. Donovan to his wife, np, 23 October 1918, in Donovan Papers, in U.S. Army Military History Institute Archives, Carlisle Barracks, Pennsylvania, 42nd Division AEF Collection (hereinafter, MHIA).

22. Duffy, *Story*, 266-67.

23. G2, 42nd Division, "Summary of Intelligence," No. 138, 8 A.M. to 12 P.M., 12 October 1918, RG 120, carton 4.

24. G2, 42nd Division, "Summary of Intelligence," No. 141, 12 P.M. to 12 A.M., 13-14 October 1918, ibid.

25. Lieutenant Ralph G. Knowles, 3rd Battalion, 165th Infantry, Patrol Report, 15 October 1918, ibid., carton 28.

26. HQ, 83rd Brigade, Field Orders no. 16, 13 October 1918 (issued as a corrected copy in pencil at 6 P.M.), ibid., carton 22.

27. Memorandum for the files, by Lieutenant Colonel Murphy, 14 October 1918, ibid., carton 10.

28. Sherwood, *Diary*, 174-75.

29. Taber, *168th Infantry*, 167.

30. Ibid., 171-72.

31. 83rd Brigade Message Center Log, 9:55 A.M., 10:00 A.M., 14 October 1918, ibid., carton 10 (hereinafter, MESLOG).

32. HQ, 83rd Brigade, War Diary, 14 October 1918, ibid. (hereinafter, 83WD).

33. R.M. Cheseldine, *Ohio in the Rainbow: Official Story of the 166th Infantry, 42nd Division in the World War* (Columbus, Ohio: F.J. Heer Printing Co., 1924), 251.

34. MESLOG, 2:05 P.M., 14 October 1918.

35. Field message from MacArthur to 42nd PC, 12:25 P.M., 14 October 1918, in RG 120, carton 11.

36. Frazier Hunt, *The Untold Story of Douglas MacArthur* (New York: Devin-Adair Co., 1954), 89.

37. Verbatim copy of a telephone message from MacArthur to Menoher, 5 P.M., 24 October 1918, in RG 120, carton 11.

38. MacArthur to Menoher, 2:35 P.M., 24 October 1918, ibid. I believe that that time of this message is incorrect and that the message arrived later at the Rainbow PC.

39. Stewart, *Rainbow Bright*, 124-25.

40. Scott to his mother, np, 24 October 1918, in Scott Letters, manuscripts in the author's collection.

41. MESLOG, 7:56, 8:20, 8:39, and 9:15 P.M., 14 October 1918.

42. G2, 42nd Division, "Summary of Intelligence," No. 142, 12 A.M., 14 October to 12 A.M. 15 October 1918, RG 120, carton 4.

43. Ibid.

44. HQ, 83rd Brigade, Field Order No. 17, ibid., carton 22.

45. Calvin Lambert Diary, manuscript, Emporia Public Library, Emporia, Kansas, 211.

46. Hogan, *Shamrock Battalion*, 239-40.

47. Ettinger, *Doughboy*, 162.

48. Donovan to his wife, np, 23 October 1918, in Donovan Papers, MHIA.

49. HQ, 83rd Brigade, Field Order No. 18, 15 October 1918, in RG 120, carton 22.

50. Ibid.

51. MESLOG, 7:04, 7:07, 7:14, 7:18 A.M., 15 October 1918.

52. Letter from Donovan to his wife, np, 23 October 1918, in Donovan Papers, MHIA. MESLOG, 7:04, 7:07, 7:14, 7:18 A.M., 15 October 1918.

53. 83WD, 15 October 1918. MESLOG, 9:20, 9:30, 10:05, 10:15 A.M., 15 October 1918.

54. Hogan, *Shamrock Battalion*, 243-49.

55. Summerall to Menoher, 12:00 P.M., 15 October 1918, in 42nd Division, field messages, in RG 120, carton 11.

56. Ettinger, *Doughboy*, 160-61.

57. Duffy, *Story*, 272-73.

58. Statement by Major Alexander Anderson, 19 October 1918, in RG 120, carton 59.

59. Field message from Donovan to Mitchell, 12:40 A.M., 15 October 1918, ibid.

60. Taber, *168th Infantry*, 198-99.

61. MESLOG, 1:16 P.M., 15 October 1918.

62. Ibid., 2:30 P.M., 15 October 1918.

63. Field message to Rainbow PC, 9:50 P.M., 15 October 1918, in RG 120, carton 11.

64. *Official History of the 82nd Division, American Expeditionary Forces* (Indianapolis: Bobbs-Merrill Co., 1929), 183-84.

65. MESLOG, 4:16 P.M., 16 October 1918.

66. HQ, 42nd Division, Special Order No. 279, 16 October 1918, in RG 120, carton 48.

67. "In the Matter of the Relief of Brigadier General Michael J. Lenihan," nd, RG 200, carton 8. Unpublished manuscript by General Lenihan, titled, "I Remember, I Remember," in MHIA. See also Chapter 12.

68. U.S. War Department, *Official Record*, 168-69.

69. William B. Amerine, *Alabama's Own in France* (New York: Eaton and Gettinger, 1919), 329-30.

70. Taber, *168th Infantry*, 197-98.

71. Henry J. Reilly, *Americans All: The Rainbow at War* (Columbus, Ohio: F.J. Heer Printing Co., 1936), 741.

72. G2, 42nd Division, "Summary of Intelligence," No. 145., 12 A.M. to 12 P.M., 17-18 October 1918, in RG 120, carton 4.

73. James G. Harbord, *The American Army in France* (Boston: Little, Brown, 1936), 442-44.

74. Hunter Liggett, *Commanding an American Army: Recollections of the World War* (Boston: Houghton-Mifflin, 1925), 101-2.

75. Pershing, *Experiences*, Vol. 2, 350-51.

76. Cheseldine, *Ohio in the Rainbow*, 256-57.

77. Duffy, *Story*, 299.

78. E.J. Sadler (ed.), *California Rainbow Memories* (Np: Private printing, 1925), 37-39. Reilly, *Americans All*, 723-24.

79. Reilly, *Americans All*, 748-49. The order of battle for the 1 November attack is found in Liggett, *Commanding an American Army*, 108-9.

80. Notes provided by Joseph O. Romano, Jr. Birmingham, Alabama, based on his conversations with his father, Corporal Joseph O. Romano, 167th Infantry. In the 1970s, Romano's son, Joseph Jr., ran a metal detector over his father's back, and the detector issued a shrill whine as it passed over that German bullet.

81. Ettinger, *Doughboy*, 169-70.

82. Patrol report by Second Lieutenant Joseph Enfield, Company C, 166th Infantry, 22 October 1918, in RG 120, carton 31.

83. G3, 1st Army Headquarters, "Operations Report" by Colonel George C. Marshall, 1 November 1918, in CMH, *The United States Army in the World War*, Vol. 9, 372.

9

From Sedan to Belgium and Luxembourg

Everett Scott, amazed that he remained unscathed after the terrible fight for the Côte de Chatillion, wrote to his mother that he believed the war would go on and dreaded another winter in France. Scott still had had no real communication from his beloved Louise, but consoled himself by thinking that nothing could be as bad as the winter march he endured less than a year before. He did ask his mother to send him some candy before Christmas, however.[1]

Martin Hogan lay between clean sheets, afraid of what the doctors were going to tell him. His bullet-shattered hand was encased in bandages. The surgeon unwrapped the bandage, revealing a deep, red hole. It would take a long time for the wound to heal, if it ever did, but the doctor now told him he was going home, to "God's country."[2]

In a driving rainstorm, the 117th Ammunition Train had to leave for the new front before the infantry men, who would, if they were lucky, hitch rides with the Indochinese lorry drivers. The rain poured down, and it seemed to Calvin Lambert that the whole Meuse-Argonne battle would be fought in a deluge. "Never have I seen such traffic," he recalled. "It was a steady stream of trucks, guns, and wagons, French and American. We went by jerks, a hundred yards at a time, then waited a half hour or so for the truck ahead to pull out. The mud was shoe top deep, the night was pitch dark and cold."[3] Lambert dozed off, but was rudely awakened when another truck skidded and crashed into his. However, his mud-covered Dodge truck could still run.

The Rainbows, short almost 7,600 soldiers,[4] left the positions they had held since 16 October and began to shift to the west. Field Order No. 50 put them on the march with little or no personal baggage, past St. Georges and Landres-et-St. Georges, where they had poured out so much blood.[5] Speed was of the essence on those crowded roads, and whenever possible the infantry moved by unused trails and in the open fields to give priority to the motor and horse-drawn vehicles. Field Order No. 51, issued on the night of 3 November, gave march unit commanders the authority to stop and disperse troops if the Germans shelled the area,[6] but not once was either MacArthur or Reilly forced to halt the fast pace. Lieutenant Colonel Judah's "Intelligence Summaries" added to the anticipation of the moment. According to the G2's report, artillery, machine-gun fire, and air activity were all "feeble," and German infantry was retreating in a disorderly manner toward the Meuse River and the city of Sedan. I Corps' G2, Colonel R. H. Williams, indicated that once the AEF had broken the German lines in the Argonne, the entire German effort to hold on the Western Front was in jeopardy. The next possible line of resistance would be the south bank of the Meuse River.[7]

On 5 November, the Rainbow would take up the pursuit, passing through the lines of the 78th, the "Lightening Bolt" Division. The 42nd reached a staging area roughly on a line from west of St. Pierremont to Verrieres to Les Petites Armoises, the Rainbow's right boundary. Across the entire divisional frontage was a heavily wooded area known as the Bois du Mont-Dieu. Mont-Dieu itself was a formidable piece of high ground, almost 300 meters high in places and heavily forested. If the Germans decided to fight there, it could be another Côte de Chatillion. Menoher, as was his custom, placed the 84th Brigade on the right and the 83rd on the left, with as much combat power forward as possible. The divisional infantry reserve would be the 117th Engineer regiment, minus two companies that were assigned to the assaulting battalions to serve as wire cutters.

At noon, the 42nd went forward from its positions in a northerly direction, and around 3 P.M. the lead elements of the Rainbow made contact with the 78th, beginning the passage of lines. So far, there had been no enemy activity to speak of except occasional machine-gun fire from German rear detachments in the towns of La Nouville à Marie and Artaise-le Vivier, just north of the Bois du Mont-Dieu. The 84th Brigade entered the town of Grandes Armoises to the delight of the French population, which rushed out to greet the advancing doughboys. The French told intelligence officers that the Germans vacated the town at 11:20 A.M., fleeing north as rapidly as possible.[8]

The Rainbow G2, Lieutenant Colonel Judah, forward with the assaulting battalions, was jubilant at the pace of the advance. He informed the division PC, "This is surely a walk....The advance is so fast and uninterrupted that I can not keep accurate check, but if anything our flanks are further advanced than stated. There is no fire. Everything is quiet. Nothing to report."[9]

As night was falling, the Rainbow halted in an irregular line running from the northern edge of the Bois du Mont-Dieu to two miles north of the town of Stonne. That night, the Division G3 issued Field Order No. 52, which simply ordered all units to continue the rapid advance at dawn the next day.[10]

There were problems, however. Just prior to crossing the line of departure, there was no ration issue. Ration wagons and trucks were caught in the extremely heavy traffic on all roads, and men were hungry. Telephone wire was also in very short supply, causing severe problems of communication between elements of the division. Colonel Screws of the Alabama 167th made his regimental headquarters in the town of Sy, on a major road. MacArthur ordered

Screws to keep his headquarters in the town and keep the telephone lines to the division open. The 167th at Sy would then be a conduit for all 84th Brigade information, while the combat troops ran their lines of communication with regiment and brigade. MacArthur was frustrated, and asked division to do everything possible to "shove rations forward."[11]

MacArthur was not the only one irritated with the supply situation in the Rainbow. The Texas 117th Supply Train had started the 5 November operation with its trucks and other vehicles in surprisingly good shape. In Company A, for example, out of nineteen Pierce-Arrow five-ton trucks, eighteen were serviceable and ready for the campaign. In Company B, all of the nineteen Pierce-Arrow three-ton trucks were serviceable. Company C had all eighteen trucks ready to go, and in Company D, only two trucks out of eighteen were broken. Company E also had all of its vehicles ready for the operation.[12] Mortorization was a technological innovation for the American Army, and the supply soldiers were doing a ground-breaking job.

However, there were three main transportation problems. The rapidity of the advance over wooded terrain with few roads made it difficult for trucks to reach the front-line units. The rain and mud slowed everything down, and there was poor management by several key officers during the movement. A few weeks after the Meuse-Argonne campaign ended, Colonel Frank Travis, commanding officer of the 117th Ammunition Train, was relieved of duty and sent back to the United States. The Kansas Ammunition Train had been a growing problem for the Rainbows for some time, and by the end of the campaign, Menoher's patience had worn thin. During the entire Meuse-Argonne operation, the work of the train was usually a subject of criticism.[13]

On 4 November, Menoher also relieved Colonel George H. Wood, commander of the 117th Headquarters Train. Having spent his career as an infantry officer in the Ohio National Guard, Wood did not have the knowledge to command and coordinate motor transport. Upon his arrival in France, Wood had been sent to staff school at Langres, and from there he was assigned to the Rainbow Division in a position for which he had no training whatsoever. Wood was a good example of the round peg-square hole syndrome that sometimes affects large armies in wartime.[14]

Given the pell-mell pursuit of the Germans, it was probably a good thing that the end of hostilities was less than a week away. In the Ohio regiment, the watchword was "Nach Sedan [on to Sedan]—and make it snappy."[15] Father Duffy marveled at the rapidity of the advance saying,

The next three days was a footrace, each battalion was taking its turn in the lead as others became exhausted. They swept from village to village, or rather from hill to hill, carefully closing around the villages, generally meeting with but little resistance.[16]

In one village, Duffy was approached by a French woman, a zealous Catholic, who asked him to hold High Mass the next Sunday. She told him that the village curé was too old, and she had preached the Word for four years: "I tell these people that God sent the German devils amongst them because of their sins." Duffy was certain that the village was in good Catholic hands when the 165th departed on its race north.

Iowa medic Stewart was having a very hard time keeping up with the infantry:

The retreating Germans were almost always only about an hour ahead of us. The rear guard put up a fight, but the columns in advance gave a lifelike imitation of a foot race. The poor old horse which hauled the medical supply cart had to be taken out of harness for the struggle through the mire in addition to its burden had now exhausted the animal.

The Iowa medics, now pulling the supply cart, had not received rations in two days.[17]

Charles MacArthur recalled:

In seven days we had averaged five meals and less than nine hours sleep, except for the occasional fifteen minutes winks on the march. Those wishing to sleep accomplished it by holding onto the carriages with their hands and dropping off their feet. The men shuffled behind each carriage, walking in their sleep. The horses snoozed the same way. So did the drivers.

MacArthur looked at the dead horses in the fields and wondered if they could be cooked. He had seen French Algerian troops do that once. Now the idea did not seem too bad.[18]

Leslie Langille's Battery B would not see the final march. The 149th's horses were too worn out to support a full regimental advance. All good horses and selected men from Langille's battery were sent to Battery A to push on to support the infantry. The rest, including Langille, were left behind.[19]

On 6 November, Pershing issued an order for the AEF to take the city of Sedan. The message stated, "General Pershing desires that the honor of entering Sedan should fall to the American First Army." Colonel George C. Marshall drafted the initial order from 1st Army to corps commands, which had been dictated to him by G3 Colonel Fox Connor.

However, before the message was transmitted, Chief of Staff Colonel Hugh A. Drum appended a final sentence, "Boundaries will not be considered binding."[20] This was in violation of everything these generals had been preaching for years. To ignore established boundaries and move willy-nilly over a battlefield was to invite death by "friendly fire" and cause untold confusion on a battlefield already afflicted by the friction and fog of war.

Although the Rainbow was the closest American unit, the tone and wording of the order made it very unclear as to who would go for Sedan. Crossing the river and taking the city would break the German defensive line and render tactically useless the German defenses south of the river, but the very ambiguity of the order plus a natural military aggressiveness were ingredients for a near disaster.

On 5 November, the 1st Division, fighting far to the right of the Rainbow, had issued a warning order to its subordinate commands to prepare the division for an attack directly to the north, passing through the 80th Infantry Division (part of I Corps) and coordinating with 2nd Division on its right flank. This was a tricky move requiring close and detailed coordination with the battle-tested 80th Division and the 2nd Division. The attack was set for 5:30 A.M. 6 November.[21] The division PC was already on the move toward a new location near the town of Nouart. The 1st Division commander, Frank Parker, and Colonel J. N. Greely, chief of staff, plus all G2 and G2 section officers and the division's signal officer were preparing to make the night move.[22]

In the mid-afternoon of 5 November, Field Order No. 61 was issued for the attack, and troops were placed in motion north of the 80th Division.[23] At 4:30 P.M., however, the message stating that Sedan would be taken by the AEF and that "boundaries will not be considered binding" arrived at Parker's PC. General Charles Summerall visited Parker's PC about two hours after the receipt of the order, and ordered the Big Red One to move immediately on Sedan.

The hard-driving Frank Parker had commanded the 1st Brigade of the Big Red One when Summerall commanded the Division. Summerall informed Parker that he should get to Sedan and take the city regardless of the tactical and operational situation on the ground.[24] This meant that Parker would have to march to his left through the 77th and the 42nd Divisions to reach the bridges across the Meuse River.

Greely and the G3 section prepared Field Order No. 62, which changed everything the 1st Division intended to do. The 80th and 2nd Divisions were now left with little direction from Summerall. The 1st Division was to march on five routes, with Parker in the lead with the hard-fighting 28th Infantry Regiment, which had its PC near the town of Stonne. This was column 4, and its route of march was from its present location to Stonne, Chemery, and the north of Chehery, then to Sedan. Column 5 was to proceed through Chemery to Omicourt to Hannogne to St. Martin, and the latter two towns were clearly in the zone of action of the 4th French Army.[25] The three regiments of the 1st Field Artillery Brigade were assigned direct support roles, and moved with the infantry. Everything was to be in motion at 10:00 P.M. 6 November. It was now a movement of almost fifty kilometers for each of the infantry regiments, through a pitch-black night, in the rain, over winding, poor roads, with no coordination whatsoever with the American or French units through which the Big Red One would pass.[26]

Dickman was furious as he learned of the movement. The PC of I Corps was not even given the courtesy of a telephone call from Parker or Summerall. This also meant that the units of the Big Red One were moving blind, with no reference as to where either the 77th or 42nd Artillery was to fire.[27] Major General James Harbord, usually one of Pershing's great supporters and a defender of the Regular Army in the Great War, was critical. Harbord relates that not even Hunter Liggett, commanding the 1st U.S. Army, had been informed by Summerall, his subordinate, of the extraordinary action.[28] Liggett was outraged that Summerall would undertake such an unprofessional and dangerous operation, and he took steps to halt the movement as soon as possible, if Parker could be found.[29]

Not only was Summerall's action a contravention of what every senior AEF commander knew to be tactically and operationally correct, it was an insult to a fellow corps commander and to the general commanding the army, his military superior. In later years, Pershing wrote,

Under normal circumstances the action of the officer or officers [here he is referring to Summerall and Parker] responsible for this movement of the 1st Division directly across the zones of action of two other divisions could not have been overlooked, but the splendid record of that unit and the approach to the end of hostilities suggested leniency.[30]

Had Pershing not wanted Sedan taken by Americans, he would not have been lenient. However, it was Summerall, Parker, and Pershing's 1st Division involved, and it appears that Pershing allowed bias to cloud his judgment.[31]

For the French, Sedan was more than just a military objective. In 1870, during the Franco-Prussian War, the Germans surrounded the French army there and captured it as well as Emperor Napoleon III. The defeat of the French at Sedan hastened the collapse of the Second Empire, and brought the humiliations heaped on France by Germany in the Treaty of Frankfurt of 1871. To see Sedan as simply a military objective was to ignore French history and national feelings since 1870. Pershing and his generals were certainly not unaware of French history, and this makes the Sedan confusion even more serious than just misplaced zeal to capture a military prize.

To add to the problem, the French Armies of the Center, under General Paul de Maistre, had assigned to Gouraud's 4th Army the task of taking Sedan, and, in turn, Gouraud assigned the mission to the IV French Corps. IV Corps had defended Sedan in the grim months of August and September 1914, when it was driven out of the city by the invading Germans. IV Corps would be the French unit to retake Sedan, thereby wiping away the memory of that bitter defeat. Hunter Liggett, obviously aware of this, shifted 1st U.S. Army boundaries slightly to the right to accommodate the French 40th Division and the rest of IV Corps' advance. Liggett stated, "The heights commanding Sedan and the Meuse Valley, and especially the great railroad line, were really all that mattered to us, and these were reached by the night of November 6-7th."[32]

Major General James Harbord confirms that those areas were items of American interest, and once the major objectives were taken, a coordinated, synchronized French-American attack would take place across the Meuse River.[33] Nowhere did the taking of Sedan by U.S. troops enter into the operational picture. Donald Smythe, Pershing's most recent biographer, understood what Sedan meant to the French as a symbol. He has written that Pershing's desire to take Sedan was "as if General Rochambeau had shouldered General

Washington aside at Yorktown in 1781 and said, 'Here, let me accept Cornwallis's surrender.'"[34] Hunter Liggett calls this blot on the AEF combat record "a sort of fetish."[35]

The warnings of history and potential tragedy, however, did not stop the Rainbow's new divisional commander, Douglas MacArthur, from pushing on toward the Meuse. On 6 November, Charles T. Menoher was selected to command the newly formed VI Corps, MacArthur was posted to command the Rainbow, and the 84th Brigade came under the capable command of Colonel William Screws. While the actual transfer of command would be officially completed in a few days, MacArthur remained forward with the combat troops.

The Alabama 167th was pushing forward, as were all other Rainbow units. In every village the French turned out with what little food they had and prepared hot coffee for the doughboys as they advanced. By the night of 6 November, the Alabamians had pushed on through a steady downpour and camped north of Bulson. The new regimental commander, Lieutenant Colonel Walter E. Bare of Gadsden, Alabama, knew that his regiment, like the others, was taking casualties from small German rear guards, but the advance continued unabated.[36]

On 7 November, Captain Thomas H. Fallaw, who had led the wild, Rebel-yell charge at Chatillion Hill, was commanding the 3rd Battalion, 167th. His unit had driven a German rear guard out of Thelonne, only a mile and a quarter from the Meuse River.[37] From the high ground just north of Thelonne, the Alabamians could see the Meuse and the outline of the town of Bazeilles, where the French marines had won undying fame in 1870 by fighting to the last round against the Germans. At 2:15 P.M., patrols from Company M pushed to the banks of the Meuse, the first Americans to reach the river. In the afternoon of 7 November, Company L, 167th, took heavy artillery fire and had five men killed or wounded.

Colonel Benson Hough received Field Order No. 54 from Menoher's headquarters about midnight on 6 November. Hough set the next day for the Ohio regiment to reach and cross the Meuse and enter Sedan. Immediately, Hough pushed his men on, and by 8:00 A.M. Company K, under the command of a diminutive but heroic Captain Ruben Hutchcraft of Kentucky, reached Chevenges, about two and a half miles from the river. Hutchcraft, a former Kentucky state legislator and professor, beloved by his men, found his advance stalled by German machine gunners in the woods just north of the town. Chevenges was on a major road leading to the one intact bridge across the Meuse. The Germans fought for that road, and Captain Hutchcraft fell, riddled with bullets. Captain Frank Radcliffe was immediately given command of Company K, and led the infuriated Ohioans as they drove the Germans from the woods and opened the road to the river.[38]

Sometime during the afternoon of 7 November, reports began to circulate that 1st Division troops were in the 42nd Division area. In fact, a patrol from the 16th Infantry Regiment had "captured" Douglas MacArthur, who had gone

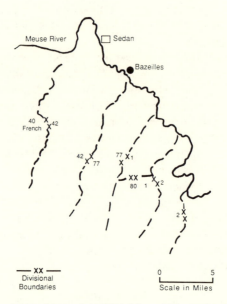

Figure 9.1 Positions of AEF Divisions, 7 November 1918

Figure 9.2 The Sedan Operation

forward to see the Iowa and Alabama regiments. MacArthur was able to clear up the confusion and apparently took the incident with good humor, but not so Menoher or Dickman.[39]

By late afternoon on 7 November, both Menoher and Dickman were complaining to Liggett, who was furious. Dickman was even talking about a court-martial for Brigadier General Frank Parker. To make matters worse, if Parker continued with his five Big Red One columns, he would soon cross over into the sector of advance held by the French 40th Infantry Division. On 5 and 6 November, the commander of the 40th had requested that American troops not wander into his sector. This request was passed down to Colonel Hough, who did his best to see that his Ohioans, those soldiers closest to the French, stayed on their side of the divisional boundary. This was fairly easy because the Rainbow divisional boundary was only about a quarter of a mile to the west of the Chemery-Chehery-Sedan road, a very identifiable key terrain feature.

To complicate matters, the French appear to have known nothing about this movement. Pershing claims that on 3 November he met with General Paul de Maistre, commanding the French Army of the Center, to whom Gouraud's IV Army was subordinate. During the meeting, Pershing suggested that, since Gouraud's forces were moving slowly, it might be wise if the American I Corps moved on Sedan. De Maistre, according to Pershing, "offered no objection, but on the contrary warmly approved."[40] If that was the case, and it is hard to believe that a French general would have been so warm to the idea of anyone not wearing Horizon Blue entering Sedan, Gouraud was not informed. His Order No. 707-3, issued on the evening of 6 November, anticipated that the French would force a river crossing the next day. There was no indication that his troops would encounter anything but retreating Germans.[41] Foch apparently knew nothing about the Americans' moving on Sedan, either. In fact, on 7 November Foch evidently believed that the American 1st Army was still operating in its zone of action.[42] Late in the afternoon of 7 November, Foch thought that the Americans would probably go into bivouac on the south side of the Meuse River.[43]

At dark, or sometime between 7:30 and 8:00 P.M., Lieutenant Colonel Bruce R. Campbell was in the 166th forward PC near Chehery. A 1st Division officer strode into the PC and stated that he was in the area to establish a forward divisional PC for the Big Red One. When he and Campbell looked at the map, Campbell was aghast to see that the proposed location was in the French 251st Infantry Regiment area of operations. A short time later, General Frank Parker came to the 166th's PC, and Campbell showed him the map, pointing out the 166th and the French 251st. Parker then told Campbell and the assembled 166th officers that he was going on, regardless of the location of 42nd or the French.[44]

Brigadier General Malin Craig, serving as chief of staff, 1st Army, telephoned Rainbow headquarters at 11:15 P.M. with a message, "SEDAN tonight, regardless of boundaries, Acknowledge."[45] Menoher was well aware of the original written message from 1st Army, but the task was much easier for a staff officer to say than for a combat division to carry out. Menoher had already taken cognizance of the orders from 1st Army, and prior to Craig's telephone call he sent a message to his subordinate commanders:

Orders from 1st Corps are most positive and explicit that the pursuit be kept up day and night, without halting and that Sedan must be reached and taken tonight, even if the last man and officer drops in his tracks. If the troops have stopped for tonight, they will be aroused at once and sent forward.[46]

This message from Menoher is significant in that he had been in possession of the order to take Sedan, with boundaries not being binding, since 6:50 P.M. when he was visited by Colonel W. S. Grant of the 1st Army staff. Colonel Grant had made Menoher personally aware of the order.[47] In Menoher's written message, he makes no bones about the nature of the relentless pursuit, but he does not restate the "boundaries will not be considered binding" phrase. Menoher knew the situation in front of him and where his troops were on the battlefield, and more important, he was well aware that the French 40th Division was moving as rapidly as possible toward Sedan. There was to be coordination between the right element of the 40th French—the 251st Regiment—and the left element of the Rainbow—the 166th Infantry. Menoher was certainly correct in pushing his troops to the limit in pursuit of a beaten enemy. He did not instruct any of his brigade or regimental commanders to violate a very critical operational and tactical principle. As far as the Rainbow was concerned, liaison with the 40th French would be made and the agreed divisional boundaries would not be tampered with. Menoher's directive to march until the last man dropped was in keeping with the nature of the pursuit.

At that time Major George T. Geran, commanding the 2nd Battalion, 166th, was at the 166th forward PC. He heard Parker tell Campbell in a loud voice that he "would proceed regardless of the 42nd Division, French, or anyone else."[48] The 166th was about to clear the woods north of Chehery as Parker and his lead units arrived. Major Robert Haubrich, commanding the 3rd Battalion, was ready to launch his attack when numerous confusing messages reached him about American troops not belonging to the Rainbow being in the woods. Ominously, some units reported that the enemy was counterattacking them on the flanks, and machine-gun and small arms fire erupted in the woods before word could be gotten down to the companies that these were doughboys of the 1st Division. The German defenders, hearing this, poured machine-gun fire into the woods, and enemy artillery fired into the mass of Americans.[49] Captain Robert Gowdy, operations officer of the 166th, received reports of numerous casualties caused by the action in the woods.

Parker's after-action report tells a very different story. For example, Column 5 marched from Stonne to Chemery to Omicourt. Omicourt was certainly in the French 40th Division zone of action, but nowhere is it mentioned that a 1st Division column had moved much farther north to St. Aignan, which was on the road to Hannogne and St. Martin, deep in the French zone.[50] Another after-action report by Parker told of the fighting in the woods north of Chevenges, but never mentioned the participation of the elements of the Ohio 166th, which had already begun their operation prior to the arrival of the 1st Division. Then Parker claims that he personally visited the PCs of the 77th and 42nd Divisions. In a masterful example of understatement, Parker wrote that the 77th and 42nd divisional commanders "seemed a bit annoyed at the First Division's appearance in their sector, but I do not believe that there was any serious feeling about the matter....Nothing but the best feeling existed at all times in all echelons."[51] There is no evidence that Parker ever visited those divisional PCs. He certainly was in the forward PC of the 166th Infantry and, evidently, never even coordinated with Colonel Hough, the regimental commander. Given Menoher's protests, Liggett's rage, and Dickman's discussion of a possible court-martial, Parker's story is just not plausible.

In an after-action report submitted to Summerall, Parker professed "only the highest professional admiration, but likewise the warmest feelings of personal friendship, [for his] comrades of the 42nd and the 77th Division."[52] In an endorsement to this report, which went to Liggett, Summerall shouldered the blame for the entire fiasco and called attention to Parker's professions of admiration and comradeship for the two divisions.

On 12 November, Parker was still trying to explain what happened. He cited in a statement a meeting between the French general commanding the 40th Division and Colonel Theodore Roosevelt, Jr., commanding the 26th Infantry Regiment, 1st Infantry Division. According to Parker, the French general, speaking to Theodore Roosevelt, claimed, "I love your father as much as I love my own."[53] That might be true, but it certainly would not have stopped Gouraud's veterans from marching all over the advance units of the 1st Division to get to Sedan. Parker ended this report with more protestations of admiration for the Rainbow and Statue of Liberty Divisions, but that does not square with his statement in the PC of the 166th Infantry when he said that he "would proceed regardless of the 42nd Division, the French, or anyone else."

By now, with five 1st Division columns moving into the area, the Rainbow was split into two unequal parts. The advanced elements of the 167th and 168th Infantry were isolated from the rest of the division, and those troops had little or no knowledge as to what was taking place in their rear. Liggett ordered the 1st Division to halt where it was and prepare to withdraw from the area of operations held by the 77th and the 42nd Divisions. Toward the end of the day, Summerall sent a report to Liggett in which he wrote:

It is a matter of profound regret if the above action was not in compliance with the wishes of the army commander, and with the meaning of the order. It was felt that the 1st Division was particularly well-placed to hurry the movement, and that a failure to take advantage of its location would not only be contrary to the meaning of the order, but would constitute a serious error. While the actual extension of the front that followed upon the movement was not anticipated, there was no question in my mind as to the necessity for the division advance.[54]

James Harbord wrote later, "As an illustration of lack of team work, and as an example of undisciplined inexperience, it justified much that our associates thought and said of us."[55]

Donald Smythe adds, "The French, who had overcome their difficulties and come storming up, panting to take Sedan, were mad as hell."[56]

About 2:00 P.M. 7 November, the advanced guard of the French 40th Division reached Checery, and it was then that it found out that elements of the 29th Infantry Regiment were in its zone of action. In fact, the lead elements of the Big Red One were on the outskirts of St. Aignan, a good nine and a half miles west of the very identifiable divisional boundary. When the 1st Division requested coordination, the French commander of the division flatly refused, and ordered the Americans to halt. The French 40th fully intended to pass through the scattered elements of the 1st Division and continue its mission, which was to coordinate with the western element of the Rainbow (the 166th) and proceed north to the bridges over the Meuse and then to Sedan.[57]

Dickman's rage was growing by the minute as the chaotic situation became clearer to him. The I Corps commander instructed the Rainbow commander simply to assume command of all American troops in his area and get the 1st Division stopped. However, Parker was in no mood to take orders from a commander of a National Guard division, and the movement went slowly forward. When V Corps was contacted by Liggett, it was discovered that the corps had lost all contact with the 1st Division and really did not know where it was. Liggett made certain Summerall understood that his division was to first stop, and then withdraw from I Corps' zone of action. Finally this was done, and around 3:00 A.M. 8 November, the Big Red One began to pull out of the area occupied by the French 40th and the 42nd and 77th U.S. Divisions.[58]

Summerall's explanation to Liggett was either false or it revealed an overly ambitious lieutenant general of the U.S. Army who could not read a map. Summerall and Dickman had been engaged in a personal feud for a long time, and what Summerall did was not only petty, but also prejudicial to the discipline and good order of the army. After the war, Frank Parker suffered from this incident, as he should have, but certainly Summerall, his commander who issued the orders to move on Sedan, did not.[59]

Summerall's report to Liggett is disturbing on other counts. He told Liggett that it was felt that the 1st Division was particularly well-placed to hurry the movement, and that failure to take advantage of its location would not only be contrary to the meaning of the order, but would constitute a serious error.[60] Brigadier General Frank Parker's after-action report to Summerall states:

The [1st] division had, within 44 hours, marched all night of the two nights and fought all day of two days and had covered *60 kilometers* [emphasis added] at the very least across country, thru woods, heavy muddy soil, for at least 40 kilometers in the face of enemy.[61]

In an annex to the report, Parker reported that to reach the areas where the

1st Division was halted and ordered to withdraw, the 16th Infantry Regiment had moved forty-three kilometers, the 26th Infantry Regiment marched sixty kilometers, and the 28th Infantry Regiment had marched forty-two kilometers.[62] If the Big Red One was so "particularly well-placed to hurry the movement," as Summerall wrote, why did it have to cover over fifty kilometers and force-march all night? The Rainbow and the 40th French were, when the 1st Division began its movement, about twelve kilometers from the city of Sedan itself. Colonel Reilly, commanding the 83rd Brigade, informed Menoher at 1:15 P.M. 6 November that his lead elements were pushing well north of Chemery, which was eight miles, on a straight line, from Sedan. He was in the process of coordinating his boundaries with the French 40th Division, which had fired its artillery into areas where elements of the 166th had entered. So concerned was Reilly with the possibility of fratricidal artillery fire that he asked Menoher to inform General Dickman at I Corps headquarters and request that he coordinate the boundary at the highest levels.[63] Division General Laiguelot, commanding the 40th French, had prepared a methodical advance with planned artillery fires, and the danger of a tragedy increased. As the 1st Division moved into the 40th's sector, Laiguelot stated that he was "obliged" to use his artillery as he had planned, but there were Americans there.[64] Evidently, the general had never been informed of any plan to allow the Americans to advance on Sedan, and probably there never was any agreement with the French.

The sketch maps included in Parker's operations report clearly show the 26th Regiment at Villers-sur-Bar and the 28th Regiment at Cheveuges when they were ordered to stop and withdraw.[65] The French had planned artillery in those areas. Parker wrote that the fault for this confusion was his, and that "there has been an absolute honesty of purpose and an entirely single minded purpose to cooperate fully and entirely unselfishly with our comrades of the 42nd and 77th Divisions."[66]

Colonel Reilly went immediately to Menoher and reported that the Big Red One's 2nd Brigade and Parker with his divisional PC had arrived directly in the rear of 83rd Brigade's lines. Menoher heard Reilly's report and telephoned Brigadier Malin Craig at I Corps, telling him, "Parker said that he had orders to make Sedan and that he was going ahead no matter what the 42nd did." Menoher stated that the arrival of the 1st Division and the subsequent mix-up of forces so confused the situation that the 166th's attack faltered, resulting in needless casualties for both the 1st and the 42nd Divisions. Menoher, who knew what the situation was as far as coordination between the Rainbow and the 40th French, warned that Parker intended to move his forces even more to the west to prepare for an assault across the Meuse River. Parker had evidently told Reilly this, and both Reilly and Menoher knew that the Big Red One would be in the French zone of action, where the 40th planned artillery fires as it advanced.[67]

French liaison officers clearly told Menoher that the 40th Division intended to continue its mission and fire. The situation was so confused that Menoher informed I Corps and 1st Army that it was intolerable, and that 1st Army had to issue orders to straighten the mess out. Menoher was given command of all American troops in the sector, and he was to ensure that the 83rd Brigade shifted slightly to the right, that coordination be completed with the 40th French, and that the Big Red One withdrawal be completed immediately.[68] While neither Summerall nor Parker addressed the cost of such an operation, James Harbord, certainly a soldier who would have first-hand knowledge, wrote later, "The Division was sent on a futile errand in executing when it sustained about five hundred casualties and marched itself to exhaustion."[69] From Rainbow operational reports, it is possible to deduce that any casualties were caused by friendly fire, when the 26th and 28th Infantries and the 166th Infantry became confused and intermingled.

MacArthur, who was now at the Rainbow PC awaiting final orders to take command, allowed the business of the division to proceed as normal since the 1st Division became no longer a hindrance to the original mission. Probably Dickman initially had urged the Rainbow to compete with the Big Red One. That was no longer an issue. On 8 November, Company D, 166th, under Captain Russell Baker of Delaware, Ohio, joined the French 251st Infantry Regiment for the advance to the Meuse.[70]

Fate had placed the Ohio 166th in a position to move to Sedan in coordination with the French 40th Division. During the day of 8 November, the Ohioans and the French pushed up to Frénois, one mile from the bridges over the Meuse and the outskirts of Sedan. In fact, the city could be seen from the Château Frénois, where the French and Americans halted for the day. That night, in coordination with the French 251st Infantry, mixed patrols went forward with a mission to enter Sedan if at all possible. Two patrols from the 166th departed the area near the Château for Sedan. One patrol from Company D was led by First Lieutenant George E. Crotinger and consisted of himself, one sergeant, thirty-three enlisted men, and one French liaison officer from the 251st. The second patrol was commanded by First Lieutenant Colvin H. Todd, also of Company D, and had two sergeants, thirty-nine enlisted men, and a French officer. Both patrols entered the town of Torcy and pushed close to the river. The Germans shelled the area heavily, and the French officers made the decision to take the patrols back to Frénois before dawn. Several things were learned: The bridge across the Meuse was intact, and German machine gunners were still in defensive positions south of the Meuse River.[71]

Companies D of both the 166th and the 165th Infantry were designated to continue operations with the French on 8 November, but for some reason, Company D of the 165th remained in its position at Bulson.[72] Consequently, it fell to Captain Russell Baker, commanding Company D, 166th, to work with the French. His troops would be the first American soldiers to enter Sedan. General Gouraud, who was not a petty man and was well aware of the contribution of the Rainbow, allowed for coordination and joint action in his plans for the day of 8 November.[73] To everyone's satisfaction, I Corps and the 1st U.S. Army reconfirmed the Rainbow's authority to take command of all American troops in their zone of action to forestall any more glory hunting by elements of the AEF.[74]

Colonel Reilly briefed Captain Baker personally, ordering him and his full company to report to Colonel Deville, commander of the 251st Infantry Regiment. Platoons of the company went with various French patrols, and one entered the city of Sedan. Once that was done, on 9 November, Company D was released and returned to Chevenges, where it paused to bury the dead from the 166th who had fallen there two days before.[75]

Between 9 and 11 November, the Rainbow remained in place, shifting positions slightly to the south to allow the French to enter Sedan and Bazeilles. General MacArthur had begun to shift the divisional PC back to the Buzancy area, anticipating another move soon after. Rumors abounded that the war would soon be over. The patrols that entered the Sedan area between 8 and 9 November reported a lessening of German fire, and from all reports the enemy army was in disarray, not spoiling for a fight. MacArthur had developed what he thought was a cold and throat infection, and was glad to get the rest as the division began to consolidate.[76]

Lawrence Stewart's Iowa medic buddies found an old destroyed house with a fireplace and chimney intact, and they built a fire to try to dry out. They had heard that on 11 November the war would be over. One of his comrades, who had been through every engagement that the 168th Infantry had fought in, said, "All the Regular Army officers will get busted now—hot-dog. That's the best thing about bein' a buck private—they can't bust you." Another soldier, a sergeant, sat in the corner of the building and just looked at a photograph of his Iowa girlfriend. The rumor, which someone had repeated, was not really believed.[77]

Charles MacArthur's Illinois gunners had not fired all day during 10 November. That afternoon, the 149th Artillery pulled back toward Buzancy, and everyone was elated at being relieved before anyone else was wounded or killed. As they passed by military police, they were told by a number of the MPs that the Rainbow was being pulled back to Bordeaux and would be one of the first divisions sent back to the United States. "A great many speculations on Bordeaux women, wine, women, omelets, women and women ensued. We even took to singing a bit," MacArthur recalled.[78]

Leslie Langille's Battery had remained behind at Harricourt when the regiment consolidated its good horses. During the evening of 10 November, the troops were officially informed that an armistice would go into effect at 11:00 A.M. the next day. They had not expected it to come so soon, and when the word was received there was mainly silence. Many of the old Chicago Board of Trade Battery ended that evening with a prayer of thanksgiving.[79] Hoosier Elmer Sherwood was in a muddy field that night just north of Buzancy when the word came that the fighting would end on the morrow. Like many of his Indiana comrades, he would believe it when it came. Right at that point, it was more pressing just to find a place to sleep.[80]

As far as Douglas MacArthur was concerned, on 11 November the 42nd would conduct business as usual, pulling units back to a divisional staging area near the Rainbow PC at Buzancy. The Rainbow soldiers had seen too much to enter into wild celebrations at 11:00 A.M. Calvin Lambert and his buddies found what had been a German bathhouse, fitted with tile floors, tubs, and fireplaces. It was time to take a bath, after fighting every inch of the way to get the 117th Ammunition Train's trucks through the mud of the Argonne. Lambert took a long bath, but really did not feel that his cooties had been washed away.[81]

John Hayes of Company I, 167th Alabama, was finally sure that he would make it back home. His regiment was marching south toward a regimental staging area near the town of Stonne when the guns stopped firing. Hayes' unit fired off flares and built fires that night, and he watched in amazement as trucks and automobiles drove past Company I's bivouac with their headlights on.[82] First Lieutenant Allison Reppy, intelligence officer, 1st Battalion, 166th Infantry, had heard rumors that the regiments would be home before Christmas, but early that night he had official word that the entire Rainbow was going to Germany as part of the Army of Occupation.[83]

On 8 November, 1st Army issued an order specifying that the Rainbow's sector would be taken over by Gouraud's 4th Army. At that time, the division would withdraw to the Buzancy area, where it would pass under the operational command of Summerall's V Corps, no pleasing prospect for the 42nd. Then V Corps would move the division back to the Mountfaucon area, where it would become the 1st Army's operational reserve, under command of III Corps.[84] That was not to happen, because five of the best AEF divisions were to be selected to form the combat troops of the new 3rd Army, which was to be the Army of Occupation in Germany.

Unknown to anyone but major players, on 8 November the Army of Occupation came into being with about 200,000 troops under Major General Joseph Theodore Dickman. On 13 November, the orders were published that officially created the 3rd Army, designated as the occupying force. The best five AEF divisions—1st, 2nd, 3rd, 32nd, and 42nd—were designated as the combat elements of the army, with 60,000 troops selected as support personnel, including army artillery troops. By 15 November, Dickman had his staff in place and could begin to plan the very complex movement of so many soldiers to Germany, to the east bank of the Rhine River.[85]

Given the area to be covered in Germany by the American Army of Occupation, it was quickly decided to add more combat muscle to 3rd Army. If hostilities began again, five combat divisions might not be enough to support operations. The 89th "Rolling W" Division, and the 90th "Tough Ombres" Division, both with fine battle records, were given orders to prepare to move into Germany. The Regular 4th "Ivy" Division was alerted also to begin the move toward the Belgian border, and the 5th "Red Diamond" Division was ordered into the Grand Duchy of Luxembourg late in November 1918. From the tiny Grand

Duchy, the 5th, in the role of an operational or army reserve, could move quickly to support 3rd Army combat operations. The National Guard 33rd, the "Yellow Cross" Division, moved into Luxembourg, while the 37th Ohio National Guard's Buckeye Division marched into Belgium to cover lines of communication between the Belgian ports and 3rd Army in Germany. Support troops from the SOS moved into Luxembourg, Belgium, and Germany as well.

Pershing ordered that every unit preparing to move east would be at full strength, with all equipment, clothing, weapons, and transportation. Several newly arrived divisions were "skeletonized" to bring the 3rd Army up to full strength. The 31st Dixie Division and the 39th Delta Division, both drawn from southern National Guards, found themselves cleaning and transferring every conceivable type of supply as quickly as possible, and preparing to send men rapidly. Needed specialists, particularly medical personnel, were transferred to the 3rd Army, and they too went to Germany.

The men of the Rainbow reacted well to the order to move to Germany, and most soldiers saw the march to the Rhine as a continuation of the great adventure they started in April 1917. Of course, there was curiosity about Belgium, Luxembourg, and especially Germany, the land of their enemies. The Rainbow became part of the III Corps under the command of Major General John L. Hines, with the 2nd and 32nd as the other corps' combat divisions. Hines, a solid Regular officer, came to France with Pershing in the spring of 1917 on the USS *Baltic*, as a major. By the St. Mihiel offensive, he was a major general in command of the 4th Division, and during the Meuse-Argonne he was in command of III Corps. He would become chief of staff of the army from 1924 to 1926.

To complete the combat corps, Dickman had IV Corps commanded by Major General Charles H. Muir, who commanded the National Guard 28th Division before rising to corps command. IV Corps was the "Regular Army" corps, consisting of 1st, 3rd, and 4th Divisions. The VII Corps was commanded by Major General William G. Haan and contained the 89th and the newly added 90th Division made up of Texas and Oklahoma National Army veterans. Haan had commanded the hard-fighting 32nd Division in combat. All in all, the three corps were the best that the AEF had to offer, and they were units which could be relied upon.

At 5:30 A.M. 17 November, the first element of the 3rd Army, the Rainbow Division, was scheduled to begin the march to the Rhine. The Rainbow, the first to enter Germany, however, would begin its trek under a new divisional commander, Major General Clement Alexander Finley Flagler, who officially assumed command on 21 November. Flagler graduated from West Point in 1889 as an engineer. During the St. Mihiel offensive, he commanded the 5th Field Artillery Brigade of the 5th Division. After St. Mihiel, Flagler got his second star as commander of III Corps artillery during the Meuse-Argonne offensive. MacArthur returned to the 84th Brigade, and Colonel William Screws resumed command of his beloved Alabama Wildmen. Reilly was replaced by Brigadier

General Frank M. Caldwell, and he went back to his Illinois artillerymen. None of these changes were demotions in any sense of the word. MacArthur related that since the war had ended, there would be no further elevation in the general ranks. There was nothing to be done except to accept the situation in good grace and humor, and this is what MacArthur, Reilly, and Screws did.[86]

The one change that did not sit well with anyone was the relief of Lieutenant Colonel Charles Dravo from command of the Irish 165th Infantry. Dravo had taken command when Brigadier General Michael Lenihan was relieved as 83rd Brigade commander, and Colonel Harry Mitchell suffered a similar fate in October. Dravo's promotion was denied and Colonel Charles R. Howland, a Regular officer, was sent to command. Howland had commanded the 172nd Infantry Brigade in the National Army 86th Division, which arrived in France just as the war was ending.[87] In many a combat veteran's eyes, this was the Regular Army's taking care of one of its own, while a soldier proven in battle was passed over. The 165th never really took to Howland, who left little impression on the tough Irishmen.

Everett Scott was not too impressed with Belgium and wished he were back in the United States, but the adventure of the march made up for his not going home right away. He hoped that the Rainbow would leave by spring, but until it did, he would continue to dream of fried chicken and lemon pies back in Iowa.[88] Leslie Langille was surprised at the welcome the Belgians gave the Americans. Many of those who had endured four years of German occupation had heard only rumors of the American participation in the war. Langille later recalled:

Cafes and private homes are jammed with our fellows, and bottles are dug out of their hiding places, covered with dust, cobwebs and age, and many toasts are drunk to their health and as many other healths as can be thought of, as with each health goes another drink. Such a "bon guerre" as this might go to the heads of the bucks; so bright and early on the next morning, November 22, we are on our way to our next one night stand.[89]

Father Duffy noticed that in Luxembourg the villages and towns were neat and not scarred by war as were those in despoiled France. He had learned that the Rainbow would stay in Luxembourg until 1 December, when it would cross over into Germany proper. On Duffy's mind was how to provide a decent Thanksgiving dinner for the troops. Duffy was a little surprised that finding good food in quantity was no real problem, except that prices were very high. Regardless, his Irishmen would have a good meal and a joyous Mass to go with it.[90]

Bill Screw's 167th Regiment would lead the Rainbow into Belgium. The column marched past the border, and as it approached the first town, the regimental colors were uncased and the band's drums began to beat. As they entered the town, the Alabama band began to play, and a roar went up from the regiment. The 167th Infantry Regiment had entered Belgium on its way to Germany, with its band playing "Dixie."[91]

NOTES

1. Scott to his Mother, 24 and 25 October 1918, in the Scott Letters, manuscripts in the author's collection.

2. Martin J. Hogan, *The Shamrock Battalion of the Rainbow: A Story of the Fighting 69th* (New York: D. Appleton and Co., 1919), 251-52.

3. Calvin Lambert Diary, manuscript, Emporia Public Library, Emporia, Kansas, 218.

4. D. Clayton James, *The Years of MacArthur, Vol. 1: 1880-1941* (Boston: Houghton-Mifflin, 1970), 229.

5. HQ, 42nd Division, Field Order No. 50, 2 November 1918, in the Reilly Papers, in U.S. Army Military History Institute Archives, Carlisle Barracks, Pennsylvania, 42nd Division AEF Collection (hereinafter, MHIA).

6. HQ, 42nd Division, Field Order No. 51, 3 November 1918, ibid.

7. G2, I Corps, Summary of Intelligence Number 111, 3 November 1918, ibid.

8. Field message from G3, 42nd Division to G3, I Corps, 4:00 P.M. 5 November 1919, in the National Archives, Washington, D.C., *Records Group 120 Records of the AEF, 42nd Division*, carton 11 (hereinafter, RG 120).

9. Field message from Judah to Murphy, 7:00 P.M. 5 November 1919, ibid.

10. Colonel Benson Hough, "After-Action Report" for 5 to 8 November 1918, 13 November 1918, ibid., carton 130.

11. Field message from Colonel Screws to Murphy, 9:00 P.M., 5 November 1918, ibid., carton 11.

12. "Weekly Motor Transport Service Report" for Companies A, B, C, D, and E, 117th Supply Train, 30 October 1918, ibid., carton 41.

13. "In the Matter of the Relief and Discharge of Lieutenant Colonel Frank L. Travis, 117 Amunition Train," 17 May 1919, in RG 200, carton 12.

14. "In the Matter of the Relief and Discharge of Colonel George H. Wood, 117th Train Hq&MP," 17 May 1919, ibid.

15. R.M. Cheseldine, *Ohio in the Rainbow: Official Story of the 166th Infantry, 42nd Division in the World War* (Columbus, Ohio: F.J. Heer Printing Co., 1924), 264.

16. Francis P. Duffy, *Father Duffy's Story* (New York: George H. Doran Co., 1919), 299-300.

17. Lawrence Stewart, *Rainbow Bright* (Philadelphia: Dorrance, 1923), 128-29.

18. Charles MacArthur, *War Bugs* (Garden City, N.Y.: Doubleday, Doran and Co., 1929), 221.

19. Leslie Langille, *Men of the Rainbow* (Chicago: O'Sullivan Co., 1933), 164.

20. G3, 1st Army, Memorandum for Commanding Generals, I Corps, V Corps, in Center of Military History, *United States Army in the World War, 1917-1919* (Washington: Government Printing Office, 1989), Vol. 9, 385. Also see: George C. Marshall, *Memoirs of My Service in the World War, 1917-1918* (Boston: Houghton-Mifflin, 1976), 189-92. Marshall's view of this situation reflects, at the heart, his respect for Pershing and the Regular Army troops of the 1st Infantry Division. Marshall's memoirs here must be taken with a grain of salt.

21. G3, 1st Infantry Division, Warning Notice for Field Order No. 61, 5 November 1918, in U.S. Army, World War Records, *First Division, American Expeditionary Forces, Regular, Field Orders, Sept. 19, 1918 to Conclusion*, Vol. 3 (March 6, 1928) (hereinafter, *First Division*). This set of documents is unusual. It is

a bound set of over 24 volumes of copies of orders, reports, war diaries, citations, all original war time copies that was assembled in the late 1920s and 1930s.

22. G3, 1st Infantry Division, "Warning Notice for Movement for Division Headquarters," 5 November 1918, ibid.

23. G3, 1st Infantry Division, Field Orders No. 61, 5 November 1918, ibid.

24. Joseph T. Dickman, *The Great Crusade* (New York: Appleton, 1927), 190-93.

25. G3, 1st Infantry Division, Field Orders No. 62, 6 November 1918, in *First Division*.

26. G3, 1st Infantry Division, Field Orders No. 63, 6 November 1918, ibid.

27. Donald Smythe, *Pershing: General of the Armies* (Bloomington, Ind.: Indiana University Press, 1986), 230.

28. James G. Harbord, *The American Army in France* (Boston: Little, Brown, 1936), 458-59.

29. Hunter Liggett, *Commanding an American Army: Recollections of the World War* (Boston: Houghton-Mifflin, 1925), 116-17.

30. John J. Pershing, *My Experiences in the World War* (New York: Frederick A. Stokes Co., 1931), Vol. 2, 381.

31. Smythe, *Pershing*, 230. This author shares Smythe's opinion that if such a travesty had occurred with a National Guard division, Pershing certainly would not have overlooked it. General Dickman is particularly bitter about this episode in his memoirs. He relates that Pershing had promised the French to investigate this action, but, by verbal order, this never took place. See: Dickman, *Great Crusade*, 193.

32. Liggett, *Commanding an American Army*, 117.

33. Harbord, *American Army*, 428-29.

34. Smythe, *Pershing*, 227.

35. Liggett, *Commanding an American Army*, 116.

36. William B. Amerine, *Alabama's Own in France* (New York: Eaton and Gettinger, 1919), 209.

37. Ibid., 211.

38. Cheseldine, *Ohio in the Rainbow*, 272-73.

39. James, *The Years of MacArthur*, 232-33. MacArthur, *Reminiscences*, 68-69.

40. Pershing, *Experiences*, Vol. 2, 381.

41. 3ième Bureau, IV Armée, Ordre pour le journée du 7 Novembre, 6 Novembre 1918 in France, Etat-Major de l'Armée, Service Historique, *Les Armées Françaises dans la Grande Guerre*, Series 7, Vol. 2 (Paris: Imprimerie Nationale, 1938), 793-96.

42. Foch to French Mission, Chaumont, 7 November 1918, ibid., Series 6, Vol. 2 (1934), 812. Also see message from de Maistre to Pershing, 7 November 1918, ibid., 811.

43. Foch to French Mission, Chaumont, 4:42 P.M. 7 November 1918, ibid., 805.

44. Statement by Lieutenant Colonel Bruce R. Campbell, 11 November 1918, in the Reilly Papers, MHIA. A copy of this report can be found in RG 120, carton 30. In fact, all of the cited statements are found in carton 30, but they are signed by those making the statement. They are also reprinted verbatim in Cheseldine, *Ohio in the Rainbow*, 281-87.

45. Telephone message from Malin Craig to Colonel Murphy, 9:15 P.M. 6 November 1918, in 42nd Division Message Log, in RG 120, carton 11.

46. Menoher to his brigade commanders, 11:00 P.M. 6 November 1918, ibid.,

carton 10.

47. Dickman, *Great Crusade*, 184.

48. Statement by Major George T. Geran, 11 November 1918, RG 120, carton 30.

49. Statement by Major Robert Haubrich, 10 November 1918, ibid.

50. G3, 1st Infantry Division, Operation Report from 6th Noon to 7th Noon, November 1918, in U.S. Army, World War Records, *First Division, Regulars, American Expeditionary Forces, Operations Reports, First Division, 12 September 1918 to Conclusion* (hereinafter, *First Division, Operation Reports*). This set of documents contains original war time orders, reports, war diaries, and was assembled in 1930.

51. Parker to Summerall, "Report on Operations of the First Division," 9 November 1918, ibid.

52. Parker to Summerall, "Crossing of Lines of Other Divisions During the Operation, Nov. 6-7th 1918," 9 November 1918, ibid.

53. Parker to Summerall, 12 November 1918, ibid.

54. Summerall to Liggett, 7 November 1918, in CMH, *United States Army in the World War*, Vol. 9, 391-92.

55. Harbord, *American Army*, 459.

56. Smythe, *Pershing*, 228.

57. American Battle Monuments Commission, *42nd Division Summary of Operations in the World War* (Washington: Government Printing Office, 1944), 85-87.

58. Ibid., 87. Dickman, *Great Crusade*, 185-89.

59. James, *The Years of MacArthur*, 235-36.

60. Summerall to Liggett, 7 November 1918, CMH, *United States Army in the World War*, Vol. 9, 391-92.

61. Parker to Summerall, "Report on Operations of the First Division," 9 November 1918, *First Division, Operations Reports*.

62. Annex to 9 November 1918, "Operations Report," ibid.

63. Reilly to Menoher, 1:15 P.M. 6 November 1918, in HQ, 42nd Division, G3 Journal and Message Log, in RG 20, carton 11.

64. Dickman, *Great Crusade*, 289.

65. Annex, Sketch Maps, 9 November 1918, "Operations Report," *First Division, Operations Reports*.

66. Parker to Summerall, "Crossing the Lines of Other Divisions During the Operation, Nov. 6-7th 1918," 9 November 1918, ibid.

67. Menoher to Craig, 3:45 P.M. 7 November 1918, in HQ, 42nd Division, G3 Journal and Message Log, RG 120, carton 11.

68. Menoher to Dickman, "Operations of 1st Division in the Sector of this Division and Misunderstanding with 40th Division (French) Regarding Sector Limits," 8 November 1918, ibid., carton 14. The order giving Menoher authority over all troops in his area is G3 Memorandum No. 84, 7 November 1918, ibid., carton 10.

69. Harbord, *American Army*, 459. The major First Division history placed casualties of all types at 10 officers and 496 enlisted men. The history does not mention the confusion and tends to gloss over the extraordinary lapse in military courtesy and discipline. See: Society of the First Division, *History of the First Division During the World War, 1917-1919* (Philadelphia: John C. Winston, 1922), 229-236.

70. Benson Hough, "After-Action Report 5-8 November 1918," 13 November 1918, in the Reilly Papers, MHIA.

71. Patrol reports by First Lieutenants George F. Crotinger and Colvin H. Todd, 8-9 November 1918, in RG 120, carton 21.

72. Monuments Commission, *42nd Division, Summary*, 89.

73. 3ième Bureau, IV Armée, "Ordre pour le Journée du 9 Novembre," 8 Novembre 1918, in *Les Armées Françaises*, Series 7, Vol. 2, 828-29.

74. Monuments Commission, *42nd Division, Summary*, 88.

75. Patrol report by Captain Russell Baker, 10 November 1918, in RG 120, carton 31.

76. MacArthur, *Reminiscences*, 71.

77. Stewart, *Rainbow Bright*, 143.

78. MacArthur, *War Bugs*, 234.

79. Langille, *Men of the Rainbow*, 167-68.

80. Elmer W. Sherwood, *Rainbow Hoosier* (Indianapolis, Ind.: Printing Arts Co. 1925), 147-48.

81. Calvin Lambert Diary, 212.

82. Hayes, *Heroes Among the Brave*, 41.

83. Alison Reppy, *Rainbow Memories: Character Sketches and History of the First Battalion, 166th Infantry* (Np: Private printing, 1919), 20.

84. HQ, 1st Army, Field Orders No. 106, 8 November 1918, in CMH, *United States Army in the World War*, Vol. 9, 398.

85. Dickman, *Great Crusade*, 198-99. Liggett, *Commanding an American Army*, 126.

86. MacArthur, *Reminiscences*, 71.

87. Duffy, *Story*, 306.

88. Everett Scott to his mother, France and Luxembourg, 13, 27, and 28 November 1919, in Scott Letters.

89. Langille, *Men of the Rainbow*, 171.

90. Duffy, *Story*, 306-7.

91. Amerine, *Alabama's Own*, 221.

10

RAINBOW ON THE RHINE

Leslie Langille was not sure about Luxembourg's welcome for the doughboys of the Rainbow. On 23 November the 149th Field Artillery arrived in the Grand Duchy town of Bushdorf, where the population seemed indifferent, if not openly hostile to the doughboys. The day before had been very different. The population of Arlon, Belgium, had turned out in a riotous welcome—liquor flowed free, and many a rugged soldier was kissed more than he had ever dared to dream. But Langille now thought as he looked around, "We have our suspicions as to the degree of neutrality practiced by the people. They are a suspicious looking lot, and seem to resent our being there."[1] Thanksgiving was spent in the Grand Duchy, and the Rainbow men remembered the sheer pleasure of warm food and being alive. The Ohio Infantry was billeted in and around Ripweiler, a small village. The regiment, while there, began a regimen of close-order drill and the manual of arms.[2]

The drill and inspections of all 3rd Army troops while on the march into Germany were prescribed for very good reasons. Constant combat did not lend itself well to a consistent reinforcement of military discipline. There was not much time spent on soldierly appearance when the troops were usually soaking wet and covered in mud. Many officers preferred not to be saluted while in the trenches, because a salute might very well be an invitation for an enemy sniper to fire. The orders sending the Rainbow on the march, therefore, stated:

The Division has earned a high reputation as a fighting unit, and while the campaigns that have brought it this reputation, have developed and intensified the combat qualities of the individual soldier, the necessary laxity of campaign life has bred a disregard of other qualities that make for the soldier, Viz., perfection of carriage, clothing, equipment and individual discipline and military courtesy. The conditions of the march do not lend themselves to the attainment of this improvement, but there will be occasional halts of several days on the march to the RHINE, and it is enjoined on all officers and non-commissioned officers to use every opportunity to restore the thoroughly soldierly bearing and conduct that characterized the Division in the early months of its training.[3]

The same order strictly forbade fraternization with anyone in any country through which the army passed. Certainly no one could have expected anything but a tremendous welcome in those areas of France that had been occupied by the Germans for four years. In Belgium, where German occupation had been harsh from the first day of the war, the indications were that the Allies would be treated as liberators, and the emotional release felt by the inhabitants would be extreme. Luxembourg could very well be another matter.

Calvin Lambert and the Kansas 117th Ammunition Train were stationed very near Luxembourg City. Lambert observed:

The people here are neutral but I think they are strongly pro-German, and we are not as welcome as they would have us believe. They have prospered from the war, and there is a great contrast between the Luxemburger and the Belgian. The Belgians received us with open arms; the Luxemburgers are only luke-warm, excepting our landlord who is a good frog. Prices are high here. I priced chickens and the boche-looking bird wanted $5 each and eggs are selling for 25 cents each. Cigars are 25 cents and drinking liquor is way up.[4]

On 27 November Monsieur Pesch, who owned the home that served as billets for Lambert and his buddies, took them on a tour of Luxembourg City. There they had a real bath and ice cream, which Lambert had not tasted since arriving in Europe.

John Hayes of the Alabama 167th was housed in the village of Hobscheid, where he and his buddies bought and barbecued a goat for Thanksgiving Day. One farmer had a rather buxom daughter, named by the Alabamians "Marguerite of Hobscheid," who was avidly courted by a number of the men from Company I. According to Hayes, that farmer's daughter was remembered long and fondly by a number of the Southern soldiers.[5]

Always the cynic and amused observer, Charles MacArthur believed, "Nobody gyps like a good Honest-to-God victim," and he was ready for the worst when they marched into Belgium. As the Illinois artillerymen marched into St. Leger, MacArthur saw people hanging from windows and waving at the soldiers. The bandmaster had had his band learn a stirring, fierce French marching song, "Sambre et Meuse," but his band had never before played it. Now, marching down the main street of St. Leger, Belgium, he raised his drum major's baton, and the band struck up the march. MacArthur was stunned:

Up from the town came a shout. That was one tune they hadn't heard for more than four years. Old men with funny hats stood in the streets and wept. The women rushed from the houses bawling louder than the men. They broke the swinging ranks to throw their arms around us and call us saviors. It was embarrassing and not in the least what we expected.[6]

The kissed, pawed, and cried-over Alabams were overwhelmed with their reception in Belgium. James F. Cogdill, the sergeant major of the 167th Infantry Regiment, was standing by a lanky Alabamian who said, "That is what I have been fighting nine months for."

At the outskirts of each town the band master, under orders from Colonel Screws, raised his baton and the 167th marched to the strains of "Dixie." Cogdill, from Inverness, Alabama, was mystified to see so many flags. "Where they got the material to make these things from no one knows," he wrote to his father, "They were probably hidden from the Germans for four and a half years."[7] Cogdill certainly did not think the Americans would be greeted with flags, kisses, and brass bands when they marched into Germany.

Outside of Arlon the men of the artillery brigade found an abandoned German supply depot, where the troops quickly exchanged wornout shoes for German boots. Many a gunner marched into Luxembourg with a German helmet on his head and an Iron Cross pinned to his blouse. Immediately, Charles MacArthur and his buddies took a dislike to the Grand Duchy, where prices were high and the people suspicious and cold. "Luxembourg was no country: it was a night club, without any of a night club's entertaining features," he said. The prices for food and chickens went steadily upward.[8] MacArthur's buddies bought an overpriced pig for their Thanksgiving fare.

On 2 and 3 December, in fairly decent weather, the Rainbow crossed into Germany. As the Irish 165th marched across the border and into the village of Bollendorf, the colors were uncased and the band struck up "Gary Owen," a favorite of Irish soldiers in any army. As he crossed the bridge, Father Duffy was startled by the sight of a bright rainbow in the sky, a fine omen for the first American soldiers in the land of their former enemies.[9]

Everett Scott was marching behind the Iowa band, which was playing "Over There," and as they crossed into Germany he too looked up and saw the rainbow. "I never went much on signs before," he wrote to his brother, "but I realy beleaved in that."[10]

Even though Americans had experienced occupying the Philippines, no one was prepared for the task before them. Reflecting a lesson learned in the actual fighting, the 3rd Army made intelligence about the enemy its first priority as the advance continued and during the occupation itself. Dickman recalled:

All the enemy's movements were carefully watched by our intelligence section. The morale of his troops, the condition of his horses, the processes of demobilization and all other items of useful information were gathered by an efficient secret service from day to day....We were at all times informed of the degree of his compliance with the terms of the armistice and were ready for any eventuality.[11]

Vast quantities of heavy equipment, arms, and supplies were turned over to Dickman's advancing army. In just a few days, 695 artillery pieces, 4,445 heavy and light machine guns, thirty-one airplanes, and thirty-eight railroad locomotives were handed over to the Americans.[12]

There was considerable interest in what the reaction of the German civilians would be to the enemy marching into their territory for an indeterminate occupation. On 1 and 2 December, III Corps was able to inform 3rd Army that, while the population seemed apprehensive over the Americans, there had been no disorder. In many of the towns, there were returning German troops, many still in uniform, lining the streets as the doughboys marched by. No one seemed to be starved or particularly ragged, and food appeared to be plentiful. The G2 at 3rd Army wrote in an intelligence summary for 2 December: "The general impression is that the German people have suffered less during the war than any of the allied peoples and probably less than the people of neutral countries."[13]

Should the armistice fall apart, the 3rd Army was to be ready to resume offensive operations. There was a military rationale for the occupation, but what was its ideological underpinning? Woodrow Wilson had sent the AEF to France on a high moral note. His famous Fourteen Points gave a sanctity to the terrible hardships the doughboy had to endure. To the doughboys, the moralistic tone behind the occupation made sense and did not sound in the least naive. There was also no question in the minds of Americans as to who caused the war and the terrible slaughter: the Germans, their kaiser, and the ruling military class. Now the doughboy was in the enemy's land, and he was to exhibit those traits that brought America to the shores of their old world. Certainly an American soldier could not himself affect the great deliberations at Versailles; neither would his voice be heard in the highest councils of Allied government. His role was to show to the Germans the disapprobabation of a democratic people. He was to stand apart, morally and ideologically untainted. He was not to fraternize with an enemy that had proven itself to be so unworthy by diplomatic action and political deed.

Leslie Langille remembered that the officers sternly lectured the troops about their duty:

We had been warned against fraternizing with the enemy, and told to be on the alert at all times, as these "Krauts" are supposed to be tricky. These orders are carried out to the letter—for exactly one day and night....A spirit of trustfulness and respect springs up between the German people and the American soldiers; and the high command is powerless to break it up, even if they tried.[14]

Too often Germany reminded the soldiers of home, and it did not take long for Dickman and his staff to realize that something was not working as far as anti-fraternization orders were concerned. No sooner were the troops billeted than they found themselves in the local bars and restaurants, making the acquaintance of the local girls. Germany was clean, unscarred by the war, full of food, filled with charming frauleins and hospitable people. By 10 December, 3rd U.S. Army decided to call all of its subordinate commands to task for their soldiers' attitudes toward the Germans. Flagler was not inclined to be harsh with his soldiers, but he followed the directives of 3rd Army and proceeded to require that each soldier receive proper instruction as to why there should be absolutely no communication between themselves and the Germans, unless official military business was involved.

By official 3rd Army policy, officers and NCOs were to instruct soldiers that Germany was responsible for the war. The locals were in support of the war, "heart and soul....until defeat made it politic for them to pretend that they were not." The German population "exulted over the atrocities of their forces," and celebrated the deaths of women and children when the *Lusitania* was sunk. The Germans "placed themselves outside the pale of civilized nations. They are not fit associates for the honest American soldier."

The American soldier, by policy, was enjoined to show a contempt and an aversion to the Germans, including the children. When meeting Germans, "their salutations are not to be recognized; no politenesses are to be indulged in when leaving billets occupied." Of special aggravation were German young people. "The children," policy stated, "are particularly ill behaved and pestiferous: They must be repulsed when endeavoring to curry favor."[15]

If the high-ranking officers believed that YMCA huts with chocolate bars and writing papers, organized tours, and other activities scheduled by the recognized American agencies such as the Knights of Columbus, Jewish Welfare Board, and the like would keep the rank and file from association with the Germans, they must have forgotten their own experiences in foreign lands.

Every unit in the Rainbow had its own story of the problems of enforcing the non-fraternization rules. The officers of the Transportation and Supply Section of the divisional headquarters found billets with a German family in the town of Ahrweiler, the Rainbow Division headquarters. The house was owned by an old woman and her two children, a daughter who was quite cross-eyed and a son very recently discharged from the German army and still in uniform. The old matron continually fussed over a fire in the stove and would ask the doughboys, First Lieutenant Marcus L. Poteet, Sergeant Major Walter Davis and Private Cooney, something in German that no one could understand. After three visits to fill the fireplace, the woman asked her question again, and Poteet responded with a frustrated, "Yah, yah," which sounded like "Ja, ja." Whereupon, a few minutes later, in marched mother, son, and daughter, and set a table for the three. The daughter carried a steaming bowl of fried potatoes, the mother a pot of ersatz coffee, and the son a set of tableware and a tablecloth.

Davis exclaimed, "For Pete's sake, they're fraternizing. What are you goin' to do?"

The private sat himself at the table, eyeing the fresh-cooked potatoes, and said "I'm going to eat." He was joined by his two superiors.

After another bowl of potatoes fortified with fresh honey, Poteet informed his men "The next man that says 'yah' to that old woman gets court-martialed. One more 'yah' and she'll be in here giving everybody a shave, haircut, and a bath, and that will be fraternizing."[16]

Father Duffy made the acquaintance of a German Catholic chaplain who had served on the Eastern Front, and they exchanged stories and talked about politics.

Duffy, who was very much aware of official policy, simply said, "Civilians hold grudges, but soldiers do not; at least soldiers who do the actual fighting." Duffy firmly believed that this was a much better approach to the conquered than a harsh and unbending occupation based on moral outrage.[17]

The 3rd Army had a bit more to worry about than innocent cases of fraternization. Influenza swept the entire AEF in late November through January, and the rising number of cases caused concern for everyone. Divisional Surgeon Jay W. Grissinger had been relieved of duty with the Rainbow and was promoted to the position of chief surgeon, I Corps. On 14 November, he became the chief surgeon, 3rd Army, and as such was responsible for medical care for the Army of Occupation. Quickly he organized the removal of very ill patients back to the more established hospitals in France. Once the 3rd Army was in place, Grissinger and his team structured a fairly comprehensive system of medical care. His observation on the early December march into Germany was that the main causes of complaint for the doughboys were very stiff, hard-to-break-in British-made shoes, respiratory ailments, diarrhea, and last, influenza.[18] In the Rainbow it became common practice for seriously sick men who were being evacuated to give their good, broken-in and waterproof shoes to someone in their unit.[19]

By the middle of December 1918, the Rainbow was in place on the west bank of the Rhine River. The divisional headquarters and troops were in Ahrweiler, which was centrally located. The 165th Infantry Regiment held the very important area of Remagen, with its large, sturdy, Ludendorff bridge across the Rhine. If hostilities broke out, the Irish regiment would secure the Remagen bridge since it offered a quick way to the east bank of the Rhine. This was the same Remagen bridge that would become famous in March 1945, when American troops captured it intact, the first such bridge across the Rhine to be so taken. Most divisional, brigade, or regimental tactical training exercises focused on a fictional scenario of the armistice failing, the Germans moving to take back the Remagen Bridge, a battalion of 165th Infantry and a machine-gun company setting up defensive positions to hold the bridge. If necessary, the 117th Engineers could blow up the bridge. The 67th Field Artillery Brigade would continuously fire on the bridge and the east bank to prevent the Germans from crossing to the west bank.[20] In another scenario, the Irish regiment, with artillery support, would seize the bridge, forcing a lodgement on the east bank of the Rhine. This would be played out later, in one of World War II's most spectacular operations.

The most difficult task for the Americans was to be an occupying power with constabulary authority over the civilian population. The administrative district, or Kreis, of Ahrweiler had 122 towns of varying size and importance, but the Rainbow had troops stationed in only twenty-one of those towns. The commanding officer in a town exercised supervisory powers over the German administration, and German offenders could be tried in American military courts. Also, the town commanders were responsible for other, smaller towns where they exercised control by visits and inspections. They were to work with the mayors of the towns, but could, if conditions warranted it, remove the mayor and prefer charges against him.

For example, the 165th Infantry headquarters and all three combat battalions and support troops were in Remagen, but due to the critical nature of duty there, the 165th had jurisdiction over only one other town. The 117th Ammunition Train, because of its available transportation, had responsibility for the headquarters town of Altenahr as well as eighteen smaller towns and villages. In this way, all 122 settlements would be under the direct control of some element of the Rainbow Division.[21]

Every Saturday, Rainbow headquarters received 122 reports that outlined a week's activities in the towns. Each report was to, "be a complete resume of any events of interest with reference to requisitions, the maintenance of order, arrests made, food conditions, and any other matter of interest that need come to the attention of higher authority."[22] If a commander could not visit the smaller settlements, he had to delegate an officer with a qualified interpreter to conduct the weekly visit. No German civilian could act as an interpreter for a visiting officer; German-speaking U.S. soldiers were selected for the duty.

The actual control of the Kreis of Ahrweiler rested on the "Twenty-Eight Rules and Regulations," which were issued by Pershing's headquarters for the Army of Occupation. Any violation of the rules could result in a German being brought before an Inferior Provost Court, under the authority of the local commander, or before the more serious Superior Provost Court, which always sat at 24 Wilhelmstrasse in Ahrweiler. A civilian, however, would be cited for a violation of the rules rather than a violation of the military regulations or Articles of War. This was not a system the Americans were especially comfortable with.

As the court policy evolved, only a Superior Provost Court could imprison a German found guilty of a violation of the rules. Fines could be imposed by either court, and those who were unable to pay were imprisoned at a rate of one day for every 10 German Reichsmarks, not to exceed three months' incarceration. Following American military procedures, the accused had the right to a speedy trial. The accused also had the right to counsel. Defense attorneys, even those military officers appointed by the court, had the right to see evidence and cross-examine witnesses. Interpreters were required to be present to avoid any misunderstandings during the trial.

The German civil authorities were also required to know the rules and regulations, post them, and enforce them in their jurisdictions. Every person was required to possess and show identification. Heads of households were required to post a list by name, sex, and age, of all persons residing in that house. This list had to be posted inside the front door of the home, much the same way hotels and motels post their rates and rules. Travel in and out of the town required passes granted by the authorities. All arms and ammunition had to be turned in to the American authorities, who would tag and keep the weapons. The only exception to this rule was made for local German police who carried side arms in the line of duty.

Rule No. 6 caused German civilians and Americans the most trouble. The AEF prohibited alcohol sales, except for beer and light wine, to American soldiers. Drinking hours were strictly prescribed, with wine and beer sales allowed from 11:00 A.M. to 2:00 P.M. and from 5:00 P.M. to 7:00 P.M. If found guilty of violating this rule, the owner of an establishment was liable to having his business closed and stock confiscated. Neither Germans nor Americans seemed inclined to obey this rule, and officers as well as rank-and-file soldiers continually violated it.

Any assembly of Germans without specific consent of the town commander was unauthorized except for school programs, religious observances, meetings of town councils, or sessions of court. Newspapers came under the watchful eye of the commander, and nothing but newspapers could be published. Mail, telephone, and telegraph was censored; at least, it was supposed to be. No German could own carrier pigeons unless he reported them to the American authorities, and all pigeonhouses were liable for inspection day or night. Any espionage, subversion, or violence committed against a soldier or property of the United States fell under a special category, and was considered to be a violation of the most serious nature. All in all, the twenty-eight categories, if fully enforced, would have made for a very restrictive life for the Germans, but there is every indication that minor infractions of the rules were overlooked as much as possible. At any rate, the military courts were busy enough with crimes committed by Doughboys, ranging from murder to drunkenness to contracting venereal disease (which did become a major problem in the Army of Occupation). The rules and instructions for enforcement of the rules covered four pages of very detailed material, but mainly, especially in the smaller towns and villages, they went unenforced.[23]

As the Americans became friendlier with the Germans, the tendency was to live and let live, a far cry from the stringent rules imposed in the French zone of occupation. At times the French were openly critical of the American attitude toward the Germans, and Pershing and his staff feared that the Army of Occupation might leave at some future date with more regard for their former enemies than for their former comrades in arms.[24] General Dickman was not blind to the fact that his troops regarded the war as over and occupation duties as onerous at best. His soldiers were young, healthy men, and he encouraged sightseeing and organized activities for his troops.[25]

This would be the second Christmas that the Rainbow spent away from home, and every effort was made to see that yuletide in Germany was as pleasant as possible. The Germans celebrated Christmas in a festive mood, and 1918 was especially joyous after four years of war. Due to the state of food preservation and shipment, the main Christmas meal reflected a great many locally purchased items. For example, the Indiana 150th Artillery at Neuenahr had baked chicken, roast pork, applesauce, cabbage slaw, and pickles, all purchased from farmers around Neuenahr. With the meal, light wine and beer were also served.

Representatives of the YMCA had arranged a Christmas Eve band concert and had small presents available for all of the regiment just prior to the dinner. The YMCA secured Christmas trees, and the regiment took over the spacious Rathaus of Neuenahr, where large tables were set up. The doughboys, veterans of many hard fights, sported the new felt three-colored Rainbow patch on their left shoulders.[26]

Father Duffy planned a special Christmas Mass for his Irish troops. The chaplain, who had celebrated open-air Mass on the Rio Grande in 1916 and in snow in France in 1917, was at once happy and sad. Bill Donovan had returned to the 165th, and Duffy found him to be a congenial roommate. For that he was grateful, but reflecting back over the year brought pain and sorrow as he thought of those now dead—Joyce Kilmer and so many others—who had marched from New York City in the late summer of 1917. Duffy had just received a sizable amount of money from the patriotic supporters of the old 69th in New York, and he turned over large sums to the mess sergeants of the regiment for local purchase in the Remagen area. Later most of the old crafty NCOs returned a good portion of the money, sheepishly informing Duffy that more could be gotten for good American, British, or French soap than for money. How did the sergeants know this, Duffy inquired; few answered.[27]

The mess sergeants from the Alabama 167th also knew about the power of a bar of soap or chocolate. As soon as the YMCA set up camp in the area occupied by the Alabamians at Sinzig (where Douglas MacArthur also had his residence) its members were besieged by Southerners who purchased all the soap and every chocolate bar the Y could have shipped in. One YMCA man was worried that perhaps the troops had developed some sort of unhealthy addiction to the candy bars. What surprised the Alabama troops was the availability of elaborate, expensive toys in the stores in Sinzig, Remagen, and Coblenz, and the ability of German parents to purchase these presents for Christmas. These were not the starving, ragamuffin Germans that the press had written about during the last several months of war.[28]

Calvin Lambert remembered that on Christmas Eve snow began to fall, and the men of the 117th Ammunition Train enjoyed a white Christmas. That evening the old German woman in whose house Lambert and his buddies had billets cooked steak and potatoes, while a number of soldiers found about twenty bottles of wine. The next morning, Christmas Day, Lambert and his friends slept through reveille formation and roll call, but most of the rest of the unit was missing as well. His Christmas was a work day, as a number of replacements arrived at the headquarters at Altenahr.[29]

Everett Scott did not find Nieder Breisig to be such a bad place on Christmas. It was beautiful in the snow, and Scott was entranced by the snow falling in the dense, quiet pine forests.[30] In his billets he had hot water, a large tub, and a huge feather mattress, a far cry from the gas-filled dugouts and soggy trenches of just a few months before.[31] On Christmas Day, Scott and a friend from Primgahar went to the NCO's mess and made taffy for the corporals and sergeants, for which they were treated to a large supper.

Word came from 3rd Army headquarters in Coblenz that leaves would start soon, and many of the combat veterans would be able to visit Paris or Brussels. The YMCA representative to the 3rd Army had informed General Dickman that the organization had around $35 million dollars to provide free entertainment, boat trips on the Rhine, and soldiers' centers throughout the leave areas in Germany. The YMCA took charge of the huge Festhalle in Coblenz, and, with Dickman's blessing, turned it into a recreation center for the off-duty doughboys.[32]

The new year also marked the official arrival of the Rainbow Division sleeve patch, even though many soldiers already had a patch sewn on for Christmas Day festivities. The distinctive shoulder insignia for the 42nd had been approved on 29 October 1918, but no AEF unit was allowed to sew on any insignia at that time, for very good reasons. Pershing simply did not want the Germans to have an easy time identifying what American units they were fighting. On 31 October, the first requisition for the felt Rainbow patches was made to the chief quartermaster of the AEF, who in turn ordered thousands to be produced by a firm in Paris. When they arrived in Germany, it was found that the specifications were not adhered to. The initial order specified that three equal arcs of red, yellow, and blue felt, one-third inch wide, were to be sewn on a piece of khaki-colored wool cloth. The patches were too big, Flagler complained, by one-half inch, and the arch of the rainbow was not clearly defined. He wanted them sent back.[33]

The issue was referred to the 3rd Army chief of staff, Brigadier General Malin Craig, who, on 6 January, told Flagler that it would be too costly to order another set at this time. They would have to use the offending patch.[34] The Rainbow soldiers, at their own expense, contracted with a local German firm that produced, at a cheaper price, a very distinct, colorful, and professionally made shoulder insignia that was totally embroidered. The patch question was symptomatic of an insignia mania that swept the 3rd Army and the rest of the AEF in late 1918 and 1919. While Pershing and Hunter Liggett did not like any distinctive insignia, they did not stop the wearing of them. The 3rd Army devised an AO, or Army of Occupation, patch, a blue circle with red border and a white A. Doughboys painted their insignia on spare helmets, and some were quite artistic. Unit insignia were painted on everything, and despite official directives specifying what could be painted on cars, trucks, signs, and so on, the doughboys painted whatever they pleased in whatever form they wanted. While this might seem frivolous to the uninitiated, it was proof that the units of the AEF, especially those in the 3rd Army, had a very high state of pride, morale, and esprit de corps.

Immediately after the holiday season, 3rd Army began a series of inspections of the various divisions training in Germany. The position of G5, Training, took on great importance within the Army of Occupation because the units arrayed on German soil were preparing for possible combat if the armistice fell apart and hostilities began again. The G5 at 3rd Army headquarters in Coblenz was a sharp-tongued, acerbic Colonel Walter Short. Short would later be the unfortunate American army general in command when the Japanese launched their surprise attack against Pearl Harbor on 7 December 1941.

Dickman was a soldier of good sense, with a real feel for his combat veterans who had proven themselves on many battlefields of the Western Front. By his directive, training was reduced to five hours per day, with the rest of the day given over to details around the units, athletic competitions, and opportunities to tour the sights of Germany. However, Dickman fully intended that the five hours' training would be serious training, tactical and realistic. He knew that Pershing was not too happy with the reduced training schedule, and believed that Pershing sent generals to his headquarters on a mission of "discreet inspection."[35]

Short inspected the Rainbow Division on 8-9 January 1919 and found it not to be in compliance with the guidance. The 166th and 168th Infantry had detailed training plans but fell short of the required five hours. Short was particularly critical of Brigadier General Gatley's 67th Field Artillery Brigade, which, according to Short's report, was doing almost nothing at all.[36] One area that was satisfactory was the procuring and use of healthy billets for the troops. The scarcity of proper, sanitary, heated quarters for the troops was a serious problem throughout the 3rd Army area, especially in smaller towns.[37] The Rainbow had never had a problem in doing its best for the troops, and the Kreis of Ahrweiler had ample space for all of the units to have comfortable quarters. Training was another matter, and Dickman immediately made his displeasure known to Flagler, ordering him to correct the training faults with the Rainbow Division.[38]

By the end of the first week, training intensified and the five-hour requirement was being met by all of the units. On 17 January a battalion from the 167th conducted an offensive tactical exercise for the division and 3rd Army inspectors. Second Lieutenant Edward Wren, the Auburn University football star and recipient of the Distinguished Service Cross, recalled that the exercise was realistic,

using ball ammunition, overhead machine gun fire, 37mm guns in action also Stokes mortar will fire some few hundred rounds. It is going to be as near like a real attack as possible just to show the generals and others how a good outfit goes over the top and captures machine guns, kills Dutch and captures prisoners. Wish you could see it. Think it will please everybody. We consider it a complement to be chosen to put this on for the Army of occupation.[39]

In the Irish 165th the drill and training, which had been approved by Colonel Short on his first inspection, continued at a strong pace, with new emphasis placed on military courtesy, appearance, and bearing. The 165th had just received over 200 replacements from the skeletonized 31st and 39th Divisions, and their training had been minimal at best before departing the

United States. Duffy was aghast to see so many men who were unable even to sign a payroll. Immediately Duffy and two other chaplains started a school to begin teaching the rudiments of reading and counting to these men and to teach English to the large number of foreign-born who were already with the old 69th Regiment.[40]

Flagler wrote to Major General Charles H. Muir, commanding the IV Corps to which the Rainbow was now assigned, that corrective action was in place and a tough program was being enforced.[41] Muir replied to Flagler's memorandum, assuring him that the G5 had sent a copy of the report to IV Corps, and that corps officers from the G5 section would continue to monitor the progress of the Rainbow Division. One of the problems for the higher headquarters and for the division surfaced on 1 February, during two follow-up inspections by 3rd Army's G3 section and Short's G5 section. Major Charles W. Foster, inspecting for the G3, could find nothing right. "It is my impression," Foster wrote, "that the state of discipline, appearance and execution of required training suffers by contrast with that of other organizations I have inspected."[42]

On the other hand, Major Charles E. Riley from Short's G5 section reported, "Those organizations of the 42nd Division which were visited for the second time on the whole show improvement and were carrying out definite training schedules."[43] Here was a case of two majors, experienced field grade officers from 3rd Army headquarters, arriving at the 42nd Division's location, seeing the same units, yet having totally different views and reporting very different things to their superiors at Coblenz. It is difficult to know what motivated each of the officers, but the situation was now in confusion. Was the Rainbow Division in conformity with training policy, or was it not? On 2 February Short sent a detailed report to Brigadier General Malin Craig, chief of staff of the 3rd Army, which stated in no uncertain terms that progress was being made. By no means did Short give a glowing report about every unit in the Rainbow Division, but it was Short's evaluation that in the space of a month, the division had made strides forward. Colonel Walter Short was known as a man who did not mince words or spare feelings, and it is possible to assume that conditions within the Rainbow Division at that time had improved.[44]

A detailed equipment inspection held by IV Corps staff officers in mid-January revealed that many items requisitioned before the Rainbow began its march to Germany had yet to arrive. There was also a shortage of troops. The 165th Infantry remained twenty-one officers and 1000 soldiers short of its required number, the 168th needed fifteen officers and 100 enlisted men, and the conditions were similar in the other units of the division. Flagler noted all this and informed Brigadier General Briant H. Wells, chief of staff of IV Corps, "Shortage of officers and men [in this division are]....beyond the control of Division Commander. Replacements have been requested weekly for months."[45] It was also an aggravation for the commander and the staff of the Rainbow that soldiers who had been wounded were being held at base hospitals in France with seemingly no provisions to restore them to their commands where their personnel and pay records were. Several hundred Rainbow veterans simply wandered away from the hospitals and made their way to Germany on their own.

An outbreak of influenza during the first week of February caused serious problems for the division, and Flagler brought the matter to General Muir's attention, asking that training maneuvers in very cold, wet weather be suspended until the disease had run its course. The divisional surgeon had recommended this action, and requested that the troops be discouraged from congregating in large groups where the threat of infection was the greatest. Divisional staff was particularly hard-hit, with a large number of officers, those required to carry on the day-to-day operations of the Rainbow, sick in quarters.[46] The situation in some regiments was critical. In the 151st Artillery, the Gopher Gunners, a full 30 percent of soldiers were sick on 3 February, and on the next day Colonel Leach had to stay in his room, ill from influenza. In January there were two deaths from the disease, but Leach felt that February could be worse.[47]

Chief Surgeon of 3rd Army Grissinger was concerned for the health of all the troops stationed in Germany. He recorded that from January to March 1919, 31,486 soldiers were admitted to the various hospitals established by the American military authorities in the alley of occupation. One-third of all soldiers diagnosed upon entry had influenza or severe respiratory illness. Of the remainder who were diagnosed after admittance, fully one-half had influenza or associated illnesses. In the same three-month period, there were 664 deaths in the 3rd Army, and Grissinger records that "575 or 89.6 percent were due to an acute infection of the respiratory tract." By the middle of February, Grissinger wrote, the temperature rose considerably and inclement weather tapered off.[48]

Muir was sympathetic to Flagler's request that outside training be suspended for a while. He did note that between 4 and 9 February the units of the corps reported fourteen cases of influenza in the 4th Division, the 3rd Division had fifty-four, while the Rainbow recorded 106 cases. Muir was more inclined to believe that infections were due to the fact that the 42nd was billeted in larger towns with more opportunities to congregate at performances, band concerts, and the like. In a slightly snide remark, Muir pointed out that the Rainbow soldiers had greater contact with the Germans than did the two Regular divisions, and consequently came into close proximity with more infected civilians in cafés, restaurants, and other such establishments. Regardless of how Muir felt, there was the danger of a number of deaths, and he agreed that the entire IV Corps would curtail training until there was evidence that the influenza epidemic was subsiding in his area.[49]

Venereal disease reappeared in the Rainbow Division with a vengeance. The number of cases had decreased dramatically when the division began intensive combat operations in July, due to the very simple fact that there were almost no opportunities to be with women. Now that combat had ended and the Rainbow was billeted in large towns, the contacts increased. The officers who commanded the AEF and 3rd Army were realistic old Regulars who had been with troops in the Philippines and elsewhere on garrison duty, and they were aware that problems would arise. Even before the Army of Occupation entered Germany there were warnings about venereal disease by various authorities, from the surgeon general of the AEF to the provost marshal general. On 26 September, Colonel H.H. Bandholtz, the provost marshal general of the AEF, directed all provost marshals at every level to enforce stringently a special set of regulations. These regulations prohibited sexual contacts with streetwalkers and placed houses of prostitution off limits. Tying liquor consumption to venereal disease, the provost marshal general restated the long-standing AEF prohibition on liquor sales, except for light wines and beer. All soldiers going on leave would be required to stay at hotels approved by the AEF, and they would be required to receive a briefing on the prohibition of hard liquor and the dangers of venereal disease. In cooperation with the French police, houses of prostitution and establishments caught selling more than the allowed light wine and beer were placed off limits, with American Military Police guards stationed at the doors. Any breach of the regulations would be automatically dealt with by courts-martial.[50]

Policies established against fraternization with the German population were in part intended to reduce the dangers of venereal infection. By the end of January, it was clear that infection in the Rainbow Division was occurring from sex with professional prostitutes who were plying their trade in the towns of the Kreis of Ahrweiler. Soldiers had settled into a routine, the fears of being in the midst of a possibly hostile population had subsided, training hours had been reduced in order to give doughboys, who had certainly earned it, some time off, and the paymasters were now regularly visiting the troops.

From the intelligence reports it is possible to deduce that there was no widespread hunger or privation among the German population that might spawn prostitution. It also appears that the major source of infection was from prostitutes from either Cologne or Bonn, the two nearest major cities, and on 1 February the Rainbow Division stated that no leaves or passes for those two cities would be allowed. There was also evidence that prostitutes from those two cities were coming into the towns occupied by the Rainbow and were practicing their trade in this area formerly free of venereal disease. By order of General Flagler, the mayors of the town were required to assist American military authorities in finding out where those women were and seeing that they were expelled from the Kreis of Ahrweiler. German doctors had been found treating American soldiers who did not want to face a court-martial for contracting venereal disease. Both doctor and doughboy would be subject to trial, with the doctor's license to practice medicine revoked. Unit commanders were required to conduct unscheduled VD inspections twice a month. The order initiating these inspections stated: "It is believed that the division as a whole frowns on sexual immorality and practices continence for the best interests of health, decency and the ambition to return home to friends and family clean morally and physically." This was a warning that lingering cases of venereal disease could very well find the soldier remaining in Germany to be cured long after his unit was back in

America.[51]

By the end of February conditions had gotten no better, with reported new cases on the increase. Flagler indicated, "The venereal diseases in this division are still abnormal." After 24 February a soldier found with VD would be tried for that offense and would face an additional charge of failing to use the available prophylaxis.[52] Rainbow authority had finally reached a point of frustration with veneral disease in mid-January, when there had been 107 new cases of VD reported in less than a month. The majority were gonorrhea, but six were nearly incurable syphilis infections. Before February, twenty-eight cases were remanded to the judge advocate general of the Rainbow Division for trial;[53] by the end of February, Colonel D.S. Fairchild, chief surgeon of the Rainbow, cited over eighty new cases for action by the legal section of the division.[54] Between 25 February and the week ending 18 March, the division reported another eighty-four cases, averaging about twenty per week. Many of the sexually transmitted diseases were contracted on leave in Paris, Charleroi, and Lyons, with only one definitely proven to have been contracted in Altenahr, in the Kreis of Ahrweiler.[55]

Colonel Grissinger at 3rd Army headquarters in Coblenz took every possible measure to reduce the VD rate in the entire Army of Occupation, which had risen dramatically to about forty per 1,000 soldiers. He approved of the policy, which had been announced throughout the entire AEF, of retaining soldiers in Europe for treatment regardless of the deployment of his unit back to America. Grissinger believed that this was a major deterrent to contracting VD. Towns like Bonn and Cologne were placed off limits because of the high rate of infection among those cities' prostitutes, but it was impossible to place Paris, Bordeaux, Lyons and Nice off limits to soldiers on leave.[56]

No person in authority believed that fraternization with local females, however, was a major source of disease. In fact, the AEF's stated and formal policy against fraternization was a dismal failure, and everyone from General Dickman on down knew it. As the occupation wore on and the soldiers got to know the families with whom they were billeted, a natural kind of amiable relationship developed. One officer recalled about the American soldiers, "At night they will sit around the firesides of the German families on whom they are billeted and drink a glass of wine or beer with the family [despite the strict orders against fraternization]."[57]

The Alabamians of the 167th Infantry, and other Southerners, had seldom seen such winter weather. The snow and the ice on the rivers gave them an interest in the type of winter sports known to their Northern comrades. The Alabams took up ice skating with many of the local girls as teachers, and, despite the rules, they learned the basics of skating and other winter sports.[58] Colonel George Leach, commanding the 151st Field Artillery, simply made the decision to close his eyes to such innocent meetings between his soldiers and the German frauleins. To Leach, this was just human nature, and very few of his men seemed to get into trouble with the local girls.[59]

Some of the local women attached themselves to particular units. Charles MacArthur recalled, "Another girl was called Kleiner, because she was little but resigned. A certain major was in hot competition with the boys in the matter of Kleiner which caused her to become known as the Officer's Mess. He got nowhere, however."[60]

In enforcing the anti-fraternization policy there were at times overly strict, unwise methods employed by military police. In some cases, soldiers suspected of seeing German girls were removed from the houses where they were staying if that girl happened to be the daughter of the family in whose house they were billeted. At times the military police saw fit to enter houses where a soldier was visiting and forcefully remove him. This caused altercations between the military police and the soldiers involved and was a source of embarrassment to all. There were open attacks on off-duty policemen, and the resentment against the MPs by the end of March forced the 3rd Army to direct all provost marshals to conduct their business with a regard for the dignity of the American soldier. The situation had become so serious that the provost marshal general in Coblenz organized a special group of "inspector-instructors" who would go throughout the command to see that enforcment of policies was carried out with "common sense and courtesy."[61]

A doughboy holding a fraulein's hand in public was one thing, but the spiraling VD rate remained another, and that had to be dealt with. In mid-March, Flagler issued an order stating that no woman would be allowed into the Rainbow area unless she had a special pass. The MPs would guard each train, and any woman without a signed pass would not be allowed to get off the train. There were instances of women traveling from areas of Germany where there were no Allied authorities, and a pass would have been impossible to obtain. These women were taken into custody and escorted to the office of the American commandant of the town. The commandant would then require that some German known to the authorities as a reputable citizen identify the woman and vouch for her respectability. If no character reference could be found, the woman was then held under guard and put on the next train passing through the town. It was also ordered that the town commandant and the military police sweep the town, round up every known or suspected prostitute, and take them under guard to the German hospital in Ahrweiler for a complete examination for venereal disease. A qualified representative of the division surgeon was required to attend every examination and certify the findings to the division headquarters. Those without venereal infection would be released, and those found with disease would be required to begin and continue treatment.[62]

The area where the doughboys of the Rainbow were stationed had been a major resort area in Germany. President Theodore Roosevelt had stopped in the Kreis of Ahrweiler to take the curative waters upon his return from a hunting trip in Africa. Prior to the war there had been a free and easy way of life in towns such as Neuenahr, Remagen, and Ahrweiler, and prostitutes had plied their trade there. During the war the same business flourished with the German troops

stationed in the Kreis. It was natural, albeit unfortunate, that they would return
to the towns, spas, and resorts when the American occupying force moved in.
The 165th Infantry intercepted a full trainload of prostitutes from Cologne who
had decided to ply their trade in Remagen. The soldiers of the 165th herded
them together and sent them back to Cologne as quickly as possible.[63]

There were cases of murder, assault, and thievery that came before the
courts-martial of the Rainbow Division, but, by and large, the predominant
charge and trial was for venereal disease. By mid-March, Flagler instructed his
subordinate commanders who heard the VD cases that a three-month confinement
and three-month forfeiture of pay was to be the minimum sentence for
contracting the disease. Having the disease was one matter; added to that was
a failure to obey the standing order to use the prophylaxis available and required.
Prophylaxis had been required since they arrived in France, and stations were set
up where the soldier, in privacy and with some dignity, could take the prescribed
treatment, which had to be done within three hours of sexual intercourse. In
addition, the soldier, especially if he were an NCO or an officer, had to face
dereliction of duty charges. The contraction of VD was regarded as a serious
matter indeed.

Dickman, Grissinger, and the unit commanders were concerned about VD
rates, and they pinned their hopes on the recreation provided by organizations
such as the YMCA, Jewish Welfare Board, Knights of Columbus, and Red Cross.
Funds were expended for shows and recreational facilities in most of the major
cities, boat trips up and down the Rhine (evidently Dickman's favorite), and the
like. Although the doughboys had a distinct dislike for the YMCA, it was to
provide the lion's share of the money and facilities.

The YMCA personnel, especially younger males, were usually suspect in the
eyes of the combat troops. Charles MacArthur, who never had anything good
to say about them, recalled, "Now that the war was over the YMCA began to
function in the matter of chocolate—at twenty cents the bar. A happy
circumstance, since the frauleins were glutted with soap and turned their minds
to candy. We again gave away a million dollars of it before we knew what it
was worth."[64] That was not what many of the representatives of the YMCA had
in mind when they opened their huts and sold candy bars, which cost five cents
or less in America.

Leslie Langille, usually not a critical commentator, was able to take a seven-
day leave in Annecy, France, a beautiful resort in the mountains. His experience
with the Y-run facility soured him considerably, as he recalled:

The YMCA secretaries of both sexes may be found here in great numbers. Those babies
know how to pick the spots all right; they can come here from Paris for a rest and to get
away from their pressing social duties....As usual the YMCA fellows stuck to their cash-
and-carry habits, even in this recreation center....Let me hasten to [add]....that the
impressions gained from the actions of the "Y" workers were those that said actions
created for themselves; I would much prefer to write about their merits, had they any.[65]

Oftentimes local Y workers were strong-willed, and failed to coordinate their actions with the town commanders. Colonel George Leach went on leave for a week, and when he returned to Neuenahr he found that the civic theater had been taken over by the YMCA for performances. His town had become a full-fledged YMCA leave area, much to his irritation.[66]

Leach was even more aggravated when on 6 February the mayor of Neuenahr came to his office to complain that an official from the YMCA had confiscated seven pianos that had been in private homes. Leach was furious, and ordered Anita Churcher, the YMCA representative in charge of the much-expanded Neuenahr recreation center, to report to him the next day. The military commander, the man responsible for the occupation of Neuenahr, was Leach, but there was nothing he could do about Churcher's high-handed actions. He did get rental payments for the pianos, but could not get them returned.[67]

The YMCA representatives had always been a problem in the area of paying for the government-issued rations they consumed during a campaign. All officers paid for their meals when not in combat, and YMCA personnel were counted as officers. In the occupation, major confusion reigned as to who ate when and what they paid. It was quite difficult to settle a bill, especially if the Y representative went from one unit to another within a division.[68] When one of the YMCA personnel got in serious trouble, it was a matter of grim satisfaction for the Doughboys. Such a case arose in the Rainbow Division in mid-March 1919 concerning accusations of sexual harassment against the senior male Y representative at Ahrweiler. On 10 March Lieutenant Colonel Robert J. Gill, the officer who had commanded the 117th Trench Mortar Battery and was now serving as the Rainbow's inspector general, received word that two highly thought of YMCA women were being ordered away from their duties at Ahrweiler. He asked the two to come to his office. When they arrived, Sara Elizabeth Buck and Lisa Gilman Todd told Gill about unwanted sexual advances by their chief, O.K. LaRoque. They also produced a written statement from Bess A. Cochrane, who also alleged sexual advances by LaRoque. Gill was outraged by what he heard and took the matter to Flagler who, in turn, felt that a breach of discipline and good moral order had probably occurred. Gill then went to the judge advocate general of the division, and they began an immediate investigation of the women's accusations against their chief.[69]

Sara Buck alleged that LaRoque was constantly trying to kiss her.[70] Todd said she had been the subject of his advances on a motor trip to Coblenz to pick up YMCA supplies. During the trip to Coblenz, she said, LaRoque began discussing the French, expressing admiration for their acceptance of sexual affairs as long as they were discreetly hidden from view. When Todd stated her disapproval of such ideas, LaRoque let the matter drop. Upon returning to Ahrweiler, however, she said he pressed her, asking her to be his lover. He began to paw Todd, who resisted his advances until he stopped.[71]

Bess Cochrane had arrived at Ahrweiler in mid-January, and said LaRoque immediately began to make sexually explicit suggestions. She claimed that in early March LaRoque tried to assault her. Cochrane had a problem with her eyes and had retired to her chamber to treat the ailment when LaRoque came to her room, ostensibly to leave some official YMCA papers. When LaRoque entered the room, Cochrane was lying in bed with a cold compress over her eyes. She said that LaRoque threw himself on her bed and grabbed her robe and gown, baring her breasts. According to the woman, he then repeatedly kissed her, threw back her covers and tried to seduce her. Cochrane resisted, and finally got LaRoque out of her room. She then had female friends sit with her and refused anything but official contact with her chief. He subsequently tried to have her removed from her post with the 117th Supply Train. Vehement protests from the unit's officers, who were not aware of the circumstances behind this move, assured that she would stay with the Rainbow Division.[72]

LaRoque, who began his service with the 117th Engineers in July 1918 but was not well-liked, was called to give a statement. He denied the accusations made against him, giving an entirely different story. LaRoque indicated that he believed Lieutenant Colonel Gill had instigated the charges because he was sending the three women away, and Gill had romantic interests in them—especially the young, attractive Lisa Gilman Todd. Lieutenant Colonel E.J. Moran of the Rainbow Divisions's staff carried out an independent investigation, and he recommended to Flagler that "Mr. LaRoque be relieved from duty with this division immediately. While I am satisfied that the charges could be substantiated before a court, trial is not recommended on account of the discredit to the YMCA that a public trial would involve."[73]

Flagler directed that LaRoque be relieved of his duties with the division and that he leave the Rainbow area as soon as possible.[74] LaRoque protested, and he indicated that he would call Colonels Johnson, Hough, and Screws, plus a host of divisional officers and YMCA workers in his defense.[75] The trial was not held for several reasons: First, the Rainbow was preparing to depart for the United States, and, second, the YMCA operation was to be rapidly phased out for the Rainbow, with Army Commissary Sales units handling the sales while the doughboys prepared for their return to the United States.[76]

It could be argued that, given the serious nature of the charge, the YMCA chief should have been brought to military trial for sexual harassment. Certainly the pressing business of preparing for return to the United States interfered with the processes of military law, but few of the AEF commanders knew how to proceed with such accusations. This was the second decade of the twentieth century, the Victorian period was in the wane, but hesitancy to deal with such a situation was prevalent. Gill and Flagler believed the women's stories, as did Lieutenant Colonel Moran, the inspector. Soldiers were slow in getting used to seeing women, except for a few nurses and YMCA or Salvation Army women, forward deployed with the armies. That many of the Y women did yeoman service in the combat areas is beyond dispute, and many, even more than the Y men, won the respect of the hard-fighting doughboys. Bess Cochrane, in her deposition, stated that she told LaRoque in no uncertain terms that no soldier had ever made such advances toward her as he had. Running through the remainder of the investigation was the idea that women were there to do a job to help the soldiers, and that they were to be regarded with dignity and respect. Most of the doughboys of the Rainbow were a rough and tumble lot with battlefield experiences akin to being in the pits of hell. Yet women, be they Lieutenant van Dolsen's nurses or the YMCA women at Ahrweiler, had earned their right to be with the army. Doughboy lore included stories of the Salvation Army's "Doughnut Dollies" who served in all kinds of conditions and the Y women who offered a welcome cup of coffee or cocoa, serving while in range of artillery and gas.

By the time the Rainbow was investigating the allegations against LaRoque, rumors circulated that the 42nd Division had been selected to return home. Officers from the 4th Division, their Ivy shoulder patches in evidence, arrived at the various headquarters looking at billets and other arrangements. The YMCA had been ordered to begin to turn its duties over a Quartermaster Corps Sales Commissary Unit, and it appeared that soon the ladies of the YMCA would be gone. O.K. LaRoque was already on his way to wherever the YMCA had decided he should go.

Old familiar faces began to disappear. Colonel Hugh Ogden of the Massachusetts National Guard, who had served as judge advocate general (JAG) of the division, was ordered to Coblenz to be the JAG for the 3rd Army.[77] Colonel Howland left the 165th Infantry regiment, and much to everyone's delight, Wild Bill Donovan took command. Still limping, Donovan would lead the old Fighting 69th back into New York. The 42nd Division could now see the end of the Rainbow.

NOTES

1. Leslie Langille, *Men of the Rainbow* (Chicago: O'Sullian and Co., 1933), 171-72.

2. Alison Reppy, *Rainbow Memories: Character Sketches and History of the First Battalion, 166th Infantry* (Np: Private printing, 1919), 20.

3. HQ, 42nd Division, Memorandum No. 320, 23 November 1918, in the National Archives, Washington, D.C., *Records Group 120 Records of the AEF, 42nd Division*, (hereinafter, RG 120), carton 1.

4. Calvin Lambert Diary, manuscript, Emporia Public Library, Emporia, Kansas, 219.

5. John B. Hayes, *Heroes Among the Brave* (Loachapoka, Ala.: Lee County Historical Society, 1973), 42.

6. Charles MacArthur, *War Bugs* (Garden City, N.Y.: Doubleday, Doran and Co., 1929), 247.

7. James F. Cogdell to his father, Luxembourg (c. 25 November 1918), in the Cogdell Letters, Alabama State Historical Archives, Montgomery, Alabama, 167th Infantry Collection.

8. MacArthur, *War Bugs*, 251, 252-53.

9. Francis P. Duffy, *Father Duffy's Story* (New York: George H. Doran Co., 1919), 309.

10. Scott to his brother, Nieder Breisig, Germany, 22 December 1918, in the Scott Letters, manuscripts in the author's collection.

11. Joseph T. Dickman, *The Great Crusade* (New York: Appleton, 1927), 233-34.

12. U.S. Army Center of Military History, *The United States Army in the World War Staff Sections and Services, G2* (Washington: Government Printing Office, 1989), 383.

13. Ibid.

14. Langille, *Men of the Rainbow*, 172-73.

15. HQ, 42nd Division, Memorandum for Brigade and Independent Organization Commanders, 10 December 1918, in RG 120, carton 1.

16. Raymond S. Thompkins, *The Story of the Rainbow Division* (New York: Boni and Liveright, 1919), 184-86.

17. Duffy, *Story*, 310-11.

18. Colonel J.W. Grissinger, *Medical Field Service in France* (Washington,D.C.: Association of Military Surgeons, 1928), 122-28.

19. Langille, *Men of the Rainbow*, 173.

20. HQ, 83rd Brigade, Training Field Orders No. 10, 31 December 1918, in RG 120, carton 19.

21. HQ, 42nd Division, General Order No. 1, 1 January 1919, ibid., carton 134.

22. Ibid.

23. HQ, 42nd Division, General Order No. 2, 2 January 1919, ibid.

24. Donald Smythe, *Pershing: General of the Armies* (Bloomington, Ind.: Indiana University Press, 1986), 245-46.

25. Dickman, *Great Crusade*, 239-40.

26. Band concert program, HQ Christmas menu, and unpublished photographs of the 150th Field Artillery Regiment's Christmas meal in the Corporal Garrett Olds Rainbow Veterans Papers, author's personal collection.

27. Duffy, *Story*, 315-16.

28. William B. Amerine, *Alabama's Own in France* (New York: Eaton and Gettinger, 1919), 229-30.

29. Calvin Lambert Diary, 227.

30. Scott to his mother, Nieder Breisig, 27 December 1918, in Scott Letters.

31. Wagoner Homer Sterns, HQ, 168th Infantry to Mrs. Scott, Nieder Breisig, 26 December 1918, ibid.

32. Dickman, *Great Crusade*, 240-41.

33. Flagler to Malin Craig, 3 January 1919, in RG 120, carton 3.

34. Endorsement by Craig, 6 January 1919, ibid.

35. Dickman, *Great Crusade*, 235, 239-41.

36. Short to Malin Craig, 10 January 1919, in RG 120, carton 19.

37. D. Clayton James, *The Years of MacArthur, Vol. I: 1880-1941* (Boston: Houghton-Mifflin, 1970), 250-51.

38. Dickman to Flagler, 11 January 1919, in RG 120, carton 19.

39. Wren to his father, Sinzig, 16 January 1919, in the Edward Wren Letters, Auburn University Archives, Auburn, Alabama.

40. Duffy, *Story*, 318-19.

41. Flagler to Muir, 28 January 1919, in RG 120, carton 19. Also see: Memorandum from Muir to Flagler, 27 January 1919, ibid.

42. Memorandum for Colonel Short from Major Foster, 1 February 1919, ibid.

43. Memorandum for Colonel Short from Major Riley, 1 February 1919, ibid.

44. Memorandum from Short to Malin Craig, 2 February 1919, ibid. Also see: Memorandum for Short from Lieutenant Colonel J.W. Anderson, 10th Field Artillery Regiment, 31 January 1919, ibid., carton 36.

45. Flagler to Muir, 16 January 1919, ibid., carton 16.

46. Flagler to Muir, 9 February 1919, ibid., carton 19.

47. Diary entries 3, 4, 10, and 11 February 1919, in George E. Seaman (ed.), *War Diary of George E. Leach, Colonel 151st Field Artillery* (Roanoke, VA: National Association of Rainbow Veterans, 1962), 100.

48. Grissinger, *Medical Field Service*, 138-39.

49. Muir to Flagler, 12 February 1919, in RG 120, carton 19.

50. Office of the Provost Martial General, AEF, Special Bulletin No. 28, 26 November 1918, ibid., carton 63.

51. HQ, 42nd Division, Memorandum No. 22, 1 February 1919, Alabama State Archives, 167th Infantry Collection.

52. HQ, 42nd Division, Memorandum No. 46, 25 February 1918, ibid.

53. Memorandum by Colonel D.S. Fairchild, 31 January 1919, in RG 120, carton 67.

54. Memorandum by Colonel D.S. Fairchild, 28 February 1919, ibid.

55. HQ, 42nd Division, Memorandum for Brigade, Regiment and Separate Unit Commanders, 19 March 1919, in Alabama State Archives, 167th Infantry Collection.

56. Grissinger, *Medical Field Service*, 143-45.

57. Letter from Lieutenant Allen, Regimental Intelligence Officer, 165th Infantry, 4 February 1919, in U.S. Army Military History Institute Archives, Carlisle Barracks, Pennsylvania, 42nd Division AEF Collection (hereinafter, MHIA).

58. Amerine, *Alabama's Own*, 230-31.

59. Diary entry, 24 December 1918, Leach, *War Diary*, 95.

60. MacArthur, *War Bugs*, 275.

61. Provost Marshal General to all MP Officials, 19 March 1919, in RG 120, carton 7.

62. HQ, 42nd Division, Memorandum No. 64, 15 March 1919, ibid.

63. Henry J. Reilly, *Americans All: The Rainbow at War* (Columbus, Ohio: F.J. Heer Printing Co., 1936), 871.

64. MacArthur, *War Bugs*, 262.

65. Langille, *Men of the Rainbow*, 180-81.

66. Diary entry, 31 January 1919, Leach, *War Diary*, 98.

67. Diary entries, 6 and 7 February 1919, ibid., 100.

68. HQ, 42nd Division, Memorandum, 9 February 1919, in RG 120, carton 74.

69. Statement by Lieutenant Colonel Robert Gill, 19 March 1919, ibid., carton 67.

70. Statement by Sara E. Buck, 19 March 1919, ibid.

71. Statement by Lisa G. Todd, 19 March 1919, ibid.

72. Statement by Bess A. Cochrane, 19 March 1919, ibid.

73. Report and recommendations of Lieutenant Colonel E.J. Moran, 19 March 1919, ibid.

74. HQ, 42nd Division, Memorandum to LaRoque, 19 March 1919, ibid.

75. Memorandum from Major George Glenn, defense counsel to judge advocate general, 20 March 1919, ibid.

76. Dickman to Flagler, 22 March 1919, ibid., carton 74.

77. Reilly, *Americans All*, 869.

11

THE END OF THE RAINBOW

On 22 March 1919, 42nd Division headquarters issued General Order No. 19, stating, "The 42nd Division is leaving the Army of Occupation of the Rhine for its journey to the United States." On 1 April 1919, III Corps and 3rd Army would relinquish the 42nd to the authority of the SOS, which was in control of the ports of debarkation.[1] The SOS had the responsibility of getting the troops onto the ships bound for America.

On 16 March, Pershing made his final review of the entire division.[2] Everett Scott had been in every fight the Rainbow had and was a jaded combat veteran. He was not overly impressed with the Sunday review held at Remagen, as he wrote to his mother:

Friday and Sat. we were busy geting ready to parade for General Parshing sunday. And sunday morning we got into trucks and went about 7 or 8 kilos and then got out and hiked about the same distance to the field where we were to parade a little after 12 oclock. And then formed a company front and waited until about 2:30 or 3 oclock for him to come. it was coald and cloudy and we had got pretty warm hiking. We carried our dinner with us. and we were alowed to eat that as soon as we got there....When the General came they blew attention and then came to present arms. And then we opened ranks and fixed Bayonets. Then he came and inspected us, which took until 5. Then he went back on the hillseid and reviewed us....After we passed him we took up the double time for about 1/4 of a mile then we were all brought togther and he spoke to us. And thanked us for what we have done and wished us a good and early trip home. They had several moving picture machines there so if you ever get the chance to see it I think that you will find it worth your time and also your money.[3]

Pershing reviewed each unit of the Rainbow. When he came to the 165th, he noted immediately that its flag was at least a foot higher than any other in the division. Every unit added silver bands to their flags for each campaign they had been in. The 165th's lineage traced battles back to the Civil War, and to accommodate the nine new bands earned in France, the regiment had to have a one-foot piece of wood added to the pole. Pershing paused a few minutes and then asked what regiment this was. "The 165th Infantry, sir," the color sergeant said.

Pershing looked at the flagpole again and asked what regiment it had been, to which the NCO replied, "The 69th New York, sir." "Oh," Pershing replied, "the 69th New York. I understand it now."[4]

As Pershing inspected the Gopher Gunners, he stopped in front of the first sergeant of the Regimental Supply Company. Something about the man jogged a memory for Pershing, and he engaged Horace "Dad" Whitmore in a conversation which, to everyone's surprise, lasted a full five minutes, with Black Jack Pershing even smiling at times. Whitmore had been a student and a cadet at the University of Nebraska when Pershing taught and commanded the corps of cadets there. The first sergeant and the general were recounting old college days.[5] Dad Whitmore had been one of the original Pershing Rifles.

The time for departure was short, as the Rainbow would turn command of the Kreis of Ahrweiler over to the 4th Division on 1 April, and troops would begin to load their equipment and depart that day. The Illinois men of the 149th Artillery threw all of their NCOs in the Rhine river.[6] 3rd Army headquarters had warned about serious consequences if the troops ran riot, but harmless pranks were overlooked.

Father Duffy spent a great deal of time getting to know Bill Donovan better. Certainly Donovan reminded him of a time when most of the men of the old 69th were still callow youths at Camp Mills. In Duffy's estimation, Donovan had grown as a man and as a soldier from his glory-hunting days. Donovan confided to Duffy that when he was finally through with getting the regiment demobilized, he was going to take his wife on a long sight-seeing trip to Japan. Duffy really doubted that Wild Bill Donovan would ever again be out of the public spotlight; neither did he believe that Donovan's usefulness to his country was over.[7]

When the official departure orders reached the 2nd Battalion, 117th Engineers, there appeared a big sign in the town square at Mayschoss that read "California or Bust." The Californians had enjoyed their time in Germany adjusting to snow, sauerkraut at every meal, fraternizing with the local girls, and sightseeing. Now they had orders that they would be one of the first Rainbow units to board trains on 1 April for the French port city of Brest.[8]

At Sinzig, the 167th Infantry had published a newspaper called the *Alabamian*, an irreverent publication with no respect for rank. In one issue it was reported: "Chaplain Smith recently returned from a pilgrimage to Cologne, where he worshipped at the cathedral. He said the beer there is excellent."[9] On 22 March the *Alabamian* ceased its publication. Corporal John B. Hayes of Company I, 167th, was almost sorry to leave his comfortable billets in Sinzig. He reflected that of the 250 Alabamians of Company I who came to France in December 1917, there were fewer than fifty left. Many of those wore more than one wound stripe. In looking over the records of Company I, Hayes discovered that nearly 800 men had passed through the company during the unit's stay in France. It had taken over 800 soldiers as replacements to keep Company I at its full combat strength of 250 riflemen.[10]

Douglas MacArthur, content in his small but very comfortable castle at Sinzig, was one of those with mixed emotions about leaving Germany. The war had brought him fame and promotion to a general's rank, but it was also unsatisfying. Despite all of his faults, MacArthur was a soldier of uncommon courage, and he left Europe as one of the most decorated AEF soldiers. General Menoher had recommended him for the Congressional Medal of Honor, but in a shocking decision the AEF board disapproved Menoher's recommendation, stating that MacArthur's actions in combat did not merit the medal. MacArthur had finished the war with seven Silver Stars and two Distinguished Service Crosses, plus numerous Allied decorations and two wound stripes. Certainly, if anyone deserved the coveted medal for actions well above the call of duty, it was Douglas MacArthur. Many irate officers of the Rainbow Division believed that it was the personal enmity of Pershing and the staff of AEF Headquarters, that denied him the decoration.[11] When Flagler left the division to become chief of the Army's Engineer School, MacArthur, who had commanded the division for a short time, was passed over. Brigadier General George Gatley, of the 67th Field Artillery Brigade, took command of the division, although his tenure was very brief.

The Rainbow did not have much time to pack for the trip to the French ports, and there were long hours spent certifying records and awarding medals and promotions. Some strange things surfaced during those last few days in Germany. Sergeant Frank Johnson, Company E, 165th Infantry, received a rather large envelope from home. When he opened it he found that he had been a lieutenant in the U.S. Army for several months. In its wartime efficiency, the War Department had sent the commission to his home in New York City, and his parents sent it on to him. By the afternoon he had on the gold bars and was filling out forms for back pay and allowances.[12]

The 149th Artillery troops decided to have one gigantic party now that departure was near. Charles MacArthur's battery had a thousand dollars in its unit fund, and several sober-minded and trustworthy soldiers took the greenbacks to Coblenz to trade them for a huge number of German Reichsmarks. They then rented the local opera house and bought all of the wine and schnapps available in Gelsdorf, with which they created a "Rainbow Cocktail," consisting of a barrel each of red and white wine, one cask of potent schnapps, twelve bottles of lemon extract, a pound of pepper, and ginger to taste! Very soon several batteries of Henry J. Reilley's 149th Illinois Artillery regiment were rip-roaring drunk. Many of them spilled into the streets of the town, where they raided the guardhouse, set a few prisoners free, and then marched onto Herr Peter Schlemmer's bar and wrecked the place. By dawn the doughboys had all passed out, and order slowly was restored to the town of Gelsdorf.[13]

On 28 March, at Neuenahr, a convention of delegates from every unit of the

Rainbow Division was held to form a division association. While that sounds like an orderly process, it was not. There were great debates over minor points, probably made major in proportion to the amount of German beer available to the assemblage. Despite all the wrangling, the association was formed and men joined for a dollar a year. Since the Rainbow's term of service was at an end, and it was known that the 42nd Division would pass into history as a unique experiment, there were hopes that this association would preserve a little of the special nature of the Rainbow Division. It succeeded beyond the grandest expectations of the founders.

The association was the most active of all the postwar divisional veterans' groups, developing an iconography of its own that was remembered with near-religious fervor as the years went by. The appearance of the Rainbow in the skies before battle and the special nature of the National Guardsmen from coast to coast became part of the Rainbow mystique. Only the U.S. Marines and the Rainbow were to have movies made about their ground combat roles in WWI: *What Price Glory* about the 5th Marine Regiment, and *The Fighting 69th*, of the Rainbow. One of the most memorable scenes from the latter was the Alabama-New York fracas at Camp Mills, New York, in 1917.

On Sunday, 30 March, Colonel Leach was in his office packing his papers for the trip back to America when a delegation from the German town administration of Neuenahr called to present the Minnesota commander with a framed resolution of thanks and an inscribed souvenir book. It was an embarrassing moment for Leach, who had led his Gopher Gunners through the hardest battles of the war. Leach was fairly certain that he should refuse the gift offered by his former enemies, but decided against rejecting it.[14]

Everett Scott had changed, but he could not quite articulate how. He wrote to his brother a warning: "For if I ever get mad you never would know what I was talking about. For I mix in what little French and German I know and then o la la. I have picked up a little German. That is I can understand a little but I cant get my tung around fast enough to talk it yet." Then Scott related the death of several of his comrades in the St. Mihiel offensive. He ended the disjointed letter with, "They say that we leave here on the 9th of April and sail the 15. Well it cant be toot sweet to suit me." Scott had received a number of letters from his beloved Louise, and, yes, they would marry, but at that point he put down his pencil just to hear the bugler, in the distance, sound Taps, the same Taps played over the graves of those dead who, that night, were so much on his mind.[15]

On 1 April, the first of the Rainbow boarded 40-and-8s for the long trip to Brest, France, and for America. On that day Colonel Benson Hough, commanding Ohio's 166th Infantry, received officers from the 39th Infantry Regiment, 4th Division, who began to take charge of supplies and billets in the Ohio regiment's area. By 6 April, Ohio would be just a memory along the Rhine River.[16] On 2 April, with the band playing "Gary Owen," Wild Bill Donovan led his Irish soldiers to the train station at Remagen. The Irish battleflag, the tallest in the Rainbow Division, was unfurled and for the last time caught the German morning sun. On 9 April, because there was a little space available on a ship, the 117th Maryland Trench Mortar Battery, which had fought so well in the Champagne, sailed for home—Baltimore. The first unit of the Rainbow was now gone.[17]

There is a strange ambivalence about leaving comrades, billets, places one knows where there were childish pranks carried on by men who had long since left their childhood behind. There were, except for the dinners and sometimes drunken revelries, few outward manifestations of joy over the departure for home. Those men, like all soldiers before and after, had developed a way of life that excluded those who had not shared in the dangers, the privations, and the few good times. For the doughboys, although America was not exactly an alien land, the hellish combat of World War I had certainly separated these soldiers from their homes. Theirs was now the "band of brothers," a closed society. The trenches, the rolling hills of the Meuse-Argonne, and now the Kreis of Ahrweiler had become a home of sorts where life was ordered and simple. It was a world of young men robbed of their youth. Brigadier General Douglas MacArthur, at Sinzig, summed it up: "When we received our orders to return to the United States, the tearful departure looked more as though we were leaving instead of returning home. We had been away from the states exactly eighteen months to the day the first convoy departed from Hoboken."[18]

The Illinois gunners of the 149th had one parting shot as their 40-and-8s were ready to depart. They fixed a banner to one of the boxcars, with a rainbow and a map of Illinois in the center. That was not too bad, but there were uncomplimentary things written about the army, officers, and military life in general. A young lieutenant saw the sign and ordered it down, a request to which the hard-bitten gunners of Battery B took umbrage, and they ran him off. Into the fracas came the indomitable Colonel Henry J. Reilly, who was not as concerned about the sign (which was probably true anyway) as he was about the crude names the enlisted men of the battery had called the officer. Reilly ignored the sign which had started the row, and ordered that a delegation of the enlisted men apologize to the newly minted officer. The men did give their regrets after a fashion, and since the train was leaving, the unsatisfied officer wisely decided to return to the officer's coach rather than delay the journey.[19]

The artillerymen were the last to leave Germany. They had the duty to turn over all battery horses and canon to the 4th Division, since their French guns were not to be returned to the United States. Leslie Langille was climbing into his 40-and-8 when he heard the regimental band strike up the now much-played "Sambre et Meuse" for the last time.[20] It seemed like such a fitting benedictory for the odyssey of the Rainbow. On 6 April, the doors of the 40-and-8s closed and the Illinois Artillery was on its way to Brest, France, and then to America.

On 8 April, Colonel George Leach spent a great deal of time alone with his thoughts. He was overcome with emotion and with that strange feeling of sadness at leaving. Everything was packed for the trip to Brest, and, true to form, Leach set aside a 40-and-8 for himself and a few officers. If his Minnesota gunners, now fewer than they were a year and a half ago, were to travel in those symbols of the Great War, he would too. The only concession to comfort for the colonel was an army cot, because (and he had not told anyone about this) he was nearly crippled at times with rheumatism and could not sleep on a hard floor. At 6:30 A.M. the 151st Field Artillery Regiment pulled out, leaving no trace of the Rainbow behind.[21]

There were no fond memories of Brest, France. Waiting for the Rainbow was Al Ettinger, who had finally gotten out of the hospital, the stockade, and numerous scraps, and rejoined his unit. Ettinger would go back with the 165th to New York.[22] Father Duffy spent his time waiting for the two ships that were to carry the 165th by preparing for the Easter celebration to be held aboard ship. He was determined that, while his Irishmen had strayed from the straight and narrow in Europe, Easter Sunday would be remembered in a "holy fashion."[23]

Not all of the 165th, however, left France in such a state of religious fervor as Duffy. The night before the New York 69th marched to the docks, a number of the men obtained passes and went into Brest, where fueled by wines and liquors, they took every last frustration out on military police who had not been in combat. The next morning, as Donovan led his men out of Camp Pontanezen to the docks, an MP captain demanded the right to seize the brawlers. Donovan ordered the first platoon of Company A to fix bayonets and precede the regiment as skirmishers. The bruised MPs and their livid captain got out of the way as the Irish Regiment, with the longest flagpole, marched by.

Regardless of the feelings of apprehension or ambivalence, the doughboys of the Rainbow felt they were ready to return home to whatever awaited them. The outprocessing at Brest was an irritation for most soldiers because they had to be cleaned, deloused, inspected for venereal disease, and newly uniformed for the trip home. It certainly did not help that many of the clerks and other troops handling the redeployment from Europe were men who did not arrive in France in time to participate in combat. There was a natural antagonism between the Rainbow soldiers and the new arrivals, and any hint of giving orders to a 42nd combat veteran was usually met with physical or verbal abuse. Colonel Leach, a man of moderate temperament, felt that his men were being treated in an unusually harsh manner by the outprocessing personnel. In Leslie Langille's battery, a number of soldiers just simply invited the clerks outside for a minute. Upon returning, it was clear that after a 149th man had punched an offending clerk in the nose, the paperwork went a bit smoother.

When the 149th marched to the docks to board the USS *Leviathan*, a huge ship confiscated from the Germans in 1917, a pious lady from the Red Cross began to chide the troops for some drinking she had witnessed. Colonel Henry J. Reilly had had enough of this sanctimonious treatment in the Brest outprocessing, and proceeded to inform the woman that what his fighting men did was none of her business. As the woman hurried off, Reilly warned his smiling soldiers not to sneak more than three bottles of liquor each aboard the ship.

The 117th Trench Mortar Battery sailed for America on 9 April 1919, and the last unit, the Kansas 117th Ammunition Train, arrived at Newport News, Virginia, on 1 May 1919. There was no final parade for the Rainbow Division. As it had come together from separate parts of the country in the beginning, it departed for those areas separately. When the regiments returned home, there were tumultuous parades in Minneapolis, Montgomery, Des Moines, Columbus, and elsewhere. In New York, as Wild Bill Donovan led his troops down Broadway, a number of 165th veterans, many missing a limb or an eye, joined in the parade. They had been sent back to America from hospitals before the regiment, but they were determined to march home with their comrades. In Montgomery, Alabama, as the train carrying the remnants of the old Bloody 4th pulled into the station, there was an honor guard of the maimed and sightless waiting for them. By the end of May, the Rainbow was fully demobilized from federal service, and those units went back under the control of the National Guards of the various states.

In World War II, the 42nd Division was activated for service, and Rainbow veterans traveled to Camp Gruber, Oklahoma, for the ceremony. The Alabama 167th Infantry passed the colors to the new regiments, but the Rainbow was not the same. While it saw good service in the European Theater of Operations in World War II, it lacked the unique character, the panache, of the division of World War I fame. In the 1990s the Rainbow exists in the New York National Guard as only a reminder of its former glory.

Where, then, does the Rainbow Division fit into U.S. military history and the story of World War I? The Rainbow Division was the premier National Guard unit of World War I, but, having said that, it is wise to point out that there were no other National Guard divisions like the 42nd. The experimental nature of the division, combining units from twenty-six states and the District of Columbia, made it unique. There appeared to be several forces at work within the Rainbow. First, there was a clear sense of regimental cohesion based on locale, such as the Alabama 167th, or ethnic background and religion, such as the Irish 165th. Each component part had its own personality, but out of this came a distinct pride in being a part of the 42nd Division. At regimental and sometimes brigade command, the National Guard nature of the division was preserved, but, more often than not, the positions that carried with it the stars of brigade and divisional command went to Regulars. The general officers developed a sense of the special nature of the Rainbow and blended in with the sometimes unruly nature of the militia soldier, a true volunteer.

The combat record of the Rainbow placed it in the top five World War I divisions. Only the 32nd Division (National Guard) came close to equalling the 42nd on the battlefield. It is difficult and probably fruitless to dispute the standings of divisions, but it is clear that time spent in the line, casualties, objectives achieved, and so on can give a good picture of the combat capabilities of a unit. Through superior leadership, experience, high morale and esprit de corps, the 42nd certainly achieved a place of high respect within the AEF and from its German opponents. It is also difficult to know if Pershing really did appreciate the combat capabilities of any National Guard division, especially the Rainbow. His personal bias for the Big Red One was well known, even down to overlooking serious breaches of military discipline. To have looked the other way during the last few days of the Meuse-Argonne, when General Frank Parker took the 1st Division on a glory-hunting expedition at the cost of 500 casualties, is a prime example of Pershing's myopia. As Donald Smythe pointed out in his biography, *Pershing: General of the Armies*, had it been a National Guard division rather than the Big Red One violating every studied principle of combat, Pershing would have court-martialed the offenders. In his final report, Pershing gave to Summerall's V Corps credit for achieving the greatest advance during the last phases of the Meuse-Argonne offensive. This distorted the picture of what actually happened in the last days.

As Pershing discussed the war he continually heaped praise upon the 1st Division, and although it was undoubtably a fine fighting unit, this was a shabby way to remember those other divisional formations that made victory possible. The Rainbow soldiers never warmed to the Regulars, except for those who came into the division and discovered what fine fighting material they now commanded. It was symptomatic of the deep rift between the National Guard and the active army that was present then and exists up to the present day.

Much has been said about the American Civil War being the first modern war, and there is some truth to that, but World War I was really more indicative of modern war-fighting. The links with the Civil War for the soldiers of 1917-18 were there, and the generals studied great battles of the Civil War, but nothing could have prepared them for the technological battlefield on which they fought in France in 1918. After the war there was a slow awareness of some of the major technological changes wrought by the war. For example, younger officers writing in the *Infantry Journal* and the *Cavalry Journal* in the 1920s and 1930s discussed the potential of observation aircraft working with traditional ground cavalry (motor or horse) to extend the reconnaissance capabilities of the army. Signal equipment became an item of interest for the army, as instantaneous communications meant rapid decisions. The motorcar and truck extended the range for supply and for quick movement of troops from one place to another. However, the aircraft was seen as infantry support in observation and close air support. There was little real interest in anything that did not support the infantry and artillery in battle, except among a handful of forward-looking officers at the Air Corps Tactical School at Maxwell Field, Alabama, who could see strategic bombing and air superiority in modern terms.

In the spring of 1917, the army general staff had wanted the war to be a "professionals' war." The Regular Army professionals, however, had no more practical experience in a modern, massive war than did the National Guardsmen. No one had ever conceived of commanding a division of 28,000 officers and men, twice the size of a Civil War corps, on a modern battlefield with chemical weapons, machine guns, aircraft, tanks and communications that made discussions and reports between commanders and subordinates instantaneous. That brilliant things were done there is no doubt, but to say that the American Army went into the war with professional leadership is to overlook the tremendous process of learning, often through trial and error, that had to take place. It was difficult for Pershing and the old army establishment to believe that a militia colonel or brigadier general might be their equal in command ability, but they were on an equal footing in learning a new art of war.

Pershing came to France with doctrinal concepts that represented the trend in army thinking for some time. Simply put, the war would be won when troops got out of the trenches and fought in the fields and hills. The principle of maneuver is one of the nine principles of war. It is difficult to achieve victory without taking the offensive and destroying the enemy. Conditions on the Western Front in 1918, when doughboys were finally committed to battle, dictated that something be done to break the logjam of trench warfare. Pershing's insistence on maneuver warfare as opposed to more of the same was, in theory, correct.

Central to maneuver was the idea that victory belonged to the infantryman with his rifle, bayonet, and hand grenade, backed up with artillery and a functioning supply system. Pershing's insistence on maneuver as the key ingredient in victory did affect generations of army thinkers who looked for ways to implement that on the battlefield. What Pershing did, then, was not in vain, but certainly what he envisioned was one thing and what actually occurred was another.

Although Pershing preached maneuver warfare, the Americans actually did little of it. There were no great flanking attacks, for example. Maneuver warfare was honored more in name than in practice. True, individual squads, companies and battalions maneuvered tactically, but as an army, Pershing's AEF did little in the way of large-scale operational maneuvering. The big battles, St. Mihiel and the Meuse-Argonne, were muscle-against-muscle affairs that produced horrendous casualties. Certainly the stalemate of the Western Front had to be broken, troops had to attack objectives, and success could not continue to be measured in a few hundred meters of ground. Casualty lists were appalling, especially in the Argonne, where solid divisions like the Big Red One and the Rainbow were used up in a few days. One has to wonder what would have been the cost to the United States had we been in combat for four years instead of about 200 days?

What did Pershing and the AEF bring to the battlefield? The American soldier was indeed the key to victory on the Western Front in that his spirit had not been worn down by four years of bloodletting. The divisions which went into battle between March and November 1918 were very large, full of vigorous and idealistic young men who believed in the task they were undertaking, and there was a steady stream of American soldiers flowing into France. The presence of this unending source of manpower had to discourage the Germans who witnessed their arrival in France. The Americans could be rash, foolhardy, and sometimes simply tactically stupid. They began to learn not to attack machine-gun nests straight on. The Rainbow found out, as did other units, that fire and maneuver, concentrations of artillery, aircraft and balloon observation, and the slow crawl were better than reckless charges against machine guns. There is a real difference between the tactics of the Croix Rouge Farm fight and the slow, methodical attack on the Côte de Chatillion a few months later. Pershing came out of the war with his faith in the infantryman, his rifle, and his bayonet intact.

It is too easy to criticize Pershing and his followers for not seeing the ultimate value of the airplane or the tank. These were new weapons systems that played spectacular roles at times but could be seen as an interesting sideshow to combat. The World War I battlefield was the first where a commander could talk quickly to a subordinate or to a higher headquarters. The balloon observer could see targets of opportunity, and, just as important, he could inform gunners in a few minutes where to fire. They could also know, just as quickly, how well they did, and artillery fire could be adjusted. This conflict spelled the doom of the horse and the mule, as automobiles and Pierce-Arrow, Ford, and Dodge trucks hauled supplies to the front and ambulances sped wounded to the rear. The new nature of the battlefield was bewildering. That critical lessons were ignored or misinterpreted should not surprise anyone, especially when we understand that the practitioners of war in 1917 and 1918 were humans thrust into a new, very lethal world, for which they had little practical training.

Their value may not have been realized, but tank and aircraft were both used on the World War I battlefield. The Rainbow had George S. Patton's tanks attached in the St. Mihiel operation, and habitually an Aero squadron and a balloon company were part of the Rainbow's combat array. The air dimension was important to the Rainbow and to the ground army in that it could yield immediate results with a minimum of problems. The future value of the tank was understood by only a few, but it was clear that the benefits to the operational planner, the intelligence officer and the artillery arm from the observation aircraft and the balloon were great. The battlefield was extended farther than any commander had ever seen, and artillerymen were capable of firing deep into the enemy's rear areas against troops, supplies, and key terrain features such as roads and bridges. Charles T. Menoher became chief of the Air Service in 1919. Like many of his fellow ground officers, he was vitally concerned with the observation squadron and the balloon as extensions of the ground commander's combat capabilities. Pursuit or fighter aircraft and long-range bombers were not a part of their combat experience. The tank broke down, got mired in mud, and had other operating difficulties. The balloon, on the other hand, made it possible to see distant targets, instantaneously inform artillerymen by telephone, and adjust artillery fires deep.

The Rainbow Division, as unique as it was, was a part of the process of growing for the entire army. The experiences of these doughboys in the Great

War shaped the army forever, producing a modern army that would be called upon to take the field again in twenty-two years in another worldwide conflict. A few Rainbow veterans would play a great role in that war. By the next war Duffy, Hough, and others were dead. While many Rainbow veterans achieved great and lasting places in local and national history, the two premier veterans of the Rainbow were Douglas MacArthur and Wild Bill Donovan. MacArthur went on to be a reforming superintendent of West Point, chief of staff of the army, the savior of the Philippines, commander of U.S. forces in the Pacific in World War II, the American proconsul in Japan, commander of U.S. forces in Korea, and a national hero of extraordinary proportions. Donovan ran unsuccessfully for governor of New York in the 1920s, but during World War II contributed his tremendous talents as chief of the vital Office of Strategic Services, the OSS. After the war he founded the Central Intelligence Agency. Both men are chapters rather than footnotes in history.

Charles MacArthur wrote his memoirs, *War Bugs*, married actress Helen Hayes, and earned a place in American literary history as a playwright. Elmer Sherwood wrote two books about his experiences as a Hoosier Gunner. Leslie Langille and Lawrence Stewart, while they also wrote their stories, went on to lead quiet lives in the American heartland. Calvin Lambert, a stalwart member of the Rainbow Association, had a solid career as a small-town Kansas journalist.

Colonel George Leach was promoted to brigadier general, served as chief of the National Guard Bureau from 1932 to 1936, and in 1937 became the mayor of Minneapolis, Minnesota. Throughout the 1920s and 1930s Leach was "Mr. National Guard" in the Gopher state. William Screws, who commanded the Alabama Wildmen of the 167th, remained in the Regular Army until he retired as a brigadier general, then served on the city commission of Montgomery, Alabama, and later as head of the Alabama Alcoholic Beverage Board. Benson Hough went on to be elected to the Supreme Court of Ohio, served as the U.S. Attorney for Southern Ohio, and rose to command of the 37th "Buckeye" Division, Ohio National Guard. Colonel Mathew Tinley of the 168th Iowa was a successful businessman in Council Bluffs, Iowa. He rose to the rank of lieutenant general and ended his career commanding the 34th Infantry Division of Iowa, North and South Dakota, and Minnesota.

Father Duffy returned to New York, where he was a leader in Catholic affairs in the city and pastored Holy Cross Church in Manhattan, a church that served the theater district. There was always something of the Irish poet in his soul; perhaps that was why he loved Joyce Kilmer so. When Duffy died in 1932, he received a state funeral with a half-million mourners lining the streets of Fifth Avenue. Later a monument was erected in his honor and a small park was named for him.

Noble Brandon Judah, the G2 of the division, became the U.S. ambassador to Cuba in the late 1920s and was honored as a trustee of Brown University. Henry J. Reilly resumed his profession as a military writer and traveler after the war. He was editor and publisher of the *Army and Navy Journal* and became a military correspondent during the Russian Kiev and Vistula campaigns of 1921 and the Manchurian campaign of 1925. In 1936 he wrote his massive *Americans All: The Rainbow at War*, and during World War II he lectured at the U.S. Army's Command and General Staff College at Fort Leavenworth, Kansas.

Major James Frew returned home to Wisconsin to practice medicine and was a regular attender at Rainbow conventions. His wife became known as Mother Frew because of her kindness and devotion to the members of the Rainbow veterans association. When she passed away in 1957, there were many old veterans who never knew her name was Estelle, for she had simply been known as "Mother" to most of them. Lieutenant van Dolsen returned from Europe a changed, sober man; his youth was left behind in the hospitals of France. He practiced medicine for the rest of his life.

Charles P. Summerall, whom some called one of the best American soldiers of the twentieth century, went on to be chief of staff of the U.S. Army. He was the only World War I general of division or corps command to have an active role in World War II. He ended his long career as president of the Citadel, and the cadets who studied under Summerall remembered him as a stern taskmaster embodying the military virtues.

In addition to Summerall and MacArthur, two other Rainbow soldiers had a definite impact on the Armed Services of the United States. Wilber M. Brucker, who served as governor of Ohio in the 1930s, became secretary of the army in the Eisenhower administration, and Donald A. Quarles served as secretary of the air force in the same administration. Brucker saw service in the 166th Infantry, while Quarles was a member of the Illinois 149th Artillery. No other World War I division produced two chiefs of staff of the army and two service secretaries.

Other Rainbow veterans who achieved notable success were: General John DeWitt, quartermaster general of the army in World War II; Robert Beightler, commander of the 37th Division in the Pacific Theater of Operations; General Miller White, G1, U.S. Mediterranean Forces in World War II; Blanton Winship, governor of the Virgin Islands; and Olin Johnson, elected governor, then senator from South Carolina. Thomas Handy, who accompanied Menoher and MacArthur on their first view of No Man's Land, rose to four-star rank and commanded all U.S. forces in Germany after World War II.

Al Ettinger remained a fighter all of his life. In 1940 he enlisted in the U.S. Marine Corps. During the Vietnam War, Ettinger organized citizens groups to support the troops serving in Vietnam, and he was devastated by the outcome of the war in Vietnam and by the shabby treatment of the returning soldiers. They had no parade, no welcome home, as he had had in New York in 1919. Ettinger "went west" in 1984.

Joe Romano, bothered continually by his wounds, lived quietly in Alabama, as did Ashton Croft. Hugh Thompson wrote his memoirs in Chattanooga in the 1930s, and he too was bothered by the severe wound he had received in the St. Mihiel offensive. Perhaps the happiest man of all was Everett Scott of

Primgihar, Iowa. A year after his return to Iowa, Scott married his flaxen-haired Louise, the woman he had loved for so long. While sitting at his kitchen table, Scott wrote out what would be their wedding announcement. At the end of the hand-written copy he added "bring cassaroles and bring money." Scott leaned back in his chair and laughed, because he had found his special pot of gold at the end of the Rainbow.

NOTES

1. HQ, 42nd Division, General Orders No. 23, 30 March 1919, in the National Archives, Washington, D.C., *Records Group 120 Records of the AEF, 42nd Division* (hereinafter, RG 120), carton 20.

2. R.M. Cheseldine, *Ohio in the Rainbow: Official Story of the 166th Infantry, 42nd Division in the World War* (Columbus, Ohio: F.J. Heer Printing Co., 1924), 320-21.

3. Scott to his mother, Nieder Briesig, 17 March 1919 in the Scott Letters, manuscripts in the author's collection.

4. Francis P. Duffy, *Father Duffy's Story* (New York: George H. Doran Co., 1919), 324.

5. Louis L. Collins, *History of the 151st Artillery Rainbow Division* (Saint Paul: Minnesota War Records Commission, 1924), 176-77.

6. Leslie Langille, *Men of the Rainbow* (Chicago: O'Sullivan Co., 1933), 183.

7. Duffy, *Story*, 325-26.

8. E.J. Sadler (ed.), *California Rainbow Memories* (Np: Private printing, 1925), 61.

9. William B. Amerine, *Alabama's Own in France* (New York: Eaton and Gettinger, 1919), 236.

10. John B. Hayes, *Heroes Among the Brave* (Loachapoka, Ala.: Lee County Historical Society, 1973), 42-43.

11. Frazier Hunt, *The Untold Story of Douglas MacArthur* (New York: Devin-Adair, 1954), 97-98. On 25 March 1942, the Congressional Medal of Honor was bestowed upon General Douglas MacArthur, more than twenty years after he had really earned his nation's highest combat decoration.

12. Duffy, *Story*, 323.

13. Charles MacArthur, *War Bugs* (Garden City, N.Y.: Doubleday, Doran and Co., 1929), 289-92.

14. Diary entry, 30 March 1919, George E. Seaman (ed.), *War Diary of George E. Leach, Colonel 151st Field Artillery* (Roanoke, VA: National Association of Rainbow Veterans, 1962), 106.

15. Scott to his brother, Neider Breisig, 30 March 1919, in Scott Letters.

16. Cheseldine, *Ohio in the Rainbow*, 322.

17. Henry J. Reilly, *Americans All: The Rainbow at War* (Columbus, Ohio: F.J. Heer Printing Co., 1936), 876.

18. Douglas MacArthur, *Reminiscences* (New York: McGraw-Hill, 1964), 72.

19. MacArthur, *War Bugs*, 297-99.

20. Langille, *Men of the Rainbow*, 185.

21. Diary entry 9 April 1919, in Seaman, *War Diary*, 107.

22. A. Churchill Ettinger (ed.), *A Doughboy with the Fighting 69th* (Shippensburg, PA: White Main Publishing, 1929), 197-98.
    23. Duffy, *Story*, 327.

Appendix A

Organization of the 42nd Division, 1917

The troop list for the 42nd Division was completed by 14 August 1917, although some units had already been alerted for movement to Camp Mills, New York. Given the magnitude of the task and the varying degrees of organization within those National Guard units, some of which had just been formed, it was a difficult undertaking. The army had no precedent to follow. Twenty-six states were involved in the process, as were five U.S. Army departments, which, for all practical purposes, had the responsibility of providing clothing and equipment, medical care, food, and transportation to those drafted Guard units. To bring order out of a very confusing process, I have listed those units involved in the formation of the "composite National Guard Division."

EASTERN MILITARY DEPARTMENT

The 3rd Battalion, 4th Pennsylvania Infantry Regiment became the 149th Machine Gun Battalion.

The 69th New York Infantry became the 165th Infantry Regiment.

The 3rd and 4th Companies Maryland Coast Artillery Companies became the 117th Trench Mortar Company.

The Coast Artillery Corps, Virginia, became the 117th Headquarters Train and Military Police.

The 1st New Jersey Ambulance Company became the 2nd Ambulance Company, 117th Sanitary Train.

The 1st District of Columbia Field Hospital Company became the 1st Field Hospital Company, 117th Sanitary Train.

SOUTHEASTERN MILITARY DEPARTMENT

The 2nd Separate Louisiana Cavalry Troop became the Divisional Headquarters Cavalry Troop.

The B, C, and F Companies, 2nd Georgia Infantry, became the 151st Machine Gun Battalion.

The 4th Alabama Infantry Regiment became the 167th Infantry Regiment.

The 1st Separate South Carolina Engineer Battalion became the 1st Battalion, 117th Engineer Regiment.

The North Carolina Engineer Train became the 117th Engineer Train.

The 1st Ambulance Company, Tennessee, became the 3rd Ambulance Company, 117th Sanitary Train.

CENTRAL MILITARY DEPARTMENT

The E, F, and G Companies from the 2nd Wisconsin Infantry became the 150th Machine Gun Battalion.

The 4th Ohio Infantry Regiment became the 166th Infantry Regiment.

The 3rd Iowa Infantry Regiment became the 168th Infantry Regiment.

The 1st Illinois Field Artillery became the 149th Field Artillery Regiment.

The 1st Indiana Field Artillery became the 150th Field Artillery Regiment.

The 1st Minnesota Field Artillery became the 151st Field Artillery Regiment.

The 1st Missouri Field Signal Battalion became the 117th Field Signal Battalion.

The 1st Kansas Ammunition Train became the 117th Ammunition Train.

The Michigan 1st Ambulance Company became the 1st Ambulance Company, 117th Sanitary Train.

The 1st Nebraska Field Hospital Company became the 2nd Field Hospital Company, 117th Sanitary Train.

The 1st Field Hospital Company, Colorado, became the 3rd Field Hospital

Company, 117th Sanitary Train.

WESTERN MILITARY DEPARTMENT

The California 1st Separate Engineer Battalion became the 2nd Battalion, 117th Engineer Regiment.

The Oregon 1st Field Hospital Company became the 4th Field Hospital Company, 117th Sanitary Train.

SOUTHERN MILITARY DEPARTMENT

The Texas Supply Train became the 117th Supply Train.

The 1st Ambulance Company, Oklahoma, became the 4th Ambulance Company, 117th Sanitary Train.

(Source: Memorandum from the War Department to the Adjutant General of the Army, Washington, 14 August 1917, in the National Archives, Washington, D.C., *Records Group 120 Records of the AEF, 42nd Division*, carton 3.)

APPENDIX B

EQUIPMENT TAKEN INTO THE TRENCHES, FEBRUARY 1918

1. The Field Service Uniform:

    Steel helmet

    Regulation overcoat

    Service coat, woolen

    Service breeches, woolen

    OD (olive drab) flannel shirt

    Woolen undershirt

    Woolen underdrawers

    Heavy woolen socks

    Woolen gloves

    Wraped puttees

    Trench shoes, hobnailed

    2 Identification tags

    Small box respirator

    French mask

2. Articles Carried in the Field Pack:

    1 Sweater

    1 Blanket

    1 Poncho or slicker

    3 Pairs heavy woolen socks

    1 Pair woolen drawers

    1 Woolen undershirt

    1 OD flannel shirt

    1 Razor

    1 Comb

    1 Cake of soap

    1 Tooth brush

    1 Towel

    1 Overseas cap

    2 Days reserve rations

3. Items to be Carried in the Field Trains:

    Rubber or arctic boots, two woolen blankets, one barracks bag for enlisted soldiers; bedding and one footlocker for officers.

4. All soldiers carried weapons plus 100 rounds of rifle ammunition for enlisted soldiers and twenty-one rounds per pistol for officers.

(Source: Memorandum No. 23, 42nd Division headquarters, 9 February 1918, in the National Archives, Washington, D.C., *Records Group 120 Records of the AEF, 42nd Division*, carton 1.)

BIBLIOGRAPHY

RAINBOW SPECIFIC

Albert, Warren J. *Battery A in France*. Danville, Ill.: Interstate Publishing Co., 1919.

American Battle Monuments Commission. *42nd Division, Summary of Operations in The World War*. Washington, D.C.: Government Printing Office, 1940.

Amerine, William B. *Alabama's Own in France*. New York: Eaton and Gettinger, 1919.

Cheseldine, R.M. *Ohio in the Rainbow: Official Story of the 166th Infantry, 42nd Division in the World War*. Columbus, Ohio: F.J. Heer Printing Co., 1924.

Cochrane, Rexmond C. *The 42nd Division Before Landres-et-St. Georges, October, 1918*. U.S. Chemical Corp Study, No. 17, Washington, D.C.: Government Printing Office, 1960.

Collins, Louis L. *History of the 151st Field Artillery, Rainbow Division*. Saint Paul, Minn.: Minnesota War Records Commission, 1924.

Duffy, Francis P. *Father Duffy's Story*. New York: George H. Doran Co., 1919.

Ettinger, A. Churchill (ed.) *A Doughboy with the Fighting 69th*. Shippensburg, PA: White Mane Publishing, 1992.

Gouraud, General Henri Joséph Eugène. "My Memories of the Rainbow Division." *The American Legion Monthly* II (November 1933).

Hayes, John B. *Heroes Among the Brave*. Loachapoka, Ala.: Lee County Historical Society, 1973.

Hogan, Martin J. *The Shamrock Battalion of the Rainbow: A Story of the Fighting 69th*. New York: D. Appleton and Co., 1919.

Johnson, Harold S. (ed.) *Roster of the Rainbow Division, Major General Wm. A. Mann, Commanding*. New York: Eaton and Gettinger, 1917.

Langille, Leslie. *Men of the Rainbow*. Chicago: O'Sullivan Co., 1933.

MacArthur, Charles. *War Bugs*. Garden City, N.Y.: Doubleday, Doran and
    Co., 1929.
Menoher, Major General Charles T. "The Rainbow." *New York Times
    Magazine Section*, 27 April 1919.
The Rainbow Reveille, 1920-1960.
Reilly, Henry J. *Americans All: The Rainbow at War*. Columbus, Ohio:
    F.J. Heer Printing Co., 1936.
Reppy, Alison. *Rainbow Memories: Character Sketches and History of the
    First Battalion, 166th Infantry*. Np: Private printing, 1919.
Robb, Winifred E. *The Price of Our Heritage: In Memory of the Heroic
    Dead of the 168th Infantry*. Des Moines, Iowa: American
    Lithographing and Printing Company, 1919.
Sadler, E.J. (ed.) *California Rainbow Memories*. Np: Private printing, 1925.
Seaman, George E. (ed.) *War Diary of George E. Leach, Colonel 151st Field
    Artillery*. Roanoke, Va.: National Association of Rainbow Veterans,
    reprint of 1923 edition, 1962.
Sherwood, Elmer W. *Diary of a Rainbow Veteran: Written at the Front*.
    Terre Haute, Ind.: Moore-Langen, 1929.
———, *Rainbow Hoosier*. Indianapolis, Ind.: Printing Arts Co., c. 1925.
Stewart, Lawrence. *Rainbow Bright*. Philadelphia, Penn.: Dorrance, 1923.
Taber, John H. *The Story of the 168th Infantry*, 2 Vols. Iowa City, Iowa:
    State Historical Society of Iowa, 1925.
Thompkins, Raymond S. *The Story of the Rainbow Division*. New York:
    Boni and Liveright, 1919.
Thompson, Hugh S. "Following the Rainbow." *The Chattanooga Times*,
    Sunday Edition. January-May 1934.
Wolf, Walter B. *Brief Story of the Rainbow Division*. New York: Rand
    McNally Co., 1919.

ARCHIVAL SOURCES

Alabama State Historical Archives, Montgomery, Alabama, 167th Infantry
    Collection.
Auburn University Archives, the Franklin Ashton Croft Diary, 1917 and the
    Edward R. Wren Letters, 1918-1919, Auburn, Alabama.
Calvin Lambert Diary manuscript, Emporia Public Library, Emporia, Kansas.
Corporal Garrett Olds Rainbow Veterans Collection, author's collection.
D. Clayton James Collection, Mitchell Memorial Library, Mississippi State
    University, Starkville, Mississippi.
Herbert W. Rowse Papers, author's collection.
National Archives, Records Group 120, Records of the AEF, 42nd Infantry
    Division, 1917-1919, Washington, D.C.
National Archives, Records Group 120, Records of the AEF, Entry 1298,
    Tank Corps, 1918-1919, Washington, D.C.

National Archives, Records Group 200, Pershing Papers, AEF, Washington, D.C.
Notes from Joseph Romano, son of Corporal Joseph Romano, author's collection.
Private First Class Everett Scott Letters, author's collection.
U.S. Air Force Historical Agency, Maxwell Air Force Base, Alabama.
U.S. Army, Institute for Military History Archives, 42nd Infantry Division Collection, Carlisle Barracks, Pennsylvania.
U.S. Army, Institute for Military History Archives, World War I Questionnaire Collection, Carlisle Barracks, Pennsylvania.

OFFICIAL PUBLICATIONS

Ayers, L.P. *The War with Germany: A Statistical Summary.* Washington, D.C.: Government Printing Office, 1919.
American Battle Monuments Commission. *1st Division, Summary of Operations in the World War.* Washington, D.C.: Government Printing Office, 1944.
————. *4th Division, Summary of Operations in the World War.* Washington, D.C.: Government Printing Office, 1944.
————. *77th Division, Summary of Operations in the World War.* Washington, D.C.: Government Printing Office, 1944.
————. *82nd Division, Summary of Operations in the World War.* Washington, D.C.: Government Printing Office, 1944.
————. *89th Division, Summary of Operations in the World War.* Washington, D.C.: Government Printing Office, 1944.
————. *32nd Division, Summary of Operations in the World War.* Washington, D.C.: Government Printing Office, 1943.
Chief of Air Service. *Final Report of Chief of Air Service, AEF to the Commander in Chief, AEF.* Washington, D.C.: Government Printing Office, 1921.
General Headquarters, AEF. *Instructions for Liaison for Troops of All Arms.* Paris: Imprimèrie Nationale, 1918.
————. *Instructions for the Defensive Combat of Small Units.* Chaumont, France: AG Printing Department, 1918.
————. *Study and Utilization of Aerial Photographs,* 2 Vols. Paris: Imprimèrie Nationale, 1918.
————. *G2, Notes on Branch Intelligence,* November 1, 1919. Chaumont, France: Base Printing Plant, 29th Engineers, 1918.
————. *Defensive Measures Against Gas Attacks.* Nancy, France: Berger et Leverault, 1917.

General Service Schools. *The German Offensive of July 15, 1918: Marne Source Book.* Fort Leavenworth, Kan.: General Service Schools Press, 1923.

Pershing, John J. *Final Report of General John J. Pershing, Commander-in-Chief, AEF.* Washington, D.C.: Government Printing Office, 1920.

U.S. Army, Center of Military History. *The United States Army in the World War, 1917-1919,* 12 Vols. Washington, D.C.: Government Printing Office, reprint, 1989.

U.S. Army War College, Historical Section. *The Genesis of the American First Army.* Washington, D.C.: Government Printing Office, 1938.

————. *The Signal Corps and Air Service, 1917-1918.* Washington, D.C.: Government Printing Office, 1922.

U.S. Office of the Surgeon General. *The Medical Department of the United States Army in the World War,* 8 Vols. Washington, D.C.: Government Printing Office, 1926.

U.S. War Department. *The Official Record of the Great War.* New York: Parke, Austin and Lipscomb, 1923.

————. *America's Munitions, 1917-1918: The Report of Benedict Crowell.* Washington, D.C.: Government Printing Office, 1919.

————. *Keeping Fit to Fight.* Washington, D.C.: Government Printing Office, 1918.

————. *Drill Regulations and Service Manual for Sanitary Troops.* Washington, D.C.: Government Printing Office, 1917.

————. *Field Service Regulations, Corrected to 1917.* Washington, D.C.: Government Printing Office, 1917.

————. *Infantry Drill Regulations.* Menasha, Wis.: George Banta Co., 1917.

————. *Minor Foot Ailments and Shoe Fitting.* Washington, D.C.: Government Printing Office, 1917.

————. *Regulations for the Army of the United States.* Washington, D.C.: Government Printing Office, 1917.

————. *Regulations for the Uniform of the United States Army.* Washington, D.C.: Government Printing Office, 1912.

PRIMARY

Azan, Paul. *The Warfare of Today.* New York: Houghton-Mifflin, 1918.

Baker, Newton D. *Frontiers of Freedom.* New York: Doubleday, Doran and Co., 1931.

Dickman, Joseph T. *The Great Crusade.* New York: Appleton, 1927.

France, Etat-Major de l'Armée, Service Historique. *Les Armées Françaises dans la Grande Guerre.* Series 6, Vol. 2, and Series 7, Vol. 2. Paris: Imprimèrie Nationale, 1934 and 1937.

Gilchrist, John W. *An Aerial Observer in World War I.* Richmond, Va.:

Private, 1966.

Grissinger, J.W. *Medical Field Service in France.* Washington, D.C.:
Association of Military Surgeons, 1928.

Harbord, James G. *The American Army in France.* Boston, Mass.: Little,
Brown, 1936.

————. *Leaves from a War Diary.* New York: Dodd, Meade, and Co.,
1925.

Horne, Charles F. and Walter F. Austin. *Source Records of the Great War,*
Vol. 7, New York: National Alumni, 1923.

Hornung, F.W. *Notes of a Camp Follower on the Western Front.* New York:
E.P. Dutton, 1919.

Langer, William L. *Gas and Flame in World War One.* New York: Alfred
A. Knopf, 1965.

Liggett, Hunter. *AEF: Ten Years Ago in France.* New York: Dodd, Meade
and Co., 1928.

————. *Commanding an American Army: Recollections of the World War.*
Boston, Mass.: Houghton-Mifflin, 1925.

MacArthur, Douglas. *Reminiscences.* New York: McGraw-Hill, 1964.

March, Peyton C. *The Nation at War.* Garden City, N.Y.: Doubleday,
Doran and Co., 1932.

Marshall, George C. *Memoirs of My Service in the World War, 1917-1918.*
Boston, Mass.: Houghton-Mifflin, 1976.

Mitchell, William. *Memoirs of World War One.* New York: Random House,
1960.

Office of Air Force History. *The U.S. Air Service in World War I,* 4 Vols.
Washington, D.C.: Government Printing Office, 1978.

Pershing, John J. *My Experiences in the World War,* 2 Vols. New York:
Frederick A. Stokes Co., 1931.

Toulmin, H.A., Jr. *Air Service, American Expeditionary Force, 1918.* New
York: D. Van Nostrand Co., 1927.

U.S. Army. *World War Records, First Division, American Expeditionary
Forces, Regular, Field Orders, September 1918 to Conclusion,* Vol. 3
(6 March 1928).

————. *Operations Reports, 12 September 1918 to Conclusion.* (1930).

Wilgus, William John. *Transporting the AEF in Western Europe 1917-1919.*
New York: Columbia University Press, 1931.

SECONDARY

Addison, James T. *The Story of the First Gas Regiment.* Boston, Mass.:
Houghton-Mifflin, 1919.

Bach, Christian A., and Henry Hall. *The Fourth Division.* Garden City,
N.Y.: Country Life Press, 1920.

Braim, Paul F. *The Test of Battle: The American Expeditionary Forces in*

the Meuse-Argonne Campaign. Newark, Del.: University of
Delaware Press, 1987.

Carter, Russell Gordon. *The 101st Field Artillery, AEF, 1917-1919.* Boston,
Mass.: Houghton-Mifflin, 1940.

Coffman, Edward M. *The War to End All Wars: The American Military
Experience in World War I.* Madison, Wis.: University of
Wisconsin Press, 1986.

Doughty, Robert Allan. *The Seeds of Disaster: The Development of French
Army Doctrine, 1919-1939.* Hamden, Conn.: Archon, 1985.

Ewart, Ernest A. *Air Men of the War.* New York: Dutton, 1919.

Greer, Thomas H. *The Development of Air Doctrine in the Army Air Arm,
1917-1941.* Washington, D.C.: USAF Historical Study No. 89,
1953.

Gregory, Barry. *Argonne 1918: The AEF in France.* New York: Ballantine,
1972.

Harris, Frederick (ed.) *Service With Fighting Men,* 2 Vols. New York:
YMCA Association Press, 1922.

Heller, Charles E. *Chemical Warfare in World War I: The American
Experience, 1917-1918.* Fort Leavenworth, Kan.: Combat Studies
Institute, 1984.

Holliday, Robert C. (ed.) *Joyce Kilmer,* 2 Vols. New York: Doran, 1918.

Hunt, Frazier. *The Untold Story of Douglas MacArthur.* New York: Devin-
Adair, 1954.

James, D. Clayton. *The Years of MacArthur, I, 1880-1941.* Boston, Mass.:
Houghton-Mifflin, 1970.

Kaspi, André. *Le Temps des Américans à la France en 1917-1918.* Paris:
Publications de la Sorbonne, 1976.

Kennett, Lee. *The First Air War.* New York: The Free Press, 1991.

Manchester, William. *American Caesar: Douglas MacArthur, 1880-1964.*
Boston, Mass.: Little, Brown, and Co., 1978.

Mayo, Virginia. *That Damned Y.* New York: Houghton-Mifflin, 1920.

Meehan, Thomas F. *History of the Seventh Division in the World War, 1917-
1919.* New York: Dodd, Meade, and Co., 1921.

Official History of the 82nd Division, American Expeditionary Forces.
Indianapolis, Ind.: Bobbs-Merrill Co., 1929.

Ottosen, Peter H. *Trench Artillery, AEF.* Boston, Mass.: Lothrop, Lee and
Shepard, 1931.

Palmer, Frederick. *Newton Baker: America at War,* 2 Vols. New York:
Dodd, Meade, and Co., 1919.

77th Division Association. *History of the Seventy-Seventh Division, 1917-
1918.* New York: Wynkoop, Hallenbeck, Crawford, 1919.

Smythe, Donald. *Pershing: General of the Armies.* Bloomington, Ind.:
Indiana University Press, 1986.

Society of the First Division. *History of the First Division During the World*

War, 1917-1919. Philadelphia, PA: John C. Winston Co., 1922.

Spaulding, O.L. *The Second Division, American Expeditionary Force in France, 1917-1919*. New York: Hillman Press, 1937.

Stallings, Laurence. *The Doughboys: The Story of the AEF, 1917-1918*. New York: Harper and Row, 1963.

Vandiver, Frank E. *Black Jack: The Life and Times of John J. Pershing*, 2 Vols. College Station, Texas: Texas A&M Press, 1977.

Wilson, Dale E. *Treat 'Em Rough: The Birth of American Armor, 1917-1920*. Novato, Calif.: Presidio Press, 1989.

ARTICLES

Arnold, H.H. "The Cavalry-Air Corps Team." *The Cavalry Journal* 38, 150 (January 1928).

Burdick, Henry H. "The Battalion Intelligence Section in Open Warfare." *Infantry Journal* 19, 6 (December 1921).

Ellis, Andrew. "On Time--On Target: The Birth of the Modern American Artillery." *Field Artillery* (August 1988).

Fickett, Edward M. "A Study of the Relationship Between Cavalry and the Air Service in Reconnaissance." *The Cavalry Journal* 32, 133 (October 1923).

Greer, Thomas H. "Air Arm Doctrinal Roots, 1917-1918." *Military Affairs* 20, 4 (Winter 1956).

Kennett, Lee. "AEF Through French Eyes." *Military Review* 52 (November 1972).

Lewis, Edwin N. "In the Argonne's Mist and Mystery." *The American Legion Weekly* (September 26, 1919).

Menoher, Charles T. "Problems of American Aeronautics." *Air Power* (April 1919).

Mitchell, William. "The Air Service at the Meuse-Argonne." *World's Work* 38, 5 (September 1919).

———. "The Air Service at St. Mihiel." *World's Work* 38, 4 (August 1919).

Rainey, James W. "The Questionable Training of the AEF in World War I." *Parameters* 22, 4 (Winter 1992-93).

Rarey, G.H. "American Tank Units in the Foret d'Argonne Attack." *Infantry Journal* 33, 4 (April 1928).

"Report of General William L. Kenly, the Director of Military Aeronautics." *Air Power* (December 1918).

Reynolds, John N. "Tactical Employment of Combat Aviation." *U.S. Air Service* (January 1925).

Smythe, Donald. "A.E.F. Sanfu at Sedan." *Prologue* 5 (September 1973).

Switzer, J.S. "The Champagne-Marne Defensive." *Infantry Journal* 20, 1-6 (January-June 1922).

Von Giehrl, Hermann. "The American Expeditionary Forces in Europe, 1917-

1918." *Infantry Journal* 19, 6 (December 1921).

————. "Battle of the Meuse-Argonne." *Infantry Journal* 19, 2-5 (August-November 1921).

Wukovits, John F. "Best-Case Scenario Exceeded." *Military History* (December 1992).

INDEX

Ahrweiler (Germany), Kreis of, 213-15, 219, 222-28, 234, 237

Air Service: Brigadier General William "Billy" Mitchell, 8, 92, 135, 145; enemy air activity, 55, 91, 157, 164; liaison with U.S. ground forces, 57, 91, 100, 145, 168; Major General Menoher's relations with, 92, 125, 157-58, 242; General Pershing's attitude toward, 8, 91, 145, 242; 2nd Balloon Company, 91-92, 168; 3rd Balloon Company, 145, 156; 12th Aero Squadron, 91-92, 125, 135; 90th Aero Squadron, 145, 158; utilization of in combat, 91; Baccarat, 91-92; Marne, 125, 135, 145; St. Mihiel, 93, 145, 156-58, 242; Meuse-Argonne, 164, 168, 188

Anderson, Major Alexander, 109, 126, 155, 177

Army of Occupation, 210, 214-16, 218-19, 222-23, 233

Atkinson, Sergeant Ralph, 179

Baccarat, France, 70-71, 75-80, 88, 90, 92, 93, 104

Baker, Newton D., 3-5, 23, 80

Bare, Lieutenant Colonel Walter E., 193

Barker, Colonel John W., 38, 76, 78-79

Battle, Major M.S., 43

Bazeilles, France, 193, 200

Bazelaire, General Georges de, 54

Belgium, American troops in, 203-04, 209-11

Bennett, Colonel Edward R., 44-45, 121-22, 128-29, 146-47

Bliss, Major General Tasker, 22

Blois, France, 23, 29, 48, 132-33

Bootz, Captain Hermann, 130, 134

Brewster, Brigadier General A.W., 44, 46, 146

Brigades (U.S.): 7th Infantry, 129; 83rd Infantry: combat participation, 126, 152, 155, 169, 171-73, 175, 177-78, 181, 199-200; Baccarat, 76; Ourcq River (Marne), 120, 124; St. Mihiel, 147-51, 156; Meuse-Argonne, 168, 170, 175-76, 180, 188; commanded by Michael J. Lenihan, 75, 84, 133, 176, 204; Henry J. Reilly, 178, 181, 199; Rolampont, 44, 47; 84th

Infantry: 17, 193; combat participation, 125, 128, 130, 150, 152, 155-58, 172-73, 176-77; Baccarat, 76; Ourcq River (Marne), 120, 123-25, 133; St. Mihiel, 146-47, 149, 156; Meuse-Argonne, 168-70, 175, 180-81, 188-89; commanded by Douglas MacArthur, 130, 132, 134, 203; Robert Brown, 44, 75, 118, 125-26, 128, 132-33; Rolampont, 44, 47; 1st Field Artillery, 170, 191; 51st Field Artillery, 123; 67th Field Artillery: Camp Coetquidan, 32-33, 35; combat participation, 87, 104-05, 109, 123, 132, 170-72, 214; Lunéville, 67; Ourcq River (Marne), 101, 104; St. Mihiel, 139-40, 165-66; Meuse-Argonne, 181; George Gatley, 171, 219, 235; Charles McKinstry, 84; Charles P. Summerall, 21, 167; 1st Tank, 147

Broussaud, Colonel François, 101

Brown, Brigadier General Robert: combat participation, 104, 120, 126; Lunéville, 47, 64; Baccarat, 75; Ourcq River (Marne), 118, 125-26, 128-29; relieved of command, 130, 132-33; Rolampont, 37, 42, 44; See also: 83rd Brigade

Buck, Sarah E., 226

Bullard, Major General Robert, 163

Camp Alvord L. Mills (New York), 5, 8, 10-19, 21, 35, 42, 62, 78, 135, 234, 236

Camp Coetquidan, France, 24, 32-35, 39, 47, 54, 67

Camp Meade, Maryland, 45

Centre de Résistance (CR), 59-60, 76, 78, 87

Chanoine, Major Charles M., 150, 152, 154

Chicago Board of Trade Battery, 12, 201

Coblenz, Germany, 217-20, 223-24, 226, 228, 235

Cochrane, Bess, 226-28

Connor, Colonel Fox, 22-23, 41, 145, 190

Corned Willie, 29, 53-54, 67, 105, 108, 134, 170

Craig, Brigadier General Malin A., 195-96, 199, 218, 220

Croft, Private Ashton, 12, 14, 16-17, 19, 36, 40, 97, 244

Croix Rouge Farm, 112, 120-23, 126, 129, 143, 242

Dickman, Major General Joseph T., 182; Army of Occupation, 202-03, 211-12, 216, 218-19, 223, 225; career in AEF, 144-45; St. Mihiel, 156-57; Sedan, 191, 195, 197-200

Divisions (French): 5th Cavalry, 163; 13th Infantry, 101, 103-04; 40th Infantry, 192, 195-200; 43rd Infantry, 101; 128th Infantry, 59; 167th Infantry, 120; 170th Infantry, 101, 103, 120

Divisions (U.S.): trained by French, 24, 30; used as replacement units, 22-23, 144, 166, 219-20; 1st Infantry, 24, 58, 93, 97, 100, 113, 117, 145; 1st

Infantry (Army of Occupation), 202; 1st Infantry (Meuse-Argonne), 163, 167-68, 179; 1st Infantry (Sedan), 191-92, 195-200; 2nd Infantry, 24, 58, 93, 97, 100, 113, 117, 181-82, 191, 202-03; 3rd Infantry, 100, 113, 117, 144-45, 202-03, 221; 4th Infantry, 100, 113, 117; 4th Infantry (Army of Occupation), 202, 221, 228, 234, 236-37; 4th Infantry (Ourcq River [Marne]), 126, 129, 131-32, 139-40; 4th Infantry (St. Mihiel), 164; 5th Infantry, 203; 26th Infantry, 23-24, 97, 100, 113, 117, 120, 123; 27th Infantry, 10; 28th Infantry, 100, 113, 117, 120, 125, 129, 163-64, 203; 31st Infantry, 203, 219; 33rd Infantry, 164, 203; 35th Infantry, 164; 37th Infantry, 164, 169, 203, 243-44; 39th Infantry, 203, 219; 41st Infantry, 23, 38, 143, 166, 179; 77th Infantry, 93, 132-33, 140, 163-64, 178, 191, 197-99; 78th Infantry, 188; 80th Infantry, 164, 191; 82nd Infantry, 163, 171, 177-78; 89th Infantry, 145, 155-56, 158, 202-03; 90th Infantry, 202-03

"Dixie", 204, 211

Donovan, Colonel William J. "Wild Bill": 2, 5, 10, 14, 228, 238-39; Camp Mills, 10; combat participation, 65-66, 70, 109, 126-27, 151, 153-55, 172-76; Lunéville, 58, 60, 64; Baccarat, 76, 80, 84, 93; Champagne, 104; Ourcq River (Marne), 111, 124, 130; St. Mihiel, 150; Meuse-Argonne, 169, 171, 177-78; decorations, 66, 70, 80, 169; early career, 2, 10; marriage, 10; occupation of Germany, 217, 236; personal relations with Father Duffy, 2, 46, 144, 234; Joyce Kilmer, 127; post-war career, 243; resists higher staff assignments, 10, 46, 146, 164; Rouge Boquet, 60, 65; training with the French, 38, 45; Rolampont, 38, 45; Vaucouleurs, 35; wounds, 176; See also: Father Duffy, Joyce Kilmer, Brigadier General Michael J. Lenihan

Dravo, Colonel Charles, 178, 204

Drum, Brigadier General Hugh A., 190

Duffy, Father Francis P.: 2, 10, 14-15, 17-18, 20; attitude toward British, 41; combat participation, 66-67, 106, 108, 133, 176; Lunéville, 60, 67; Baccarat, 76, 78, 84-85, 93; Champagne, 103; Ourcq River (Marne), 112, 118, 126, 134; St. Mihiel, 143, 150, 164; Meuse-Argonne, 180, 189-90; early career, 2, 10; occupation of Germany, 204, 211, 214, 220; post-war career, 243; relations with William J. Donovan, 2, 10, 35, 46, 176, 217, 234; with Joyce Kilmer, 2, 45, 103, 127; religious activities, 14, 16-17, 20, 30, 35, 53, 76, 112, 144, 169, 217, 238; training: Camp Mills, 10, 17; Rolampont, 36, 38, 45;

Vaucouleurs, 30; *See also*: William J. Donovan, Joyce Kilmer, 165th Infantry Regiment

Dussauge, Colonel André, 65

Ettinger, Private Albert: 14, 19-20, 238; assigned as dispatch rider, 19, 78-79; combat participation, 66, 103, 174; Lunéville, 53, 61, 65, 71; Baccarat, 79; Champagne, 103; Ourcq River (Marne), 134; St. Mihiel, 143, 154, 164; Meuse-Argonne, 174, 176; discipline problems, 14; post-war career, 244; Rolampont, 36; Vaucouleurs, 29-30, 40; wounds, 103, 182; *See also*: William J. Donovan, Father Francis Duffy, 165th Infantry Regiment

Fallaw, Captain Thomas H., 179, 193

Flagler, Major General Clement F., 203, 212, 218-27, 235

Fraternization: instances of, 212-14, 223-24, 234; policies against, 210, 212, 222-24

Frew, Major James W., 14, 34-35, 63, 108-09, 244

Garnett, Colonel Ruby, 157-58

Gatley, Brigadier General George, 105, 140, 171, 181, 219, 235

GHQ, AEF (Chaumont): Intelligence, 82, 84; Rainbow Division, 21-22, 38, 41-42, 44, 46-47, 70, 111-12, 132-33, 146-47, 158, 240-41; staff, 30, 36-37, 43, 235; supply, 55, 58, 145;

training, 34; venereal disease, 68; YMCA, 79

Gill, Lieutenant Colonel Robert, 104, 107, 226-27

Glover, Lieutenant Edmund P., 63

Gouraud, General Henri, 98, 100-01, 103-05, 109-10, 112, 182, 192, 195, 197, 200, 202

Greely, Colonel John, 191

Grissinger, Lieutenant Colonel John W., 43-44, 69, 85, 214, 221, 223, 225

Groupe de Combat (GC), 59-61

Handy, Captain Thomas T., 58, 244

Harbord, Major General James, 22-23, 46, 80, 117, 133, 145, 163, 191-92, 198, 200

Hayes, Private John B., 19, 61, 97, 107, 118, 121, 143, 152, 164, 202, 210, 234

Hine, Colonel Charles, 30, 37-38

Hogan, Private Martin J.: 2, 10-11, 13, 18-19; combat participation, 108, 126, 174; Lunéville, 53, 61, 65, 71; Champagne, 102; Ourcq River (Marne), 112; St. Mihiel, 154; Meuse-Argonne, 167; joins 165th Infantry, 13; training: Camp Mills, 10, 18; Rolampont, 35, 40; Vaucouleurs, 29; wounds, 70, 134, 175-76, 187; *See also*: 165th Infantry Regiment, Shamrock Battalion

Hough, Colonel Benson W.: combat participation, 154, 177-78, 193-94, 196; Ourcq River (Marne), 131; St. Mihiel, 146;

Meuse-Argonne, 171, 177-78;
early career, 45; conflict with
Regular Army, 44-45;
occupation of Germany, 227,
236; post-war career, 243;
Rolampont, 44; *See also*: 166th
Infantry Regiment
Howland, Colonel Charles R., 204,
228
Hughes, Colonel William N., 36-
37, 58, 76, 83, 130, 133, 147-48,
157, 164, 170, 178
Hutchcraft, Captain Ruben B., 193

Influenza, 147, 168, 214, 221

Janice, Elsie, 139
Jewish Welfare Board, 213, 225
Judah, Lieutenant Colonel Noble
B., 58, 83, 133, 170, 174, 181-
82, 188, 243

Kelly, Colonel William, 37, 46,
67, 87, 131, 180
Kelly, Private Eddie, 65-66
Kilmer, Sergeant Joyce, 2, 10-11,
45-46, 66-67, 103, 127, 217, 243
Kriemhilde Stellung, 167-68, 178-
81

Lambert, Sergeant Calvin: 1, 9,
11, 13, 15, 18, 118, 202; early
career, 1, 9; combat
participation, 109, 122; St.
Mihiel, 151; Meuse-Argonne,
174, 187; injured in hospital, 39;
post-war career, 243; recruiting
for 117th, 11; training: Camp
Coetquidan, 34, 39; Camp Mills,
11, 13, 15; Kansas Ammunition

Train, 9, 11, 140, 210, 217
Langille, Leslie: 3, 201, 204, 209,
212, 225, 237-38; combat
participation, 87-88, 110, 151;
Lunéville, 67; Baccarat, 76;
Camp Coetquidan, 32-33, 54;
Champagne, 93; Ourcq River
(Marne), 139; St. Mihiel, 166;
Meuse-Argonne, 190; University
of Illinois, 3; post-war career,
243
LaRoque, O.K, 226-28
Lawton, Colonel Frank, 57
Leach, Colonel George: Camp
Coetquidan, 33; early career, 12;
occupation of Germany, 221,
223, 226, 236-38; post-war
career, 243; St. Mihiel, 155; *See
also*: 151st Field Artillery
Regiment
Lenihan, Brigadier General
Michael J.: 17; combat
participation, 124, 152, 155,
174-76; Lunéville, 47, 64;
Baccarat, 75, 84; Ourcq River
(Marne), 120, 124, 133; St.
Mihiel, 143, 148-50; Meuse-
Argonne, 168-69, 174-77;
relieved of command, 178, 203;
reassigned to 77th Infantry
Division, 178; Rolampont, 42;
Vaucouleurs, 30; *See also*: 84th
Brigade
Liggett, Major General Hunter:
36, 47-48, 218; I Corps, 125,
129-30, 132, 163, 178, 180;
Sedan, 192-95, 197-98
Lunéville, France, 47-48, 53-56,
59, 67-71, 75-76, 78-79, 83-85,
102-04, 118, 120

Luxembourg, 202-04, 209-11

McAndrew, Brigadier General
    James W., 56, 132
MacArthur, Brigadier General
    Douglas: 1, 3, 13, 23, 244;
    Chief of Staff, Rainbow
    Division, 4, 37, 57, 59, 98;
    combat participation, 126-27,
    151-52, 154-56, 158, 168-69,
    173-74, 176-77, 180-81, 193;
    Lunéville, 54, 58; Baccarat, 71,
    80, 83; Ourcq River (Marne),
    113, 132-33; St. Mihiel, 146,
    148-50; Meuse-Argonne, 168,
    171-72, 188-89, 193, 195;
    commander 84th Brigade, 130,
    132-34, 203; commander
    Rainbow Division, 193, 200,
    204, 235; courage of, 235; early
    career, 33, 37, 57; formation of
    the Rainbow Division, 4;
    occupation of Germany, 201-03,
    217, 235, 237; organization
    of the Rainbow Division staff, 4,
    13, 23, 37, 56-58; post-war
    career, 243; relations with
    General Mann, 22; with General
    Menoher, 47-48, 57, 71, 132,
    164, 172-73; with General
    Pershing, 22-23; with General
    Summerall, 169; training: Camp
    Mills, 5, 13; Rolampont, 38, 41,
    44, 46-48; wounds, 59
MacArthur, Major General Arthur,
    1-2
MacArthur, Private Charles: 12,
    19, 97, 110; Army of
    Occupation, 224, 235; Lunéville,
    54, 67, 76; Baccarat, 88;

Belgium, 210; Camp Coetquidan,
    32; Luxembourg, 211; post-war
    career, 243; St. Mihiel, 151;
    Meuse-Argonne, 167, 190, 201;
    University of Illinois, 3; YMCA,
    79, 225
McCoy, Colonel Frank, 103, 112,
    127-28, 143-44, 146
Machine Gun Batallions: 149th,
    44; 150th, 104, 106, 124; 151st,
    98, 104-05, 107, 124
McKenna, Major James A., 126,
    134
McKinstry, Brigadier General
    Charles H., 21, 84, 101
Mann, Brigadier General William,
    4-5, 13-14, 17-18, 20, 22-23
Marsh, General Payton, 24
Marshall, Colonel George C., 98,
    145-46, 182, 190
Menoher, Major General Charles
    T.: 244; attitudes toward air
    service, 92, 125, 157-58;
    command, 46, 57, 100, 173, 193-
    97, 199-200; combat
    participation, 125-26, 128, 173-
    75; Lunéville, 54, 58, 64;
    Baccarat, 71, 78, 80, 85;
    Champagne, 111; Ourcq
    River (Marne), 113, 129-33; St.
    Mihiel, 147-48; Meuse-Argonne,
    173-75, 177-78, 181, 188-89;
    early career, 20-21; with
    Douglas MacArthur, 41, 44, 47-
    48, 57-58, 132, 164, 172-73,
    235; with General John J.
    Pershing, 21; post-war career,
    242; Rolampont, 36-37, 39, 43,
    45, 47; Vaucouleurs, 47; See
    also: Douglas MacArthur

Meuse-Argonne Campaign:
59, 121, 134, 156, 187, 189,
203; American combat forces,
163, 193-95, 198-200, 237;
Pershing plans for, 144;
casualties, 163, 182, 240-41;
commits Rainbow Division, 168;
terrain, 164, 168-69, 173, 176,
178, 189, 195; weather, 168-69,
175, 178; German defenses of,
163-64, 167, 172, 175, 177-78,
181-82, 188, 200; See also:
Frank Parker
Mitchell, Brigadier General
William "Billy", 8, 92, 135, 145,
164
Mitchell, Colonel Harry D., 146,
176-78, 204
Muir, Major General Charles, 203,
220-21
Murphy, Colonel G.M.P., 133,
147-49, 151-52, 157-58, 170
Murphy, Colonel P.A., 44

National Guard: 1-4, 10-12, 22,
32, 38, 57, 97, 100, 103, 106,
113, 117, 129, 135, 144, 203,
239-40; draft of, 3-4, 7, 11, 68;
Pershing's attitudes toward, 22,
113; relations with Regular
Army, 2-4, 7-8, 44-45, 48, 113,
117, 139, 164, 198
Naulin, General Pierre, 100-01,
111
Neibaur, Private Thomas C., 179
Norman, Lieutenant John, 65
Nurses, 69, 102, 109, 111, 227-28

Ogden, Major Hugh W., 15, 19,
29, 58-59, 228

117th Ammunition Train, 11, 17-
18, 34, 39, 75, 87, 118, 122,
140, 151, 174, 187, 189, 202,
210, 215, 217, 239
117th Field Signal Battalion, 44,
157
117th Mobile Ordinance Repair
Company, 47
117th Sanitary Train, 29, 34, 44,
56, 87, 123, 151
117th Trench Mortar Battery: 17,
226; Camp Coetquidan, 29;
combat participation, 87, 107;
Lunéville, 56; Baccarat, 87-88;
Champagne, 104, 107, 146;
Ourcq River (Marne), 123; St.
Mihiel, 146; return to U.S., 237,
239; See also: Lieutenant
Colonel Robert Gill

Parker, Brigadier General Frank,
191-92, 195-200, 240
Patton, Colonel George S., 145,
147-50, 152, 155, 242
Pershing, General John J.: 3, 42,
48, 59, 79-80, 105, 145, 147,
180, 190, 193; AEF
Headquarters, 22-24, 42, 47,
133, 182; Chaumont, 24, 30, 41,
147; air service, 8, 91, 145, 242;
attitudes toward 1st Infantry
Division, 17, 93, 167, 192, 240;
National Guard, 21-22, 68, 113,
233-34, 240; relieved officers,
20, 133; develops doctrine, 38-
39, 241-42; early career, 8, 234;
plans St. Mihiel operation, 144,
146, 156; Meuse-Argonne
operation, 144, 163; regulations
for occupation of Germany, 203,

215-16, 218-19; reliance on
infantry, 8, 100, 113, 117, 164;
relations with the French, 40-41,
55-56, 64, 68, 70, 98, 102, 195;
with Douglas MacArthur, 13,
235; with subordinate officers, 8,
47-48, 64; selected to command
AEF, 3
Poste d'Appui (PA), 59-60
Pretelat, General André, 101

Quigley, Sergeant Lawrence, 105,
110

Regiments (U.S.): 1st Gas and
Flame, 145, 149, 152, 168, 170;
2nd Alabama, 12; 3rd Iowa, 124,
146; 4th Alabama, 1, 10, 14; 4th
Ohio, 45; 28th Infantry, 191,
199-200; 47th Infantry, 126-29;
69th New York, 2, 9-11, 13-14,
67, 106, 108, 217, 220, 228,
234, 236, 238; 117th Engineer:
227, 234; casualties, 87; combat
participation, 66-67, 89, 132,
214; Lunéville, 59; Baccarat, 75,
87; Champagne, 104; St. Mihiel,
1, 149-50; Meuse-Argonne, 169-
70, 175-77; used as infantry
troops, 104, 131, 139, 180, 188;
Rolampont, 37, 44, 46; See also:
Colonel William Kelly; 149th
Field Artillery: 201, 209, 244;
Camp Coetquidan, 55; called to
service, 1917, 12; combat
participation, 88, 90; Lunéville,
55, 58; Baccarat, 75-76, 90;
Champagne, 104; St. Mihiel,
140; Meuse-Argonne, 181, 190;
discipline problems with, 54,

234-35, 237-38; prior service,
12; See also: Chicago Board of
Trade Battery, Leslie Langille,
Charles MacArthur, Henry J.
Reilly; 150th Field Artillery, 12,
90, 104, 156, 216; 151st Field
Artillery, 12, 64, 104, 156, 221,
223, 238; 165th Infantry
Regiment, "The Fighting 69th":
13, 15-16, 45, 140, 143-44, 146,
228, 233-35, 238-239; combat
participation, 66, 70, 173-78;
Lunéville, 58, 60-61, 64-66, 68,
70, 108-09; Baccarat, 76, 78, 86;
Champagne, 104, 106, 108-09,
111-12; Ourcq River (Marne),
124, 126-28, 130, 134; St.
Mihiel, 150, 153, 155; Meuse-
Argonne, 164, 167, 169-78, 180-
82, 190; discipline problems, 36,
41-42; Irish background of, 239;
occupation of Germany, 200,
204, 211, 214-15, 217, 219-20,
225; riot with 167th Infantry, 15;
training: Camp Mills, 18, 20;
Rolampont, 37-38, 43, 46; See
also: Colonel William J. "Wild
Bill" Donovan, Father Duffy,
Private Al Ettinger, Corporal
Martin Hogan, Sergeant Joyce
Kilmer; 166th Infantry
Regiment: 45, 244; combat
participation, 108, 127, 196-200;
Lunéville, 62, 76; Baccarat, 84,
86, 88-90; Champagne, 100,
104; Ourcq River (Marne), 124,
131; St. Mihiel, 146, 150, 154-
55; Meuse-Argonne, 170-72,
174-75, 177-78, 180-82;
occupation of Germany, 200-02,

219, 236; Sedan, 193-97, 199, 200-01; training: Camp Mills, 18; Rolampont, 44; *See also*: Colonel Benson Hough; 167th Infantry Regiment: 12, 16, 19, 45, 239, 243; called to service, 1917, 10; combat participation, 172-73, 180-81, 193-97; Lunéville, 55, 61-64; Baccarat, 76, 80-81, 84, 90, 93; Champagne, 97, 106-08, 111; Ourcq River (Marne), 111, 120-22, 124, 128-29, 132; St. Mihiel, 143, 150, 152, 155-58; Meuse-Argonne, 164, 170-73, 179-81, 188-89; Croix Rouge Farm, 120-23; health problems, 20; occupation of Germany, 202, 204, 210-11, 217, 219, 223, 234; relations with 165th Infantry, 15, 64, 76, 108, 111, 170; with 168th Infantry, 59, 64, 76, 84, 106, 111, 120, 129, 132, 150, 170; training: Alabama, 10; Rolampont, 37; Vaucouleurs, 36; *See also*: Private John B. Hayes, Corporal Joseph Romano, Colonel William Screws; 168th Infantry Regiment: 15, 143-44, 146-48, 201, 219-20, 243; called to service, 1917, 11; Chatillion Hill, 17, 173, 177, 179; combat participation, 63, 66, 82, 89, 128-29, 197; Lunéville, 59-60, 62-64; Baccarat, 76, 78-79, 82, 84, 90; Champagne, 103-04, 106, 111; Ourcq River (Marne), 124-25, 131-32, 134; St. Mihiel, 150, 153, 158, 166; Meuse-Argonne, 169-70; Croix Rouge Farm, 120-

21; training: Rolampont, 36, 44, 53; Vaucouleurs, 30, 32; *See also*: Colonel Edward Bennett, Private First Class Everett Scott, Colonel Matthew Tinley

Reilly, Brigadier General Henry J.: 237-38; combat participation, 199, 201; Baccarat, 98; Ourcq River (Marne), 128; Meuse-Argonne, 179, 181, 188; commands 83rd Brigade, 178, 181, 199; early career, 12, 33, 167; occupation of Germany, 203-04; post-war career, 243; training: Camp Coetquidan, 34, 54; Camp Mills, 12; *See also*: 149th Field Artillery Regiment
Remagen, Germany, 214-15, 217, 224-25, 233, 236
Reppy, First Lieutenant Allison, 182, 201
Rolampont (Training Area 7), France, 35-40, 43-44, 47-48, 53, 68, 70-71, 75-76
Romano, Corporal Joseph: 1, 5, 10; Camp Mills, 16; combat participation, 83, 107, 121-22; Lunéville, 55, 71; Baccarat, 81, 88; Champagne, 97, 118; St. Mihiel, 152; Meuse-Argonne, 181; early career, 1, 81; post-war career, 244; Rolampont, 36, 40; wounds, 81, 181; *See also*: 167th Infantry Regiment
Roosevelt, Colonel Theodore, 197, 224
Ross, Major Lloyd, 171-72, 179
Rouge Bouquet, 60, 65, 67

St. Mihiel Operation: 93, 158,
163-64, 166-68, 177, 203, 236,
241, 244; American combat
forces, 144, 146, 156-57;
German defensives of, 149, 153;
Pershing commits Rainbow
Division, 145-46; Pershing plans
for, 132, 144, 146, 156; tanks
used in, 145, 147-50, 152, 154-
55, 158, 242; terrain, 149, 152,
155, 242; weather, 150, 156
Scott, Private First Class Everett:
1, 5, 11, 14, 17, 19, 236; combat
participation, 66, 89, 128;
Lunéville, 66; Baccarat, 89;
Champagne, 102, 110; Ourcq
River (Marne), 128; St. Mihiel,
143; Meuse-Argonne, 173, 187;
joins 168th Infantry regiment,
11; occupation of Germany, 204,
211, 217, 233; post-war career,
244-45; training: Des Moines,
11; Rolampont, 40; Vaucouleurs,
30; wounds, 66, 89; See also:
168th Infantry Regiment
Screws, Colonel William: 203-04;
combat participation, 55, 129;
Lunéville, 61; Champagne, 104;
Ourcq River (Marne), 129;
Meuse-Argonne, 188-89;
command of the 84th Infantry
Brigade, 193; early career, 10;
occupation of Germany, 211,
227; post-war career, 243;
training: Alabama, 10;
Rolampont, 37; See also: 167th
Infantry Regiment
Sedan, France, 182, 188-200
Service of Supply (SOS), 23-24,
38, 55, 105, 133, 143, 145, 168,
180
Shamrock Battalion (3rd, 165th
Infantry): 13, 64, 76; Lunéville,
69-70; Champagne, 102, 104,
109, 112; Ourcq River (Marne),
126, 134; St. Mihiel, 154;
Meuse-Argonne, 167, 169-70,
174-75, 177-78; See also:
Martin Hogan
Sherwood, Private Elmer, 110-11,
123, 139, 138, 170, 201, 243
Shoes, Army, 8, 13, 18, 30, 35-36,
38, 41, 43-44, 58, 211, 214
Short, Colonel Walter, 219-20
Sinzig, Germany, 217, 234-35,
237
Slum (Slumgullion Stew), 29, 60,
62, 78, 89, 93, 105, 108, 110,
134
Smith, Captain Emmett P, 55
Smythe, Donald, 144, 163, 192,
198, 240
Stewart, Private Lawrence: 201,
243; combat participation, 68,
89; Lunéville, 54, 62; Baccarat,
78; Champagne, 102; Ourcq
River (Marne), 129, 133; St.
Mihiel, 150; Meuse-Argonne,
173, 190; Rolampont, 53; See
also: 168th Infantry Regiment
Summerall, Lieutenant General
Charles P.: and the 1st Infantry
Division, 21, 117, 145, 167;
commands 67th Field Artillery
Brigade, 21, 181; early career,
167; Meuse-Argonne campaign,
168-69, 176, 181; post-war
career, 244; relations with
Douglas MacArthur, 169; with
Charles T. Menoher, 177-78;

with Frank Parker, 191-92, 197-98, 200; with John J. Pershing, 240; with Henry J. Reilly, 178, 181; relief of Brigadier General Michael J. Lenihan, 178; Sedan, 191-92, 197-200, 202

Tanks, 145, 147-50, 152, 154-55, 158, 168, 175-76, 241-42
Taylor, Lieutenant James O., 16-17
Thompson, Second Lieutenant Hugh: combat participation, 81-83, 89-90, 108, 152-53; Lunéville, 60, 62; Baccarat, 71, 78; Champagne, 103; Ourcq River (Marne), 134; St. Mihiel, 144; commissioned in army, 32; post-war career, 244; Valbonne, 32; wounds, 90, 103, 108, 153; See also: 168th Infantry Regiment
Tinley, Colonel Matthew, 146-47, 171, 243
Todd, Lisa Gilman, 226-27
Tours, France, 24
Travis, Colonel Frank, 122, 189

Underwood, Captain Oscar W., Jr., 18, 58

Valbonne Training Area, 32
Van Dolsen, First Lieutenant William W.: 2, 228; combat participation, 69, 109; Lunéville, 63, 68-69; Baccarat, 71, 80, 85; Champagne, 102, 105, 111-12; Ourcq River (Marne), 124; St. Mihiel, 151; as mess officer, 34, 39, 102; and

nurses, 69, 109; post-war career, 244; training: Rolampont, 39-40; Vaucouleurs, 29, 34; See also: 117th Sanitary Train
Vaucouleurs Training Area, 24, 29, 32, 35, 38, 40, 47
Venereal disease, 68-69, 80, 216, 221-25, 238

Wilson, Woodrow, 1, 3, 7, 10, 23, 48, 80, 212
Wolf, Major Walter B., 58, 88-89, 156
Wood, Colonel George H., 189
Wren, Lieutenant Edward, 121, 219

Young Mens' Christian Association (YMCA), 14, 16, 54, 79-80, 109, 166, 174, 213, 217-18, 225-28

About the Author

JAMES J. COOKE is Professor of History at the University of Mississippi. He spent the academic year, 1992–1993, as Visiting Professor of History at the U.S. Air War College. His last book was *100 Miles From Baghdad: With the French in Desert Storm* (Praeger, 1993).

ISBN 0-275-94768-8

9 780275 947682

HARDCOVER BAR CODE